D0871914

More Praise for *The Sensible Guide to Forex*

"This is the one forex book aimed at conservative mainstream investors who might never otherwise consider forex, but should because we all need currency diversification. Even those who never plan to trade will find a wealth of information that will make them better investors. This step-by-step guide to less demanding and lower-risk ways to trade or build a currency-diversified investment portfolio offers a less intimidating path to forex profits."

—Yohay Elam, Founder of Forex Crunch

"Cliff Wachtel's book provides pragmatic counsel and guidance. A must read for serious investors seeking to diversify beyond stocks, bonds, and gold."

—Dave Lemont, CEO, Currensee

"A must read for *any* informed investor or trader that deserves to become *the* classic introduction to forex. This book is the ideal shortcut to simpler, safer forex trading or investing. As Cliff succinctly puts it, 'The need for currency diversification is one of the most important lessons of the Great Financial Crisis.' This book details—with genuine respect for his readers' money and intelligence—a range of solutions, offering something for readers of every skill level and risk tolerance. Wachtel provides full details and illustrations to show you how to actually make money, without overloading you with secondary details or information you can find elsewhere."

—Eric Harbor, CEO, Caesartrade.com

"One of the best starting points I have read about forex. Understanding both the big picture and the essential, practical details of how to identify, plan, and execute a profitable trade is the manna of successful traders. Cliff delivers both. He explains what e. e. cummings called 'the root of the root and the bud of the bud and the sky of the sky of a tree called life,' but applied to the forex world. A really good tool, whether you're a newbie forex trader or a long-term traditional investor trying to build a diversified portfolio. Read it and you will get 'forexpertise.'"

—Mauricio Carrillo, FXstreet.com U.S. Manager, @MCarrilloFX

"This book is an insightful introduction to the world of forex. Wachtel leads the novice trader on a journey of discovery from the most basic concepts in the forex market to more sophisticated trading strategies. What stands out is his honesty. Wachtel doesn't sugarcoat the FX market; instead he shares the idiosyncrasies of this market and debunks a few FX myths along the way. He also introduces some of the latest developments in the retail forex market, from social trading to binary options. Wachtel's broad knowledge of this market makes this book an interesting read for those who want a thorough insight into the world of FX."

—Kathleen Brooks, Research Director, Forex.com

"In an ever-evolving field, it's rare to find a guidebook so helpful and timeless as Cliff Wachtel's *Sensible Guide to Forex*. This book gives both current traders and new traders the perspective they need to take their forex trading to the next level."

—Tal Holtzer, CEO, DailyForex.com

"This is a fantastic, comprehensive, and up-to-date overview and practical guide to succeeding in the foreign exchange market, with an insightful, qualitative, and nonintimidating approach. Whether you are a novice considering a move into the foreign exchange market or an experienced trader looking for a deeper understanding of various concepts or some new approaches, Cliff's book does a stellar job of covering all the bases."

—Joel Kruger, Currency Strategist, FXCM

"Cliff's book is a must-read, cogent, cohesive compendium of the realities of forex. I've been in the trading business for 35 + years and believe that success is all about intelligent risk management. The book's relentless emphasis on risk and money management is the reason that this is the first investment book I've bothered to finish in the past 20 years. For the novice, first he arms you with the relevant information to keep you from immediately losing your shirt, so that you survive the learning process with most of your cash and confidence intact. Then he takes you step-by-step through a number of paths to profitability. For the professional, he reminds us of the rules we all strive not to violate every day because we're human. He also provides the first in-depth coverage of two new and potentially very useful ways to tap forex—social trading and binary options. This book is the only source I've found for in-depth and objective coverage of either of these intriguing new ways to trade forex markets with potentially less effort and better returns."

—David Israel, Chief Market Strategist, White Wave Trading Strategies, Ltd. www.whitewavetradingstrategies.com

The Sensible Guide to Forex

The Sensible Guide to Forex

Safer, Smarter Ways to Survive
and Prosper from the Start

CLIFF WACHTEL

WILEY

John Wiley & Sons, Inc.

Published by John Wiley & Sons, Inc., Hoboken, New Jersey.
Published simultaneously in Canada.

For general information on our other products and services or for technical support, please contact our Customer Care Department within the United States at (800) 762-2974, outside the United States at (317) 572-3993 or fax (317) 572-4002.

Wiley also publishes its books in a variety of electronic formats. Some content that appears in print may not be available in electronic books. For more information about Wiley products, visit our web site at www.wiley.com.

Library of Congress Cataloging-in-Publication Data:

Wachtel, Cliff, 1959–
    The sensible guide to Forex : safer, smarter ways to survive and prosper from the start / Cliff Wachtel.
        pages cm. – (Wiley trading series)
    Includes index.
    ISBN 978-1-118-15807-4 (hardback); ISBN 978-1-118-26403-4 (ebk);
    ISBN 978-1-118-23745-8 (ebk); ISBN 978-1-118-22605-6 (ebk)
    1. Foreign exchange market.   2. Foreign exchange futures.   I. Title.
    HG3851.W324 2012
    332.4′5–dc23

                                                                                    2012005565

Printed in the United States of America

10 9 8 7 6 5 4 3 2 1

This book is dedicated to:

The Almighty, for everything
My wife, Michelle
My parents, Dr. Arthur and Phyllis Wachtel
My children, Sarah, Binyamin, Eliana,
Gavriel, and Maayan
To Rabbi Noach Weinberg, OBM

Finally, it is to you, dear readers, the sincere, serious traders or investors who seek the prudent path to currency diversification via conservative forex, either as active traders or as passive investors, that this book is ultimately dedicated.

Contents

CHAPTER 6   Essentials of Fundamental Analysis   169

CHAPTER 7   Pulling It All Together with Trade Examples   205

CHAPTER 8   Technical Analysis: Basic Momentum Indicators   227

CHAPTER 9   Technical Analysis: Future Study   255

Read This First

What You Absolutely Must Know

R ead this first ... or at least skim it. There are things you must know here.

First, congratulations! You've just found something few forex (foreign exchange or currency) beginners ever find—an ideal starting point.

CURRENCY RISK: EVERY INVESTOR'S DILEMMA

You can't live with them, and you can't live without them. They're often complex, exasperating, unreasonable, and irrational, and they always want more of your time and money. I am referring to trades or investments that give you currency diversification, of course. We all need it, but few succeed in currency markets. The methods commonly used are too risky, complex, and time-consuming for most people.

Unfortunately, it's very hard to find the right guidance for getting started. Virtually all of the so-called "Beginners' Guides" are either:

- too superficial to give you the practical skills needed to start making money, or
- too complex and detailed to provide clear step-by-step ways to actually start making money
- too focused on the usual methods of forex trading that are too risky, complex, and time consuming for most people to use successfully.

We've dedicated years to creating a book that avoids these pitfalls. It gives you a variety of approaches to get started via safer, simpler, more profitable ways to lower your risk and increase your returns, either as a conservative forex trader or as a more passive longer-term investor seeking exposure to assets in the best currencies.

Unlike other beginners guides, this book has the right balance of practical information and methods you use to actually make money, without burdening you with too much information or the wrong kinds of information. It provides the shortest path to actually making money as soon as your circumstances allow; or in the worst case, to avoid the mistakes and losses that drain your cash and confidence before you have had enough time to find your path to success.

Currency Risk and How to Fight It

Currency risk is today's great hidden portfolio risk. The governments behind the most widely held currencies are trying to inflate away their debts via low interest rates and "stimulus" (technically not money printing!) programs. It's unclear whether these policies serve the "greater good;" however, they are likely to devalue their currencies, and any portfolios denominated in them. So, for your own financial self-defense against that risk, you obviously need to diversify into assets exposed to sounder currencies, or those currencies themselves.But it's very tough to find solutions suitable for most traders or investors.

- For aspiring forex (foreign exchange) traders, most of the material available is about complex, demanding, time-consuming, high-leverage, high-risk methods unsuitable for the average risk-averse trader seeking steady profits rather than gambling thrills. Yet the materials aimed at beginners tend to be far too superficial to prepare anyone to actually make money. This book seeks to bridge that yawning gap with safer, smarter, and less demanding ways to trade forex, with the details and examples needed to get you ready to start trading or investing as quickly as your personal circumstances allow.
- For longer-term investors, there's plenty out there about foreign stocks or bonds, but almost all of it ignores the prospects of the currency behind these. A falling currency can turn a good investment into a bad one. This book shows you how to identify the currencies most likely to hold their value and provides ideas about how to apply that knowledge to a long-term portfolio for both income and capital appreciation.

THE SOLUTION

I'm not the only one to recognize the problem of currency risk.[1] I'm just the first to offer a book with the most cost-effective solutions to the problem that will actually work for most people, not just the few who are suitable for short term high risk trading. I'm not seeking to manage your money for a high fee (typically unconnected to actual performance), nor am I trying to sell you an expensive newsletter subscription or trading system.

Here is one source to take you step-by-step straight from ignorance about forex markets to competence needed for profiting from them, either as:

- A trader: using safer, smarter techniques than those usually advocated. These will allow you to survive the learning period with your capital and confidence intact, and to become profitable sooner. Those with some background can cut straight to the parts they need.
- A longer-term passive investor: Most sensible investors practice asset and sector diversification, yet ignore this basic principle of diversification when it comes to currency exposure, and have almost all of their assets denominated in a single currency, be it the USD, EUR, GBP, JPY, and so forth.

  This failure to diversify into assets in the strongest currencies is uniquely reckless. That's because the governments behind these and other currencies are pursuing stealth inflation to cut their debt loads. They'll never admit it, but historically low interest rates combined with repeated stimulus programs betray their true intentions—they want to slash the real value of their debt load through inflation (rather than more responsible but politically harder policies like cutting spending or raising taxes), even if they gut your net worth in the process. We'll teach you how to identify the currencies with the strongest long-term trends, and the kinds of assets that will ride them, for lower risk and higher, for more reliable returns.

The need for currency diversification is one of the most important lessons of the Great Financial Crisis that began in 2007. Ignoring it involves some toxic combination of ignorance, foolishness, laziness, or recklessness.

I can help cure the ignorance, though if you're reading this book the other three probably don't apply to you.

SOME BACKGROUND

Decades ago, while settling in as a U.S.-trained accountant and new immigrant to Israel, I started teaching English to earn some extra money. Teaching anything I understood well always came easily, but I was frustrated because the available textbooks were neither especially clear nor efficient. Teaching with them just made the whole process more painful and time consuming. I kept finding so many shortcuts and better ways to organize the learning process that I soon started writing my own materials. Over the years these evolved into a full set of courseware.

With these in hand, I was able to take absolute beginners to a sixth- or seventh-grade level (per standards of the Israel Ministry of Education) in under 30 hours, instead of the hundreds of hours typically required by our local school system or private teaching companies, and had a successful and fun teaching practice.

Years later, while working with forex traders, I found the same situation but worse. There was no Education Ministry to certify the materials, no structured program of what to learn in what order. There were plenty of training materials, some quite good, but most would just waste your time and money spent acquiring, studying, and applying them without success. Even if you were lucky enough to catch some of the better materials, after countless hours, books, articles, courses, you got some useful information and trading techniques, but you still had to figure out how to integrate it all into a plan of action. You still lacked a clear step-by-step roadmap toward actually making money, or at least not losing much while you learned and practiced.

Figuring out how to get started with forex, either as a trader or as a long-term investor looking for conservative ways to profit from forex trends, can be frustrating.

Still, you've got to start somewhere. Welcome to somewhere.

WHY ANY TRADER OR INVESTOR NEEDS THIS BOOK

The following expands upon, and at times repeats, what I've said above. The repetition is intentional because it's needed to get the message through.

As governments sacrifice the value of their currencies, and your savings, to further their own policy goals, currency diversification is no longer optional for prudent investors; it's critical for your financial survival. With both the U.S. dollar and Euro suffering wild swings over recent years, this lesson is beginning to reach mainstream investors.[2] You have to do something. Unfortunately, most forex materials focus on time consuming, complex, high-risk, high-leverage trading strategies. The majority of forex traders fail with this approach within a matter of months, while an elite few prosper.[3]

So where to turn? There are so many books, courses, blogs, and webinars, but most will waste your time and money because they're either too complex or too superficial.

Relax—you don't have to become another lamb to the slaughter.

If you're serious about succeeding in forex, you just need the right guidance toward the trading or investing style that best suits you. Welcome to that guidance.

Finally, here's a sane, conservative approach to forex for rational adults interested in gains, not gambling, either as traders or even just longer-term investors with no interest in directly trading currencies.

Unfortunately, forex's reputation has been tarnished by too many books and brokers pushing high-risk, reckless trading methods that are unsuitable for most of us. While most new traders fail within months, the elite 20 to 30 percent enjoy a lucrative, stimulating part-time or full-time career. Most of them aren't geniuses or connected insiders. You can join them, but you need the right start.

Welcome to that start. You're going to need it.

Do one or more of the following sound like you?

- I'm a short-term forex trader seeking to lower my risks and improve my profits.
- I'm an aspiring forex trader but I'm uncomfortable with the time-consuming, high-leverage, high-risk day trader methods and mentality that permeate most of the forex world. I want guidance on how to trade longer-term positions that ride the exceptionally stable longer-term trends with less risk and less need for constant monitoring.
- I'm a conservative, longer-term traditional equities or income investor with less interest in short-term trading. I'm seeking to diversify my currency exposure in order to lower my risk and boost my capital gains and income by having my growth- and income-oriented assets in the currencies most likely to appreciate over the long term.
- I'm too busy to waste weeks on books that are unclear, lack detailed explanations, or bury me in too much information to use. I just want that one book that provides:
  - What I need to get started actually making money while controlling risks.
  - Fully detailed, well-illustrated explanations.
  - Explanations of the different ways to profit in forex markets in addition to the standard methods.
  - Guidance about how to continue my education and development as a trader.
- I need a clear introduction to forex basics and the different ways to play this market, and enough analytical and risk management tools that are sufficiently explained so that I know how to combine them into simple trading systems that I can quickly start applying without too much complexity.

- I'm intimidated by forex, though I know I should tap into it somehow. I hear a lot about how most people lose money in online currency trading, and how it is riddled with brokers who just want to push you into risky, high-leverage trading before you're ready, so before you know what you're doing you've already lost everything. I'm looking for low-risk ways to break into forex, but don't know:
  - How to get started.
  - What trading styles are right for me.
  - How to locate the right online broker and sources of further training and market analysis.
- I want currency diversification before the @#%∗! government destroys the purchasing power and value of my dollars/yen/euros through endless money printing and inflation, but I don't want to trade.
- I'm seeking an asset that isn't correlated to all the other markets, and where there's always a playable trend or trading range regardless of what stocks or bonds are doing.

If any of these needs are yours, then you've come to the right place.

What This Book Offers

Here's what you get.

- An intelligent introduction to forex. Instead of time-consuming, high-risk methods unsuited for most people, this book provides:
  - Focus on a variety of lower-risk, simpler, less time-consuming trading methods, styles, instruments, and time frames to suit different personalities and needs.
  - Detailed coverage of the key aspects of trader psychology, risk, and money management that are in fact the real foundation of trader success.
  - Unique, exclusive, in-depth coverage of new, alternative ways and instruments for forex traders that are less risky and demanding—social trading and binary options.
  - Ways for longer-term passive investors to identify the most stable, reliable long-term forex trends and the best assets for riding them for higher returns and lower risk via currency diversification.
- A practical introduction to forex. Going beyond simplifications and theory, it provides a practical, well-illustrated, step-by-step guide to actually identifying, planning, and executing lower-risk, higher-yield trades and investments for a variety of traders and investors.

Why Listen to You, Cliff?

The short answer is: As trader, writer, advisor, and chief analyst in one form or another for over 30 years, I've been both ringside seat spectator and combatant in the markets. You can find further details through a simple online search from various online profiles.

Rabbi Noach Weinberg once told me that a fool learns from his own mistakes, but a wise man learns from the mistakes of others.

Here's my offer to help you learn like a wise man, from my mistakes and experience. Credentials aside, let the ideas speak for themselves.

What This Book Will Not Do

- Pretend to teach you hidden secrets of trading.
- Suggest that forex trading or investing is a likely road to fast riches requiring little effort.
- Focus on the high-risk, overly complicated, or very short-term hyperactive trading styles typically advocated in so many forex books. These strategies alone virtually guarantee failure for all but the few with exceptional experience, powers of concentration, temperament, risk tolerance, and capital. The only positive thing these strategies reliably produce is high trading volume fees for the brokers. In one recent survey, most online forex brokers reported that only 20 to 25 percent of their traders were profitable.[4]
- Burden you with interesting but unnecessary historical background information about forex.
- Overload you with more kinds of fundamental and technical analysis tools than you can use, and leave you without guidance about which tools to start with and when to add or use others. That, in turn, risks causing traders to:
  - Abandon attempts to learn how to methodically combine different kinds of indicators into simple systems and how to test them. Instead, they attempt random combinations of analytical tools without any controlled method for evaluating which work and which don't.
  - Succumb to paralysis from analysis, unable to act under the weight of a vast flow of often conflicting information.
- Include long tracts of pages repeating information that's been said better elsewhere and is easily available. Where possible I've tried to strike a balance between comprehensiveness and brevity, referring you to quality, free, online resources when appropriate.
- Focus exclusively on leveraged spot market trading. From other forex books, you'd think there's no other way to play forex. Hardly. For both traders and longer-term investors, there are worthy alternatives

to consider in the right conditions, like forex binary options for simple shorter-term trend trading, and forex exchange-traded funds (ETFs) for those seeking exposure by means of an unleveraged instrument that behaves like a stock and can be accessed via a standard equities account.

What This Book Will Do

- The short version is pretty much the opposite: It will provide an alternative introduction to forex, one aimed at the sensible, rational investor and trader, instead of the madcap gambler or get-rich-quick sucker.
- Virtually every investor needs this kind of guidance, because today, the hard fact is that everyone needs currency diversification.
- We can't afford to ignore currency markets any longer, so we need to learn sensible ways to benefit from them.

For traders or aspiring traders, that means it will:

- Teach you how to find and execute only the lowest-risk, highest potential yield trades via relatively simple tools and easily available information. In other words, you'll learn to be a successful beginner with the right tools for your level, rather than a failed imitation of an experienced, prepared professional.
- Show how to use forex to profit in bear markets more easily than with other asset classes like stocks.
- Counteract the get-rich-quick day trader mentality that pervades so many other forex books and leads most traders to failure. Instead, we'll set you up to succeed by showing you how to keep losses low relative to your gains so you make money even when most of your trades don't. We'll push you to make defensive trading your top priority.
- In place of purported secrets, give you the best of what's been said distilled from over 30 years of experience and a small library's worth of study.
- You'll get enough details and tools so that you can identify, plan, and execute relatively simple, low-risk, high-potential yield trades, while avoiding information overload. These include plenty of step-by-step examples of each step of the trading process, including the critical risk and money management so you avoid fatal damage to your capital or confidence. The idea is to give you enough information to make smart but simple trades with relatively low risk and high reward so, in the

shortest time possible, you're trading and, if not making money, at least not losing much while you are learning.

- Give you more than enough of the core skills you need to get started, and then offer guidance on how to continue your education—what to cover next and where to learn it.
- Focus on trading styles, methods, and time frames that are best suited for less experienced traders, the kind that increase the odds of keeping your capital and confidence intact while you gain skills and suffer the normal setbacks.
- Provide a full toolbox of technical and analytical tools and guidance on how to combine them into a variety of simple trading systems that you can back test before risking your cash.
- Show how to combine your analytical risk and money management (RAMM) tools into a complete trading plan.
- Demonstrate how to record and organize your trading plans so you can review every trade and learn from your successes and failures.
- Offer alternative ways to benefit from forex markets beyond the usual leveraged spot market trading of most online forex brokers. Even those who ultimately don't have the inclination or time for forex trading will find there are multiple ways a more passive, long-term investor can benefit from nonleveraged forex exposure.
- In what may be the most important section of the book, present the first widely published objective look at the two newest ways to profit in forex:

  1. Forex social networks and social trading: Use a community of fellow traders and ranked experts with published performance data to improve your skills. Or even better, let the best traders trade for you and earn better, more reliable returns with far less work. This is probably the most reliable way for those new to forex to get started actually making money, because you're using proven pros.

  2. Binary options: We present the pros and cons of a new, little known, and potentially very useful new forex trading instrument when used properly, binary options. In the right circumstances, these simplify your trading, give you more control over risk, and can up your odds of success.

For longer-term investors with little interest in trading, we show you how to use your knowledge of currency markets to:

- Enhance your capital gains and income.
- Reduce the risks from lack of currency diversification.
- Achieve all this without ever needing to directly trade currency pairs.

For both traders and investors, the book will:

- Guide you to some of the best free online sources of information on a wide range of forex topics, like trade advice, continuing trader training, broker reviews, and daily and weekly fundamental and technical analysis of specific currency pairs and overall markets.
- At the end of the book, leave you with specific ideas on what to do next to get started trading forex.

Yes, I'm offering you a lot. If you're investing your valuable time to read this, I owe you no less.

In sum, this is the forex book for:

- Profit-maximizing, risk-averse traders: Those seeking a sensible introduction to forex trading, who are more focused on steady monthly profits rather than gambling, via safer, easier, more profitable ways to trade than the short-term, high-leverage, high-risk methods most people associate with forex trading.
- Long-term investors with little or no interest in trading forex: Those seeking to lower currency risk and increase returns by diversifying into assets denominated in the currencies most likely to hold their value and appreciate over the long term.
- Anyone seeking an asset class that works in any market condition: Unlike stocks or bonds, the very nature of forex markets means there's always a bull market in some currency pair.

Whether you're a trader or a traditional, conservative, long-term investor seeking capital gains or steady income, this is the one forex book written specifically for you, not the wild-eyed action junkie day trader so beloved (and quickly fleeced) by many in the forex industry.

VISIT THESENSIBLEGUIDETOFOREX .COM FOR ADDITIONAL ONLINE CONTENT

Additional related content resides on the book's companion website at www.thesensibleguidetoforex.com. This website provides:

- Updates and additional content.
- Much clearer versions of the charts, in color and with much better resolution.

- Trade simulation exercises to practice what you've learned with the option for interactive feedback.
- More in-depth information on a variety of topics found in the book.
- A continual stream of articles on ideas for trades or investments for currency diversified income.

Go to www.thesensibleguidetoforex.com. The breadth and depth of the site's content will expand over time. We hope the site becomes a must-read for those seeking currency diversification, either as traders or investors seeking capital gains and/or income denominated in a variety of currencies.

Acknowledgments

Zack Miller, Managing Director of Lighthouse Capital Ltd, publisher of NewRulesofInvesting.com, and author of the seminal work on social networks and social trading, *TradeStream Your Way to Profits*. In addition to repeated and invaluable mentoring when I needed him most, he provided the first contact with...

SeekingAlpha.com CEO David Jackson and his editorial team. Together they've provided me and so many with the chance to prove ourselves with nothing more than our writing as a credential. That led to connecting with...

John Nyaradi, publisher of WallStreetSectorSelector.com and author of *Super Sectors: How to Outsmart the Market Using Sector Rotation and ETFs*, who in turn who introduced me to...

Senior Editor Laura Walsh of John Wiley & Sons, who paired me up with Senior Development Editor Judy Howarth, both of whom merit special thanks for their expert guidance, insight, and enormous patience in shepherding the manuscript into its finished form.

Anna Olswanger, my agent, guide, and interpreter throughout the journey through the world of publishing.

Longtime friend and wise counsel Shelly Freedman, Esq., for support, advice, and a special assist on the title.

Those whom I've met only through their writings:

In no particular order, Kathy Lien and Boris Schlossberg (Bkassetmanagement.com), John Kicklighter and Joel Kruger (d=DailyFX .com), Brian Dolan (Forex.com), Kathleen Brooks (Forex.com), John Mauldin (www.johnmauldin.com), Marc Chandler (Brown Brothers Harriman, marctomarket.com), James Chen (FXDD.com), Dr. Alexander Elder (Elder.com), Ed Ponsi, and the others referred to as resources for further information in Appendix A.

Samantha McGarry (Inkhouse Media and Marketing), and Alon Levitan (eToro), for their help on the forex social networks and trading chapter.

Shay Ben Asulin, CEO of Anyoption.com, for his cooperation in freeing up the time needed for this project.

It's easier to stand tall on the shoulders of giants.

Finally, my deepest thanks in advance to you, dear reader, for spreading the message contained herein. It's through you that we'll strike a blow against governments that want to steal our money through inflation, and brokers who seek a quick buck at our expense.

The Sensible Guide to Forex

CHAPTER 1

Three Must-Know Forex Facts

Forex's Top Three Lessons

The three most important lessons you'll ever learn about foreign exchange (forex) markets are:

1. **Everyone needs forex diversification.** Just as every competent investor needs to diversify by asset classes and sectors, so too they need exposure to assets in multiple currencies and an understanding of forex trends and what's driving them. Yet most have almost all their assets denominated in one or two currencies. Today, that is an especially fatal error, because the governments behind most major currencies intend to get out of debt by causing inflation, which allows them to repay their bonds with depreciated money. That's good for those governments, and disastrous for those holding their weakened currency and anything denominated in it. They won't admit it, but historically low interest rates and a steady stream of economic stimulus programs betray their real intentions. They want to reduce their real debt, and, in the process, your wealth, through the subtle tax of inflation. To protect yourself, you need as much of your assets as possible to be denominated in the currencies that are likely to hold their real value or appreciate in the long run, and lift your portfolio along with them. Having some commodities exposure is also a means of hedging this currency risk and playing forex trends, so both forex brokers and traders typically also deal with commodities. Thus while they're different asset classes, in practice forex tends to include commodity trading and investing.

1

2. **Forex markets offer significant advantages over other asset markets.** If trading with leverage, there is more risk, but that can be controlled and managed if you invest the time to learn and practice proper risk and money management (RAMM). You can benefit from forex without dealing with the added complications of RAMM issues (covered in Chapters 10 through 12).

3. **You can succeed using forex trading or investing if you learn and practice what follows.**

FACT 1: EVERYONE NEEDS FOREX DIVERSIFICATION EVEN IF YOU DON'T TRADE ACTIVELY

All those responsible for managing assets need some forex exposure and awareness of what drives forex markets.

You're Exposed: Cover Your Assets

Like it or not, you're exposed to currency risk. Every asset is denominated in some kind of currency. For example, consider the case of the US investor. Even if your portfolio has done well in U.S. dollar (USD) terms, over the past decades, the picture is less rosy against other major currencies and commodities. Because we all use imported products, this means your purchasing power and wealth are melting away if your assets are in a declining currency like the U.S. dollar.

For example, anyone whose assets are too concentrated in U.S. dollars has paid the penalty countless times whether they realize it or not. Remember oil at $10 per barrel, or gas at $0.35 per gallon? Remember the bestselling guide for frugal tourists in the late 1950s, *Europe on $5 a Day*? The final version came out in 2007, *Europe from $95 a Day*.[1] Remember how in the 1960s and early 1970s durable Japanese cars were considered inexpensive?

This decline in purchasing power isn't just due to inflation. For example, the U.S. dollar has been in steady decline for decades against many other important currencies.

- Since 2000, the USD is down 32 percent versus the Canadian Dollar (CAD).
- Since 1990, the USD is down 52 percent versus the Japanese Yen (JPY).
- Since 1970, the USD is down 75 percent versus the Swiss Franc (CHF).

Today, currency diversification is no longer optional. As governments maintain historically low interest rates and assorted stimulus plans that risk devaluing their currencies and your savings, currency diversification is as essential for your portfolio as sector and asset class diversification. Failure to do so is foolhardy. You don't have to be an active trader to ride the strongest long-term forex trends. We'll show you many ways that passive, longer-term investors can protect themselves.

While Americans may be waking up to the need for currency diversification, that's hardly news to most of the world, which has dealt with this issue for years. In other areas of the world, like Japan or Italy, with histories of weak currencies, participation in forex trading is a widespread middle-class phenomenon. For example, Japanese housewives are such prominent participants in forex that they're referred to collectively as "Mrs. Wantanabe."[2]

As an American student in Israel in the 1980s, I watched families run to spend their monthly pay check because its purchasing power would fall every day due to high inflation. In the mid-1980s, friends with dollars could exchange them for local currency at higher black market rates and purchase anything from cars to apartments in the local currency at a 40 percent discount.

Even Long-Term Buy-and-Hold Investors Need Forex Diversification

Therefore, just as wise investors diversify into different kinds of assets and sectors, they must also diversify into the different kinds of currencies, particularly those likely to appreciate versus their peers. As we'll discuss in Chapters 10 through 12, even long-term buy-and-hold passive investors who don't actively trade currencies can protect and grow their wealth by allocating portions of their portfolios to instruments denominated in the most promising currencies.

Although most forex market participants are short-term speculators, currencies can be excellent long-term plays, because currency pairs tend to form stronger, more stable long-term trends compared to stocks. Why? Because the fundamentals of the underlying economies that drive currency prices change much more slowly than those of individual companies. It's a longer, more complex process to change the relative growth rates of entire economies (or currency unions in the case of the Euro) than it is for an individual company. Even better, unlike stocks, currencies don't all move together in the same direction, nor do they all respond in the same way to other markets or global indexes. Indeed, some currencies move in the opposite direction, providing a genuine bear market hedge without the complications (or periodic bans) involved in shorting stocks.

In short, currency markets produce some of the most stable long-term price trends that are ideally suited for long-term passive investors, and also can provide simple, effective ways to profit in bear markets. As we'll discuss in Chapter 12, the right currency investments can provide long-term appreciation as well as steady income yields.

FACT 2: POTENTIAL FOR BETTER RISK-ADJUSTED RETURNS

There are more reasons to have forex exposure beyond currency diversification. Once you do some homework, you'll realize that forex is arguably among the most rewarding asset classes for traders and investors. Even though forex is dominated by short-term, high-risk speculators, there are investing/trading styles suitable for both:

1. More conservative active traders who use longer-term holding periods and specific methods and instruments to reduce risk.
2. Long-term investors who know how to:
   - Ride stable, proven, long-term forex trends for capital gains.
   - Earn steady income from "carry trades" or from investing in bonds, dividend stocks, and other income vehicles denominated in the right currencies.

Forex Markets Often Provide Advanced Warnings of Changes in Other Markets

Forex markets often react to changing conditions before other markets, providing valuable advanced warning of possible trend changes. As we'll learn later, certain currencies tend to move same direction as "risk assets" like stocks or industrial commodities, and others tend to act like "safe haven assets" like bonds. When these correlations break down, that too can often be a warning of a change in direction for other markets. We'll delve further into this kind of intermarket analysis in Chapter 9.

Forex Needn't Be Any Riskier Than Other Markets

Forex has a gotten a reputation for being excessively risky due to a combination of:

1. High failure rates due to beginner traders who failed to do their homework and understand the risks associated with the high leverage (see borrowed funds in Chapter 2) commonly used in most forex trading.

2. Brokers who failed to provide sufficient training to deal with the risks of using leverage.

However, you can reduce and manage the risks. There are:

- Brokers, like etoro.com, that allow you to adjust your leverage down to what you can handle, and they will provide guidance on the appropriate level.
- Unlevered ways to play forex, which are no riskier than an exchange-traded fund (ETF) or a stock.
- A variety of techniques to reduce risk in forex trading, as well as new instruments for simpler, safer forex trading (see Chapter 11).

As we'll see further on, making money trading forex can be easier than in stocks and other more traditional asset markets, particularly in bear markets. However, you do need to do your homework, especially if trading with leverage, which adds risk as well as reward. Part of that homework is to learn more conservative, simpler techniques that make it easier to succeed at forex than those most commonly used. Until recently, there was no single source for learning this more sensible, conservative forex. No longer. This is the only book to gather these methods into one collection.

Part of forex's reputation for excessive risk comes from stories appearing in the mainstream media. The typical plotline runs like this: Some gullible novices believed a broker's get-rich-quick pitch about how they'd score fast money with little effort or background in forex. These geniuses were shocked (shocked!) to find out otherwise. The conclusion: Forex should either be avoided altogether or is unsuitable for most people.

If you're smart enough to be reading this book, you will see the absurdity of that reasoning. Just because there are individuals who behave stupidly with cars or power tools doesn't mean that these should be avoided altogether. The same goes for forex, including the typical leveraged trading. If you've had the right preparation and have the discipline to practice proper trade planning risk and money management (RAMM), you can keep the risk to acceptable levels, just as with any other kind of investing or trading. As with driving, there are ways to simulate the experience until you're ready for the real thing, and ways to then start slowly under less challenging conditions until you're ready for more challenging conditions

No Uptick Rule: Just as Easy to Profit in a Falling Market as in a Rising One

Just as it's easier to row with the current than against it, it's easier to profit by trading in the direction of an established market trend. Unlike with stocks (and other financial markets), in forex it's as easy to profit from falling markets as from rising ones. This is a huge advantage of forex markets.

During an uptrend, when prices are rising, most traders go long, meaning they buy the asset with the hope of selling it at a higher price. They're attempting to buy low and sell high, the classic way most people view investing.

During a downtrend, when prices are falling, it's easier to profit by trading with that downtrend. So, the more sophisticated equities traders try to exploit that downward momentum and sell short; that is, sell borrowed shares with the hope of buying them back later at lower price, returning the borrowed shares, and profiting on the difference—for example, sell borrowed shares for $100 per share, buy them at $80, return them to a broker, and pocket $20 per share.

However, most stock exchanges are controlled and regulated by those who have an interest in keeping stock prices high. The politicians who oversee market regulations and the executives who run the listed companies look better when prices are up and are more likely to keep their jobs. Falling prices make them look bad, and extended downtrends can be toxic for their careers.

Many of the major stock exchanges tend to make profiting from downtrends harder. For example, many exchanges have some kind of uptick rule that permits shorting the stock only when price is rising. That keeps short sellers out when prices are moving lower and the odds are in their favor, and forces them to sell into rising prices and absorb losses until the downtrend resumes. During the strongest downtrends that offer the fastest profits, upticks are rare so many have no chance to ride the move lower at all. In times of market panics, which can be incredibly profitable for short sellers, exchanges have banned short selling altogether. Since the start of the Great Financial Crisis, short selling has been periodically banned during the juiciest downtrends in both the United States and Europe:

- In the United States, the Securities and Exchange Commission (SEC) did so in September of 2008.[3]
- Regulators in Spain, Italy, Belgium, and France banned short selling of their banking stocks in August of 2011.[4]
- Some markets employ circuit breaker rules that automatically stop trading once an instrument has fallen a certain percentage in a given day.

Though ways exist to circumvent these restrictions, they can be more complicated, expensive, and riskier. These added obstacles effectively exclude many individuals from playing strong downtrends even as the big institutions and professionals feast on them.

As we'll learn in Chapter 2, no such restrictions exist against selling a currency, or more precisely, a currency pair (they always trade in pairs), so it's as easy to profit during a downtrend as an uptrend. Indeed we'll see that the essence of trading a currency pair always involves buying (being long) one pair and selling (being short) another, depending on whether you buy or sell the pair.

Low Correlation to Other Financial Markets

In other words, because some currencies move in the opposite direction of stocks and other risk assets, there's always a bull market somewhere in forex. This is a critical advantage. As we'll learn later, most globally traded assets tend to move together. For example, most equities move in the same direction as their relevant index. With forex, however, different currencies move in different directions under the same market conditions. So, you have a way of profiting from fear even when regulators ban or limit short sales of stocks or refuse to recognize the rights of those holding insurance against sovereign bond defaults to collect.[5]

One reason it's easier to profit in bear markets with forex is that the process of profiting from a decline in a currency pair is no different than it is for profiting from its appreciation. We'll explain that in detail later.

Another reason it's easier to profit with forex than with stocks is the availability and ease of commodities trading at most forex brokers, which enhances your chances of profiting regardless of market direction because, as we'll see later, certain commodities like oil can and do lose their normal market correlations. At least one commodity, gold, isn't connected with market optimism or pessimism like other assets but moves with something else entirely, the need to hedge against loss of purchasing power of the major currencies.

As we'll see when we discuss intermarket analysis as a trading tool, currency traders frequently find currency and commodity trading to be nearly interchangeable. You use the same account, trading platform, and analysis. Whether they trade a currency or related commodity often depends on which offers a better way to exploit the same idea.

The Most Flexible Hours

Forex markets trade in a seamless 24-hour session, 5.5 days a week, from Sunday 5:15 P.M. EST until Friday 5:00 P.M. EST. So, those with work or family commitments can trade a fully liquid market whenever convenient.

Forex Markets Offer the Best Liquidity

A liquid market is one that has many buyers and sellers. The more buyers and sellers at any given moment, the more likely you are to get a fair market price when you buy or sell. The more liquid a market is, the less likely it is that a few otherwise insignificant orders or players can move prices in wild, unpredictable movements. Indeed, unlike in stock markets, even the biggest players will have trouble manipulating the price action in major currency pairs beyond a matter of hours. Two exceptions to that, which we'll discuss later, are a few central banks and crooked forex brokers. Fortunately, dishonest brokers can be identified and avoided with some research,[6] and central bank intervention risk is usually known or soon uncovered after the first incident, putting markets on guard.

The more liquid the market, the easier it is to be profitable. Prices are fairer and more stable, less subject to sudden unpredictable movements. You should generally avoid trading in illiquid markets, except on rare occasions when trying to enter positions at bargain prices offered by those desperate to close a position.

Forex markets trading volumes dwarf those of equities. Latest estimates put average daily forex turnover at around $4.71 trillion, of which individual retail traders alone account for about $1.5 trillion.[7] For perspective, look at Figure 1.1 to see how this volume dwarfs that of the world's leading stock exchanges individually and combined.

That huge trading volume, going on 24 hours a day, means abundant buyers and sellers are usually present at any given time. That means you're more likely to get a fair price no matter when you buy or sell. It means that you rarely see partial fills, which are cases in which you can only buy or

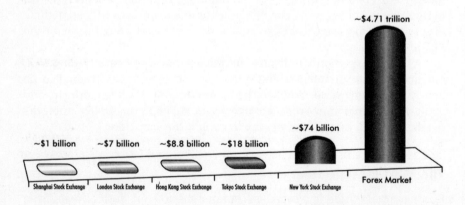

~$4.71 trillion

~$74 billion

~$1 billion ~$7 billion ~$8.8 billion ~$18 billion

Shanghai Stock Exchange London Stock Exchange Hong Kong Stock Exchange Tokyo Stock Exchange New York Stock Exchange Forex Market

As of late 2010
Per Dow Jones Newswires as of July 2011

FIGURE 1.1 Average Daily Trading Volume

sell part of your intended order. For more on the most liquid hours of the trading day, see Appendix C.

No Centralized Exchange with Specialists Holding Monopoly Power to Regulate Prices

In most stock markets, the specialist is a single entity that serves as buyer and seller of last resort and controls the spread, which is the difference between the buy and sell price for a given stock. Though in theory they are regulated and supervised to prevent their abusing that power to manipulate prices at the expense of the trading public, specialists are experts at knowing when they can get away with a degree of this and force you to buy higher or sell lower.

In forex, no single specialist regulates prices of individual currency pairs. Rather, multiple exchanges and brokers are competing for your business.

Though the lack of centralized exchanges can complicate regulation, competition and easy access to pricing information has brought competitive pricing.

Less Slippage

Slippage is the difference between the stated price on your screen and the actual price you pay or receive. The less liquid the market, the more often slippage happens because fewer traders are present to take the other side of your trade. For example, let's say you buy 1,000 shares at $30, and to protect yourself in case the price falls, you place a protective stop loss order to sell the shares at $29. However, if there are no buyers at $29, then the price "gaps" lower until it hits the next buy order, so you incur a greater loss.

Because forex markets are:

- typically running at full speed in at least one if not two continents 24 hours a day, over five days a week
- have no specialists controlling prices, and
- trade at such larger volumes than equities,

forex players face lower risk of slippage. Indeed, many forex market makers provide some kind of "no slippage" policy that lessens the degree of price uncertainty.

The Best Risk/Reward Potential

Forex trading or investing offers some of the best risk/reward opportunities of any financial market IF (big if here) you know how to exploit it. The availability of leverage, meaning the use of borrowed funds to control large blocks of currencies and thus magnify gains and losses, creates unmatched profit potential for those with limited trading capital IF (again, really big IF here) they learn how to control the downside risk. For example, with 100:1 leverage, a 1 percent move means 100 percent profit. It also means 100 percent loss.

Understanding and controlling this risk, and knowing how much is appropriate in a given situation, is what distinguishes the winners and professionals from the losers on whom they feed. Risk and money management (RAMM) is what allows you to survive the learning stages with your funds and confidence intact.

Therefore, throughout this book we will cover how to reduce risk of large losses while retaining the exceptional profit potential. This involves learning the right attitudes, expectations, as well as the key analytical and trade planning skills. If you do what we teach, and continue your education in the ways we suggest, then if you have the talent, you'll have a chance to earn more with less capital than in other markets like stocks or bonds. At the same time, you'll keep losses from the losing trades at affordable levels so that you remain consistently profitable over the long run.

The Lowest Startup and Trading Costs

- Forex trading has among the lowest entry or startup costs in money and time of any financial market, in terms of trading capital and training/equipment costs, as follows: Unlike most markets, you do not need many thousands of dollars to get started. That's because in forex, we can trade with leverage (borrowed funds), typically 100:1 or more. This allows us to make substantial profits on small price movements. However, as noted above, that also means:
- For every $1 you have at risk, you control $100. For every $1,000, you control $100,000.
- For every 1 percent move in price, you have a 100 percent profit or loss. Much of this guide is about how to minimize that risk of large losses while maximizing the odds of profiting. It involves learning to cut losing trades short and let winners run so you can be profitable even when wrong on most of your trades.

    In theory, you can often start with as little as $100. However, you'll learn that you'll lower your risks and have more chances to profit by starting with at least a few thousand dollars (or the equivalent) if possible. As we'll see later, the small position sizes available from mini and micro accounts allow those with limited funds to trade smaller positions, which keeps the percentage of capital risked per trade acceptably low. More on that later.

- Training and equipment costs: Forex brokers typically provide free full-featured trading platforms and data feeds, and the better brokers offer extensive archives of free training materials and market analysis. With online stock brokers, traders typically need to maintain minimum balances or minimum trading volumes to get free quality charting and trading platforms from their brokers or get access to worthwhile research.
- Risk-Free Practice Accounts: Even better, they typically provide full-featured practice or demo accounts that allow smart beginners to simulate most of the trading experience and practice with play money until they feel ready to risk their capital.
- Low transaction costs: Most forex brokers charge no fees, commissions, or hidden charges. They earn their money on the difference, called the spread, between the buy and sell price, typically a few ten-thousandths, called pips, of the price. Depending on the lot sizes traded, a typical two-pip spread, four pips total to open and close a position, can cost anywhere from $0.40 to $40. In general transaction costs are very competitive compared to those of online stock brokers

In sum, you can earn more with less investment. Better still, you can do it while keeping your current job. The first step is to study this book.

FACT 3: YOU CAN DO THIS

As with any kind of financial market trading, you need to be able to answer the following question:

How Can I Compete against the Pros and Big Institutions?

Whenever you are trading in global asset markets, most of your competition consists of the top professionals who are responsible for most of the trading volume. They have nearly every advantage over you: skill, experience, and any advantage that money can buy, the best equipment, information sources, industry insider contacts, whatever.

You have no better chance of beating someone like David Woo or Stephen Jen at short-term forex trading than you do at beating Michael Jordan or Lebron James at basketball.[8]

So how can you compete?

You don't.

The real answer obviously is, don't even try to trade like they do.

That's fine; there's plenty of money to be made if you know the secret, which is really no secret. It's just common sense.

In the beginning, don't try to be a bad imitation of an experienced pro. Instead, focus on becoming a great beginner. That means finding and using the trading techniques, styles, and instruments that even a beginner can, in measured stages, start to implement successfully. You'll spend most of your time calmly and persistently searching the charts for those few easier opportunities, rather than spending long hours glued to your computer, frenetically making lots of trades based on rash decisions, based on short time frames in which price movements are harder to predict, with the odds firmly against you.

How do you identify and execute these simple, low-risk, high-yield trades? Funny you should ask. The following is a summary of how we'll do it.

How David Beats Goliath: More on What This Book Will and Won't Do

As I've said before, you have to start somewhere. Welcome to the some-where. We'll teach a variety of ways to harness the power of forex markets that are safer, simpler, and more likely to be profitable than the higher-risk methods most commonly practiced. Regardless of your skill level or risk tolerance, there are solutions here to suit you.

A prime focus of this book is to be a trader's roadmap for finding, planning, and executing trades that are safe and simple enough for beginner to intermediate skill levels. More specifically:

- We will teach you how to identify and trade only the lowest risk, highest potential yield opportunities with easy to identify low-risk entry and exit points. When prices are rising, that means finding the trades where you can buy close to the likely near-term low price, called support, and sell at the likely high price, called resistance, for a given holding period. When prices are falling, you'll do the opposite. In other words, sell a currency at its likely high, and buy it back at a lower price, and profit on the difference, which is called "going short" a given currency pair. If that seems confusing, don't worry because we'll explain it in depth later. Just know it can be done.
- Unlike almost every other forex book, we will show you simple ways to trade the more predictable, persistent, and thus safer, longer-term forex trends. We will show you alternative instruments to the usual high leverage spot market forex trading.

- We will show you to how to be a disciplined trader, focused on profits, not gambling. This includes doing something you'll rarely see in forex books. We will NOT encourage you to trade short-term intraday moves in which you enter and exit within a matter of minutes or hours. Day trading forex is suicidal for most traders, particularly the less experienced ones. Why? Intraday price movements are dominated by short-term, unpredictable money flows from large players. Most traders don't have the technical skills and information resources to monitor and interpret what these large institutions are doing, why they're doing it, and what these large orders suggest about future price movements. Intraday trading is great for broker trading volumes and profits, which is why so much of the free analysis they provide focuses on this kind of short-term cowboy trading in which you enter and exit within minutes or hours, rarely longer than a few days. For all but the most skilled traders, trading those time frames is just gambling. This book's aim is to help you make money, or at least minimize the losses that are an unavoidable part of the learning process.
- New or uneducated forex traders who attempt to day-trade forex really aren't even attempting to be serious traders. Instead, they're looking for some gambling fun. They'd be better off at a casino, where at least they might get some free food and drinks. This widespread gambler's mentality is a prime reason why the failure rate for new traders is so high. Many new traders never treat trading like a business. *They fail to prepare, so inevitably they've prepared to fail.*
- We will coach you to manage risk so you can be profitable even when most of your trades lose money. That means:
  - Know when and how to exit quickly and minimize losses when the odds go against you, and accept those losses as part of the business.
  - Know when and how to stay in the trade until your indicators show the odds are no longer with you, and know to avoid the temptation to grab a quick profit and get out too soon.
  - Create a simple but thorough trading plan so your decisions about position size and entry and exit points are made beforehand and not under the emotional duress of an ongoing trade with money at risk.
  - Manage your trading capital so you can survive sudden unanticipated losses.
  - Help you practice the techniques we teach with some trade simulation exercises.
- We will explain the basics of trader psychology so you don't defeat yourself with the wrong expectations, and you will learn how to handle winning and losing streaks.

A War Story: One View of the Typical Forex Trader

A smart CEO of one forex company once said this about his typical customers: "Just between us girls, most of them would just as soon take that
money and go to Atlantic City or Las Vegas, but for whatever reason they
trade forex instead." (I'm quoting from memory, but this is the jist of it.)
   Even though there's nothing wrong with having some fun if you like
gambling, this book is aimed at the serious minority seeking not just fun
but profit.

What's the Catch?

There is a catch: Forex trading requires time and effort as with any other
competitive, lucrative field. In Chapters 10 and 11, I will show you some
approaches that are easier than the usual trading methods, but even these
require study and practice. Like achieving anything else worthwhile, especially a lucrative, stimulating career, you'll need the discipline for a sustained investment of time, effort, and money. You'll suffer some uncertainty, frustration, and failure, with no guarantee of success, as you would
in achieving anything else worth attaining.

   Sorry if I'm bursting anyone's bubble. Fortunately, you've got the right
book to minimize the drain on your time, emotions, and finances.

Most Traders Fail within Their First Two Years

While I'm trashing get-rich-quick illusions, here's a helping of fear to
keep you motivated and paying attention. In case you forgot (or skipped)
what I wrote in the Read This First section earlier, here's a little fact
I've never seen acknowledged in any forex book, though it's a well-worn
topic of forex trader forums on such major forex content websites like
ForexFactory.com.[9]

   The fact is this: Per available data, the odds are firmly against you. Most
forex traders lose money and are gone within a matter of months.[10]

   U.S.[11] regulators have reported that the vast majority (around 80 percent or more) of forex traders fail within their first two years. Few manage to last at day trading in general.[12] At least one large publicly traded
forex brokerage reports that 70 percent of its traders are unprofitable,
close enough to provide additional confirmation.[13]

   Many take a rather simplistic view that because most traders fail, forex
trading should be avoided altogether by amateur traders or investors. By
that same reasoning, one should avoid real estate and insurance sales and

any other field that offers low barriers to entry, is potentially lucrative, and attracts intense competition from which only a minority prosper.

Consider that one cannot even begin to practice in most lucrative, skilled professions without years of professional training, typically costing over $100,000 in tuition, related expenses, and lost wages. After that, there's a demanding battery of exams, followed by years of relatively low-paying jobs with grueling hours, commuting, office politics, and ass kissing thrown in as you learn how the job is done.

Even after passing through all those hoops, only a minority will make the big money. From my own experience working in large accounting firms, I'd be surprised if 10 percent of the new hires out of college eventually become partners or find equally lucrative roles in the field.

Having worked with traders for years in various capacities as fellow trader and chief analyst tasked with advising clients, it's clear that most traders don't do the preparation needed to have even a chance to succeed. The small minority that attempt a serious program of study and practice have the huge additional obstacle of needing to somehow figure out how to design their own training program to duplicate the theoretical, practical, and mentoring aspects of other professional training programs. What sources to study? Which skills to learn in which order? What websites or forums to browse? What trading styles to start with?

I wrote this book for those like you, the sincere, serious traders or investors who seek the path to better results.

Here is the good news:

- The failure rates are inflated by all those casual gamblers who were never serious traders.
- That you're reading this book puts you in a different category of trader altogether. You're doing the right preparation as you would for any profit-making endeavor, and you're going to get sound, conservative advice. If you heed my lessons, the losses you incur as part of your learning will be well within your means, and if you've the ability and discipline, you'll be on the road to real success.

Even if in the end forex trading isn't for you, you'll have learned valuable ways to profit from forex as a long-term investor.

In sum, I can't guarantee you success, but I can make you better, and put you miles ahead of the rest of the unprepared suckers.

CHAPTER 2

Forex Basics

This chapter covers:

- Basics of Currencies and Currency Pairs
- Currencies Trade in Pairs and Why That Matters
- Size Matters: Types of Currency Pairs
- Pips—The Universal Currency of Currencies
- Leverage and Margin: Their Relationship and Impact on Risk
- The Three Facets of Risk and Risk Control
- The Core Four: The Most Important Skills for Success

BASICS OF CURRENCIES AND CURRENCY PAIRS

Here we are going to cover only what you really need to know about currency pairs in order to understand the material that follows. At some point, perhaps even before you proceed to the next chapter, you'll want to know more and can search the Internet to explore answers to such questions as:

- What are the unique aspects of a given currency or pair?
- What news is most important for a given currency or pair?

- When is the best time to trade a given currency or pair?
- What currencies or pairs do better in which situations?
- What's carry trade and how do you use it to earn steady income?
- How are currency markets changing and what do I need to know about that?

Trade Only the Most Liquid Currencies

Though most currencies are convertible and tradable, most traders stick to the eight major currencies (known as majors) because they have the most liquidity or availability, meaning that lots of buyers and sellers are usually present at any given time That means you're likely to get the best price and avoid slippage (discussed in Chapter 1).

For example, if you want to buy or sell something, you'll get a better price if thousands of counterparties are competing for what you have to offer, as opposed to just one or two.

The Major Currencies

Here are the eight major currencies, along with their symbols and nick-names, ranked in order of liquidity:

Symbol	Country	Currency	Nickname
USD	United States	Dollar	Buck, Greenback, The Reserve Currency
EUR	Euro Zone members	Euro	Fiber, The Unified Currency, The Single Currency, The Anti-Dollar
JPY	Japan	Yen	Yen, Jippy
GBP	Great Britain	Pound	Cable
CHF	Switzerland	Franc	Swissy
CAD	Canada	Dollar	Loonie
AUD	Australia	Dollar	Aussie
NZD	New Zealand	Dollar	Kiwi

Currency Labels Explained   Why these symbols? In general, the first two letters stand for the country, and the last letter signifies the currency (see Figure 2.1).

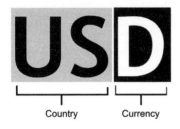

Country	Currency

Currency codes are three letters.
Usually the first two signify the
country and the third stands for
the currency name.

Other Major Currencies

GBP
Great British Pound

AUD
Australian Dollar

JPY
Japanese Yen

CAD
Canadian Dollar

NZD
New Zealand Dollar

CHF
Swiss (Confoederatio
Helvetica) Franc

The slight exception to this rule is the Euro
(EUR), which just uses the first three letters of
the word Europe.

FIGURE 2.1 Decoding Currency Symbols

Risk versus Safe Haven Currencies: Definition and Ranking

Depending on how they behave, these major currencies are classified as one of two kinds: risk and safety or safe haven currencies. For now, just know that in general:

- Risk currencies are those that appreciate in value in times of optimism and depreciate in times of pessimism like other risk assets such as stock indexes or industrial commodities.
- Safe haven or safety currencies depreciate in times of optimism and depreciate in times of pessimism like other safety assets that are in demand when markets are fearful, such as investment grade bonds.

Here's a table showing how these currencies rank on the risk-to-safety spectrum:

RISK					SAFE HAVEN		
RISK CURRENCIES					SAFE HAVEN CURRENCIES		
AUD	NZD	CAD	EUR	GBP	CHF	USD	JPY

In other words, the AUD is the currency that tends to rise the most when markets feel optimistic and want risk assets, and the JPY tends to fall the most. In times of fear, when risk assets are selling off, the opposite occurs.

- These labels refer solely to how these currencies behave relative to other assets. These categories do NOT refer to the safety of these currencies as a store of value. For example, the JPY generally behaves as the ultimate safety currency, however few would dispute that the CAD is a better long term store of value given Canada's better fiscal health.
- While the above general ranking works over a given period of days or weeks, it rarely applies perfectly on a daily basis. For example, even if markets are feeling very optimistic, and classic risk barometers like the S&P 500 are trending higher, currency specific news events can cause lower ranked risk currencies to outperform the AUD and NZD.

We'll review the concepts of risk and safety currencies later, and cover them in more depth, because they're critical for understanding and predicting how currencies and markets will interact in different situations.

CURRENCIES TRADE IN PAIRS AND WHY THAT MATTERS

Like everything else, currencies need to be priced in a currency, so currencies always trade in pairs. This fact makes forex markets different from other markets in two critical ways.

Price Movements Are Always Relative to Another Currency

Here's the first big difference.

Thus, unlike how traditional asset markets price stocks or commodities in terms of a given currency, foreign exchange (forex) prices are the product of the movement of one currency relative to another.

For example, when traders talk about the price of the U.S. dollars (USD), they're referring to the dollar value relative to another currency, depending on which pair they're considering.

This is a critical difference from other asset markets.

- For example, on a given stock exchange, traders need only consider how share prices change relative to the local currency, which is assumed to have an essentially fixed value regardless of what's actually happening in forex markets. However, forex traders must consider how a currency will move relative to multiple currencies, all of which are moving at the same time. For example, it's common for a given currency to be up versus some currencies but down versus others. That often complicates an assessment of its overall strength. There is no single definitive index like the S&P 500 for currencies. Even popular currency indices like the USD index only capture the USD's strength relative to a limited basket of currencies, and may not tell how the U.S. dollar is faring relative to others. For example:

- If traders wants to benefit from the USD's strength the most over a given period, they must also choose the currency against which it will be strongest during the anticipated time span of the trade, be it an hour, year, or anything in between.
- Even when the New Zealand Dolar (NZD) is relatively weak, if the USD is doing even worse, you can still profit from buying the NZDUSD.

It's Just as Easy to Profit in Bear Markets as in Bull Markets

This is such a huge advantage over other markets such as stocks that it alone justifies learning to trade forex, because forex trading gives you an easier, more reliable way to play bear markets.

- In other markets, there are often technical rules that make it harder to profit from downtrends. These include the periodic outright bans on short selling (typically when that's most profitable), and the Uptick Rule mentioned in Chapter 1, which often prevents less sophisticated traders from catching the most profitable sharp downtrends, and keeps them away until the trend is moving higher, thus making short selling riskier.
- When you short stocks, your broker must borrow shares from someone who owns them. These aren't always available when you want them, because other short sellers want to borrow them too.

However, such bans are impossible in currency markets, because currencies trade in pairs, which means you're always selling one in order to buy the other, that is, shorting (selling) one and going long (buying) the other. Some currencies (safe haven currencies) rise in times of pessimism or bear markets; others (risk currencies) rise in times of optimism or bull markets. Profiting from bear markets is just a matter of buying safe haven currencies and selling risk currencies to pay for them. In bull markets you do just the opposite. Unlike specific stock exchanges, currency markets are too international and interlocked for anyone to ban selling a given currency at a given price. Even central banks' attempts at manipulating prices are rarely sustainable for long.

Confused? Stay with me here—the details of how we're always buying one currency and selling another, and how we profit from bear as well as bull markets, will be clarified further on when we learn about the anatomy of a forex pair price quote and better understand what actually happens in a forex trade.

How to Read a Forex Pair Price Quote

Table 2.1 shows a sample forex price quote that you'd see on your trading platform, with explanatory notes added. To make the table easier to follow, I'm going to intentionally repeat definitions and examples. It's important that you take the time to go through this carefully until all is clear.

In other words:

- Read the pair as the Euro-U.S. Dollar or the Euro-Dollar.
- The currency on the left, the EUR, is called the base currency. That's because price movements of the EURUSD are "based" on the base currency. *The EURUSD price will rise on the charts if the EUR is rising versus the USD.* In other words, when this pair is trending higher, it means the EUR is rising versus the USD (and vice versa, the USD is falling versus the EUR). When the EURUSD is falling, that means the EUR is falling versus the USD, and the USD is rising versus the EUR.

  Thus, when you think the base currency will rise versus the counter currency, you buy or "go long" the pair. For example, if you think the Great Britain Pound (GBP) will appreciate most relative to the Japanese Yen (JPY), you would buy the GBPJPY. If you believe the opposite, you'd sell the pair. Relax, we'll teach you how to determine that later.

- The currency on the right, in this case the USD, is usually called the counter currency because the price of the pair moves "counter" to the value of the USD versus the EUR. That is, if the EURUSD is rising, the value of the USD relative to the EUR is falling. The currency on the right is also called the quote or terms currency, because price movements of the EURUSD are "quoted" in "terms" of the USD. Price is read as counter currency per base currency. In other words, do not read the pair like a fraction. Instead, we read the EURUSD price as: U.S. Dollars per Euro and not Euros per Dollar. For example, if the EURUSD price is 1.4000, that means the price or exchange rate is 1.4000 USD per EUR, or, the EUR costs 1.4 USD.

TABLE 2.1 Sample Forex Price Quote

Pair	Bid Price	Spread	Ask Price
EUR/USD or EURUSD (Read as Euro-U.S. Dollar or Euro-Dollar)	1.3921	3	1.3924
The currency on the left, the EUR, is called the base currency, because the EURUSD's price is "based" on whether the EUR rises versus the USD. When you buy (go long) the pair, you are buying (going long) the base currency—in this case the EUR—and selling dollars to pay for it. When you sell (go short) the pair, you are selling (going short) the base currency, to pay for the counter or quote currency, in this case the USD	The currency on the right, the USD, is called the counter, quote, or terms currency because the EURUSD price moves "counter" to the value of the USD versus the EUR, and the EURUSD's price is "quoted" in "terms" of the currency on the right, in this case, the USD. When you buy the pair, you sell (go short) the counter currency (the USD here) to pay for the base currency (the EUR here). When you sell (go short) this pair, you are buying (going long) the counter currency (the USD here) and selling the base (the EUR).	When you sell the EURUSD, *you sell at the lower bid price.*	This is in place of the fee or commission the market maker or broker would get for matching buyer and seller.	When you buy or go long the pair, *you buy at the higher ask price.*

- The above price quote means you could do one of the following:

Buy the EURUSD pair at the (higher) ASK price.	OR	Sell the EURUSD pair at the (lower) BID price.
That Means:		That Means:
You buy Euros and pay for them buy selling dollars, paying the higher ask price. For every 1 EUR you buy, you're selling $1.3924 USD, regardless of whether your account is funded with JPY, GBP, EUR, and so on. Amounts are converted as needed.		You sell Euros and get U.S. dollars in exchange for them at the lower sell or bid price. For every 1 EUR you sell, you're being paid $1.3921 USD.

- In sum, you're always buying at the higher price and selling at the lower price so that the broker can earn the spread in lieu of fees or commissions.
- When you buy or go long the EURUSD, you're long the base currency EUR and you're short the USD. When you sell the pair, you're doing the opposite. Thus, you're always long one currency and shorting the other, so it's as easy to short one currency versus another and, thus, benefit from its downtrend as it is to be long that same pair.
- **When you enter or exit a position you buy at the higher ask price, and sell at the lower bid price**. Why? The difference or spread between the bid and ask prices is the profit the market maker or broker earns for pairing buyers and sellers instead of charging a commission like stock brokers.

Figure 2.2 shows how a price quote might appear on a typical trading platform.

Don't worry about understanding the details in the above order window. The only thing you really need to know is that you buy at the higher price and sell at the lower price. To profit, you first need to overcome the transaction costs, in this case the spread, as you would in any other kind of market, whether they call it a commission or anything else.

Summary of Currency Pair Basics

- You buy the EURUSD at the higher ask price if the following occurs:
  - You want to open a new buy position for the pair (go long the pair), you're betting that the price of the EURUSD pair (in Dollars per

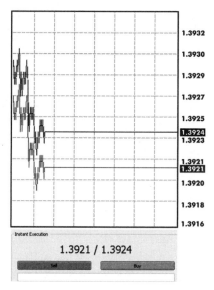

FIGURE 2.2   Euro versus U.S. Dollar (USD)

Euro) will rise. In other words, you think the EUR will rise in price versus the USD.
  - You want to close an existing short position in which you had bet the opposite, that the pair would drop, (the EUR would fall versus the USD), either to take your profits or to cut your losses on your short position.
- You sell the EURUSD at the lower bid price if the following occurs:
  - You want to open a new sell position for the pair (go short the pair), betting the price of the EURUSD pair (in Dollars per Euro) will fall. In other words, you think the EUR will fall versus the USD.
  - You want to close an existing long position in which you had bet the opposite (that the pair would rise in value, meaning the EUR would rise versus the USD), to either take profits or to cut losses on your long position.

Why It's Just as Easy to Profit from Falling Prices

Do you see now how benefiting from a downtrend in a currency is no harder that riding an uptrend? Let's review.

Whenever you buy or sell a currency pair, you're always buying (going long) one and selling (going short) the other. In times of optimism (bull markets), you want to be long pairs that have risk currencies as the base currency (one on the left) or short pairs that have safe haven currencies as the base currency. In times of pessimism (bear markets), you want to do the opposite, because:

- When you're long a currency pair, you're long (buying) the base currency and paying for it by shorting (selling) the counter currency.
- When you're short a currency pair, you're short (selling) the base and buying (going long) the counter currency.
- Pairs that have risk currencies as the base currency are called risk pairs. Those with safety or safe haven base currencies are called safety or safe haven pairs.

For example, if you think markets will favor risk currencies and that the EUR (a risk currency) will be strong relative to the USD (a safety currency), then you buy the EURUSD. When you do that, you will be buying the EUR and paying for it by selling (shorting) the USD. If you believe the opposite, sell the pair. That means you're selling the EUR and using the proceeds to buy U.S. dollars.

In sum, whether you buy or sell a currency pair, you're always buying (going long) one and selling (going short) the other.

Thus, unlike other asset markets, profiting from a downtrend is as easy as profiting from an uptrend. Currency traders are always long one currency and short the other. Regulators can't ban shorting one currency without banning all forex trading of all pairs that include that currency. Even if there were widespread will to do this, the lack of a single exchange would make such a ban difficult to enforce. Even central banks have a hard time manipulating currency prices for more than a short time.

Remember: Currency Pair Prices Are "Based on" the Base Currency   Currency pair charts move in the direction of the base currency (the one on the left), and in the opposite direction of the quote, terms, or counter currency. When you think the base currency will rise versus the counter currency, you buy the pair because you're buying the base currency and paying for it by selling the counter currency. When you believe the opposite, you sell the pair because then you're selling the base currency to buy the counter currency.

Let's see this in action.

Pounds Sterling/U.S. Dollars (GBPUSD)   For example, in the GBPUSD chart shown in Figure 2.3, which currency is rising versus the other?

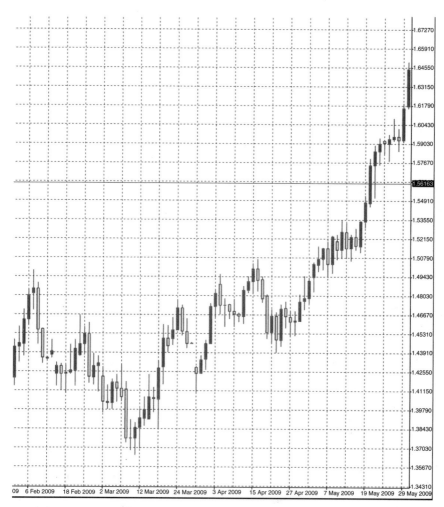

FIGURE 2.3 GBPUSD Daily Chart
Source: MetaQuotes Software Corp.

The GBP is the base currency. Overall the trend is up. That means:

- The GBP has been rising versus the USD.
- The USD is the counter, quote, or terms currency, so the prices are read as US dollars per British pounds, and the USD has been falling versus the GBP.
- The GBP trend is up versus the USD, the USD trend is down versus the GBP.

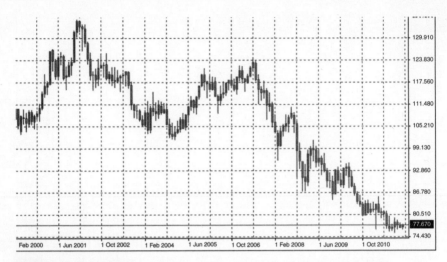

FIGURE 2.4 USDJPY Daily Chart, September 10 to November 4, 2010
Source: MetaQuotes Software Corp.

Analyze This!

Question: If you think the GBP will be stronger than the USD, would you buy or go long the GBPUSD, or would you short it? Why?
Answer: You'd buy it. The GBP is the base currency, so the pair should rise.

U.S. Dollar/Japanese Yen (USDJPY) Figure 2.4 shows another example. In the USDJPY chart, which currency is rising versus the other?

The USD is the base currency. Overall the trend is down. That means:

- The USD has been falling versus the JPY.
- The JPY is the counter, quote, or terms currency, so it has been rising versus the USD.
- The JPY trend versus the USD is up, and the USD trend versus the JPY is down.

Analyze This!

Question: If you think the JPY will be stronger than the USD, would you buy or go long the USDJPY, or would you short it?
Answer: You'd short it. If you thought the trend was reversing, you'd buy the pair.

SIZE MATTERS: TYPES OF CURRENCY PAIRS

Three types of pairs are available, categorized by the size of their average trading volume or liquidity:

1. The majors
2. The crosses
3. The exotics

The Major Currency Pairs: The Most Liquid

The most liquid pairs, that is, those that have the highest average daily trading volume (and lowest risk of slippage), are generally some combination of the USD and one of the other majors, that is, the EUR, JPY, GBP, Swiss Franc (CHF), CAD, NZD, and the Australian Dollar (AUD). Specifically, here are the major currency pairs, ranked by trading volume: EURUSD, USDJPY, GBPUSD, AUDUSD, USDCHF, USDCAD, and NZDUSD.

More on Risk and Safe Haven Currencies

Virtually all widely traded financial assets can be categorized as risk or safe haven (or safety) assets. Basically, risk assets are those that rise in times of optimism and evidence of accelerating growth, like stocks, industrial commodities, real estate, and so on. In contrast, safety assets appreciate in times of pessimism and fears of slowing growth, like investment grade bonds.

As noted above, there are also two basic types of currencies: risk and safe haven (or safety) currencies. Those that tend to move up or down with other risk assets like stocks, and move in the opposite direction of safe haven assets like bonds, are referred to as risk currencies. Those that move in the same direction as safe haven assets and in the opposite direction of risk assets are called safe haven currencies.

Again, here's how the major currencies rank on the risk spectrum:

RISK				→		SAFE HAVEN	
RISK CURRENCIES					SAFE HAVEN CURRENCIES		
AUD	NZD	CAD	EUR	GBP	CHF	USD	JPY

In later chapters, you will learn more about these. Understanding this distinction is critical for understanding and anticipating currency pair movements. For now, just know that the distinction exists, that there are risk and safe haven (or safety) currencies.

Beware: Again, This labeling has nothing to do with the quality of a currency as a store of value. It refers only to how these currencies and pairs behave relative to other asset types.

The Signs of the Crosses: Divine Revelations about Currency Strength

The cross currency pairs, or crosses, are pairs of major currencies that don't include the USD. By removing the USD's direct influence, the cross currencies reveal much about other currencies' strength. Though most aren't as liquid as the majors, as Figure 2.5 shows, the most popular Euro crosses are equally liquid. For example, below are more widely traded that some of the majors:

- EUR/JPY
- EUR/GBP
- EUR/CHF

Figure 2.5 shows a rough breakdown of forex trading volume by currency pair.

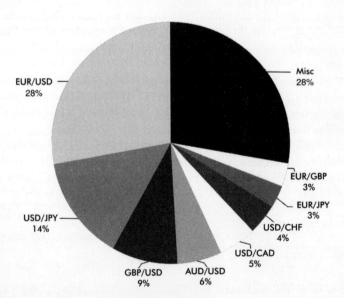

FIGURE 2.5   Currencies Traded Most Actively

Revealed Truth from the Crosses: True Strength or Weakness of a Currency Studying the cross currency pairs of a given currency can provide insights about its real strength or weakness. Because any given currency's most widely traded pair is usually the one including the USD, the relative strength of the USD can obscure a currency's true health. Indeed, when trading the major currencies, the basic choice is whether to be bullish or bearish on the USD, and then just decide which other currency to best trade against it. Because the crosses don't directly involve the USD, they:

- Allow trades that are purer plays on a given currency with less interference from movements in the USD.
- Serve as a barometer for the true strength of a currency.

Purer Plays on Currency Strength For example, if great news comes out that is bullish for the GBP, but the USD is strong that day, the GBPUSD might not move much. Buying (going long) the GBPJPY or GBPNZD could be a more profitable way to play GBP strength. The Internet is a good source for more information on currency crosses. Also, see the article titled, "Make the Currency Cross Your Boss: from forex analyst Boris Schlossberg at Investopedia.com.

Using EUR and USD Crosses to Better Assess EUR and USD Strength Throughout much of the European Union (EU) debt crisis, the EUR managed to hold its value even though its underlying fundamentals were terrible given the de facto insolvency of a number of the Euro-zone (EZ) governments and many of the largest EZ banks that held the related sovereign bonds. The entire existence of the Euro-zone, and thus the Euro, was in question, but that day of reckoning wasn't believed to be a near-term threat during most of 2010–2011. However, for various reasons and for much of this period, the USD's short-term prospects were actually even less appealing.

Because the EURUSD pair alone accounts for approximately 28 percent percent of all forex trade, a weaker USD automatically drives up demand for the EUR and vice versa. That's because for every three to four Euros bought, a USD is sold and vice versa. Thus, the EUR and USD push each other in opposite directions like children on a seesaw. Its relative strength versus the USD helped it appear steady.

However, if you looked at certain EUR crosses like the EURJPY or EURCHF, you'd have seen that:

- In times of optimism, the EUR didn't rally as much as other risk currencies versus safer currencies like the JPY and CHF.

- In times of pessimism, the EUR was weaker versus these safe havens than other riskier currencies that should have done worse.

Thus, the Euro's relative strength versus the USD made it look stronger than it actually was.

Similarly, when Greece appeared at risk of a default, which could have set off a chain reaction of additional sovereign and bank insolvencies, the EUR tanked and the USD looked great versus the EUR even though the Dollar's underlying fundamentals hadn't improved. However, those watching the more trusted safe haven currencies like the JPY and CHF could see these gaining against the USD and thus knew the USD's safe haven strength was only relative to the EUR.

In Chapter 9, we'll discuss how intermarket analysis, which is the observing and comparing of different asset markets to currency pairs, can provide additional insights into how these pairs might behave in the future.

Walk on the Wild Side: The Exotics

The exotic currency pairs are those comprised of at least one emerging market currency. Though these can be profitable given the growth in some emerging market economies, they are less liquid and should be avoided until one is profitable with the more liquid pairs and then is profitable with these on practice accounts. Examples of the exotics include:

USDBRL: U.S Dollar versus the Brazilian Real
USD/ZAR: U.S. Dollar versus the South African Rand
USD/MXN: U.S. Dollar versus the Mexican Peso
USD/SGD: U.S. Dollar versus the Singapore Dollar
USD/TRY: U.S. Dollar versus the Turkish Lira
EUR/TRY: Euro versus the Turkish Lira

PIPS: THE UNIVERSAL CURRENCY OF CURRENCIES

Because the price in which currency pairs are denominated varies with the counter currency, traders measure price changes in pips, which are universally recognized as the smallest unit of price movement measured, roughly like a tick for stock prices or basis point for bonds. The value of a pip varies depending on the currency pair and quantity traded .

For currency pairs in which the JPY is the counter currency, like the USDJPY, EURJPY, or GBPJPY, a pip is 0.01 yen. For all other pairs, a pip is 0.0001 of the counter currency.

You need to know how much each pip is worth so you know how many pips you can afford to lose and can manage your risk and money accordingly. Serious traders generally don't risk more than 1 to 3 percent of their accounts on any one position, so they need to know how many pips equal that much cash. Once they know this, they can set their stop loss orders (discussed below) on their trading systems to automatically close their trades after losing that number of pips.

As we'll learn later, one of the primary criteria for choosing a trade is whether the likely maximum move against your position, per your technical analysis, is one you can afford, meaning one that doesn't exceed 1 to 3 percent of your account size. If it does, don't take the trade because it's too risky.

Calculating Pip Values

In practice, any decent trading platform will have a pip calculator to perform this function quickly and easily. Still, it's helpful to know how to calculate a pip if you need to monitor a position when you are away from your computer. See Appendix B for more information.

Three Ways to Limit Risk: Lot Size Usually the Easiest

There are three ways you can keep your maximum loss risked per trade to between 1 and 3 percent of your total capital.

1. Increase the size of your account, so a given loss represents a smaller percent of your capital. This is usually a function of your wealth, which is often beyond your control in the short-term.
2. Decrease the leverage used, so a given percentage move in price against you represents a smaller loss for a given position size. This may or may not be within your control, depending on your broker.
3. Limit your position size.

Position size is usually the easiest one of these to control and, at times, is the only one. So, let's look at that first.

Lot Sizes Matter Obsessive focus on risk and money management (RAMM), meaning keeping your risk per trade as low as possible or avoiding relatively large losses, however you phrase it, is what separates the elite long-term survivors from the majority that eventually drop out. The size of your positions is a key part of risk management because the smaller the lots you trade, all else being equal (leverage, number of lots, and more), the less each pip is worth. So, smaller lots mean that for each percentage move in price, there's less profit, but more importantly, less loss. It's the losses that can wipe out your capital, your confidence, and thus your trading career.

For a number of reasons based in the history of forex trading, currency pairs usually trade in standard size lots of 100,000 units of the base currency. To make trading affordable to the individual trader of average means, online retail brokers invented mini accounts with lot sizes of 10,000, and micro accounts with lot sizes of only 1,000 units.

We don't just like these newfangled innovations. We love them.

Because smaller lot sizes reduce your risk per lot traded, they give you a number of important advantages over standard lots.

They provide greater flexibility to adjust your position sizes with the circumstances:

- When you're hot, you can increase position size by adding lots.
- While you're learning, making the transition from practice to real accounts, or in a losing streak, small lots help you keep losses down until your trading improves and is consistently profitable most weeks or months.
- When you want to enter or exit a position in stages with only part of your planned position (another risk management technique), smaller lots make that easier to do while keeping the total cash risked within 1 to 3 percent of your capital.

In sum, the smaller the lot size, the lower the risk because we reduce the following:

- The value of each pip.
- The cost of each 1 percent move against you.
- The potential loss if your stop loss order is hit (see Order Types further on). We measure risk not by the total position size but by the potential loss if your stop order is hit.

Yes, smaller position sizes mean lower profits when prices move in your favor, with lower interest income from carry trades (discussed in Chapter 11). However the priority is to keep losses low. Always. As we demonstrate in Chapter 5 and Appendix E, a given percent loss requires a larger percent gain to recover your loss because you're trading from a reduced capital base.

Once you find the right combination of trading styles, instruments, and analysis that suits you, you will have time to increase lot size, risk, and profit potential. Until you're consistently profitable over many months (regardless of your percentage of winning trades), the priority is to keep risk and losses on any given trade to within 1– to 3 percent of your account size. Profiting with only a minority of winning trades is okay, because many profitable traders succeed that way, as we'll discuss later on.

LEVERAGE AND MARGIN: THEIR RELATIONSHIP AND IMPACT ON RISK

In finance, leverage refers to the percentage of your total position that is from borrowed funds used to magnify your returns. Margin is the actual cash portion of your position; it's a security deposit set aside from your total account as a provision against loss and the need to repay the borrowed funds. Leverage and margin are just two ways of viewing the amount of borrowed funds used to magnify your gains or losses, your opportunities and risks.

For example, 100:1 leverage means you set aside a margin deposit equal to 1 percent, $100, of your total $10,000 position. That $100 allows you to control $10,000 of the EURUSD or $10,000 worth of Euros. Thus, a 1 percent price movement means a $100 or 100 percent gain or loss. Using a 50:1 leverage implies a 2 percent margin deposit of $100 that is set aside from your account to control $5,000 of the EURUSD or $5,000 worth of Euros. A 1 percent price movement would bring a 50 percent gain or loss.

Leverage: Greater Risk and Reward

Leverage is a dual-edged sword that can work for or against you. The easy availability of leverage in forex is what attracts the risk seekers and repels the risk-averse investor. Leverage is neither inherently good nor bad by itself. Like a car or firearm, it is easy to learn how to use it safely and effectively if you have enough training, self-control, and the common sense needed to wield it without hurting yourself. Those lacking any of the above should avoid it until successful using practice accounts; otherwise, the results will be gruesome. Even after that, when first trading real money, opt for the lowest leverage settings possible.

Understanding and managing leverage is one of the primary characteristics that separate the winners or future winners from the eternal losers and suckers on whom the others can feed. Therefore, we will invest a lot of time in this book covering RAMM.

Permitted Leverage Varies with Place and Time

As of October 18, 2010, the Commodity Futures Trading Commission (CFTC) set the legal limit for U.S. forex brokers at 50:1 (2 percent margin) for the major currency pairs, and 20:1 (5 percent margin) for the less liquid and more volatile exotic pairs. The CFTC's definition of major currency pairs is much broader than the generally accepted definition noted earlier; therefore, it includes a wider variety of currency pairs than those mentioned above. See Appendix D for full details.

Forex brokers outside of the United States commonly offer 100:1 or 200:1 leverage, sometimes as much as 400:1 or more, though other countries like Japan are moving toward reduced legal leverage limits.

Some brokers like etoro.com allow you to adjust how much leverage you use. Some don't. Consider avoiding those brokers when starting to trade live money.

How Margin, Lot Size, and Leverage Interact

Again, the margin is the minimum percentage of the cash value of your position that your broker requires you to set aside for each trade. Margin and leverage are two different aspects of the same feature, reflected in how little cash you need to control a standard, mini, or microsized lot.

For example, using 100:1 leverage or a 1 percent margin requirement means the same thing. You need $100 to control $10,000 worth of a given currency pair, which is one mini lot. Every 1 percent price move would bring a $100 gain or loss. You'd need $500 to control five lots, and each 1 percent price move would bring a $500 gain or loss.

The higher the leverage or lower the margin, the greater the percent profit or loss for every 1 percent price movement and the greater the reward and risk.

Your margin deposit is *not* your maximum possible loss. Instead, it's the minimum amount you need to open a position and keep it open. If the price moves against you, your broker will automatically set aside more cash and increase your margin deposit to cover that drawdown to in your account

Your maximum loss on a trade depends on where you have set your stop loss order (described in the section on order types later), the size of your position, and whether you had enough cash in your account to cover that loss and any other you may be taking. If you didn't, your broker can terminate some or all of your positions to keep your account from going below zero, via what's called a margin call.

The Importance of Adequate Capital

One of the most common beginner mistakes is trading without enough cash to absorb normal drawdowns.

It's possible to forecast the trend but still have a losing trade because asset prices typically gyrate within a rising, falling, or horizontal channel. Even if you're right about price direction, you will need to have enough cash on hand to absorb temporary drawdowns without having your account wiped out and your position automatically closed by your broker via a margin call before price starts to move in your favor.

For example, let's say you open a one mini lot (10,000 units of base currency) of the EURUSD at 100:1, which requires $100, and assume this is your only open position. The pair moves 2 percent against you, causing a paper loss of $200. If you have that cash available, your broker will commit or allocate another $200 to that position and leave the position open. If not, your brokers will issue a margin call and close the position (to protect themselves and you from incurring losses beyond what you've got in your account). Typically, they'll send you a warning so that you've time to add funds if you want to keep the position open.

In sum, to avoid margin calls that can turn winning trades into losers, it's critical that you understand how much cash you need to keep in your account. That means you must be clear about:

- How much each 1 percent move costs you, based on your lot size and leverage.
- How much loss you can typically expect to absorb from random price movements and the maximum loss you'll allow via your stop loss (much more on this in Chapter 5).
- How many positions you can, therefore, afford to have open at any one time.

The key point to understand is that if you don't keep enough cash in your account to cover a normal price move against you, you risk having your position automatically closed by your broker before a correct trend forecast can play out in your favor.

Again, beware—your margin deposit is not your maximum possible loss. Instead, it's a minimum deposit to keep the position open.

Insure You Have Adequate Capital   The best way to avoid a margin call is to never risk more than 1 to 3 percent of your account in any one trade before your stop loss order (see the following section) is hit. That way your account should never take a big surprise loss, and you'll have the needed cash on hand. Unless you can absorb the temporary losses from normal price fluctuations, you are virtually assured of a losing trade even you were ultimately right about the trade.

Margin Calls: Your Account's Circuit Breaker

A circuit breaker is a safety device in your home's electrical system. When too much current is flowing for the wires to bear without melting down or catching fire, it cuts off the flow of electricity. Similarly, margin calls are a safety device for your account, preventing you from going into debt when losses threaten to become greater than the cash in your account. Margin calls automatically close out your position before you find yourself owing the broker money, possibly a lot of money in fast moving markets.

When your electrical or account circuit breakers are tripped, it can be frustrating. You're stuck in the dark, or you're stuck with a loss as you watch the price turn in your favor and become what would have been winning trade if you'd had the cash needed to avoid the margin call.

However, they both serve as valuable protection against being fatally burned.

Margin calls serve another valuable function. Like tripped circuit breakers, they tell you something needs to be fixed in your trade planning and risk and money management. That's a critical red flag because good trade planning is another essential characteristic that separates the winners from the losers.

Fortunately, trade planning is a key component of RAMM and is not rocket science, so even beginners can know how to keep losses affordable so they live to fight another day with funds and confidence intact.

Your first goal is to survive long enough to learn to be profitable. That means learning enough of the four key skills that make a successful trader or investor in the forex market or any other market. First, you'll need some background information on order types so that you can understand those skills and their illustrations.

Order Types

Forex brokers offer the same kinds of entry and exit orders used in other major financial markets. So, if you already trade in some kind of financial market then you'll be familiar with these and can skip this section.

In this section, we'll give just enough information on these as needed to:

- Reinforce what we've covered thus far in related topics.
- Give you enough background on order types to understand what immediately follows.

In later chapters on risk, money management, and trade planning, we'll fill in the details about how to use the different order types to your best advantage.

Entry Orders: Opening a Position   Unlike market orders (orders to buy or sell immediately at the current price), entry orders (or entry limit orders) are pending orders entered in advance to enter or open a new position at some future price that the trader deems more favorable than the current price. These will execute automatically and don't require any action from the trader at that time. This ability to choose entry points in advance is very valuable for two reasons:

1. You can enter these orders at your convenience, whenever you have time. That's important for those with limited free time to trade, yet want to enter at a certain price level or better. This is an essential feature even for full-time traders (never mind those with jobs and lives beyond trading) because they can't be available 24 hours a day.
2. It removes emotion from entry decisions, and that, friends, is critical. Like drinking and driving, trading and emotion don't mix. When they do, you risk becoming road kill. Few can avoid the pull of fear or greed when trading in real time with money at stake. You want to do your analysis and objectively choose entry points isolated from the pull of fear or greed that might make one hesitate to seize an opportunity. You don't want to jump in when it's too late or too early.

For example, I can't remember how many times I've left open orders to enter at some deep support level, forgotten about them, then felt a wave of fear when notified weeks later that the order was filled. There were so many reasons that price could fall further, and things seemed so bleak (which was why, of course, long-term deep support was hit). Usually, the greater my fear when I find I've "assumed the position," the higher the profit because I bought near the point at which the bad news had drained away the sellers and few were buying. I probably would not have entered the trade if I were making the decision in real time instead of well in advance. But that was the time to buy.

These orders are supposed to execute when a certain price level is hit or breached. Usually, the intention is to enter a position at a specific price. However, under certain conditions, prices can jump or "gap" below (when opening long positions) or above (when opening short positions) the intended price, so the order takes effect at better price than that which was entered.

Order Types for Buying or Going Long a Currency Pair   Buy Limit is an entry order to buy a currency pair at a future price below the current price, typically used by bargain hunters seeking to buy on a pullback from the current price at what they believe is at or near a level that has served as a floor or support in their chosen time frame, be it an hour, day, week, month, year, or longer. They are seeking to buy low and sell high. They're comparable to value buyers in equities markets.

Buy Stop is an entry order to buy at a future price above the current price, typically used by traders who believe that once price breaks above a certain price level that has served as a ceiling or resistance level in the past, the price should continue a sustained move higher. Their goal is to buy as the price begins to make a sustained move higher. They're comparable to momentum buyers.

Order Types for Selling or Going Short a Currency Pair   In Chapter 2, we said that because currencies trade in pairs, you're always long one currency and short another. When you sell or go short a currency pair, you're buying the counter currency (the one on the right) and paying for it by selling the base currency. No restrictions exist against shorting a pair because selling and buying a currency pair are essentially the same type of transaction. All forex trades involve buying one half of the pair and selling the other to pay for it, regardless the currency in which your accounted is denominated.

Sell Limit is an entry order to sell the pair short at a future price above the current price, typically used by bargain hunters seeking to go short a currency pair at what they believe is at or near a price level that has served as a ceiling or resistance in their chosen time frame. They believe that around this price level the currency pair will start to drop. They are hoping to sell high and buy low. As we learned earlier, really what they're doing is trying to buy the counter currency at a lower price relative to the base currency, and then sell it for a profit at a higher price relative to the base currency.

Sell Stop is an entry order to sell at a price below the current price, typically used by momentum-type short sellers, those who believe that once the pair breaks below a price that has served as a floor or support in the past, the pair will make a sustained move lower.

The OCO Order: To Open a Long or Short Position Depending on How Price Moves   The one cancels the other (OCO) order allows you to place two future orders depending on which of two possible but mutually exclusive outcomes occurs. This way you're ready to profit from multiple possible scenarios.

For example, on July 10, 2011, the USDCAD was in between near-term support and resistance on its daily chart (see Figure 2.6). For now, just know that support is the recent low price and resistance is the recent high price (we'll go much more in depth on these concepts later).

Let's say you want to play the next multiday trend, which, for simplicity's sake, we'll assume would be indicated solely by the break higher above key resistance or the break lower beneath strong support. These are marked by the upper and lower horizontal red lines. You'd use an OCO order that would include the following two entry orders:

1. An entry buy stop that executes when price breaks above the resistance level (upper horizontal line), the theory being price is beginning a move higher.

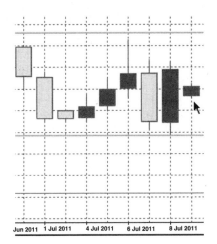

FIGURE 2.6 USDCAD Daily Chart, June 30 to July 10, 2011
Source: MetaQuotes Software Corp.

2. An entry sell stop that triggers when price breaks below the support level (lower horizontal line), the belief being that the EURUSD is about to make a move lower.

When one order executes, the other is cancelled. Figure 2.7 shows what happened.

Depending on where you set your entry points, your entry sell stop would have been executed between July 13 and 15 (In reality, you'd consider other technical and fundamental data besides these support and

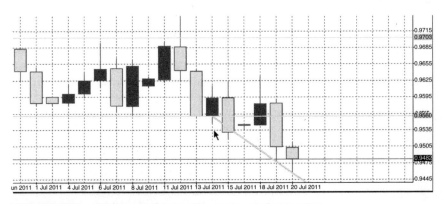

FIGURE 2.7 USDCAD Daily Chart, June 30 to July 20, 2011
Source: MetaQuotes Software Corp.

resistance (s/r) lines, but we'll stick to these for now for the sake of illustration.)

The break below support did signal a move lower over the coming days.

Beware Temporary Reversals before Breakouts   For a variety of reasons, it's common for breakouts to begin, retrace somewhat, then resume. Note how the downtrend reversed during July 17–18 before it resumed. This is another reason we discourage very short-term trading because you can easily get shaken out of a correctly identified trend by mere random price movements. Much more on that later when we discuss RAMM, trade planning, and recommended trading styles and timeframes. For now, know that even if your analysis is good, expect some kind of countermove against you. A big part of risk management and trade planning will involve selecting situations in which fake reversals are easier to identify and will involve deciding how much of a to accept before you cut your losses.

At some point during the above trade, you'll decide it's time to take profits, or if the trend reversed, to cut losses when they're small. To do that, you'll need to use one of the following exit position orders.

Exit Orders: Ways to Close a Position

The main difference between them is whether you're closing a losing trade to cut your losses or a winning trade to take profits.

Stop Loss Orders: Fixed and Trailing Stops   As the name implies, stop loss orders are pending orders that automatically close your position to stop a loss from getting any worse than your predetermined maximum amount you were willing to risk. That maximum may be determined by either:

- Risk management considerations: broken price support of some kind (many exist as we'll soon see) or other indications that you were wrong about the price direction.
- Money management considerations: you don't want to lose more than 1 to 3 percent of your account on any given trade.

There are two basic kinds of stop loss orders:

1. Fixed or Simple Stop Loss: As the name implies, this order automatically executes when a fixed predetermined loss is reached or if the market gaps past it, and the loss is exceeded. Any good trading

platform will allow you to set that loss in terms of pips, cash loss, or percentage loss from your entry price.

2. Trailing Stop Loss: As the name suggests, this kind of stop loss order trails or follows the price as it moves further in your favor, and it automatically closes your position after the currency pair price moves against you by a fixed number of pips, cash amount, or percentage change in price against you. Thus the trailing stop loss not only to limits losses, but also locks in gains from winning trades that have started to reverse against you by more than what you believe to be normal random price movements or "market noise."

Stop loss orders are a key part of risk management. We can enter them in advance and have our trading system automatically cut our losses. They help keep emotion out of our trading

Exit Limit Orders: Taking Fixed Maximum Profit   Just as a stop loss limits your losses, exit limit orders lock in, but limit, your gains. They are triggered after a predetermined gain instead of a predetermined loss, be it in registered in pips, cash, or a percentage move in your favor from the entry price. If, for some reason, a trailing stop is inappropriate, an exit limit order locks in profits in case a price reverses against you. Typically, it is set near what you believe will be strong resistance to further gains.

The exact names of the assorted order types may vary on some trading platforms, so be sure to clarify before you trade real money.

Market Order: Executing in Real Time at Current Price   As the name implies, market orders are buy or sell orders at the current market price, used by those who are usually present at their trading station or who have been waiting for a particular price, chart setup, or news event and want to enter or exit immediately. Though placing a market order in advance is possible during times when markets are closed to buy or sell at the opening market price, this is rarely advisable for a number of reasons, chief among which is that you don't know what you'll be paying.

Though market orders have their uses (they're good for getting out of a trade quickly if you've a good reason to change your plan for that trade), they can be dangerous for all but the most disciplined, cold-blooded unemotional traders who can think quickly and objectively when their money is at risk. Even if traders have a solid predetermined trading plan, fear, greed, and ego can cause them to abandon it in the heat of the moment via a market order.

Thus, beginners and those not yet consistently profitable on a monthly basis should stick with predetermined entry and exit points as based on a solid trading plan. By the way, I specifically refer to profitability over a period of time as a means of evaluating success rather than percentage of winning trades. You can be profitable with a low percentage of winners (the question is whether you emotionally can handle that, and also be unprofitable with a high percentage).

THE THREE FACETS OF RISK AND RISK CONTROL

Now that you know about pips, lot sizes, leverage, margin, and order types (particularly stop losses), we can summarize what risk is and how we control it.

If risk is the planned maximum percent loss of your capital on a trade, then here's how each of the above elements influence your risk:

Leverage: Determines the percentage loss or gain for every 1 percent price movement per lot. It determines the margin deposit needed to control a given lot.

Lot size: Determines the nominal cash loss for a given amount of leverage and percent price move because it determines how much each pip is worth (see Appendix B for details).

Account size: Determines how large a loss we can absorb without exceeding 1 to 3 percent of our capital, so we can survive a string of losses and still have a good chance of recouping our losses (see Appendix E for details). Thus, account size determines how far away our stop loss orders can be set from our entry points, and so also determines how much flexibility we have to take trades that demand wider stop loss settings that risk more cash

Example

We'll see more of how these elements influence our RAMM later. Here's an illustration of how the above elements influence the amount we risk per position, and how they influence each other. For example, the larger the account, the larger the loss one can afford per position, and the larger the leverage and position size one can afford.

Example:

Pair Traded: USDCAD

Account size: $20,000, denominated in US dollars, the base currency, which implies we can afford a $200–600 loss to keep risk per trade to 1 to 3 percent.

Lot size: 10,000 units of base currency (the one on the left of the currency pair symbol). As shown in Appendix B (Rule of Tens), each pip is worth $1, so we can afford to set our stop loss no more than 200–600 pips from our entry point.

Leverage: Assume we use 100:1 leverage. For every $10,000 of base currency, we will need to have $100 on deposit, and every 1 percent loss means our position loses $100, and we'll need enough cash in the account so the broker can set aside another $100 for each 1 percent move against us.

Result:

If using 100:1 leverage, trading the USDCAD, and entering at 1.0500, a 1 percent loss equals 105 pips, or $100 USD. So, we can afford a loss of between 210 pips ($200) and 630 pips ($600). We would be careful to set our stop loss orders no farther than 210 to 630 pips from our entry point. For each 210 pips move against us, our broker would need to set aside another $100 deposit to keep this position open. If that cash was unavailable, we'd have to have a margin call and the position would be automatically closed.

THE CORE FOUR: THE MOST IMPORTANT SKILLS FOR SUCCESS

There's a common misconception that success in trading or investing is all about the right analytical techniques, finding the right trade setups, algorithms, secret chart pattern, and so forth, and that everything else is secondary. By all means do your best with these since they help, particularly if you can afford to hire the best mathematical and programming talent, and provide them with the best equipment and time needed to develop winning systems. Generally, that's a game that only wealthy funds and institutions can play.

However, if you want to bet on your chances of ever figuring out even a part of the markets, consider the following:

- Most actively managed funds fail to beat the returns of passively managed index funds that simply mirror the relevant benchmark index.[1] Remember, these people are supposed to be the best, smartest, best trained, and funded, with unparalleled access to all the resources they need. They survived a rigorous selection process to be hired and promoted to the rank of fund manager and have convinced people smart enough to accumulate wealth to invest with them.

- Recent history has witnessed numerous spectacular hedge fund failures. Some were based on complex strategies and algorithms, some on value investing. The most famous of all was that of Long-Term Capital Management (LTCM). Its principal managers included two Nobel prize-winning economists and team of highly regarded market veterans whose reputation alone managed to attract over $1 billion before the fund even started operating.[2]

- Automated trading systems sound great in theory, and are promising for those who understand technical analysis and programming or can hire those who do. However, for the rest of us, unless you're comfortable with investing in something you don't understand (generally a bad idea unless you're getting good advice), leave consideration of these until a later time when you have the skills and experience to evaluate them properly. Trading systems often lack transparency. Developers understand how they work, and most of the time, you won't. Even if the system has a verified track record, they're typically designed to work in a specific kind of market environment, be it a trending market, a range bound market, a risk-seeking market that favors carry trades, and so on. Once the market changes, the system's performance breaks down. Systems that function in multiple kinds of markets over long periods are considered as rare and treasured as the legendary Holy Grail. Do you really believe that anyone who actually created such a system would be hawking it on the open market at prices retail traders can afford? We'll look into autotrading systems more in Chapter 10.

The point here is that even good analysis by bona fide geniuses and market legends is so often wrong that analytical skills, though still essential, rank at the bottom of the top four keys to trading success. Here they are, in order of importance:

1. Trader psychology, which includes your mindset, discipline, unemotional decision-making ability, attitudes, expectations, awareness of what trading styles they're suited for, and so forth.
2. Risk management.
3. Money management.
4. Technical and fundamental analyses, which includes knowing how to use the two together.

Trader Psychology

This includes having right attitudes toward winning and losing trades, realistic expectations, knowing your risk tolerance level, discipline, the mistakes you're prone to make and how to monitor and compensate for them, keeping fear and greed out of trading decisions, having the discipline and humility to cut losses, let winning trades continue, etc. Many books cover this topic alone, but keep in mind the following attitudes and expectations.

Mind Your Business　It's no secret that much of the 75 percent or more of retail forex "traders" who fail aren't really even attempting serious trading. They want some fun and excitement by betting on an outcome. Forex brokers love to aim marketing campaigns at this herd of sheep, which so willingly runs to the slaughter. For them, it's a game and not a business.

For you, dear reader, that's good news. The mere fact that you're reading this book suggests you're not one of the madcap cowboys or at least don't want to be one of them. The high failure rate doesn't apply to you. Continue doing your homework, and expect do all the things you'd do if you were starting a business that faces lots of competition from bigger, more skilled players. Expect to invest plenty of time in study, and practice, be it over a shorter period as a full-time trader or over a longer one as a part-time trader. Expect frustration and failure, a need to develop means of monitoring your business, how to identify and correct problems, and more. In Chapters 10 through 12, we'll show you easier ways to profit, but even these require education and effort.

Trade Defensively　Just as new or accident-prone drivers drive defensively, proceeding slowly and taking extra precautions, so should those who are not yet consistently profitable trade defensively.

Until you have found the trading or investing styles that are keeping you consistently profitable, trade defensively.

Assume most of your early trades will be losers. That's fine; it's quite possible to be profitable with a less than 50 percent winning trade percentage. It's a normal part of the learning process. With this expectation in mind, don't trade real money until you're profitable on practice accounts for about six months.

Learn from Every Losing Trade　Accept losses as the tuition expenses. To get the most for your money, you should keep a trading log in which you record, among other things, your trading plan, the trade rationale, and a post-mortem of why it did or didn't work. We'll show you examples of these in Chapters 5 and 7. Again, expect failure, and embrace it as an unavoidable and necessary learning experience. By all means, make every effort to learn from every failed trade. If you don't know, find someone or some resource to help you. Many are available. Some forex brokers will offer a degree of free mentoring. Many online forex content sites have writers responding to questions. There are online trading forums, along with many offering courses and mentoring for a fee. As with anything else, do your due diligence.

Risk and Money Management (RAMM)

In light of the above, if you've got a professional's mindset, you'll be serious about RAMM. Theoretically, they're separate, but in practice, you apply them together and both are essential for your survival while you are learning and finding yourself as a trader or investor.

> Risk management: Because even successful traders commonly experience a high percentage of losing trades, you're goal is to keep losses from losing trades low relative to the gains from winning trades, so you can be profitable with fewer than 50 percent of your trades being profitable. That is what risk management involves.
> Money management: While risk management is about keeping losses small relative to your gains, money management is about ensuring that loss per trade is small relative to your total account size. As we will discuss in Chapter 5 and Appendix E, small losses of about one to three percent of your total account are survivable and relatively easy to recoup, large ones are not, and repeated large losses will destroy your account and confidence.

Technical and Fundamental Analysis

As the examples at the start of this section suggest, those decisions will often be wrong even for the best traders and investors, so the other three allow you to prosper despite the unfortunate reality that markets are too complex and dynamic for the vast majority of traders to outsmart by analysis alone.

Despite their being at the bottom of the "core four," technical and fundamental analyses are essential because they're the basis for your trading decisions, including those involving your risk and money management because you need both:

- Solid technical analytical skills to identify low-risk entry and exit points.
- A firm grasp of fundamental analysis for grasping the big picture needed to anticipate long-term price moves and events that could influence short-term price movements.

So, analytical skills are not only important in their own right, they are also essential to good RAMM.

CHAPTER 3

Technical Analysis (TA) Basics

I f you understood most of Chapter 2, you now have enough background so that we can begin to cover the analytical skills that will help you succeed in forex or any other kind of trading or investing. This chapter will cover:

- What is technical analysis (TA).
- Understanding the basics of candle charts and the simple goals and theory behind all those complex looking lines, charts, patterns, and more.
- How to understand and use some of the most important of these, including various ways we identify support and resistance (s/r) and trends.
- Examples to illustrate and apply what we've covered.

Those with some experience in TA from other kinds of trading will be glad to know that nearly everything they know applies to TA of forex markets. The charts, their common patterns, and their indicators work the same way. The main difference is the unique fundamentals driving these charts. These readers can feel free to just skim the following for anything they may have missed or want to review.

TA is typically defined as the study of price behavior, which is a reflection of mass trader behavior. Repeating chart patterns or persistent support or resistance levels don't form from thin air, but rather from the repetitious nature of how traders respond to past experience, each other, new information, and how each tries to anticipate how the other will react

49

to that information. Trader behavior is based on unchanging human psychology. It's logical, then, that the repetitive nature of chart patterns and other technical indicators simply reflects that repetitive nature of human and crowd behavior in similar circumstances.

However, even the best TA is often wrong for various reasons, and the signals it provides often conflict.

That's why we obsess over risk management. We can't control the outcome of a trade. However, we can control what we risk and can make sure that we keep our losses affordable, and only enter trades that have both a high probability of being profitable, and a high risk-to-reward ratio (explained later).

Unlike fundamental analysis, TA ignores speculation about what may be influencing supply and demand. Instead it focuses purely on how (not why) prices move and what that movement suggests about future price behavior.

Of all the four core skills mentioned in Chapter 2, we'll cover TA first because it's the basis for much of our risk control decisions, such as:

- Defining what trades offer the lowest risk, highest potential yield entry and exit points, so that we can buy low and sell high (or vice versa in the case of short positions).
- Identifying price levels for cutting losses or taking partial profits if the trade threatens to turn against us.
- Deciding position size and partial position entry or exit.

TA occurs mostly on charts, which are pictures of trader behavior over a given period, regardless of what fundamentalists may speculate is the reason behind that behavior.

So, the first step in learning TA is to read and understand the price charts.

CANDLE CHART BASICS

To understand a book, you need to be able to read the words. To understand sheet music, you need to be able to read the notes. To understand price behavior, you need to be able to read and interpret the charts.

Candle Anatomy and Meaning

Charts come in different styles, but we will focus on Japanese candlestick or candle charts, which have become by far the most popular because they provide the quickest visual grasp of price action and the market sentiment behind it. Much has been written about the advantages of candle charts

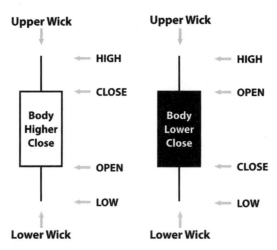

FIGURE 3.1　Anatomy of Chart Candles

and why they've become the dominant charting style since they were first introduced to the West by analyst Steve Nison in 1989, and popularized in his seminal book, *Japanese Candlestick Charting Techniques*, nearly a decade later.[1] However, we'll stick to an overview of what you need to know to make money. So, let's get to one of the cornerstones of TA, which is understanding candle charts.

First, study the parts of each candlestick, shown in Figure 3.1.

Figure 3.1 is self-explanatory, but here are the key points to understand about candlesticks:

- Candles usually have a body and wick (called a shadow) on both ends; however, any of these individual parts may be missing from a given candle as we'll see below. Together, they cover the entire price range over the given period the candle represents. The body alone represents the range between the open and closing price for a given period, and the wicks, or shadows, show the upper and lower price ranges.
- Each candle displays all price information: the high, low, and open and closing prices for a given period, depending on the chart's time frame. Here are two examples of candle information:
  1. Each candle on a one-minute chart covers the opening, closing, and high and low prices for one minute.
  2. Each candle on a daily chart shows this price information for an entire day.
- Any good trading platform should provide candlestick charts ranging from one second to one month.

- Body color tells us the price direction for the given period. The most common color coding is green bodies for higher closes and red for lower ones. In this book, we generally use dark gray for higher closes and light gray for lower ones, as seen in Chapter 2, Figures 2.3, and 2.7.

Relationship between Body, Wick, and Its Significance

The length of the bodies and the wicks, in absolute terms and relative to each other, can tell us a great deal about market sentiment over the duration of a given candle. That can be significant for candles covering longer periods like an entire day, week, or month. As with any technical indicator, candles and their patterns over shorter durations are less meaningful because price movements within a given day or less often can be caused by random money flows unrelated to any real market sentiment.

Here's the key to understanding the relationship between wick (or shadow) and body length and the meaning of an individual candle: The longer the wicks are relative to the body, the greater the indecision and the greater the back and forth struggle between buyers and sellers, and the more likely the current trend will cease or reverse. Conversely, the shorter the wicks are relative to the body, the more decisive the move up or down, and the more likely that the move will continue in the same direction.

Figure 3.2 represents the Bullish "Marubozu" Type and suggests strong buying pressure. A long higher close body with few or no shadows shows buyers outnumbered sellers and were in control during the entire period

FIGURE 3.2 Bullish "Marubozu" Chart

FIGURE 3.3   Bearish "Marubozu" Chart

covered by the candle, steadily pushing price higher. The longer the candle body, the greater the buying strength.

Figure 3.3 illustrates a Bearish "Marubozu" Type and suggests strong selling pressure. A long lower close body with few or no shadows shows that sellers outnumbered sellers and were in control during the entire period covered by the candle, steadily pushing price lower. The longer the candle body, the greater the selling strength.

Figure 3.4 illustrates the Doji Type which is neutral or indecisive, with sellers and buyers evenly matched. Similarly, small body relative to the wicks suggests the same indecisiveness to a lesser degree. If the body was red, the sellers were modestly stronger; if green, the opposite is true.

Lower Wicks   A relatively long lower wick suggests initial strong pessimism and selling which reversed as buying increased at the lower bargain price, and short sellers took profits. In other words, a lower price level was tested and held firm, turning back attempts to drive price lower. A short lower shadow suggests less indecision, less testing of lower prices, and lighter selling pressure that required few buyers to reverse it.

If the currency pair closes at its low for the period covered, the candle won't have a lower wick.

Upper Wicks   Conversely, a relatively long upper wick suggests initial optimism or buying pressure that reversed as sellers stepped in and buyers took profits. In other words, a higher price level was tested and held firm,

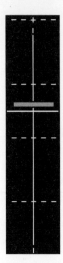

FIGURE 3.4 Doji Chart

turning back attempts to drive price higher. A short upper wick shows less indecision, less testing of higher prices, less struggle between buyers and sellers.

If the closing price is the high for the period covered, the candle won't have an upper wick.

SUPPORT AND RESISTANCE (S/R) BASICS

Before proceeding, you'll need a basic understanding of s/r. We'll deal with these both in greater depth later, but for now just understand that when we discuss price support or resistance, we mean exactly what these terms imply. For the sake of simplicity, assume we're referring to long positions, that is, trades for which the goal is to buy low and sell high. As we'll discuss further on, definitions of support and resistance are reversed for short positions, so we'll ignore those for now.

- Support, as the name suggests, is a price level, trend line, or other indicator that acts like a floor, preventing price from falling lower. It's where buying tends to occur repeatedly over a given period. Support draws in new buyers because it's seen as the lowest, bargain price for a given period. If support is breached for more than a brief period, that usually means market perception of the asset's value has fallen, and price will continue lower until the next support level. The stronger the support, the more bearish (pessimistic) the signal if that support level is breached.

- Resistance is just the opposite of support. It is a price level, trend line, or other indicator that acts like a ceiling, preventing price from rising. If resistance is breached for more than a brief period, that usually means price will continue higher until the next resistance level. The stronger the resistance, the more bullish optimistic the signal if that level is breached.
- Support or resistance (s/r when discussing these together) are rarely exact price points, but rather are defined zones or areas, with their range depending on a variety of circumstances covered later.

S/R can be as simple as a price level at which price tends to reverse direction, or it can be made up of multiple trend lines or other technical indicators (that we'll learn about later) that all converge on an area and mutually reinforce the s/r zone

The strength of an s/r area depends on various factors, such as age (older is better), how often it has been tested and held firm, the number and quality of various kinds of s/r indicators that converge on a given price level, and whether or not it's near a large round-number price level. Let's look at some real-life examples.

As shown in Figure 3.5, the EURUSD daily chart of June 10 to July 25, 2011, you will see the following:

A. June 21–22: The pair of long upper wicks (a "tweezers tops" pattern, covered in Chapter 4) showed strong resistance level around 1.4400, caused by selling pressure from some combination of those who were long the pair taking profits and short sellers opening new positions. The June 14–15 candles show prior resistance around 1.4400. Round numbers have a psychological appeal as natural buy or sell points, so certain round numbers tend to become significant s/r points.

B. June 23: The lack of much upper wick tells us that prices mostly fell from the start of the day. The long lower wick indicates that the pair managed to recover over half of its losses before the official close of the day's trading in the New York session. The lower wick shows sellers tested all the way down to around 1.4130 before buyers stepped in and short sellers took profits. Think of the long lower wick as a blind man's cane, probing for obstacles.

C. June 23–26: This 1.4130 support level was tested each day as selling continued, but this level held firm. The June 24 (Friday) candle's lower opening and even longer red body shows continued firm selling pressure, but roughly equal upper and lower wicks reflect some indecision

FIGURE 3.5   EURUSD Daily Chart, June 10 to July 25, 2011
Source: MetaQuotes Software Corp.

about how low to go. The June 26 (Monday) candle is a small light gray (this would be shown in red) body with small wicks, meaning price direction was mostly straight down but with weakening selling pressure. This weakening selling pressure was confirmed by the rally that followed.

D. June 27: A strong reversal as prices rebounded off this support level. The long dark gray (this would be shown in green) body shows decisive buyer control, with prices closing near the top of the day's range, and it "engulfs" or retakes the prior two days' losses. Such candles are called "bullish engulfing" patterns because they "consume" and recoup the prior days' losses.

E. June 30: Long upper wick again serves like a blind man's cane hitting an obstacle as the market gropes around to locate near-term resistance. Combined with the short dark gray (green) body near the bottom of the daily price range, which means there was little gain on the day, suggests the uptrend is weakening, as indeed it was.

F. July 3–4: Taken together, we see that the market opened above the 1.4550 resistance level twice but couldn't advance. On July 4th, after six straight days of gains and having hit resistance, sellers began taking control, probing lower before buyers stepped in, but could not prevent a lower close on the day. In Chapter 4, we'll learn that this kind of candle, with a small body, little or no upper wick, and a long lower wick relative to the overall candle range is a bearish sign when it occurs during an up-trend and is confirmed by the next candle closing lower (as was the case on July 6th). It's called a "hanging man." Its long lower wick, topped by a small body, combined with a lower close in the next candle, presents an intuitively clear picture of the market rejecting higher prices.

G. July 12: This is essentially the same form of candle as on July 4; how-ever, during a downtrend (and especially after an eight-day long down-trend and close at what was strong long-term support around 1.4000), this is considered a bullish reversal sign, called a hammer, as sellers probe lower support but buyers send sellers retreating and recover most of the day's (or any other period's) losses. In other words, this long lower shadow is a graphic image of the market rejecting lower prices. Once again, the lower wick may have hit bottom. Like the bear-ish hanging man shown on July 4th, this bullish twin hammer required confirmation from the next candle and got it with the next day's bullish engulfing candle (it engulfed or recouped the prior day's move). It sig-naled the start of a move higher over the coming sessions.

H. July 17: The candle had a mere line instead of a body, meaning that the opening and closing prices were the same or nearly so—price un-changed. The market ruled undecided, a tie between buyers and sellers. Such candles are called dojis. As signs of indecision, they often sug-gest a possible reversal of the current trend. This form of doji, with its prominent lower wick, that occurs after a downtrend near strong sup-port around 1.4000, suggests a market groping for a bottom. That was the case, as the following days confirmed this bullish sign and buyers took over and sent prices higher.

I. July 25: This doji, with equidistant wicks, shows complete indecision or perfect balance between buyers and sellers.

Analyze This!

What do you think happened to the EURUSD after the indecisive doji of July 25 (H)? Consider the following evidence:

- The EURUSD has had five straight days of gains, the last three with increasing strength.
- Looking at the month covered by this daily chart, the current price level of 1.4409 has served as near-term resistance because looking at the far left, middle, and far right sides of the chart, the pair has failed twice before to make a sustained move above it.
- The current price level of 1.4409 is essentially the same as 1.4400. As we'll learn in greater detail when we study s/r, round numbers tend to

serve as natural support or resistance because humans are psychologically wired to think in terms of round numbers. The more zeros, the more psychologically significant the number. That's why $4.99 feels cheaper than $5.00.

• July 25 (H) shows a doji candle, a classic sign of indecision.

For the sake of simplicity, we'll ignore the overall bearish fundamental factors that were behind the July price declines.

So, what do you think happened? Do you think the pair finished the day higher, lower, or the same? Here's what happened. If you thought the price would pull back, you were right. In Figure 3.6, after the undecided doji, the pair made a head-fake higher and pulled back (note the 2 candles that follow H). We'll talk more later about these "false breakouts," why they happen, and what you can do to protect yourself against being fooled by them.

FIGURE 3.6 EURUSD Daily Chart 20, June 3 to August, 2011
Source: MetaQuotes Software Corp.

Ideally, your reasons should have gone something like this.

The pair was at a significant near-term resistance level and was showing indecision. The more likely move is a pullback as long positioned traders take profits from the prior solid run higher. Markets expect some pullback, so unless new bullish news arrives, the element of self-fulfilling prophecy operates. Traders create the reality they expect.

CANDLE CHART TIME FRAMES: LENGTH MATTERS

Before concluding this section on candle charts, you need to know more about chart time frames and which ones you should use when starting out. As in other areas of life, longer is better.

We mentioned earlier that each candle presents the price action over a specific period, or to use traders' jargon, a time frame. Most trading platforms' charting modules allow you to view candles representing time frames ranging anywhere from a second to a month.

As you'll see, the time frame of the chart from which you trade matters. It matters a lot. The short version—stick to trading off of longer time frame charts, like four hour, daily, weekly, or monthly candles, until you are successful trading moves over these longer periods. Only then should you even consider trying to day trade currencies.

Different Time Frames, Different Trading Techniques, and Styles

The following is an overview of the differences in trading techniques and styles:

1. Those trading over short time frame charts, that is, short holding periods and trading off of charts with candles that form over a matter of minutes or hours:
   - They rely almost exclusively on TA and especially risk management. In these time frames, prices move with unpredictable large block trades of big players, most fundamentals except for news items are irrelevant, and most technical indicators are less reliable, so keeping the frequent losses low is key.
   - They actively monitor their positions more closely, so be on the lookout for breaking news that could change everything. They must make many real-time decisions quickly and must not let emotions shake them from their trading plan.
   - They allow only small losses because gains over short periods are smaller than over longer periods.
   - They tend to stick to trading highly leveraged spot (cash) market instruments, that is, trading currency pairs themselves via an online broker's trading platform because they need:
     - 24/5 access in order to catch opportunities that come and go quickly.

- High leverage in order to earn adequate profits from the small price moves that occur over a matter of minutes or hours without needing to commit six-figure sums that would be beyond the means of most traders.

2. Those holding positions over weeks, months, or years, using charts with daily, weekly, or monthly candles:
   - In addition to using technical analysis to plan entries and exits, will add a heavy dose of long-term fundamental analysis involving the health of the underlying economies of the currencies they trade, like trends in rates of interest, growth, employment, consumer spending, and so on. These factors can matter, and because they don't change quickly, multimonth trends are reliable; they don't reverse often.
   - Allow larger total pip losses and looser stop losses because of the larger moves that occur over longer periods, and because riding established, reliable long-term trends requires looser stop losses.
   - Don't need to actively watch positions. They can plan trades and enter orders to enter and exit in advance and thus can monitor trades less frequently.
   - In addition to directly trading currency pairs with online brokers, they have the option of trading unleveraged instruments like currency exchange-traded funds (ETFs) or monthly binary options, or other instruments. They are playing longer-lasting, larger price moves, and so may neither want leverage (which makes it harder to stay in a position for a long time and wait out the moves against you) nor need it (because the price moves are large enough already). As we'll discuss later, that absence of leverage makes it simpler to trade because you don't need the same degree of risk and money management.

Different Time Frames, Different Trends

The trend, meaning the overall price direction, that you'll see on any chart depends greatly on your time frame. Seeing a variety of trends nested within longer-term trends is common.

For example, look at this AUDJPY monthly chart shown in Figure 3.7.

During this period risk assets like the AUDJPY were in an overall downtrend. The AUDJPY is a classic risk pair, meaning that it tends to move in the same direction as other risk assets, like stock indexes or oil, because the two currencies occupy opposite ends of the hierarchy of risk currencies. The AUD is the number one risk currency, and the JPY is typically the ultimate safe haven. In times of optimism or risk appetite, the AUD is usually strong and the JPY is weak, so the pair tends to move sharply

FIGURE 3.7 AUDJPY Monthly Chart, October 1, 2007, to June 1, 2011
Source: MetaQuotes Software Corp.

higher. In times of pessimism or risk aversion, it moves firmly downward because the JPY tends to be strong and the AUD tends to be weak. Remember, pairs move in the direction of the base currency.

Note how the picture changes for someone viewing a daily chart anytime from September 2010 to February 20 2011, as shown in the chart in Figure 3.8.

Although the pair was in a long-term downtrend, embedded within this downtrend was a shorter term, multimonth uptrend that was tradable even for conservative longer-term (multiweek or month) forex traders. In particular, note:

- By November 2010, the AUDJPY was in an established uptrend because it had formed a series of both lower highs since August 2010 and higher highs by early November.

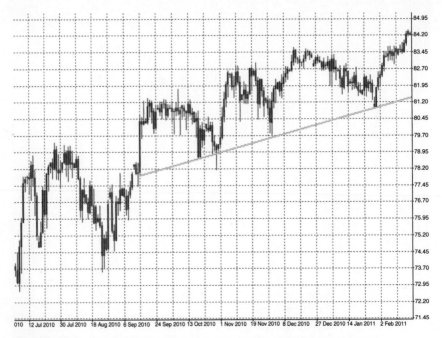

FIGURE 3.8   AUDJPY Daily Chart, July 12, 2010, to February 20, 2011
Source: MetaQuotes Software Corp.

- As shown in the chart in Figure 3.9, by late December, the pair
  had formed an ascending channel (two parallel trend lines) that was
  formed by three higher highs and two higher lows. As we'll see later,
  these upper and lower channel lines are useful indicators of s/r that
  we use (usually in combination with other indicators for confirmation)
  to select low-risk, high-yield entry and exit points when planning and
  executing our multiday, weekly, or monthly trades.

In sum, the time frame you choose to trade will influence every aspect
of your trading. As we'll discuss in Chapter 5, longer time frames can help
put the odds of success in your favor and, when used properly, will reduce
your risk.

IDENTIFYING SUPPORT AND RESISTANCE (S/R) TO BUY LOW, SELL HIGH, OR VICE VERSA

Here's another useful oversimplification. The whole point of TA is to help
us buy low, sell high, or vice versa when shorting a currency pair. That

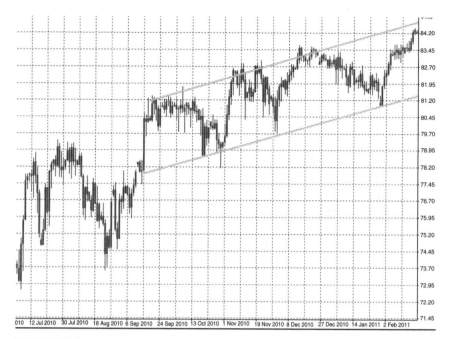

FIGURE 3.9 AUDJPY Daily Chart, July 12, 2010, to February 20, 2011
Source: MetaQuotes Software Corp.

is, we use TA to more precisely identify the likely low and high prices for a given period. These become our low-risk entry points and high-yield exit points.

Definitions of S/R Are Reversed for Long and Short Positions

Definitions of s/r can get confused when discussing short positions, so let's clarify this now. Though definitions of s/r are reversed for long and short trades, they are conceptually the same:

- When we're buying (or going long) the pair, the likely low price is support, and the high price is resistance.
- When we're selling (or going short) the pair, the likely high price is support, and the low price is resistance.

In other words, we define support as the area where you want to open a position because it's the floor that you hope will *support your trade* and protect you from losses. Resistance is the area where you want to close positions because it acts like a ceiling that *resists further gains. You always enter near support (whether that's the high or low price) and sell near resistance (whether that's the high or low price). Conceptually, s/r are the same regardless of whether you're long or short. Understand this, and you'll avoid a lot of confusion.*

With these definitions of s/r clarified, we can now state the general principle for locating low-risk, high-yield trade situations.

The General Rule for Identifying Low-Risk High-Yield Trades

Once we know how to use TA tools to identify likely s/r in a given time frame (for example daily, weekly, or monthly candle charts), we can scan charts for situations where the distance between the support and resistance is the greatest and where price is approaching support, which allows us a low-risk entry point to buy or sell the currency pair.

We then:

- Place entry limit orders to open positions near support. For long positions, support is near the likely low, and for short positions support is near the likely high for a given period. We enter near support because the odds of price moving against us are lower, and if support is breached, that's a signal to exit while our losses are small.
- Place exit limit orders (for taking profits) near resistance. For long positions resistance is near the likely high, and for short positions it's near the likely low.

There are details and exceptions, but that's what you're seeking when you scan charts looking for opportunities. Whether you choose to enter slightly before or after price hits support is a judgment call that is influenced by a variety of factors. For example, if you're more worried about missing the trade and are confident it will work as planned, or think support is very strong, you might want to jump in earlier. If you feel the opposite, you'd set your entry limit order a bit below support.

Finding S/R Is Key to Identifying and Executing Low-Risk High-Yield Trades

Identifying s/r is arguably the most important goal of TA. Here's why. If you can find situations that allow you to enter at strong support zones and plan exits near strong resistance that is a much greater distance away from your entry point than your stop loss, then you will have a low-risk, high-yield setup that even a beginner can turn into a profitable trade.

Some would argue that identifying trends, momentum, or cycles of price movements (all discussed later) are equally or more important. However, trends are sequences of s/r levels, and trend lines are mostly used as a type of s/r. Momentum is the speed at which trend lines change, and cycle analysis like the Elliott Wave Theory is the timing of when these change. Granted, momentum and timing indicators can have important predictive value beyond their relationship to s/r.

In other words, by using TA to find likely s/r at which to enter and exit, we can hunt for trades that offer both the lowest probability of loss and highest probability of gain:

1. **The lowest probability of loss:** For example, we open long positions near what our TA tools tell us is the likely support or low price for a given period we set an entry limit order to open a long position near support. We also enter a stop loss order to close the position a short distance (in pips) below this estimated low price because if the price breaks below this level, that's our signal that we were wrong about support and that in fact the pair could fall much lower. With the stop loss order, our trading platform automatically closes the position for us with only a small loss. Similarly, we want to open short positions by entering a sell limit order near what our TA tools indicate is support. With short positions, support is the high price for a given period. As part of good risk management, we enter a stop loss order a short distance (in pips) above this level, so that if we were wrong and the price breaks higher, that stop loss automatically executes and closes our position with an affordable small loss.

    How we choose where to place our stop losses will depend on a number of factors that we'll discuss in more detail later. For now, know that we'd consider these factors:

    - Money management criteria: What size loss can we take and not lose more than 1 to 3 percent of our trading capital.
    - Risk management criteria: Aim for a 1:3 risk-to-reward ratio. In other words, the distance in pips from our entry point to stop loss should be no more than about a third of the distance from our entry point to our profit-taking point (near the high in the case of long positions, near the low in the case of short positions). That way our winning trades produce gains that make up for multiple losses.
    - Normal or average price fluctuation or candle length is for the given time frame so we don't get "stopped out" of our position by random market noise.
    - Market conditions: For example, if we have a lot of confidence in the prevailing trend, we might compromise on certain RAMM criteria because we believe the chance of a loss from the trend stalling or reversing is exceptionally low.

2. **The highest probability of gain:** Using our TA tools to identify s/r, we hunt for and trade situations where the distance from our entry point to the likely resistance or high price is triple (or more) the distance (in pips) from our entry point to our stop loss point.

Good Risk Management Requires Good TA

Do you see why technical analysis is so, well, fundamental to good risk management? You need good TA to determine likely s/r to identify situations that offer low-risk, high-yield entry and exit points. In short, TA tells you when you're buying low and have a good chance of selling at a much higher price (or the opposite in the case of short positions).

Think of S/R as Zones or Areas

As we mentioned earlier, support and resistance are not precise prices but rather price ranges. For example, in Figure 3.10, our labels assume a long position on the EURJPY. If we were short the pair, the labels would be reversed. For example, SUPPORT 1 would be labeled RESISTANCE 1.

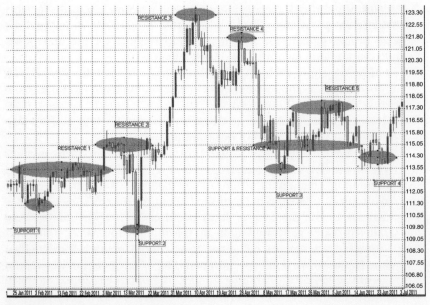

FIGURE 3.10 EURUSD Daily Chart, January 16 to July 3, 2011
Source: MetaQuotes Software Corp.

Support and resistance are not precise points but rather areas. Depending on circumstances, some may determine s/r points based only on opening or closing prices, while others will consider the wicks as well.

There are many reasons for why s/r should be viewed as zones rather than precise points, including:

- Differences in perception of s/r: The application and use of many s/r indicators depends on human judgment and is to varying degrees subjective. For example, different traders will draw the same trend line a bit differently. These differences will cause some variance in where traders chose to buy or sell.
- Trader temperament: Buy and sell orders tend to cluster around popular s/r levels, so the effects of these are felt above and below them. For example, as a currency pair rises toward resistance, more conservative traders will have exit orders to take profits set somewhat before resistance (or what they think it is) is hit in order to beat the crowd and exit before price might start to reverse. More aggressive traders will place profit-taking sell limit orders closer to or above resistance in hope of getting a few extra pips of profit.
- Large institutions and brokers are aware of key s/r levels and will often use their ability to place huge orders to move prices so less savvy individual traders get fooled into making premature buy or sell decisions from which these players reap profits. The mechanics of this are beyond the scope of this book, but the point here is that there are those who can and will try to influence very short-term perceptions of s/r, thus further blurring where an objective s/r point lies. These attempts at short-term price manipulation are part of the reason why so many seemingly random, unpredictable intraday price movements are seen on the short time frames (1 to 60 minutes, one- to four-hour charts, etc.). More on how to deal with these attempts to fool you later when we discuss topics for further study.

So Stick to Trading Longer Time Frames—They're Safer

This is another reason we urge less experienced or profitable traders to avoid day trading forex until they're consistently profitable on a monthly basis with multiday/week/month positions. They avoid becoming victims of random price movements or attempts at short-term price manipulation. That happens in any kind of short-term trading and not just forex. As noted earlier, stock markets are ruled by market makers for a given stock, who, ahem, have been known to succumb to similar temptations, all for the sake of maintaining an "orderly market, of course" Your Honor.

Few beyond the central banks of sovereign nations have the ability to exercise longer-term influence on prices, so longer-term trends are far less subject to manipulation by even the most powerful players.

Reasons to Consider Using Multiple Entry and Exit Points

When you enter a position, support might not appear exactly where you think it should be, and you could find your trade moving against you. Similarly, resistance might appear earlier or later, causing you to miss a profit-taking opportunity or to exit too soon (if you're not using a trailing stop).

So, consider entering positions and taking profits in stages. For example, consider closing half of your position when your profit equals the size of your stop loss (plus a few pips extra to cover transaction costs). Then move up your stop loss order to this first exit or break-even point so even if the trade reverses, you break even. If it continues to move in your favor, switch to a trailing stop loss to ride the move for whatever gains you can get.

More on this in Chapter 5, when we discuss the value entering and exiting positions in stages rather than all at once. Staged entries and exits are another aspect of trade planning, risk management, and trader psychology because if you've taken some profits or will at least break even, this relieves some of the stress of trading.

Once Broken, Resistance Becomes Support and Vice Versa

Markets are comprised of human traders who study past support and resistance levels. Look again at Figure 3.10 for reference.

Note how often former resistance becomes support and vice versa. For example, compare:

- Resistance area 1 and support area 3 both center around 113.55.
- Resistance area 2 and s/r area A both center around 115.05.

Why Resistance Becomes Support and Vice Versa   The short answer is that traders remember recent highs and lows and are watching charts like the one in Figure 3.10. They tend to perceive breaks above resistance as a sign the asset has hit a new plateau, and they treat former resistance as support until proven otherwise. At least part of the reason for this is that those who sold near resistance and regret having sold too soon see a return to that price as a chance to reverse their mistake.

The same holds true when support is broken. If prices rise back toward that former support area, traders who are still holding the asset, who had expected price to move higher and are sitting with losing positions, see this level as a chance to get out and break even.

Don't "OD" on TA

It's easy to get carried away with TA in your early years of trading and to clutter your charts indicators in the hope that more is better.

It isn't, so don't. Here are two reasons:

1. While I'm oversimplifying a bit, most indicators measure s/r, trend, trend strength (aka momentum), or the cyclical movements of prices, so the marginal benefit of additional indicators drops after you have one or two of each kind because they're tracking the same thing in different ways. So, stick to around five (plus or minus 2) of them as a rough guide. By all means experiment with various tools for various asset classes or pairs, but limit the number you're using at any one time.

2. You risk the common beginner's malady of paralysis from analysis, as you struggle to reconcile conflicting or ambiguous signals. For example, though a group of trend or momentum indicators may be attempting to track the same thing, the difference in how they do it could be enough to send conflicting signals.

It's far better to focus on mastering a limited number of technical tools (four to seven as a rough maximum), mixing trend, momentum, and timing indicators, as discussed in Chapter 9. Together these give you enough information about likely s/r points and where to enter and exit for best results.

Therefore, know that you'll put the odds more in your favor by first focusing on building expertise with the tools we'll be covering and applying them to a limited number of currency pairs and time frames. For example, some traders will gravitate toward how a given currency pair responds to moving averages or other kinds of trend lines. Others will focus more on Double Bollinger bands or Fibonacci retracement and extension levels. In Chapter 9 we'll show you how to test the forecasting power of different combinations of indicators through a process called back testing. Over time you can then expand your repertoire of tools used as well as pairs and time frames traded.

Why Specialize in a Few Currency Pairs and Time Frames?

When starting out with forex, you'll progress faster by becoming familiar with the price behavior and fundamentals of a few pairs in a few time frames, preferably longer ones for reasons cited above. As each economy and currency has its unique characteristics, so too do individual currency pairs. For example, different kinds of events impact some more than others. Correlations can be different. The EUR and USD tend to move in opposite directions because the EURUSD comprises 25 to 33 percent of all forex trade, so every time three to four EUR are bought, a USD is sold, and vice versa. That means the pair can be subject to wild swings depending on which currency is in favor at a given moment. However, the USDCAD tends to be less volatile because the Canadian economy is more closely linked to the fortunes of the USD, a destination for about 75 percent of Canadian exports. We'll go deeper into intermarket correlations and how to use them in Chapter 9.

By specializing, you'll develop expertise faster, and you won't be sacrificing much in terms of trading opportunities because, as we'll see, there are only two kinds of currency pairs: risk currencies and safe haven or safety currencies. Members of each group behave similarly relative to the overall market movements, so you can ride bullish or bearish market trends with only a few currency pairs.

What Determines Whether a Currency Is a Risk or a Safe Haven?

In Chapter 2 we said that there are 2 kinds of currencies, risk and safe haven, which respond in opposite ways to market sentiment.

- The higher the risk ranking (think AUD, NZD, CAD, EUR and GBP in that order), the more the currency tends to appreciate versus those lower on the risk spectrum in times of optimism, when markets seek risk assets like stocks or industrial commodities. In times of fear, the opposite happens.
- The higher the safety ranking (think JPY, USD and CHF in that order) the better the currency performs versus those lower on the safety spectrum (or higher on the risk spectrum) in times of fear, when risk assets sell off and safety assets, like quality bonds, rally.

Once again, here's the general ranking.

RISK	➡️				SAFE HAVEN		
RISK CURRENCIES					SAFE HAVEN CURRENCIES		
AUD	NZD	CAD	EUR	GBP	CHF	USD	JPY

What causes a given currency's risk ranking?

The main reason is interest rates. The higher the currency's benchmark short term yields, the more closely it moves with other risk assets, and so the higher it tends to rank as a risk currency. That's because in times of optimism, high-yielding currencies are in greater demand due to carry trading. In other words, carry traders buy higher-yielding currencies and sell lower-yielding ones to fund these purchases, with a view to profiting on the interest rate differences. In times of fear, carry traders close these positions, causing a sell-off in risk currencies and a rally in their safe haven counterparts. If you're confused, don't worry; all this is explained in Chapter 6.

For now, just know that a currency's short term benchmark interest rate, set by its central bank, is the most important reason behind a given currency's ranking.

There are other factors that can affect risk ranking, but their influence can vary with multiple factors. Interest rates provide most of the explanation for whether a currency behaves like a risk or safety asset, that is, like a growth stock or like a quality bond.

Understanding the Risk/Safety Asset Distinction Is Lucrative

Whether the base currency (the one on the left) of a forex pair has a higher risk or safety ranking than its counter currency determines whether the pair is a risk or safety currency pair, and thus determines how it correlates with other kinds of assets. When we see a divergence in that correlation (that is, the pair isn't behaving like other risk or safety assets), that's usually a warning of a possible change in market direction or in the currency pair.

For example, forex and bond markets tend to pick up changing conditions before stock markets, so those who watch forex or bond markets can often see advanced warnings of what may happen with stocks or other markets. That advanced knowledge can be very profitable.

The opportunities to spot these divergences from the normal correlations between currency pairs and other asset types is one of the best reasons why everyone needs some awareness of forex markets.

With experience, you'll become increasingly sensitive to any divergences from normal correlations between asset types. The study of these relationships is called intermarket analysis, and we'll explore this critical topic in Chapter 9.

Note however, that because currencies trade in pairs, the significance of currency's risk ranking is in how it affects the behavior of one of its pairings. The farther apart a given pair's component currencies are on the above risk spectrum, the more sensitive the pair will be to market movements. We'll explain that in much greater depth later on.

CHAPTER 4

Technical Analysis

Types of Support and Resistance (S/R)

N ow you understand some basics about charts, support and resistance (s/r), and risk and money management (RAMM). You're ready to get to the meat of TA and learn the tools to identify the likely support area at which to enter or open a position and the likely resistance zone at which to exit or close it.

This chapter will cover:

- Price levels
- Trends and trend lines
- Fibonacci retracements
- Bollinger Bands (BBs) in range-bound markets
- Introduction to Japanese candle chart patterns
- Introduction to Western chart patterns
- The importance of having multiple s/r indicators

I have selected the following tools and indicators of s/r based on importance and ease of use. The idea is to give you a powerful toolkit you can learn quickly and easily.

Though opinions about the value of TA vary, most would agree it's necessary to know if you're buying low or selling high. And though many disparage TA, I've yet to meet a serious trader or investor who doesn't use it. The main reasons include:

- Much of it makes intuitive sense. Some of it doesn't, but works anyway. For example, the Fibonacci retracements we will discuss further on are based on a common ratio found in nature, music, and other fields of study. Why it applies to price behavior is unclear, but it does, so look at it like electricity. You use it even though you don't understand how it works.

- Used properly, it improves your performance.
- It is so widely used that you need to watch the popular indicators to know what the rest of the market is thinking. That self-fulfilling prophecy factor alone makes it worthwhile.

Let's focus on that last point. *Successful trading or investing depends on anticipating what the crowd will do, and doing it first, or even better, early, just as they've already started to bid up the price but before most of the gains are realized. In other words, the key to success isn't knowing what's necessarily true, but rather correctly anticipating what the rest of the market will soon believe is true.*

Savvy traders ignore their personal opinions and focus on what they think the crowd will do. These traders buy when price is low before the herd rushes in and bids it up, and they sell before the masses sell and drive price lower, regardless of whether they think the move is justified. Ironically, many with great academic credentials and analytical skills often struggle because they can't anticipate what they see as an irrational behavior of markets, while others of more average credentials who have a better feel for the emotions of market participants prosper.

While fundamental analysis (see Chapter 6) is valuable, it tells us little about the likely best entry and exit prices in a given time frame and, except for news trades, it tells us nothing about short-term price action. Fundamental analysis is also notoriously bad for timing entries and exits. In contrast, technical indicators can tell you when the crowd has begun buying or selling.

Regardless of whether you believe in TA, you need to understand and use it because the crowd uses it. That makes TA invaluable in anticipating what they see as s/r, and thus when they are likely to be buying or selling. The more popular the indicator, the more it creates a self-fulfilling prophecy of how markets may react.

Though some theorize that TA works solely because of this self-fulfilling prophecy phenomena, that line of reasoning fails to explain why markets originally accepted TA. It had to produce some results before it could gain acceptance. Moreover, as we'll see next, most of the commonly used s/r indicators have a clear logic to them.

PRICE LEVELS

Simple price levels, like those in Figure 4.1, are the most basic building blocks of most s/r indicators. As noted earlier, think of them more as areas or zones rather than precise price points.

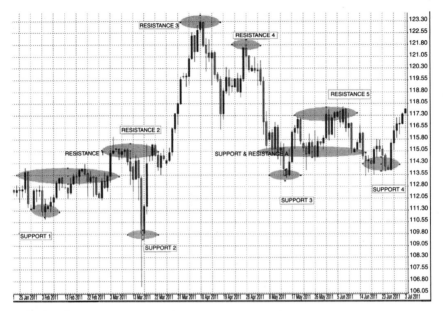

FIGURE 4.1 EURUSD Daily Chart, January 16 to July 3, 2011
Source: MetaQuotes Software Corp.

They don't appear out of nowhere. As experienced food shoppers remember a low price (support) or a high price (resistance) for apples, price levels are the product of collective trader memory over a given period and time frame. That perception of what is a low or high price can change with news about the fundamentals (see Chapter 6) that affect supply and demand, be it for apples or a currency. For example, reports that apples cure impotence would raise demand and price for apples. Similarly, rising interest or growth rates increase demand for a given currency.

For Lowest Risk, Enter Near Strong Support

If you enter near strong support, and that support doesn't hold, then you will immediately know you were wrong about how low price should go and you can exit the trade with only a small loss. For example, if you open a long position, the farther that entry is *above* solid support, the bigger your loss before price tests that support level, and the greater your risk of loss if support is breached.

Similarly, when you enter a short position, the further that entry is *below* the next major support level, the larger your risk of loss before discovering that support isn't holding and it's time to exit with a small loss before it becomes too large. Remember, with short positions, support is the likely high price.

Therefore, correctly identifying strong support is essential to choosing low-risk entry points.

What Makes Some S/R Points Stronger Than Others?

We'll discuss these criteria for strong s/r as they apply to price zones, but these characteristics apply to any kind of s/r points and not just price levels.

Four factors that make s/r points stronger are:

1. Round numbers: They're easier to remember and use. The bigger the round number, the more psychologically important it tends to be. For example, in stock markets, it's significant when the Standard & Poor's 500 Index (S&P 500) breaks above or below some multiple of 50 or 100, or when the Dow Jones Industrial Average (DJIA) breaks through a multiple of 100 or 1,000. The same holds true for currency pairs. For example, using the long-term monthly charts, the EURUSD's most significant levels have been 1.2000, 1.3000, 1.4000, and 1.5000, with lesser but still significant s/r roughly every 200 pips (1.4800, 1.4600, etc.) and more minor s/r every 100 pips, and so on. Traders are human and humans are wired to attach significance to round numbers. Note the charts shown in Figures 4.1 and 4.2.

2. Age: The longer a given price level has held, the stronger the support or resistance and the more significant a signal when it is broken. For example, support that has not been broken for over a year is considered stronger than support that has held for only a few weeks or hours. In Figure 4.1, note how the strongest, major support and resistance levels are the oldest and rarely reached or breached.

3. The number of times tested: After age, this is the next most important criteria for judging strength of a price level as s/r. The more times price hits a given level and that level holds, the stronger it is and more significant if broken. Often age and number of times tested go together. See Figures 4.1 and 4.2 for examples of how repeated tests of a price level define it as an s/r area.

4. Multiple types of s/r converge: The more kinds of s/r that meet at one price or narrow price range, the more they reinforce each other and strengthen that s/r point. The stronger each of these are (older, tested, etc.), the stronger that s/r area. We'll see an example of mutually reinforcing s/r indicators at the end of this chapter.

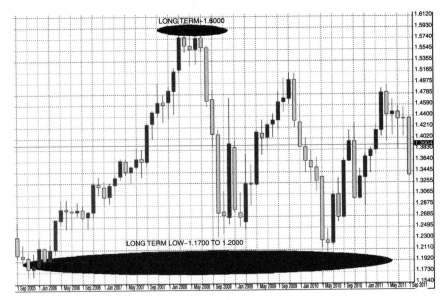

FIGURE 4.2 EURUSD Monthly Chart, September 1, 2005, to September 1, 2011
Source: MetaQuotes Software Corp.

Longer Time Frames Offer More Reliable S/R Indicators

The longer the chart's time frame, the more established and reliable the key price levels and other s/r indicators.

For example, the EURUSD monthly chart shown in Figure 4.2 shows the major long-term s/r levels from a nearly six-year period from late 2005 to late 2011. Deep support is around 1.1700 to 1.2000. Strong resistance is around 1.6000. During this period, each represented extreme market sentiment and a major reversal point. We can see that around 1.5000 and 1.4000 are significant levels.

Having more reliable data is one of the advantages that come from working on charts with daily or longer time frame candles. We'll look at more advantages of longer time frame trading in Chapter 5.

Check Shorter Time Frames to Detect Interim S/R Levels

As we see above, different time frames contain different s/r points and trends. Over any given time frame, a number of minor s/r points from shorter time frames can be nested within the upper and lower price extremes that serve as the strongest s/r of different price levels of longer time frames. The longer the time frame you're viewing, the more these minor levels appear.

Whatever time frame you trade from, you need to check shorter-term time frames (typically, about a fifth of the time frame from which you trade) to be aware of these so you can anticipate possible pauses or reversals and a possible need to exit a position at these levels. Sometimes, these are short-term gyrations or pauses, and sometimes they can be the start of longer-term reversals.

For example, additional minor s/r levels show up more when we look at the same period covered in the monthly chart in Figure 4.2 for the EURUSD, but a finer resolution is present via the weekly chart shown in Figure 4.3 with some of the price areas that serve as more intermediate-term s/r.

The areas around 1.2600, 1.2800, 1.300, 1.4200, and 1.4800 serve as important s/r levels. Look closer, and you'll find others as well.

The EURUSD daily chart in Figure 4.4 gives a clear view of the major s/r levels:

- Firm support around 1.4340 and 1.4375
- Firm resistance at 1.4515 and lesser resistance at 1.4440 and then 1.4410.

Within this same period, note the lesser s/r levels on the EURUSD hourly chart in Figure 4.5 for the same period.

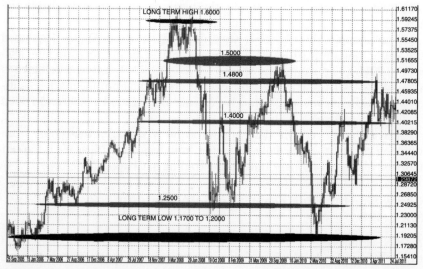

FIGURE 4.3   EURUSD Weekly Chart, Week of September 25, 2005, to Week of July 24, 2011
Source: MetaQuotes Software Corp.

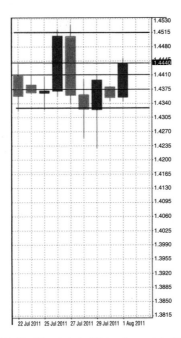

FIGURE 4.4 EURUSD Daily Chart, July 22 to August 1, 2011
Source: MetaQuotes Software Corp.

FIGURE 4.5 EURUSD 1 Hour Chart, July 22 to August 1, 2011
Source: MetaQuotes Software Corp.

For example, we can see lesser s/r levels worth noting: 1.4255, 1.4345, 1.4360, 1.4375, 1.4480, and so on.

TRENDS AND TREND LINES

In addition to being an essential element of TA in their own right, trend lines are one of the most basic forms of s/r, along with price levels. First, here are some principles that apply to all kinds of trend lines.

Trends Vary with Time Frame

Over any given period of time, price can only move up, down, or sideways in a trading range. The sequence of candles in a given time frame forms the trend. I keep emphasizing time frame because the strength and trustworthiness of trends (and other technical indicators) varies radically with time frame, because they are more established and tested on the longer time frame charts. For whatever time frame you trade from, remember to always check:

- At least one longer time frame to get a sense of the bigger overall trend within which you're trading. Ideally, you want to trade in the direction of that larger trend although there will often be tradable counter moves within the longer-term trend. As a rule of thumb, the longer time frame should be four to six times longer than the chart from which you trade. For example those trading off of daily charts would check weekly charts for the bigger trend.
- At least one shorter time frame to check the minor trends and s/r levels nested within your trading time frame so you know where the trend may pause or reverse and be a possible exit point to take profits or cut losses. Again the rule of four to six times applies. For example, those trading off of daily charts would look at four-hour charts.

Similarly, time frames of much greater or lesser magnitude can usually be ignored.

Defining Trends, and Constructing Trend Lines

Here's how we define and construct trend lines:

Uptrend definition and trend line construction: An uptrend is comprised of a series of at least two (preferably more) higher lows and higher highs. To construct an uptrend line, we will need to connect at least two higher lows. For example, see the long rising line on left side of Figure 4.6? From the start of the uptrend on May 2 until May 27, 2011, we had an uptrend. Note the brief downtrends within the overall uptrend. Such temporary counter moves are common and normal within longer-term trends.

Downtrend definition and trend line construction: A downtrend is a series of at least two (preferably more) progressively lower highs and lower lows. To construct a downtrend line, we will need to connect at least two lower highs. For example, see the long falling line on the right side of Figure 4.6. Note that there was also a normal shorter-term counter move higher in the middle part of this downtrend in the first half of July 2011.

Like much of TA, a degree of subjectivity exists about how you apply and interpret these tools. For example, some may choose to connect only closing prices to form their trend lines, and others may include wicks to better reflect the overall direction or reflect a more conservative strategy of catching only the deepest tests of support or resistance as entry points. Traders have different strategies concerning how close to a trend line to enter or exit positions As with other kinds of s/r, view trend lines as bands rather than precise lines of s/r.

Finally, in Chapter 2, you learned currencies trade in pairs. When we speak about a pair trending higher or lower, remember that we're really referring to how the base currency (the one on the left) is moving relative to the counter currency. In any given pair, one currency is moving up or down versus the other. So, when traders see the EURUSD dropping, they may say the pair is falling or the USD is rising versus the Euro. They're saying the same thing, just from opposite perspectives of the base and counter currencies.

Types of Trend Lines

Trend lines come in four basic types:

1. Single up or downtrend lines
2. Channels, including flat trading ranges
3. Moving averages (MAs)
4. Bollinger Bands (BBs), a variation on MAs

These are the must-know basic tools of trend analysis. For further study, you'll want to learn about Average Directional Index (ADX),

Directional Movement Index (DMI), and others, which you can research on the Internet.

Here you will learn how to use a set of analytical tools not just separately but in combinations, because that's how you'll actually make trading decisions. That way you can get started making intelligent, well-planned trades on practice accounts and then with real money. Unlike many forex books, we'll avoid overloading you with superficial understandings of more tools than you can or should use, with little idea of which to use, when to use them, or in what kinds of combinations.

Single Uptrend or Downtrend Lines

Let's look more at single trend lines. As the name suggests, these individual trend lines are lines we draw to better highlight the overall price direction over a given period. Figure 4.6 provides an example of how we plot up, down, or flat range trading trend lines.

The figure suggests:

> An uptrend is a series of higher lows and higher highs, as we see from
> May 2nd to the 22nd. To plot an uptrend line, draw a line that con-
> nects as many of the higher lows of the candle bodies as possible,
> while best capturing the overall upward slope, even if that means
> having some candlesticks either not touching the line or crossing

FIGURE 4.6 USDCAD Daily Chart, April 29, 2011, to July 22, 2011
Source: MetaQuotes Software Corp.

it. Trends rarely move in neat straight lines, so varying degrees of overlapping candles are okay.

A downtrend is a series of lower highs and lower lows. To plot a downtrend line, you want to connect as many of the lower highs as possible while best showing the overall downward slope even if that means having some outlier candlesticks.

Again, as with any other kind of s/r, trend lines should be viewed as bands or areas of s/r rather than precise points, and candlesticks rarely line up in a straight rising, falling, or flat line. Thus, you can have a few outlier candlesticks or wicks above or below your uptrend line. *The goal is to best capture the overall slope of the line.* Again, variations in speed and direction within the overall trend are expected.

Channels: Better Than Single Trend Lines

Instead of single trend lines, you can draw their clearer, more useful version: channels.

As the name suggests, channels (aka tunnels or sleeves) are parallel trend lines that surround a rising or falling trend at an angle that shows the overall slope of the trend up, down, or sideways. *As with single trend lines, the goal is to draw lines that show the overall slope of the trend.* We want to capture the likely trading range, so don't worry if you've some outlying candles that extend beyond or fall within your channel lines when keeping them parallel.

Figures 4.7 and 4.8 show some examples of a rising, flat, and falling channel.

The big advantage of channels over single trend lines is they provide clearer, more useful information than single trend lines. In addition to trend direction, they provide the following advantages.

Channels Provide Guidance for Both Entry and Exit Points As long as you're trading in the direction of the trend, these upper and lower limits may be attractive entry and exit points if, as always, confirmed by other indicators.

Be cautious, however, about using these to trade against the trend (i.e., opening short positions at the top of a rising channel or long positions at the bottom of a falling channel). Playing both ends of the channel works well when you trade in the trend's direction, or if the slope of the channel is very mild and the channel is wide. Don't trade against the trend if the trend is steep and/or the range of the channel is narrow, because you may run out of room to exit profitably if the price doesn't move in your favor fast enough. When you trade against a channel, resistance gets closer with each candle and the odds of a successful trade drop rapidly.

FIGURE 4.7   Rising Channel AUDJPY Daily Chart, September 6, 2010, to February 21, 2011
Source: MetaQuotes Software Corp.

Beware of Trading against the Trend Using Channels as S/R for Entries and Exits—An Example

In Figure 4.9, see how an otherwise well-planned trade can be foiled by trading against a channel that is sloping too steeply or is too narrow.

Look what can happen when you trade against the slope or trend using channel lines as entry and exits:

1. You correctly identify a good entry point for a long EURCHF position near the bottom of the downtrending EURCHF.

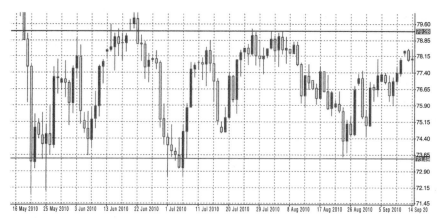

FIGURE 4.8 Flat Channel or Trading Range AUDJPY Daily Chart, May 16, 2010, to September 14, 2010
Source: MetaQuotes Software Corp.

FIGURE 4.9 Falling Channel EURCHF Daily Chart, April 11 to June 24, 2011
Source: MetaQuotes Software Corp.

2. You entered near the low of the day around 1.2485, with a planned sell limit to take profits entered in advance on your trading platform around 1.2701, a realistic target which the price had hit two out of the three prior days.

3. You used solid risk management. Your planned loss was only about a third of your likely gain. You'd earn about 216 pips, so you could afford to set a generously wide stop loss order 63 pips down at 1.2422 and have a better than 3:1 reward-risk ratio. If you're correct, you gain over three times what you'd lose if your stop loss is hit. When we cover risk management, you'll see how these kinds of reward-risk ratios are what we want to remain profitable even when we're wrong the majority of our trades.

4. Theoretically, this looks like a worthwhile trade setup backed by sound risk management. You've a low-priced entry, and your likely loss is only about a third of the likely gain.

5. However, even though the channel was wide enough to trade profitably (over 300 pips) and you had entered near the bottom of it, the trend was falling hard and, by May 16, the upper trend line (resistance) was below what had been an otherwise realistic profit-taking point only five days earlier. Now that profit target was right at resistance and no longer a good bet.

6. If you were alert and lucky, you might have decided to exit that day, even at the low for the day at 1.2565 with a profit of 82 pips, not bad, but about the same size as your stop loss of 63 pips, a reward-risk ratio slightly better than 1:1. To stay profitable over the long run, you will want your gains from winning trades to produce at least two to three times the losses from your losers. That way you're profitable even with fewer than 50 percent winning trades. More on this when we cover RAMM.

7. If you weren't monitoring the trade, your stop loss was hit May 20 as the falling upper trend line held as resistance and price kept falling.

The big lesson here is don't trade against a channel's trend unless the slope is gentle and the channel is wide. When in doubt, don't. Use the resistance line only as an area for taking profits.

Channels Offer Stronger Trend Reversal Signals from Breakouts in the Opposite Direction of the Channel   The other big advantage of channels over single trend lines is that when the lower line of a rising channel or upper line of a falling channel is breached, that is a potentially significant trend reversal signal because such a move requires a significant change in market sentiment. Breakouts in the direction of the channel are not a signal of changing sentiment and often signal the trend may have spent itself as the final supporters of the trend have joined in.

Trading sideways moving markets like that shown in Figure 4.9 requires the use of channels to gauge the height of that range and locate s/r. Their distance should capture the overall range even if some candlesticks extend outside or remain well within the lines.

Even though trend lines are useful tools, their construction can often be subjective, and that's why we view them as areas or bands of s/r rather than as precise, discrete lines.

To avoid the subjective human element of trend lines, we turn to moving averages, the product of an objective mathematical calculation.

Moving Averages (MAs)

As the name implies, moving average (MA) lines for a given period don't plot the price at a given moment. Instead, each point on these lines is the average closing price for a certain number of prior completed candlesticks or periods.

For example, at any given point in time, a 200-period MA plots the average price over the past 200 periods. On a one-minute chart, in which each candlestick shows price movement over one minute, the 200-period MA is comprised of a series of average closing prices for the past 200 one-minute candles. On a daily chart, the 200-period moving average shows a series of average closing prices over the past 200 days.

As each new closing price is added, the oldest one is dropped from the calculation, hence the term moving average, or MA. In other words, what makes these MAs is that for each new candlestick, the calculation replaces the oldest closing price with the latest one. For example, over a 251-candlestick period, the 200-period MA calculation would drop the closing price from the 250th candle and replace it with the one from the most recent, the 251st period. These 200 most recent closing prices would be totaled and divided by 200 to give the latest price level of the 200-period MA. This is the formula for the most basic MA, the Simple Moving Average (SMA).

Advantages of MAs   MAs have two advantages over the other types of trend lines previously discussed:

1. They clarify trend direction: As a series of average prices over a given period rather than real-time prices, MAs filter out random price movements and present a smoother, clearer picture of the trend for the period they cover versus the series of candlesticks. Because MAs are

dynamic and changing trend lines, MAs can provide a useful look at the more subtle price fluctuations within the overall trend that hand-drawn straight trend lines or channels will miss.

2. They are often more reliable s/r because everyone's MAs look the same: They're built from an objective mathematical formula, so unlike trend and channel lines, a given type (SMA, EMA, WMA) and duration of MA for a given time frame looks the same on everyone's chart and presents the same picture of trend and s/r for all viewing it. That's a valuable attribute. By watching the most widely followed MAs, you have a better idea of what the rest of the herd believes to be the s/r of these trend lines. That allows you to anticipate and exploit their moves.

Disadvantages of Simple MAs and Their Alternatives   The main disadvantage of using single SMA lines is that by their nature of being a series of average prior prices, they lag the current price. We'll see later in Chapter 8 that using multiple MA lines together can turn MAs from lagging indicators into leading indicators.

To partially remedy this time lag for individual SMAs, Exponential Moving Averages (EMAs) and Weighted Moving Averages (WMAs) are available. Leaving aside the mathematical distinctions, know that though SMAs weigh the oldest and newest prices equally, WMAs and EMAs assign greater weight to the most recent data and are a bit more responsive to recent price changes. No clear consensus exists on which is better or more popular. Whether one or another works better for you will be a matter of experiment (see later discussion of back testing). The more responsive WMA and EMA are more accurate if recent prices are more indicative of where the trend is going. Sometimes that is true, and sometimes it's not.

The Most Important MAs to Watch   The 5-, 10-, 20-, 50-, 100-, and 200-period MAs are widely followed in most markets and time frames. They are the standard sampling of shorter and longer-duration MAs and provide a degree of self-fulfilling prophecy. They indicate s/r because traders believe they are s/r points. The longer-duration MAs are particularly popular s/r indicators. For example, even the mainstream financial press aimed at laymen will usually mention if a major stock index crosses its 50- or 200-day MA. The forex media (which exists almost exclusively on the Internet) will quickly note if a major pair hits or crosses one of the longer-duration MAs like its 50-, 100-, or 200-day MA. Similarly, because MAs in longer time-frames are older, 20-, 50-, or 200-day, week, and month MAs get more attention because they provide much more significant s/r than those durations in shorter time frames.

By all means, tinker with slight variations on these. For example, some prefer to shorten their sampling period to get a head start on the crowd (at the risk of getting a premature, false signal). Slightly longer or shorter sampling periods have their advantages and disadvantages. Following is a summary.

MA Duration and Age: Advantages and Disadvantages   To understand and use MAs, you need to understand the relative strengths and weaknesses of the longer- and shorter-duration MAs, and the older ones you'll see on daily to monthly charts versus the younger MAs in the shorter time frames. Here's what you need to know.

Shorter Durations (5, 10, 20 Periods): More Responsive to Price Changes, Weaker, Less Significant S/R

The advantages:

- More responsive to price changes and are quicker to indicate a change in trend.
- Are better at showing short-term trends.
- May provide warning of trend changes when they cross longer-duration MAs (see Chapter 8 on MA crossovers).

The disadvantages:

- Weaker, less significant s/r, so they don't provide as reliable signals of trend continuation or reversal as the longer-duration MAs when they are breached or when they hold.
- Shorter-duration MAs don't display the overall trend as well as longer-duration MAs when prices are bouncing around because the shorter-duration MAs follow each price move so closely.

Longer Duration (50, 100, 200 Periods): Less Responsive to Price Changes, Stronger, More Significant S/R

The advantages:

- Stronger, more significant s/r provide more reliable signals of trend continuation or reversal when they are breached or when they hold.
- They are better than the shorter-duration MAs at displaying the overall trend when prices are volatile because a more sustained trend is needed to move these MAs.

The disadvantages:

- The longer the duration, the further they lag current price action.

The Same Advantages and Disadvantages Apply When Comparing Younger versus Older MAs The same durations on longer time frame charts are older than those on shorter time frame charts.

Thus a 200-day MA is a much more significant s/r than a 200-hour MA but is less responsive to price and trend changes.

Examples of Long- and Short-Term MA Behavior Let's look at some examples of how long- and short-term MAs behave. In Figures 4.10 and 4.11, the shorter MAs, the more closely they follow price. The longer the MAs, the smoother they are and the less often they tend to be breached.

This is a EURUSD weekly chart, meaning each candlestick shows a week's price movement for the Euro-USD currency pair. Thus, the 10-period EMA line is a 10-week EMA, the 50-period EMA is a 50-week EMA, and the 200-period EMA is a 200-week EMA.

Notice how:

- Shorter-term MAs show price changes faster than longer-term MAs: The shortest duration 10-period MA follows price more closely than the others, whereas the longer-duration 50- and 200-period MAs are progressively more smoothed, with the 200-period MA almost flat, reflecting how minimal the net price was over the period shown despite the volatility. That's a potentially important point that you might have missed by looking at only the candles.
- Longer-term MAs provide better s/r: The shorter-duration 10-week MA is breached seven times, far more often than the 50-week (two times)

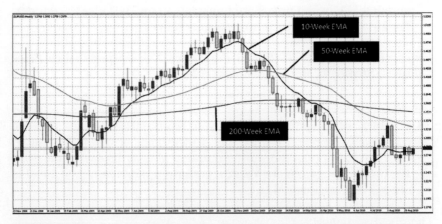

FIGURE 4.10 EURUSD Weekly Chart, November 23, 2008, to October 1, 2010
Source: MetaQuotes Software Corp.

FIGURE 4.11 USDCAD Daily Chart, September 5, 2010, to August 4, 2011
Source: MetaQuotes Software Corp.

or 200-week. Shorter-duration MAs are less reliable s/r than longer ones.

- Again, note the tradeoffs: See how the shorter-duration MAs are more responsive, and how the longer-term MAs are better at showing the overall trend because they don't jump with every short-term move. The longer-term MAs are breached much less frequently. Indeed, if the 200-day EMA is breached, we will have to consider whether this longer-term downtrend is reversing.
- Because this is a daily chart, these are 200-, 100-, 50-, 20-, and 10-day EMAs.

Additional Points about MAs: Watch and Respect the Most Popular Ones Most Popular Durations: Trading has nothing to do with discerning what logically should happen. Instead, it's all about anticipating what the crowd will do and doing it first in your chosen time frame before they bid up your entry price or bid down your selling price.

Don't Think: What logically should happen?

Think: What will the crowd think the other investors will do?

This kind of thinking is important for short-term trades meant to be concluded within a few days at most, or intraday trades and trades based on short-term reactions to news events. For example, during 2010–2011, despite the worsening situation in the Euro-zone (EZ), the EUR would repeatedly rally on flimsy excuses like:

- Rumors of rescue plans.
- Rescue plans that were badly flawed and failed to address the real problems in the EZ.
- Bank stress tests that were so lenient that banks which passed the tests were nationalized or dependent on government or European Central Bank (ECB) support within a matter of months after the tests.

So why did the EUR rally? Enough traders believed that expectations had sunk low enough that anything resembling good news would spark at least a short-term rally, and they were right.

Applying this lesson to technical indicators, it pays to keep the most widely followed indicators like the 10, 20, 50, (100?), and 200 MAs on your charts so you know where everyone else is seeing these widely followed forms of potential s/r.

For example, if you want to buy low, you need to have identified what everyone else believes is the likely support so you're ready to buy if the crowd buys and proves the support level is valid. In planning your profit-taking exit, you need to know where the masses are likely to begin selling and be ready to take profits before price hits real resistance and a wave of selling.

This principle of watching the popular indicators holds true for all kinds of technical indicators.

You don't have to keep them all on your chart at the same time if you find your chart getting cluttered. You can keep multiple charts of the same currency pair and time frame with different templates (groups of technical indicators), so that you can watch everything yet still keep uncluttered charts. That's one reason that traders love to use computers with multiple screens.

For Further Study, Experiment   Though you should watch the most popular MAs, traders can and do experiment with less or more radical variations on these. Some will use slightly shorter-duration MAs when seeking more responsive trend lines in order to catch trend changes before the rest of the crowd, but at a cost of catching more false signals. Others will opt for slightly longer durations in order to filter out all but the most proven trends. That may reduce the number of losing trades at a cost of missing some moves or accepting reduced profits on winning trades due to later entries and exits. The MAs that work best for you will depend greatly on your risk tolerance, skill level, ability to monitor trades in real time, and thus your chosen time frame and trading style. When we cover MA crossovers in Chapter 5, we'll see that this kind of tinkering can be useful for developing entry and exit signals.

Before you start tinkering with MA durations or any of the most popular TA tools, get comfortable with those covered in this book. Only then will you have the background needed to start customizing your tools.

FIBONACCI RETRACEMENTS (FIBs): THESE FIBs DON'T LIE

Fibonacci retracements (Fibs) provide a valuable kind of s/r information that the previous s/r indicators don't.

As in any financial market, forex price trends don't move in a straight line. Instead, trends move in a zigzagging pattern as they periodically retrace parts of their primary move and continue it, steadily testing progressive levels of s/r as they move higher or lower.

For example, in the period covered in the EURUSD daily chart shown in Figure 4.12, note not only the retracements within the overall uptrend (like October to November 2010 on the right side of the chart, or May to

FIGURE 4.12 EURUSD Daily Chart, September 2, 2010, to August 4, 2011
Source: MetaQuotes Software Corp.

early August 2011 on the left), but also the smaller reversals within these countermoves.

Fibs help us determine where prices are likely to either:

- Make these repeated short-term reversals as they zigzag within their longer-term trend.
- Make a longer-term reversal within an even longer-term trend or begin a longer-term reversal.

Fibs are based on certain mathematical relationships, expressed as ratios, between numbers in a series, that were identified (at least for the Western world) by thirteenth-century mathematician Leonardo Fibonacci. They have application in fields as diverse as biology, music, and art. You can search online for the details of how these are derived, but we'll stick to what's relevant to trading.

Traders found that trends tend to retrace prior moves according to these same ratios, which in percentages come to 23.6 percent, 38.2 percent, 50 percent, 61.8 percent, and 100 percent of a given trend. By drawing these percent retracements of a trend on their charts, they could better predict where future price moves might stall or reverse.

That is, they found that when trends retrace they tend to retrace 23.6 percent, 38.2 percent, 50 percent, 61.8 percent, or 100 percent of their prior move.

It's unclear why these ratios work, but they do, so they became widely accepted, thus strengthening their influence as markets accept them as likely s/r points.

For example, Figure 4.13 is the same chart as we saw in Figure 4.12, with Fib levels (horizontal lines) drawn for the range of the downtrend of December 2009 to June 2010. Note how well the Fibs predict s/r as the EURUSD retraces that downtrend.

Applying Fibs to Your Charts

Because the application of technical indicators varies with charting packages, we usually don't cover how you insert a given indicator. With Fibs, however, it's worth reviewing the general mechanics of how you get them on your chart.

So, where did these lines come from? How do you draw them?

To create Fib levels, you select a major high and low for the period in question. Your charting software divides that price range by the key Fibonacci ratios of 23.6 percent, 38.2 percent, 50 percent, 61.8 percent, and 100 percent, and it draws horizontal lines at the prices that correspond to

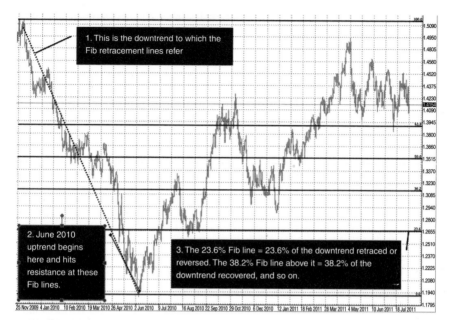

FIGURE 4.13   EURUSD Daily Chart, November 25, 2009, to August 5, 2011
Source: MetaQuotes Software Corp.

these percentages of that range. These price levels are where s/r levels are more likely to occur.

Your charting software will describe the mechanics of this, which typically involve nothing more than the following procedure steps:

- Identify the price range to study. For example, in Figure 4.13, we wanted to see the Fib s/r points as the EURUSD rallied and retraced the downtrend of December 2009 to June 2010, highlighted by the dotted line on the left side of the chart.
- Select the Fibonacci retracements option.
- **To plot the fib retracements for an uptrend that occurs after a downtrend,** you first need to define the range of the prior downtrend so that the charting software can calculate the percent retracement points that the new uptrend will hit as it retraces through the range of the prior downtrend. To do that:
  - Place your mouse cursor at the high point where the downtrend began, left click and hold the left mouse button down in order to drag the mouse cursor to the low point where the downtrend ends, then release the left mouse button.

- The fib retracements will appear. These serve as s/r points for the uptrend that follows. As price rises, each level it approaches is resistance until decisively breached, and then that level becomes support unless price falls back below it.
- **To plot the fib retracements for a downtrend that follows an uptrend**, you do the same thing. The only difference is that you first need to define the range of the prior uptrend so that the charting software can calculate the percent retracement points that the new downtrend will hit as it retraces through the range of the prior uptrend. To do that:
  - After selecting the Fibonacci Retracements option from you menu of technical indicators, place your mouse cursor at the low point where the uptrend began, left click and hold the left mouse button down in order to drag the mouse cursor to the high point where the uptrend ends, then release the left mouse button.
  - The fib retracements will appear. These serve as s/r points for the downtrend that follows. As price falls, each level it approaches is support until decisively breached, and then that level becomes resistance unless price falls back below it.
  - The software fills in the price levels that correspond to 23.6 percent, 38.2 percent, 50 percent, 61.8 percent, and 100 percent of the price range you selected.

Fibs Within Fibs

Traders must choose the period to which they apply Fibs, so there is a degree of human judgment as to the range to which a given set of Fibs will be applied. At any one time, millions of traders will be looking at different Fib levels for different periods and time frames. So, it's helpful to draw Fibs for a time frame above and below the one from which you trade so that you can see both:

- The longer-term s/r from longer-term Fibs that cover a wider price range and possibly a different trend altogether.
- The shorter-term s/r from Fibs nested within your time frame that covers a narrower price range and possibly a different kind of trend.

For example, let's say we wanted more information about likely s/r for the EURUSD downtrend from April to August 2011, as shown in Figure 4.13. We could draw another set of Fibs for the uptrend of February to May 2011 that occurred within the broader overall downtrend that began in late 2009 to early 2010, which would provide possible support points as the EURUSD retraced this uptrend lower.

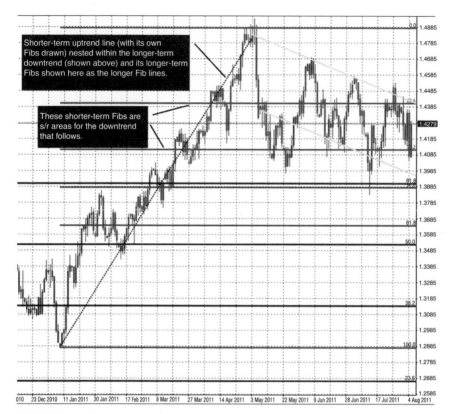

FIGURE 4.14 EURUSD with Fibonacci Retracements from January 11, 2011, to August 4, 2011
Source: MetaQuotes Software Corp.

The resulting Fibs, in Figure 4.14, served as useful predictors of s/r during this downtrend. Like any s/r points, see them as center lines for bands or zones of s/r within which the candles cluster, rather than as precise points of s/r. Some retracement levels are stronger than others. The 23.6, 38.2, and 61.8 percent retracement levels tend to be stronger than the others.

For perspective, examine the chart in Figure 4.15. This uptrend and its Fibs nest are within the broader overall downtrend and its Fibs.

You can use different sets of Fibs to gauge possible s/r points for the overall trend and various moves higher or lower within it. In this case, we plotted Fibs for the longer-term overall downtrend from November 25, 2009, to June 2, 2010, and also plotted the Fibs for the shorter-term uptrend from January 12, 2011, to May 4, 2011, within this overall downtrend.

FIGURE 4.15   EURUSD Daily Chart, November 25, 2009, to August 4, 2011
Source: MetaQuotes Software Corp.

BOLLINGER BANDS (BBs): USE AS S/R IN RANGE-BOUND MARKETS

Bollinger Bands (BBs) are a simple yet powerful combination of channels and MAs. BBs consist of an SMA surrounded by an upper and lower band plotted by a certain number of standard deviations above and below the SMA. Think of them as flexible channels whose width varies with price volatility. The wider the price swings over the period of the SMA, the wider the channel; the narrower the price range over this period, the narrower the channel.

The default settings on most charting software will be a 20-period SMA with the bands at a distance of two standard deviations (discussed next) from this SMA. Figure 4.16 shows what they look like using these "20, 2" default settings.

You can change these settings to suit your needs, and later we'll look at one useful variation: Double Bollinger Bands (DBBs). However, the standard settings are popular and are worth watching for the sake of knowing what the herd is seeing as potential s/r from the lower and upper bands.

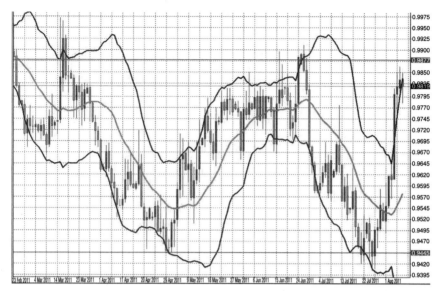

FIGURE 4.16 USDCAD Daily Chart, February 23 to August 8, 2011
Source: MetaQuotes Software Corp.

Support/Resistance (S/R) for Flat or Gently Sloping Trends: The Bollinger Bounce

The two standard deviation width of the channel means that the statistical probability of price hitting the bands given the price range of the past 20 periods is only about 5 percent. However like any statistical measure, it assumes that all elements of the sample, in this case the 20 periods, are the same.

That assumption works for flat, range-bound markets or gently trending markets, which by definition are times when no change occurs in the markets' perception of a currency pair's value. Under those conditions, the upper and lower bands provide reliable s/r points. In flat or mild trends, the price tends to fluctuate between the upper and lower bands, as price bounces off the upper and lower bands like a ball bouncing off the floor and ceiling. Even if price swings widen or narrow, Bollinger bands adjust for those conditions and widen or narrow with the price swings, providing s/r points that adjust with volatility (a uniquely valuable feature of BBs). In Figure 4.16, price usually bounces off these bands back toward the middle, particularly when price makes a sudden sharp move up or down.

Using the standard default settings of a 20-period SMA middle band with each band two standard deviations distance from the middle band, there is only a 5 percent chance that the price will ever touch the outer bands. Again, this calculation assumes (as with any statistical measure) that all sample elements (the past 20 periods) were the same and all prices equally probable. When there's no strong trend or no trend at all, that assumption applies. Flat price action suggests that market perceptions about the value of a currency pair haven't materially changed.

However, that assumption doesn't apply in a strong trend, which by definition indicates market perceptions about value are changing.

Bollinger Bands Don't Provide Meaningful S/R with Strong Trends

BBs are useful s/r points only when the pair (or any other asset) is in a flat trading range, as in Figure 4.16, where you can see how price tended to bounce off the upper and lower bands. However, if a currency pair or any other asset is in a clear trend, you won't see that tendency for price to bounce off these bands. If the trend is strong, as in Figure 4.17, the bands provide no useful s/r at all as price can climb up or down the BBs for long periods repeatedly. The price continued to climb the upper band from April to mid-June 2010, September to October 2010, February to April 2011, and July 2011 (all periods highlighted).

You don't need to know why this is true, but just in case you're interested, here's a basic layman's explanation.

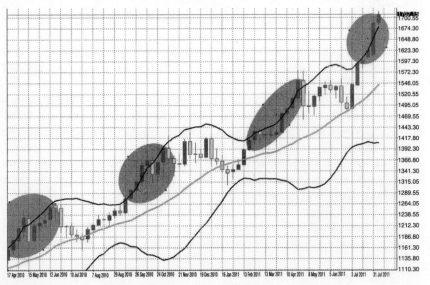

FIGURE 4.17 Gold Weekly Chart, April 17 to August 8, 2011
Source: MetaQuotes Software Corp.

Assuming the two standard settings mentioned previously, then statistically speaking, 95 percent of the 20 closing prices were supposed to fall within two standard deviations from the middle band. However, as noted, statistics assume that all data or elements of the sample (in this case, the past 20 closing prices for the each candle) are equally probable. That's not the case for strongly trending markets, which by their nature indicate that perceptions of value are changing. So, the 20 (or other) past 20 data points or closing prices were not equally probable. For example, during a rising trend, higher prices are more likely than lower ones. Changing perceptions of value mean that the latest prices have a higher probability of hitting the upper band in an uptrend or lower band in a downtrend.

In sum, strongly trending markets reflect a change in how the asset's value is perceived, so the BBs don't work as meaningful support or resistance in strongly trending markets.

However, BBs have additional uses besides gauging s/r in flat or gently trending markets. We'll cover that in Chapter 8.

INTRODUCTION TO JAPANESE CANDLE CHART PATTERNS

Chart patterns are another technical indicator and form of s/r. The two styles most widely followed are Japanese candle and Western style chart patterns.

A few key differences exist between them:

- Scope: Though Western chart patterns can serve as the centerpiece of certain trading strategies, Japanese candle patterns are not intended to comprise a stand-alone trading system; instead, they confirm or are confirmed by other technical indicators. Japanese candle patterns typically forecast what happens over the next few candles, whereas Western patterns can suggest longer-term movements covering a longer period and can suggest specific price targets.
- Pattern types: Japanese candle charts mostly indicate reversal or indecision (i.e., possible reversal), whereas Western charting patterns tend to indicate continuation (trend pausing before resuming) or reversal.

What both kinds of chart patterns share in common is that both are useful because:

- They help us understand market sentiment and are easy to interpret because they make sense. For example, it's intuitively clear that candles comprised solely of long bodies with no wick, meaning that price went straight up or down, suggest strong, decisive bullish or bearish sentiment with buyers or sellers in control. Candles comprised almost solely of upper and lower wicks, with only a line for a body, show price moved back and forth but ended almost unchanged. They suggest indecisiveness or a balance of power between buyers and sellers.

• Both kinds of chart patterns present graphic images of mass trader psychology, which doesn't change over time, hence these patterns do tend to repeat and are valid indicators of s/r points and how price may behave in the future.

Candle patterns are a vast topic. Our goal here is to introduce you to the most important among them. You can search for more information, a great deal of which is available online free. Some are so good that I admit I

TABLE 4.1   Summary of Basic Japanese Candle Patterns

Number of Bars	Name	Bullish or Bearish?	What It Looks Like
Single	Spinning Top	Neutral	
	Doji	Neutral	
	White Marubozu	Bullish	
	Black Marubozu	Bearish	
	Hammer	Bullish	
	Hanging Man	Bearish	
	Inverted Hammer	Bullish	
	Shooting Star	Bearish	
Double	Bullish Engulfing	Bullish	
	Bearish Engulfing	Bearish	

TABLE 4.1 (Continued)

Number of Bars	Name	Bullish or Bearish?	What It Looks Like
	Tweezer Tops	Bearish	
	Tweezer Bottoms	Bullish	
Triple	Morning Star	Bullish	
	Evening Star	Bearish	
	Three White Soldiers	Bullish	
	Three Black Crows	Bearish	
	Three Inside Up	Bullish	
	Three Inside Down	Bearish	

couldn't do a better job, so use these and print the parts you want as hard copies:

- BabyPips.com
- investopedia.com
- stockcharts.com

Table 4.1 is a brief summary of the candle patterns with which you should become familiar. It will be easier to remember what price movements these patterns suggest if you see the logic behind them even if you don't remember their names.

Note that the table classifies candles and patterns as bullish, bearish, or neutral. The adjective "bullish" refers to candles that show price rising or patterns that suggest price will rise, because a bull gores its adversary in an upward motion. "Bearish" is used to refer to candles that show price falling or patterns that suggest price will drop, because a bear swipes at its adversary in a downward motion.

Notes on Single Candle Patterns

- Spinning Top

Depends on whether higher or lower close. Significance increases if occurs after an extended move in the opposite direction of the close. In this example, the most recent candle showed a black, lower close. If these spinning tops occurred at the top of an extended uptrend, it would suggest a coming reversal. If they occurred at the bottom of a downtrend, they'd merely suggest continued downtrend, already the default assumption in an ongoing downtrend.

- Doji

Neutral: The more wick relative to body, the more indecision because buyers and sellers are more evenly matched. The lack of a body means that dojis suggest indecision and possible end or reversal of trend. Thus they're more meaningful when found after a long move up or down, because they suggest the move may end and perhaps reverse.

- White Marubozu – Bullish/Black Marubozu – Bearish

Conversely, the more body relative to wick, the more decisive the move and the clearer the dominance of buyers or sellers. White suggests buyers dominant, so usually suggests more upside. The black version suggests the opposite.

- Hammer – Bullish/ Hanging Man - Bearish

Hammer and Hanging Man have same shape:

  Long lower wick, little or no upper wick two to three times the length of the body

Opposite meaning depending on the following:

  a. Occurs after extended move lower = Hammer, bullish, suggests market probing and hitting a bottom.

  b. Occurs after extended move higher = Hanging Man, bearish, suggests market hitting a top.

In either case, higher or lower close unimportant.

- Inverted Hammer - Bullish/Shooting Star - Bearish

Inverted Hammer and Shooting Star share same shape and are the inverted forms of the Hammer and Hanging Man shown above

It has a long upper wick, little or no lower wick two to three times the length of the body. As usual, needs to occur after a move higher or lower, needs start of reversal to confirm the pattern.

Opposite meaning depending on the following:

  a. Occurs after extended move lower = Inverted Hammer, bullish, suggests markets hitting bottom, confirmed by a bounce higher

  b. Occurs after extended move higher = Shooting Star, bearish, suggests markets hitting a top, confirmed by bounce lower

In either case, higher or lower close unimportant though if it's in the opposite direction of the prior candles, it's a bit more suggestive of a halt or reversal of prior candles' trend.

Notes on Double Candle Patterns

- Bullish Engulfing

  Occurs when a bearish candle (lower close) is followed by a noticeably longer bullish candle (higher close), which "engulfs" the range of the prior bearish candle. The longer the bullish candle, the more it "engulfs" or exceeds the range of the prior bearish candle, the more bullish the pattern. Obviously, as always, context and timing matter. The pattern is more bullish if this pair appears after an extended downtrend, at strong support, or both, because these other signs confirm that the odds are higher that the downtrend is exhausted.

- Bearish Engulfing

  Occurs when a bullish candle (higher close) is followed by a noticeably longer bearish candle (lower close), which "engulfs" the range of the prior bullish candle The longer the bearish candle, the more it "engulfs" or exceeds the range of the prior bullish candle, the more bearish the pattern. Obviously, as always, context and timing matter. The pattern is more bearish if this pair appears after an extended uptrend, at strong resistance, or both, because the odds are higher that the uptrend has become exhausted.

- Tweezer Tops – Bearish

  Looks like a pair of tweezers at the top of an uptrend. Ideally:
  - First candle closes in the direction of the uptrend, the second closes down.
  - Upper wicks are longer than the bodies, and should be about the same length and terminate around the same resistance (confirms resistance to further upward progress), hence the tweezers shape.

  Think of these wicks as knocking against a ceiling of resistance, or the market rejecting a certain higher price as it probes for a top.

- Tweezer Bottoms – Bullish

  The opposite of the above. Looks like a pair of tweezers at the bottom of a downtrend. Ideally:
  - First candle closes in the direction of the downtrend, the second closes up.
  - Lower wicks are longer than the bodies, and should be about the same length and terminate around the same resistance (confirming a floor preventing further downside), hence the tweezers shape.

Think of these wicks as knocking against a floor or support, or the market rejecting a certain lower price, as it gropes for a bottom.

Notes on Triple Candle Patterns

- Morning Star – Bullish/ Evening Star – Bearish
Evening Star and Morning Star are the bearish and bullish variations on the same theme:
    - The first candle is in the direction of the trend, ideally with a long body that suggests a strong final push that exhausts the move.
    - The second candle is a doji, suggesting indecision and that the first candle was the last big push for the trend.
    - The third candle is in the opposite direction of the trend, and should close beyond the midpoint of the first candle, preferably with a long body showing a decisive reversal move.
- Three White Soldiers – Bullish
This pattern is comprised of three long-bodied bullish (higher close) candles after a downtrend, and signals a longer-term reversal higher.
To be a valid pattern:
    - The second candle's body should be longer than that of the first, and should close near its high with little or no upper wick.
    - The third candle's body should be the same size or larger than that of the second and also should close at or near its high with little or no upper wick.
- Three Black Crows – Bearish
The opposite of the above Three White Soldiers
This pattern is comprised of three long-bodied bearish (lower close) candles after an uptrend, and signals a longer-term reversal lower.
To be a valid pattern:
    - The second candle's body should be longer than that of the first, and close near its low with little or no lower wick.
    - The third candle's body should be the same size or larger than that of the second and also should close at or near its low with little or no lower wick.
- Three Inside Up – Bullish
Found during a downtrend and signals its possible end. Characterized by:
    - First candle closes lower and has a relatively long body in the direction of the downtrend.
    - Second candle closes higher to about the midpoint of the first candle.
    - Third candle closes above the high of the first candle.

In sum, this is a very basic bullish swing pattern. The longer the second and third candle, the more convincing the reversal signal.
- Three Inside Down – Bearish
The opposite of Three Inside Up.
Found during an uptrend and signals its possible end.
Characterized by:
  - First candle closes higher and has a relatively long body in the direction of the uptrend.
  - Second candle closes lower to about the midpoint of the first candle.
  - Third candle closes below the low of the first candle.
In sum, it's a very basic bearish swing pattern. The longer the second and third candle, the more convincing the reversal signal.

More Key Points about Japanese Candle Patterns

Though the patterns are classified as reversal (indicate reversal of the trend's direction), continuation (indicate trend continuation), or indecision, depending on which is their more common role, these are generalizations. Like any technical indicator, they don't always work and should be used in combination with others that confirm or refute them. The evidence from TA is useful for timing entries and exits but is rarely unequivocal. It's up to you to weigh contradictory or inconclusive signals from the total of your TA and fundamental analysis and discern where the balance of evidence points. Your interpretation of these patterns, and any other indicator, depends on the context in which it occurs.

Context and Timing Matter

As with everything, context and timing make a difference when interpreting Japanese candle patterns:

- A bullish reversal pattern (like a hammer or bullish engulfing pattern) is more suggestive of a bullish reversal pattern if it comes after an extended downtrend than it is after a brief one, especially if that brief one comes within a longer-term uptrend.
- That same bullish reversal pattern will have more credibility if it happens to occur at a strong support level where we'd expect a downtrend to be more likely to reverse.

If the picture isn't clear enough, look for another opportunity. Remember, some of the best trades you'll ever make are the ones you decide not to take. Missed opportunities only hurt your ego; bad trades hurt your capital.

INTRODUCTION TO WESTERN CHART PATTERNS

Like Japanese candle patterns, Western chart patterns are indicators and forms of support and resistance.

Western chart patterns are commonly classified as reversal or continuation patterns, but these are rough generalizations that help us organize these patterns in our minds. Reversal patterns are often not followed by trend reversals, and continuation patterns are often followed by breakouts up or down.

This chapter will just introduce the most widely followed Western chart patterns (as opposed to those of Japanese candle charts). As with candle charts, this topic is vast and is worthy of its own book. The following is meant to present a few sample chart patterns and a list of the others you should learn.

As with candlestick patterns, you'll have a much easier time remembering what these patterns mean if you understand the logic behind them.

Classic Western Reversal Patterns

Here are some samples of reversal patterns, and a list of others to learn from the previously mentioned websites or other sources as time permits.

Double and Triple Tops, Double and Triple Bottoms   These are all variations on the same theme:

- An s/r level is tested and holds, forming the first top or bottom.
- Price retreats for a time and the farthest extent of this pullback is called the neckline.
- Price rebounds to the s/r price level, which holds again, followed by another retreat, which this time, extends past the neckline for a move equidistant to the distance from the top or bottom to the neckline.
- A third test of the s/r level makes this a triple top or bottom.
- These are all reversal patterns, that is, they suggest that the current trend will reverse.
- The key difference:
  - A double or triple top by definition comes after an uptrend.
  - A double or triple bottom comes after a downtrend.

Example: Double and Triple Top   A double top signals (see Figure 4.18) the reversal of an uptrend. The tops are peaks that are formed during an uptrend, when the price hits strong resistance, bounces down,

FIGURE 4.18 NZDUSD Daily Chart, January 29 to May 14, 2008, Double Top and Neckline, a Break Below Which Suggests an Equidistant Move Lower (within a few weeks, on June 13, 2008, the price hit and exceeded the 365-pip drop from the neckline, hitting 0.7490, over 400 points)
Source: MetaQuotes Software Corp.

and repeats this process, forming a double top. Ideally, this resistance will be confirmed by other forms of resistance at the peaks, like a long-established price level, a Fib level, a long-duration MA, and so on. If this process repeats a third time, that's a triple top.

The logic of these being reversal patterns is clear: If resistance has held up through two to three tests, odds are the uptrend is finished, so the price will likely stay below that resistance until new fundamental factors favor the base currency and fuel a break above resistance. For example, these could be:

1. A change in market sentiment, bullish or bearish, that favors the base currency. For example, rising risk appetite from improving global economic data would help the risk currencies to rise versus the safe haven currencies, so the AUDJPY, NZDCHF, or EURUSD could rise higher on an improvement in risk appetite.

2. An interest rate increase becomes more likely for the base currency than for the counter currency.

3. Improving growth data (GDP, jobs, spending, etc.) in the base currency's economy relative to that of the counter currency's economy.

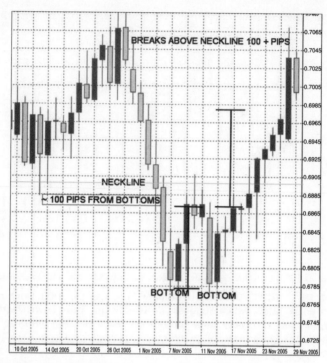

FIGURE 4.19 NZDUSD Daily Chart, October 10, 2005, to November 29, 2005
Source: MetaQuotes Software Corp.

Remember, currency pairs move in the direction of the base currency (the one on the left of the pair symbol). When it's stronger than the counter currency, the pair rises. When it's weaker, the pair falls.

How to Trade the Downtrend Following a Bearish Double Top Pattern

When price falls below the neckline (the lowest closing price between the two tops), that is a confirmation of the reversal. So, that's the area where you would place your sell limit order to open a short position because you'd be anticipating a new move lower, typically about the same distance again as the distance from the peaks to the neckline, as illustrated in Figure 4.18. The same rules apply for a triple top.

Double and Triple Bottoms As you can see from the chart in Figure 4.19, double and triple bottom patterns are inverted forms of the double and triple tops. They occur after a downtrend, as price repeatedly tests and fails to break below a support level. That suggests the downtrend is finished, the selling is exhausted, and the odds are higher for some kind of reversal as support is likely to hold at least until new fundamental factors favor the counter currency over the base currency, which would fuel a break below support.

How to Trade the Reversal Higher In the chart in Figure 4.19, the farthest pullback from support forms the neckline, which is where we place an entry buy limit order to open a long position, with a profit target of twice the distance in pips from the double bottoms to the neckline. In practice, we would consider this trade if it fit with our risk management rules that we'll cover in Chapter 5. Here's a sneak preview of those rules. We'd consider taking this trade if we believed:

- The distance in pips from the neckline to our profit-taking target was about three times the distance from the neckline to our stop loss.
- The neckline provided solid enough support to place that stop loss order far enough beneath it to avoid getting hit by random price movements.

Double bottoms, like double tops, are trend reversal patterns. You'll want to look for these after a strong downtrend and wait until price reverses above the neckline (the farthest point of the bounce off support) as likely confirmation of the reversal.

The above applies for triple bottoms, too. They include a third test of the same support level.

Beware False Breakouts, Shake Outs, and Other Fake Outs

False breakouts often occur at widely anticipated breakout points like the neckline of a double or triple bottom. Vast flocks of inexperienced traders will attempt to go long at these points. So, big experienced players may attempt to use these breakout points to fool you into selling too early near the bottom or buying to late near the top.

For example, the neck line of a double or triple bottom will attract a lot of buy orders from traders attempting to buy just as the widely anticipated breakout higher begins. As it starts, big players may join the buying to briefly pump up the price and lure in more buyers. They may then attempt to drive price back down with some large sell orders (taking a quick profit on those new long positions and opening new short positions) so that enough stop loss orders get hit to start a wave of selling that drives price down further as the selling "shakes out" more long positions. That is a basic "false breakout."

The big players are now sitting with large short positions they accumulated in creating the mini sell off. The pair is now lower, so the big boys take profits on these shorts by buying back the pair at a lower price from the inexperienced retail traders. Ideally, that buying lures in enough others to get price back past the neckline and start the real breakout, which pros may feed by taking more long positions, perhaps attracting more buyers and driving price higher. At some point they then take profits on these long positions, and so on.

That's why you use stop losses. It's why you might wait to enter until the break past the neckline is a bit more advanced (at a cost of getting in later on the move up and losing some profit), and you might wait until price has made a false breakout pullback and has resumed its break past the neckline. In addition, you could get other kinds of confirmation of the reversal.

We'll discuss more on how to protect yourself against these and other head-fakes in Chapter 9.

Other Reversal Patterns to Know

Here are some more reversal patterns you should be familiar with: Head and Shoulders Top and (Inverted) Head and Shoulders Bottom. This pattern works the same way as double and triple tops and bottoms except there's a single top or bottom to create the head, and the neckline is formed by the lows between the two shoulders (lesser tops or bottoms) as shown in Figure 4.20.

Head and Shoulders Top   Perhaps this pattern is more intuitively appealing because the right shoulder shows a reversal starting.

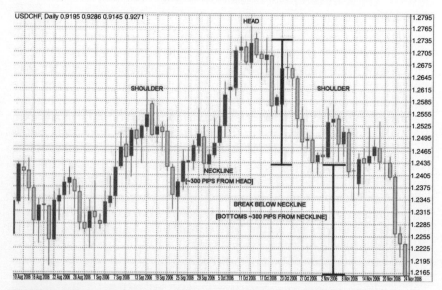

FIGURE 4.20   USDCHF Daily Chart, August 10 to November 24, 2006
Source: MetaQuotes Software Corp.

To be a bearish reversal pattern, it must occur during an uptrend (so there can be a bearish reversal), and the bullish inverted Head and Shoulders bottom needs to occur during a downtrend.

Once the neckline is broken, we expect a move roughly equal to the distance from the head to the neckline as we saw with double and triple tops and bottoms.

Inverted Head and Shoulders Bottom   This is a flipped over version of the Head and Shoulders Top, and all rules apply.

Classic Western Continuation Patterns

Let's get familiar with some classic Western continuation patterns. As the name suggests, these patterns imply trend continuation rather than reversal.

Cup and Handle   As the name suggests, the cup-and-handle pattern resembles the shape of a tea cup and handle on a chart. It's a bullish continuation pattern. In other words, it occurs during an uptrend, and it suggests a coming breakout past established resistance and a new move higher. The cup-shaped part of the pattern should be rounded, not V-shaped, formed over a minimum of about seven weeks, and its right side forms on low volume.

Like most chart patterns, this one shown in Figure 4.21 makes sense as a picture of mass trader behavior.

Stage 1: An uptrend must precede this pattern. The longer the uptrend, the more the pool of potential buyers is reduced until it is exhausted, either because of strong technical resistance, new bearish news, or lack of new good news to fuel the up trend. The combined lack of new buyers and profit taking (or shorting) sellers creates a resistance price level where sellers prevent further moves higher.

Stage 2: The pair sells off as sellers, either profit takers or short sellers, drive the price lower. This selling forms the downtrend that is the left side of the cup. When there are no more sellers, the price stops falling, the left side of the cup is completed, and the price stabilizes, forming the bottom of the cup. The downtrend that forms the left side of the cup typically retraces one-third to two-thirds of the prior uptrend. Ideally, it should be as smoothly rounded as possible because that reflects a steady draining of sellers.

Stage 3: Price then moves in a flat trading range. With seller gone price, price stabilizes. The ones left holding the pair are the longer-term believers who won't sell and may add to their positions and help fuel the uptrend that forms the right side of the cup once buying resumes.

FIGURE 4.21   Example of Cup-and-Handle Pattern EURCHF Monthly Chart, January 1, 2003, to November 1, 2007
Source: MetaQuotes Software Corp.

Stage 4: Buyers recognize support has been established and at some point buying resumes, due to a positive change in underlying fundamentals, a change in overall market sentiment that favors the base currency, or bargain hunting that causes buying to resume, driving price back to its old high, forming the right side of the cup. The longer this cup takes to form, the more established the resistance or rim, *and thus the stronger the signal* for a new move higher when the pattern completes, and this resistance is decisively broken.

Stage 5: The typical selling pressure that occurs when a pair hits significant resistance at this old high causes a pullback for the usual reasons. Those who bought at the bottom take profits, or those who bought near the top and held seek to sell and break even. However, the fundamental change that drove the rise back to recent highs at the rim of the cup has now attracted enough believers so new buyers step in after a shallow pullback (no more than about a third of the distance to the low of the cup). This brings the price back to the recent high or rim of the cup, creating a short-term double top (bullish because it's part of a larger bullish cup-and-handle pattern) or an inverted bullish head-and-shoulders pattern.

Stage 6: A decisive break above this resistance level or rim often signals a new leg higher, marked by the arrow. The uptrend that followed was almost as long as the one that preceded it.

We Repeat: False Breakouts Happen

The initial breaks above resistance (or beneath support) will often fail. These are called false breakouts, and can happen one or more times before the real one occurs.

Analyze This!

Can you spot such a failed break within the cup of the pattern in Figure 4.21? In which month did it occur? Where was the resistance or rim that it tried and failed to breach? (See Figure 4.22.)

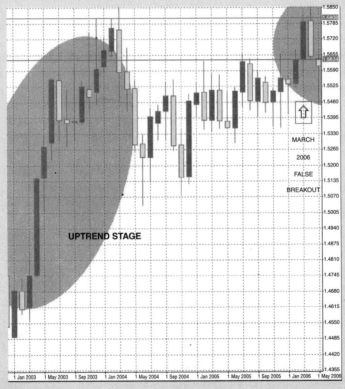

FIGURE 4.22 Example of Cup-and-Handle Pattern and False Breakout, EU-RCHF Monthly Chart, January 1, 2003, to November 1, 2007
Source: MetaQuotes Software Corp.

In Figure 4.22 we see the March 2006 (marked with an arrow) candle was an initial failed breakout for a smaller cup-and-handle pattern (with resistance or rim at around 1.5634) within the larger pattern shown in Figure 4.21 that ultimately did produce a major upside breakout in August 2006.

Again, there are ways to protect yourself; more on that in Chapter 9.

Other Continuation Patterns

Here are other common continuation patterns that should be part of your further education, all easily searchable online.

- Bearish rectangle
- Bullish rectangle
- Bearish pennant
- Bullish pennant
- Bearish flag
- Bullish flag

Patterns That Can Be Continuation or Reversal

These can serve as reversal or continuation patterns. What they share in common is that the price range converges into a narrower range until price breaks out either in the direction of the trend (continuation) or in the opposite direction (reversal).

Triangles   There are three kinds: symmetrical, ascending, and descending. There are lots available on these online, so we'll only present one of them, the symmetrical triangle pattern.

Symmetrical Triangle   For example, note what happens with a symmetrical triangle (see Figure 4.23).

Eventually the range narrows and price breaks out of the triangle higher or lower. In theory, the initial breakout is about the same distance as the base of the triangle. In this case, it broke lower as concern grew about the European Union (EU) debt crisis (see Figure 4.24).

The Underlying Logic of Chart Patterns

These patterns don't come about by magic. Like the other patterns we've seen, they're pictures of unchanging crowd psychology. The patterns repeat because crowd behavior repeats when subject to fear, greed, and indecision, as these feelings permeate the markets in response to current events and how markets interpret them based on their prior expectations.

FIGURE 4.23 EURUSD Weekly Chart, February 6 to August 21, 2011
Source: MetaQuotes Software Corp.

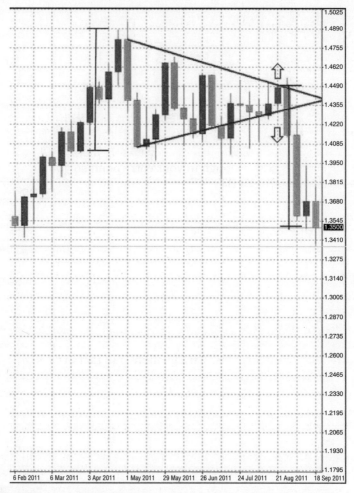

FIGURE 4.24   EURUSD Weekly Chart, February 6 to August 21, 2011
Source: MetaQuotes Software Corp.

By recognizing these patterns, you're better able to anticipate the likely s/r levels these patterns create.

These patterns are widely recognized. As with any widely followed kind of s/r, you need to be aware of it to anticipate the likely s/r levels. In other words, patterns are another way of anticipating what the crowd is likely to do.

Remember, trading success has nothing to do with knowing what is true or right and has everything to do with anticipating what the crowd will do, be it rational or not, and doing it first.

THE MORE S/R INDICATORS, THE BETTER

Technical indicators should almost never be used in isolation but should be used in specific kinds of combinations (discussed in Chapter 9) that provide you enough information to decide whether you've got sufficiently strong support and resistance in the right places to suggest a low risk high potential yield trade. Specifically:

- Strong support close enough to your entry point so you can set a stop loss order far enough away from that support, so that the stop loss won't get hit by random price moves, but only by a move against you that is strong enough to indicate that you were wrong and that price is reversing against you.
- The distance from likely resistance (your profit-taking point) to your entry point is two to three times farther than the distance from your entry point to your stop loss. That way you have reward-risk ratio of 2:1 or 3:1. That kind of reward-risk ratio is a central requirement of good risk management and trade planning because it allows you to be wrong on the majority of your trades and remain profitable. Under those conditions, even a less experienced trader can succeed despite constant mistakes and losing trades. We'll go more into that in Chapter 5.

Here's another concept about s/r you must remember: *The quality of an s/r level depends on the quality of the indicators (age, number of times tested, etc.) and on the number of them that converge on a given area and mutually reinforce each other.*

The more s/r indicators you have converging on a given price level, the stronger the s/r levels and the easier it is to find trades with great reward-risk ratios, meaning trades with small risk of loss and large potential for gain. If you only take trades in which your worst-case loss is a third of your gain, you can be wrong on most of your trades and remain profitable.

Multiple Mutually Reinforcing S/R Indicators: An Example

For example, in the daily EURUSD charts in Figure 4.25, the strong resistance to further price gains around the $1.3800 price level is formed by the convergence of five kinds of resistance around March 17, 2010 (highlighted by the arrow in Figure 4.26).

Figure 4.25 is the first "zoomed-in" chart to show the multiple kinds of resistance that converged on the area around the1.3800 price level in detail.

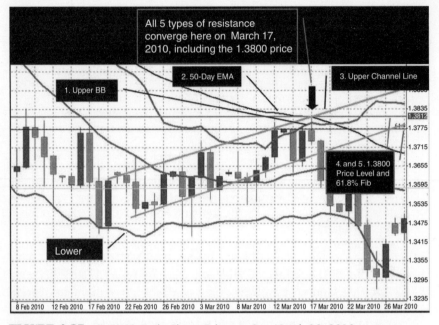

FIGURE 4.25 EURUSD Daily Chart, February 8 to March 26, 2010
Source: MetaQuotes Software Corp.

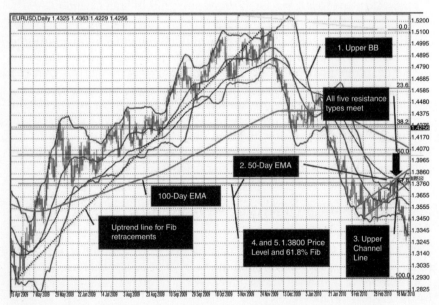

FIGURE 4.26 EURUSD Daily Chart, April 15, 2009, to March 29, 2010
Source: MetaQuotes Software Corp.

Figure 4.26 shows the "zoomed-out" big picture for perspective, so you can see how long established some of these s/r indicators were. Note the highlighted arrow and upper channel line to see where the chart in Figure 4.25 fits.

In particular, examine how long established the 1.3800 price level, 50-day EMA, and Fib levels were, and what reliable support or resistance they had proven to be.

Here are the five kinds of resistance present in Figure 4.25.

1. **Price level:** The 1.3800 level is a round number that has repeatedly served as proven support or resistance during most of the period shown. In the longer-term daily chart, the level repeatedly served as s/r from May to July 2009 and from January to March 2010.

2. **Upper channel line:** A rising month-old trend line from February 18 to March 18.

3. **Established EMA:** The 50-day EMA, which served as reliable s/r during the period shown, nearly a year, making it a strong s/r indicator.

4. **Fibs:** The 61.8 percent Fib level (under the arrow) from the low to the high of the period from April 2010 to the end of the year, nine months. That age earned these lines more respect. Note how well these lines served as s/r over the year covered in the chart. In particular, note how the 61.8 percent Fib line held for the March 2010 high discussed here.

5. **BBs:** The upper BB (settings: 20 days, two standard deviations). BBs are primarily momentum indicators and are not reliable s/r in strongly trending markets. In range-bound markets as shown here over the weeks prior to March 17, they provide a degree of s/r.

In addition to these kinds of resistance, there were chart patterns suggesting a reversal:

- Western chart pattern: During February to March 2010, a bearish flag or rectangle formed.
- Japanese candle pattern: The candle after the March 17 convergence was a bearish engulfing pattern that confirmed the March 17 bearish hanging man. The candle of March 26 was a bullish engulfing pattern that suggested a coming bullish reversal, which began in the following days as shown by the right most candles.

Don't worry if terms such as EMA, Fibs, and BBs are still unfamiliar to you. Together, they form multiple types of s/r converging on a given area that reinforce each other. Review this chapter for the basics on these kinds of s/r indicators.

Given the above, it's no surprise that price peaked on March 17. The entire market was watching these and other basic indicators of s/r, so a pullback was likely unless some great news about the EURUSD changed trader perceptions and gave buyers a reason to step in even with five layers of resistance converging on the 1.3800 area.

Here, we see a good example of how s/r levels are zones or areas and are not precise points. Even in this example, from February 9 to March 17, daily highs ranged from about 1.3775 to 1.3835, showing a perfectly normal, nearly symmetrical range of +/− 25–35 pips around the 1.3800 round number.

CHAPTER 5

Trader Psychology and Risk and Money Management (RAMM)

N ow that you know some foreign exchange (forex) basics and technical analysis (TA), you have the background needed to understand the real foundation of successful trading and investing: proper trader psychology and risk and money management (RAMM). No matter how skilled and compelling your analysis, it will often be wrong. Worse, you'll endure losing streaks that can irreparably damage your account balance and confidence unless you've got the right preparation.

Welcome to that preparation. This chapter covers these core nonanalytical aspects of trading:

- Basic trader psychology issues like mindset, attitude, expectations, discipline, finding a trading style that fits your personality, and understanding the conditions you need to succeed.
- Top RAMM issues, including:
  - Why trading longer time frames lowers risk.
  - Risking no more than 1 to 3 percent of your account per trade with your stop loss.
  - Proper risk-to-reward ratios (rrrs) for each trade.
  - How to set stop losses.
  - How account size influences RAMM issues like stop loss settings, position size, and leverage used.
  - Planning trades in advance to remove emotion from your decisions in a trade journal.
  - Learning from your victories and losses via your trade journal.
  - The importance of having a business plan.

In this chapter, we'll review the key elements of proper mindset and RAMM because they are intimately related.

RAMM: PRESERVING CAPITAL IS YOUR TOP PRIORITY

Warren Buffett is considered one of the greatest investors ever. Here are his top two rules for success:

Rule No. 1: Never lose money. Rule No. 2: Don't forget Rule No. 1.[1]

Paul Tudor Jones, the founder of Tudor Investment Corporation, has an estimated net worth of $3.3 billion and is ranked as the 336th richest in the world by *Forbes* magazine as of March 2011.[2] Here's his take on the key to trading success:

At the end of the day, the most important thing is how good are you at risk control.[3]

Cliff Wachtel doesn't deserve to be mentioned on the same page as these giants, but heck, it's my book, so here goes:

The key to succeeding is controlling your bleeding.

In other words, your ability to survive long enough to succeed is less a matter of how much you make when you're right than how little you lose when you're wrong. That's because while you're learning (and often afterward), you're likely to be wrong at least as often as you're right, probably more often.

The reason RAMM is so essential is this: Your losses hurt you more than your gains help you. That's not just because of the damage losses do to your confidence and motivation. After you suffer a drawdown, you're working with a smaller principal. For example, let's say you start with $1,000. If you lose 10 percent, you will need to earn over 11 percent on your remaining $900 to recover your losses. If you lose 15 percent, you will need to earn almost 18 percent on your remaining $850 to get back to $1,000. Though profits are the goal, it's the losses that can stop you from achieving it. See Appendix E for more on this.

Having this professional trader's risk aversion is a key part of trader psychology that will determine as much as anything else whether you survive your mistakes like a professional or get killed by them like an amateur.

Mastering the psychological component of trading is the root of success because ultimately trading is based on having the right mindset, attitude, expectations, discipline, and trading style that fits your personality and doesn't drain your energy.

So, let's begin by reviewing what you must know about the psychology of successful trading. Getting it may take a long time, but at least you know what you've got to do, and that puts you ahead of most investors.

THE INNER GAME: TRADER PSYCHOLOGY BASICS

In Chapter 2, in the section on the Core Four Skills, we said that the psychological aspects of trading are the basis of trading success because otherwise:

- There won't be proper RAMM, without which traders are doomed no matter how brilliant their analyses, strategies, or trading plans. The inevitable mistakes will eventually inflict too much damage on their capital, confidence, or both.
- You won't know how to handle the dangers of both losing streaks and winning streaks. Both can be fatal. Losing streaks obviously can drain your capital and confidence, either of which is fatal to your trading career. Winning streaks can lead to overconfidence, which encourages sloppy habits that ultimately hit your bottom line, possibly permanently.
- There won't be realistic profit expectations, so you could get discouraged too soon when in fact you're doing fine.
- Minimizing risk (versus fastest or largest potential profits) won't be your primary criteria for choosing trading styles and durations. For example, you may attempt to day trade for faster profits before you're ready.
- There won't be proper focus on finding trading styles that suit your personality, and that could cause you to burn out from stress even if you're successful. For example:
  - High-leverage, short-term day trading will drain the energy of those who are risk-averse or lack the time and concentration needed to constantly monitor intraday trades.
  - Action junkies who have the time, risk tolerance, and ability to stay focused will find longer-term positions boring and frustratingly slow.
  - Many extroverts will need contact with others to feel energized and stimulated, and they may find trading rooms and online forums are a better way to learn than hours of study in isolation, which they may find tiresome.
  - Introverts may find such venues distracting and draining. They need quiet and will learn better via self-study resources, and via more limited personal an online contacts.

As you gain experience, you'll realize how the following basics of trader psychology are the true foundation of success. Until you're psychologically ready to trade, until you've got the right attitudes, expectations, trading methods, and environment, all the analytical skills in the world won't help. This topic is worthy of a book in itself, but here are the basics for further study.

Lesson 1: Seek Trading Styles and Methods That Fit You

Regardless of what kind of trader you fantasize about being, the cold truth is that you're far more likely to succeed by finding trading styles and techniques that fit you, rather than trying to fit yourself to the wrong kinds of trading.

What to Consider When Seeking Trading Styles and Methods

In other words, find ways to trade that suit your:

Skill level: Those with only basic analytical skills need methods that don't require sophisticated and complex analysis. Beginners should also avoid short-term day trading that requires more technical analysis skills and faster decision making. Those with strong analytical skills may want to move as quickly as possible to designing and refining their own algorithm-based trading systems.

Lifestyle: This includes considerations like time and energy available. If you don't have the time or energy to monitor positions in real time, you need a trading style that doesn't require constant trade monitoring, or a short-term trading style in a market that's liquid when you're available to watch it.

Temperament: This includes aspects of your personality like:
1. Mental discipline and emotional control: Different traders feel different degrees of stress when risking their money.
   A. Some have the discipline and lack of ego to do the following when money is at risk:
      i. Resist the temptation to take a quick, small profit when they know the trade has room to run until it hits resistance.
      ii. Admit they're wrong and cut their losses when their pre-planned stop loss order is hit.

      These traders at least have the key psychological foundations to succeed in short-term intraday trading that demands real-time decision making. Skills are another issue.
   B. Others are more emotional and struggle to stick to their plans, such as:

     i. They take profits too early out of fear they'll lose them, even though they know there is still room before price hits resistance.

     ii. They let losses run too far because it hurts them to admit they were wrong, and they don't exit until they've incurred losses too large for their egos or accounts to survive.

These more emotional traders need trading styles that allow them to plan and enter entries and exits in advance so they don't have to make real-time decisions.

Risk tolerance: If you don't handle risk well, you'll need more conservative, lower-risk ways to trade. Lower (or zero) leverage, smaller positions, and longer time frames are a few ways to keep trader stress at acceptable levels.

How you make decisions: If you're a deliberate, analytical type who likes to look at lots of information, consult with others, mull things over, and research, then you need to make sure you have enough time to do so. That kind of trader will want slower, longer time frame-based trades. Having the time you need is important in the early stages while you're learning. If you don't like a lot of analysis and prefer quicker decisions based on limited data, you may be more comfortable with faster, shorter time frames and simple sets of indicators and trading rules.

Patience versus a need for action: More patient traders can sit with trades for weeks or months. Action junkies need shorter time frames; otherwise they risk entering bad trades out of sheer boredom.

Need for wins versus profits: There are trading systems that have lots of small losses and just a few huge gainers that make the whole system profitable. However, many traders get depressed if 70 percent or more of their trades are losers. They quit altogether or become so desperate for winners that they exit winning trades too soon and they miss much of the profits that would have made up for their losers. Other traders don't care about winning percentages as long as monthly or quarterly profits are satisfactory.

The key point of this is: If something about a trading style causes you too much pain, be it too many hours, too much stress, risk, boredom, complexity, discipline needed, or whatever, then you won't last.

Finding Your Trading Approach Lowers Your Risk   Finding the right trading style may not sound like it's related to risk management, but it is. Without the right trading style and methods, your risk of stress, frustration, and of quitting forex is much higher even if you're prospering.

Accept That It Takes Time to Find Your Way   Those getting started won't know what trading styles, analytical tool sets, currency pairs, or time frames work best for them. That's okay, since finding out is a big part of the learning process. That's why we spend months using practice accounts before we start risking our money. Successful traders will even return to practice accounts when trying new methods.

Getting to know yourself as a trader isn't a phase in your development that you can skip or cut short. All the advice in the world won't help if you're trading in ways that don't fit you. You probably won't be earning steady profits until you find what kind of trading feels comfortable. Steady profits over time will be the confirmation that you've found your niche.

Tips to Finding Yourself Faster   To expedite that process of finding your niche, here are some tips:

- Avoid day trading currencies (or anything else) until you've built up the requisite successful experience on demo accounts for about six months of part-time trading. After that, start with real money but with small positions, because practice accounts can't prepare you for the stress of having cash at risk. Know that few find they have the needed skills, concentration powers, and information resources to succeed at day trading currencies.
- If the time you can dedicate to forex trading is limited, seek out styles of trading that require only periodic monitoring at your convenience. For example, employees in an office should be careful about attempting any kind of trading that would require monitoring during work hours. You risk being distracted and underperforming in both capacities.
- Those who are risk-averse or have limited risk capital would need to avoid any combination of high leverage and large position sizes relative to their account size. As we'll discuss next, losses per trade must be kept around 1 to 3 percent of your available trading capital.
- Traders should never trade with money they can't afford to lose. The stress will likely prevent you from letting winners run or cutting losses short. You must learn to view trading capital as special funds set aside for trading that you can afford to lose with relative calm because you don't view losing trades as losses, but rather as your tuition for learning how to trade.

Lesson 2: Basics of the Trader's Mindset—Minimizing and Accepting Risk

Here are two tips on how the professionals deal with risk:

1. Their top priority is to minimize losses: Amateurs think first about how much they can make. Professionals focus first on how much they could

lose. They accept calculated risk as part of the business but focus more on minimizing losses than maximizing gains. Study Appendix E to see how losses hurt you more than profits help you.

2. They stick to their plans and accept losses as the cost of experience: Once professionals have taken all the precautions they can and have a solid trade plan in progress, they stick with it and don't let risk of loss shake them out of that plan unless circumstances or assumptions on which they based their plan change and justify a change in their trading plan.

   - They create plans that allow profitable trades to run until they hit resistance, and that include preset stop loss orders that will cut losses short. They avoid temptations to deviate from their plans and do the opposite. Once they enter a trade based on a solid plan, they don't deviate from it to take a quick profit during a normal pullback. They don't cancel stop loss orders that are about to be hit, they accept taking a small affordable loss rather than risk a larger one. They do this because they accept mistakes as a normal part of the business and admit to them. They don't need to be consistently right, just profitable. As long as their plan was solid and they stuck to it, they take satisfaction in their discipline, and if the loss bothers them, they review the trade and discern what they might have done wrong or how their read of the market may have been wrong.
   - They view their trading accounts not as savings but as risk capital, funds set aside to take calculated risks, which over time should be profitable if they've done their jobs well.
   - They view losses not only as part of the business, but also as the tuition for their ongoing training, as the cost of experience.
   - To make sure they get the full education that they've "paid for" with losses, they keep a trade journal and analyze what went wrong to locate the problem or mistake so it's less likely to be repeated. We'll cover planning and trade journals later in the chapter.

Lesson 3: Dealing with Losing and Winning Streaks

Losing and winning streaks offer their own challenges.

Losing Streaks   Losing streaks sap confidence and capital. Professionals know that when they hit a losing streak, it's time to do one or more of three actions:

1. Cut position sizes and/or leverage used: Until they figure out what's wrong and break the streak, they reduce the amount risked per trade.

2. Take fewer trades, limiting themselves to only the most compelling situations with the lowest potential losses and highest potential yields (more on that later).

3. Take a break from trading: This is especially true if they're under stress from their personal life or have gone too long without some genuine rest (as opposed to a week or more traveling with children or touring for 12 hours a day to see a month's worth of sights in 10 days).

Winning Streaks   Winning streaks are great for our accounts, but they can also be too good for our egos. We can become overconfident and sloppy because we don't need our plans or trading rules now that we're on a hot streak. That bad idea can become dangerous if rewarded with a few more winners, which encourages further recklessness that puts the odds against you and eventually ends in losses.

When I close out a big winning trade I usually take the rest of the day off from trading, and I've known many others who would do the same when they start to feel invincible. They believed they were saving money by waiting until they calmed down because they felt they were too likely to get sloppy and make bad trades that violated their rules.

Conclusion   We could go deeper in trader psychology, but we won't. You've seen enough to be aware of its importance and how it influences the kind of trading you do and how well you manage your risk and capital. Many sources of free information on the psychological aspects of trading are available, as well as professional trader coaches and other vendors of materials on the topic.

Now let's get into the specifics of RAMM.

WHY TRADE LONGER TIME FRAMES

Here's the most important step in reducing risk.

Seek Safer Trading Styles

The first step to lowering risk is to choose a low-risk trading style. Professional football and ice hockey players wear more protective padding than professional golfers or tennis players and have referees to prevent dangerous behavior. Yet the golf and tennis players suffer far fewer serious injuries due to the far safer nature of their sports.

The same goes for trading. The best path to low risk is low-risk trading styles. One key component of lower-risk trading is longer time frames.

Though day traders avoid risks from holding positions overnight, most people will find that trading from daily, weekly, or monthly charts is a more profitable, lower-risk approach. This section details why.

Beginning traders, or experienced traders who are still unprofitable, should avoid trying intraday time frames, those in which you open and close positions within a matter of minutes to the close of one to two trading days. Instead, stick to trading price moves that occur over a number of days, weeks, or months. That means using four-hour, daily, weekly, or monthly charts until you are consistently profitable on a monthly basis for about six months on a practice or demo account, then a similar period using small positions with real money. If, after that time, you still want to day trade currencies, then use practice accounts and go through the same process. Yes, I understand you can, in theory, make money faster on shorter time frames and this style is exciting. If your goal is to have the fun of gambling with money you don't mind losing, rather than earn a steady income, then by all means, pour yourself a drink, put on some music, and have fun.

Beware, however, that most short-term traders in any market, not just forex, fail. Your odds of success are much higher with trading off of longer-term time frame charts.

As with Driving, Speed Kills

Trading off short time frames moves at a faster pace. In addition to the added difficulties of short-term trading discussed below, this faster pace brings additional challenges that are too much for most traders. These include the need for fast decisions with money at risk. That might not be a problem for proven, experienced traders, but it's a potentially fatal problem for those lacking a track record with a simple manual or more complex automated trading systems. Because:

- There is often no time to create well-designed trading plans. Failing to plan means planning to fail.
- Having no time for advanced order placement risks emotion-driven decisions. Short-term price moves can be so unpredictable and quick that it's often not possible to enter entry and exit orders in advance. That means making real-time entry and exit decisions when your money is at risk. That leaves the door wide open for emotions to creep in and cause you to
  - Cut profits short even when there is plenty of room before the next resistance point.
  - Let losses run beyond what you can afford in the often vain hope that the trade will turn around.

- You must constantly monitor your positions and make decisions while money is at risk rather than making them in advance under calmer circumstances with orders placed in advance. That added stress can be dangerous because:
  - Few have the sufficiently strong concentrations skills.
  - There is risk of bad decisions from decision fatigue (the tendency to make poorer decisions after a long day of making decisions or other mentally taxing work as the mind tires). Professional traders know not to trade when they're tired, stressed, or otherwise suffering from impaired mental focus.

    It's not uncommon for day traders to make 10–20 or more trades per day when markets are volatile. That can and does lead to decision fatigue. It causes those who make many mentally demanding decisions to make bad decisions toward the end of a workday.

    For example, a study of Israeli judges showed that the deciding factor in which prisoners got parole was not whether the prisoner was Jewish or Arab. Instead, the deciding factor was how long the judge had been on duty that day.[4] Prisoners on trial early in the morning received parole about 70 percent of the time, but those who appeared late in the day were paroled less than 10 percent of the time. Decision fatigue is a known problem for day traders.[5]
  - Traders using longer time frame charts are less likely to encounter this problem. The more reliable trends, chart patterns, and support and resistance (s/r) levels on longer-term charts take more time to develop, so decisions about whether to take a trade are much less frequent. Usually, those trading off of daily or longer time frame charts can reach a tentative conclusion, and then sleep on it before reaching a final decision and executing the trade.
- There is less time to evaluate the available evidence or check with more experienced trades or analysts. This is a particularly serious problem for:
  - Newer traders.
  - Traders who have yet to find a trading style with which they are both comfortable and successful.
  - Those prone to making slower decisions and/or to examining lots of evidence before making financial decisions.

A More Level Playing Field

Remember what we said in Chapter 1 about not trying to compete with the big boys who have every advantage? Day trading currencies is the worst form of that. The traders running the forex departments of large financial institutions have decisive advantages that are most prominent with short-term intraday trading than with longer duration trades. They usually have:

- More experience because it's their full-time job (and the newer hires have access to their veteran supervisors).
- Better training and access to analysis, at times from top in-house gurus or private advisory services charging prices only institutions or the wealthy can afford.
- More natural ability. Competition for these lucrative institutional trading jobs is naturally fierce. Those who survive it tend to be the fittest.
- Access to the best information resources and equipment available. Assume they will know everything before you do. That puts you at a huge disadvantage when you're holding positions over a matter of hours or a few days. However, over weeks or months more of the important information becomes widely known. For example, a big institutional trader might have ways of knowing about a major central bank announcement a few hours in advance. However, over the coming weeks that bank's policy bias will be clearer to all.
- Access to enough capital to move prices over a given number of minutes or hours to their advantage and start false breakouts or other fake price moves that can fool the herd into buying or selling at the wrong time. (More on that later and what to do about it over longer durations.)
- Even if you could afford to buy most of that, here's what no amount of money can buy (short of buying a majority share in one of these firms):
  - Direct or indirect access to their firms' order books, allowing them to know what price levels their own customers chose for their buy and sell orders.
  - Various inside contacts at other institutions with whom this information can be shared and traded for future tips. It's like playing cards with someone who can see your hand when you can't see theirs.
  - Pure insider information. This information is the only rational explanation for why markets seem so consistently good at anticipating certain major news events. For example, in the days before Greece agreed to terms allowing its second bailout in the spring of 2011, the Euro and other risk assets strengthened. Weeks later, just before Standard & Poor's (S&P) downgraded America's credit rating from AAA to AA+, markets were selling off. A coincidence? The SEC suspected otherwise. Days after the announcement, the SEC began investigating the firm on suspicion that news of the downgrade was leaked ahead of time. Insider trading scandals have become a regular occurrence. Given their record in recent years, it's safe to assume that regulators catch only a portion of the most egregious offenders.

However, over a period of days or weeks, insider information tends to leak out, or if it doesn't, it still may show up on the charts as unexplained steady buying or selling pressure. That too can alert you to an opportunity. The longer your time frame the better your chances of seeing this, because those accumulating large positions try to be discreet and build them gradually. So the longer your time frame—multiple days, weeks, or longer—the more you can neutralize the natural advantages of the big players, especially if you're selective about the trades you take.

More and Better Information Means Better Trade Decisions

Intraday price movements are harder to predict. You don't have much information on which to base a good decision. Some of the following is repeated from above to make sure you get it clear.

First, random price movements or "market noise" is more influential over the course of a given number of hours, during which time trades can be made or broken based on the movements of 10 to 20 pips.

In addition to the attempted manipulations noted earlier, there are the more innocent short-term money flows from large players conducting their normal business. For example if a Chinese company buys an Australian firm, that payment or installment on that purchase could influence short-term AUD prices. These price movements are difficult to predict even for experienced institutional traders with every advantage available.

Those lower on the food chain, particularly the least experienced and skilled at the bottom of it, lack the training, experience, and information resources needed to identify and interpret the resulting short-term price movements, which can include a lot of sheer random movements.

The widely available technical indicators are less useful, and the publicly available longer-term fundamentals and trends of the underlying economies of a currency pair are irrelevant over the course of a given number of hours.

Trends Are More Reliable in Longer Time Frames

Currencies often perform as if we're really trading shares in entire national (or regional in the case of the EUR) economies. The economic fundamentals of a country (GDP, employment rates, consumer spending, etc.) change much more slowly for countries than for publicly traded companies. That stability in economic fundamentals creates equally stable trends (or flat trading ranges) in forex pairs that can persist over weeks, months, or years. So why not trade with longer holding periods that exploit these longer, stronger, more reliable trends?

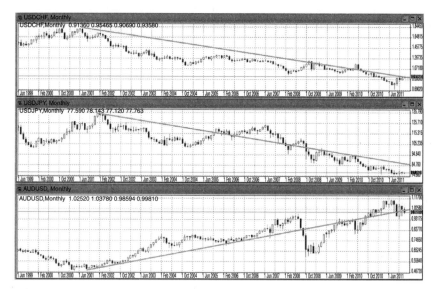

FIGURE 5.1 Top to Bottom: USD versus CHF, JPY, AUD from June 1999 to December 2011. Note the steady, persistent trend in these pairs.
Source: MetaQuotes Software Corp.

Let's look at some examples.

Note how stable the long-term trends have been for the USDCHF, USDJPY, and AUDUSD from June 1999 to December 2011 (see Figure 5.1).

From January 2000 to mid-August 2011, the CAD gained over 32 percent against the U.S. dollar (USD) (see Figure 5.2).

Long-term forex trends can persist for even longer than those shown in Figure 5.2.

From 1970 to 2011, the Swiss Franc gained 75% versus the USD. Imagine how well you'd have done with the right Swiss stocks and/or bonds since you'd have asset and currency appreciation in your favor.[6] We'll go deeper into that topic in Chapter 12.

In both cases, the monthly charts show that, with few exceptions, the trends were smooth and stable over the periods in question.

This tendency toward stable long-term trends is a huge advantage for forex traders with the intelligence, patience, and capital needed to play them because so much of successful trading is based on betting in the direction of the longer-term trend.

So why not take advantage of these safer, more easily predictable multiweekly, monthly, and yearly trends and trade them instead of their riskier, less predictable short-term counterparts? The pips are worth as much for easy trades as for hard ones.

One word of caution: Long-term positions mean there's more time for wider price swings, so if you're using leverage you need to be sure you have

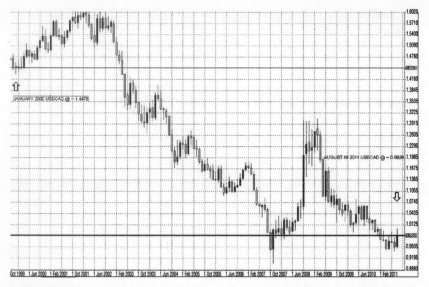

FIGURE 5.2   USDCAD January Monthly Chart, December 1999 to August 18, 2011
Source: MetaQuotes Software Corp.

enough cash in reserve to afford the wider distances between your entry point and your stop loss orders. For example, a given pair might typically move only 50 pips over a given day but move hundreds of pips in the course of a month. You need enough cash in your account relative to your position size and leverage used to be able to absorb those temporary drawdowns as the longer-term trend makes its normal countermoves within its longer-term trend. If you don't want the risks associated with leveraged trading for a given position size, you can cut your position size, or use instruments like forex, exchange-traded funds (ETFs), and exchange-traded notes (ETNs), which we'll cover in Chapter 10.

These easily seen long-term national economic fundamentals create these persistent, reliable long-term trends. The ability to play such reliable trends is a great advantage of long-term trading over short-term trading, which lacks trends of comparable trend reliability.

Ideal Trends For Long-Term Investors

Should you continue to play the trends in Figure 5.2? Unless they've reversed by the time you read this, why not? These are decade-long trends that are assumed valid until proven otherwise. The only questions are when to enter, what stop loss settings make sense, and whether you are able to afford to ride out the likely price swings along the way for a given position size and leverage. For long-term investors, or those with limited analytical and RAMM skills, these are some of the lowest risk trends you can find. As we'll see in Chapters 10 through 12, you don't even have to play them by directly buying or selling the currency pairs themselves. There are multiple ways to ride these trends which long-term investors may find more suitable.

Other Technical Indicators Are Better in Longer Time Frames

As noted at the start of Chapter 4, the easily available TA indicators found on most popular charting platforms used by retail traders all work better on longer time frame charts because they're older, more established, and provide more meaningful s/r and better signals when they're breached or when they diverge from normal price behavior, regardless of whether they are:

- Forms of s/r that we've covered previously or those in later chapters: chart patterns, Fibonacci retracements (Fibs), price levels, and so forth.
- Momentum indicators: assorted oscillators, moving average (MA) crosses, Double Bollinger Bands (DBBs), and so on.
- Cycle or timing tools: Fibonacci, Gann, Elliot Wave or other price cycle indicators.

Publicly Available Fundamental Data and Analysis Matters in Longer Time Frames

Over the course of weeks and months, the fundamentals of the underlying economies of a currency pair have time to affect its trend and price. For example, trends in interest rates, national debt levels, employment, consumer spending, and more may not matter over the course of a few hours or days (except as news items before and after the most recent figures are announced), but they become increasingly meaningful over weeks and months. Though the big players will still be better at fundamental analysis (FA), their advantage is less pronounced. With some experience, small traders and investors get a good grasp of the longer-term fundamentals of the major currencies. There's a lot of good information online for free or low cost, and there are only eight major currencies. Seriously, you don't need to pay thousands a year for a subscription to Nuriel Roubini or Charles Nenner to have had a firm grasp of how the EU or U.S. debt troubles are likely to influence their respective currencies. An hour a day on some top free websites like those listed in Appendix A will get you free access to some superb analysts and articles on forex and related macro and fundamental topics. When you're playing multiweekly or monthly trends, it usually wouldn't matter much if you read them a few days after their subscribers.

Lower Trading Costs

The potential trading range over a few minutes or hours is usually going to be a mere fraction of that which is possible over a period of many days or weeks. Let's say each transaction to open and close a position costs you on average 2 pips, so each trade costs about 4 pips. If you're striving for the 10–30 pips profit per trade of a typical day trader, transaction costs consume up to 40 percent of your profits. That kind of expense implies a trader needs a high percentage of winning trades to be profitable.

In contrast, those in positions that take multiple weeks to develop commonly earn 150 pips or more on winning trades because the trend or trading range has more time to cover a greater range of pips. That means transaction costs consume a much smaller percentage of profits and allow traders to be profitable with a much lower percentage of winning trades.

Start Out with Longer Duration Trades

In sum, trading longer-term positions from longer time frame charts increases your odds of success for six reasons:

1. A more level playing field: Longer duration positions allow you to compete by neutralizing much of the big institutions' advantages, which are more pronounced in the short term.

2. More and better information: The better the information, the greater the time to digest that information, with more reliable trends and technical indicators and less decision fatigue risk, combine to foster better decisions and a higher percentage of winning trades.

3. More time, less stress: You have more time to analyze and reconsider before placing a trade, with the ability to place trades in advance without greed and fear weighing on you as you decide in real time what to do, less pressure to decide, and lower chance of decision fatigue.

4. Work smarter, not harder: Longer time frames demand less active trade monitoring and less work. In addition to being better rested and less stressed, you can choose to put that extra time into finding the lowest risk trades, furthering your trading education, market research, and related reading. Or (dare I say it) you could do other things for a more balanced, rewarding life.

5. Lower transaction costs: The larger trading ranges over longer time frames mean that transaction costs consume a much smaller percentage of your revenues and allow you to be profitable with a much lower percentage of winning trades.

6. We believe these benefits far outweigh the potential excitement (or stress) and potential faster profits (which few achieve without considerable experience and skill) of the day traders.

To trade longer time frames, it helps if your broker provides the tools you need, particularly quality longer-term analysis.

Content Quality: The Sign of a Quality Broker

While we're encouraging trades on longer time frames, which depend on good long-term focused analysis, here's a related bit of critical advice for selecting a forex broker. Even though you have a number of criteria to consider, here's one you can use as a first screening to filter out the obviously lower quality operations.

The Best Forex Brokers Provide Quality Guidance to Trade Longer-Term Positions The more quality content they provide that makes it easier for you to trade longer time frames (as well as shorter durations), the more they're oriented toward serious traders rather than casual gamblers and the better a chance of success they're giving you.

There are four signs to look for.

1. Price data going back at least 10 years, preferably more

An important sign of the quality of your charting tools is how far back you view the price action on a given asset or currency pair. There will likely be times when you will want a big picture view of the price action of the past decade or more. If your broker can give you only a few years or shorter for the assets or currency pairs you trade, that signals a bad trading platform. It suggests the broker is focused on encouraging the short-term trading to be avoided by all but the more experienced and successful traders or that the broker is focused on fleecing casual gamblers who are trading more for fun than profit. This is a warning to trade elsewhere.

2. Free access to quality longer-term as well as short-term analysis

A broker who's serious about helping you profit will provide quality technical and fundamental analysis for periods extending beyond hours or days. If a broker provides only news updates you could find on any financial or forex news site, poor quality analysis, or analysis covering only the next few days at most, then move on. The broker is either unwilling or unable to invest in the resources you need for success playing the safer, more reliable longer-term trends.

The best will provide specific trade advice, including suggested entry and exit points. Some decent brokers don't do this out of liability concerns though there are ways to avoid that, and few traders would publicly admit to being stupid enough to believe that a given analyst was guaranteeing a winning trade (especially when nearly all analysis web pages contain legal disclaimers).

3. Free quality trader training

   Similarly, a broker that's on your side will make a serious effort to educate you with free or low-cost extensive training materials. We don't mean a superficial 30-page beginner's guide that barely covers basic s/r, plus a few brief, superficial webinars. We mean a full set of courseware on all aspects of trading.

4. Quality content means your broker is stable and on your side

   Quality shows a genuine effort to help you succeed and says a lot about the broker's financial stability. Good analysts and full-featured websites represent a serious investment that suggests both financial stability and the intention to build a lasting business based on a large base of successful traders. The forex industry is young and has many small brokers started by those who come from the online gambling industry. Many of them retain that mentality, and continue to view traders as lambs to be slaughtered rather than long-term clients who will provide a lasting corps of repeat customers, who therefore should be nurtured. Cheap or nonexistent content suggests the broker isn't focused on helping you succeed. Instead, it's assuming high client turnover (read: you lose all your money) and is focused on bringing in the next group of suckers before the current group is wiped out.

In general, if a broker is not helping you survive and succeed in the long run, not teaching you to trade or is limiting your ability to take longer-term positions, then move along. Remember this advice when you explore binary options, an alternative way of trading forex that we'll look at in detail later.

For now, just note that most binary options brokers offer expirations of a day or less. Don't waste your time with them as these are just glorified gambling sites. View them as you would any other casino, as adversaries, not trusted brokers. You'll want to stick to the ones that offer weekly and monthly durations. At the time of this writing, only anyoption.com offered both of these though we hope more brokers do so by the time you read this.

THE ESSENCE OF GOOD RAMM

To be motivated to practice good RAMM, you first need the right mindset, discussed previously. RAMM is all about the following, which we cover in detail in this chapter:

- Trading with safer styles and methods, as discussed previously.
- Making sure your gains from winning trades are larger than your losses from losing trades, as discussed later in the chapter on risk-to-reward ratios (rrrs).
- Increasing the odds of favorable rrrs. We'll consider only the trades that offer entry near strong support, with a reasonable stop loss that's much closer to our entry point than the next likely resistance area, which would serve as our likely exit point. Again, see the upcoming section on rrrs for details.
- Preventing a fatal loss from one or a series of losing trades from which you're unlikely to recover without adding funds. In essence, that means keeping your maximum loss per trade to a maximum of 1 percent to 3 percent of your trading capital.

THE THREE PILLARS OF RAMM

As in Chapter 2, the size of this maximum allowable loss per trade depends on three conditions:

1. Account size: Determines the cash value of the 1 to 3 percent maximum loss you can afford. Thus, it determines how far you can set your stop loss orders from your entry point. The larger the account, the wider the stops you can afford, and the more choices of trades you have available to take. For a given account size, that maximum loss you can safely afford is a function of the following two factors.

2. Leverage or margin used: Fixes the percent loss you incur for each 1 percent price move against you per lot traded. The greater the leverage (or the lower the margin), the greater the percent loss for each 1 percent price move against you, and the smaller the percent price move against you that you can afford without exceeding that 1 to 3 percent. The higher the leverage, the higher the risk and profit potential per trade. Some brokers allow you to adjust the leverage you use, some don't.

3. Position size: Determines cash value of each pip or 1 percent loss. For a given leverage setting, the larger the lot size used (more on that later), the more every pip move against you costs. The larger the lot size, the higher the risk and profit potential.

Let's look at these in greater detail. All focus is on insuring that your stop loss setting doesn't risk more than 1 to 3 percent of your capital and that gains per winning trade are much larger than losses per losing trade.

ACCOUNT SIZE AND AFFORDABLE LOSS PER TRADE

One of the core money management rules of professional traders is not to risk more than 1 to 3 percent of their capital on any one trade.

They understand the mathematics of losses, and how a given percent loss requires an even larger percent gain to recoup that loss. See Appendix E for illustration. This 1 to 3 percent refers to the amount risked by your stop loss, not position size. In other words, account size determines how far you can set your stop loss from your entry point without risking more than 1 to 3 percent of your account.

For example, those with a $10,000 account would not set their stop losses so far from their entry point that they risk more than $100–$300 per trade. Those with $100,000 accounts could accept $1,000–$3,000 loss per trade and so could set their stop loss orders further from their entry point.

The reason for keeping loss/trade to within these 1 to 3 percent limits is that you can then afford a string of 5 to 15 losses and still have about 85 percent of your capital left.

SETTING STOP LOSSES: BASIC TECHNIQUE AND PSYCHOLOGY

For a given position size and leverage, you limit your maximum loss per trade through your stop loss settings. The following rules on stop loss setting assume you're entering near strong support, because if you aren't, you shouldn't even consider entering the trade. If the trade moves against you, that nearby support is quickly breached and you have a signal to exit before a small loss becomes a large one.

Where to Set Stop Losses: Two Criteria

When setting your stop loss order, you're always striking a balance between two conflicting criteria:

1. The stop loss price is close enough to your entry point so if it's hit, the loss doesn't exceed 1 to 3 percent of your account value, as noted previously.

2. It's far enough away from your entry point and the likely support level so it doesn't get hit by normal random price movements and close your position before price has had time to move in your favor. Rather, it's triggered only by price moves that are big enough to suggest that you were wrong and overestimated the strength of a given support zone,

and now a loss is more likely than you thought. It's time to close the position before a small affordable loss becomes a large one. There are different ways to determine normal or average price movement to expect during a given period. Some manually determine average or typical candle length over a given period. Some will use a certain percentage of the range as determined by the Average True Range (ATR) indicator (more on this soon). Price volatility varies with market conditions and time frame as must the distance from entry point to stop loss.

Viewed from another perspective, setting stop losses means striking a balance between:

- Less frequent but larger losses from wider (or looser) stop loss settings: The farther your stop loss from your entry point, the larger the losses on losing trades relative to your gains from winning trades. However, you have less chance of having your stop loss hit before price starts to move in your favor (being "stopped out"). The main advantage of this approach is a higher percentage of winning trades (which you may need for encouragement), at least when you're right about the ultimate price direction. The main disadvantage is that you risk too many large losses and lower profits compared to the following approach to setting stop losses.
- More frequent but smaller losses from tighter (or narrower) stop loss settings: The closer your stop losses to your entry point, the smaller the losses on losing trades relative to your gains from winning trades. However, you'll have more losses from being "stopped out" on trades that would have ultimately worked, because your stop loss will be hit more often, before price has had time to move in your favor.

More Capital Allows Wider Stop Losses and a Wider Choice of Low-Risk Trade Opportunities

A larger account means:

- You can afford to set stop loss settings that are wide enough to avoid getting prematurely "stopped out," yet still only risk 1 to 3 percent of your capital, because you have more capital to risk. That means there are more trades available to take that have entry points that are both close enough to strong support and only risk 1 to 3 percent of your capital.
- You can afford the wider stop losses needed to ride the more stable longer-term trends via longer-term positions. As noted previously, forex markets produce many stable long-term trends. However, the longer you hold a position, the larger the normal price swings and the

farther the stop loss must be from your entry point. For example, a pair may have average daily price swings of 50 points, but weekly or monthly average price swings could be many times larger. A bigger account allows you to set those stop losses far enough from your entry point (near strong support, of course) to ride the wider short-term fluctuations within the more predictable long-term trends. In sum, a larger account allows you a wider choice of trades in any time frame, and also offers more chances to ride the most stable, predictable, and safer trends that are the basis of lower risk trading.

Not surprisingly, studies suggest certain minimum account sizes increase your chances of being profitable.[7]

Balancing Risk versus the Need to Win

While a larger account allows for wider stop losses, you need to accept the added risk that comes with them. Wider stop losses can increase your percentage of winning trades, but risks lower profits because losing trades cost more.

The right balance between winning percentage and loss sizes varies for each trader.

Some need a higher percentage of winning trades that comes from wider stop losses in order to avoid getting too discouraged, even if it comes at a cost of higher losses and lower overall profits.

Others are less emotional. As long as they achieve realistic profits at the end of the week, month, or quarter, they can accept taking more (but smaller) losses as long as the gains from the winners outweigh those losses enough to keep profits healthy. Few, however, are cool enough to accept very high losing percentages, such as 70 percent of their trades, no matter how profitable the trading style.

So, as you experiment with trading styles, be sensitive to what you need most to keep going. For some traders, particularly when starting out, the priority will be a higher winning percentage to build confidence. Others will need lower losses per trade and can accept the tradeoff of more "stopped out" trades and less frequent wins as part of the learning process.

When in doubt, err on the side of tighter stops and smaller but more frequent losses. Deal with the discouragement that may come from those by:

- Reminding yourself that it takes time to be successful, especially given the profit potential and competition it attracts. You need to learn and practice a lot to know enough and know what kind of trading suits you (e.g., your risk tolerance, time available, patience).

- Taking a break from trading to review your losing trades in your trading journal and identifying and correcting your mistakes.
- Taking a break from trading, period. I'm amazed at how much clarity can come after a good night's sleep or a few days off from a given dilemma.

Do not underestimate the importance of managing your mood and attitude, and of finding trading styles that give you enough of a winning percentage to keep going even if they are perhaps less profitable.

So how far (in pips) from strong support do you want to set your stop loss? First, it must be close enough to your entry point so that if hit your loss is less than 3%. Second, want it beyond the range of random price movements. So we need a way to define the range of "normal random price movements." There are many ways to do this; here are a few simple ones.

Method 1: Recent Range

The simplest, perhaps most intuitive way to set stop loss orders is to look at recent highs and lows for the period in question. In other words, the stop loss should be at least as far away from support as suggested by the recent price volatility, which of course varies dramatically depending on the circumstances and time frame. See our trade examples in Chapter 7.

Method 2: Average True Range (ATR)

Rather than using your own judgment, some statistical measures of price volatility are available. One of the most popular is the Average True Range (ATR) indicator, which measures the average movement for a given currency pair (or stock, commodity, etc.) for a given time period. Typically, the default setting is 14 periods, that is, 14 days on a daily chart, 14 hours on an hourly chart, and so forth, but over time you may want to experiment with that setting.

Knowing the ATR for a given period, traders can chose to place stops a given percentage of that range away from the entry point. For example, traders with great confidence in the direction of the trend who want to avoid having their stop loss hit would place their stop loss 80 to 100 percent of the ATR beyond their entry point near strong support. They'll accept the larger loss if that stop is hit because they believe the likelihood of that happening is low. Those with less confidence and more risk aversion who want smaller losses (even if there are more of them because the stop gets hit) might place their stop closer, perhaps 50 percent or less of the ATR away from the entry point.

Once you know the average volatility for a given period via the ATR, you have a better idea of how far away your fixed or trailing stop loss order needs to be to avoid getting hit by random price movements.

Later in this chapter and in Chapter 7, we'll see examples of how to use ATR.

So How Much Capital Is Enough?

By the time you've graduated from practice accounts, you should have a an initial idea about what kinds of trading you like to do, and your trading journal (more on that later) should provide a record of the amount you need to allow for realistically wide stop loss settings per trade and still be able to absorb a string of 5 to 15 losses. That amount will vary with trading styles and methods. For example, positions held for weeks or months need wider stop loss settings to absorb wider price swings than positions held for a few days.

We offer 5 to 15 losses only as a rough guide. We're not suggesting you rack up 10 straight losses before stopping. After you see five losing trades out of the past six to seven, you should consider stopping to identify the problem by studying your trade journal (discussed later on in this chapter). You may well repeat this process a few times before you've fixed the problem, suffering periodic losing streaks of about 15 losses as part of your tuition for your trading education.

Again, you should have about six profitable months of trading with practice accounts (and very small positions with real money) before doing any serious trading with live money. Thus you should have some experience with the process of fixing losing streaks before you "go live" with larger position sizes. Furthermore, you'll have extensive records of your past trading to guide you. Again, we'll cover trade plans and journals later.

If the account size you need and can afford is unclear, and it may well be, don't worry. You're allowed to make mistakes with your account size in the early stages. Start with an amount that meets the following criteria:

- You can afford to lose it as an investment in your education.
- Based on your limited experience with the size of your positions, leverage, and stop losses, you can absorb a string of 5 to 15 losses and still have about 85 percent of your capital left.

Practically speaking, most people will have limited control over what they can afford to lose. Instead, most people will adapt their trading style, position size, and leverage to their account size. So, let's move on to those aspects of RAMM.

LEVERAGE AND MARGIN

We covered this second pillar of RAMM earlier in Chapter 2 and provide additional details in Appendix D. However, no discussion of RAMM would be complete without a reminder that the higher your leverage, the higher your risk. Until you're an accomplished trader, or at least good at RAMM, you want to keep it as low as your broker will allow and add more as your success warrants. Many brokers have fixed leverage levels, so you have to adjust your account size or position size.

POSITION SIZING

Of the three pillars of RAMM, position size is usually the easiest one to adjust, at times the only one.

As you may recall from Chapter 2, you typically have three choices of lot sizes you can trade.

1. Standard Accounts: 100,000 units of the base currency (the one on the left).
2. Mini Accounts: 10,000 units of base currency.
3. Micro or super mini accounts: 1,000 units of base currency.

Just to give you an idea of what that means, if:

- The account is denominated in Euros.
- The Euro is the base currency (the one on the right), which is common with the major currency pairs.

Then the cost per pip is €10.00 for a standard lot, €1.00 for a mini lot, and €0.10 for a micro lot. See Appendix B for details.

In practice, you may not have much control over your account size because that's largely fixed by how much you're able to afford. Many brokers don't offer much choice on leverage used. So, lot size is the one thing everyone can use to keep risk down.

When you first graduate from practice to real accounts, no matter how successful you were with demo accounts, stick to trading one or a few lots of the smallest lot size offered. The one big weakness of practice accounts is that they can't simulate the pressure of having money at risk, so many traders struggle to attain the same success they had with demo accounts when they start trading real money.

Expect your performance to suffer when you transition to trading and risking real money. That's normal.

So when you start trading with real money, use small positions that keep your losses to around 1% or less of your total account. You can increase your position size after you see a number of months of profitable trading. Because you'll be working with small lots, evaluate your performance based on percentage rather than nominal gains. Don't view this period as a delay. View it like you would a paid internship. You accept less money for the sake of gaining better experience. After you see that you've maintained or improved on your performance with practice accounts, then you can consider moving up to larger position sizes. If you hit a losing streak, strongly consider cutting down your position sizes until your performance recovers.

AVOID HAVING TOO MANY OPEN POSITIONS

Closely related to position sizing is the common mistake of overtrading with too many full-sized (versus partial) open positions. This can be distracting, and it defeats the purpose of keeping position sizes small by increasing the percentage of your account at risk at any one time. How many open positions are too many? This is a judgment call and depends on your skill level and time frame. Trades that occur over days or weeks require less active monitoring than those that complete in a matter of minutes or hours.

ENTRIES NEAR STRONG SUPPORT, EXITS NEAR STRONG RESISTANCE

Regardless of whether you enter or exit all at once or in stages, a key part of good risk management is to base your entries and exits on the location of strong s/r.

Entries

If you're playing trading ranges (bounces off lower and upper channel lines that form resistance or support), only enter the near strong support of one channel line and at least plan to take some profits near the likely strong resistance around the opposite channel line unless you're using a trailing stop.

If you're a momentum trader who enters trades on breakouts past resistance levels, enter only after a strong resistance level is decisively broken (based on personal judgement that will improve with experience), and plan to take at least partial profits near the next strong resistance level.

Exits: Use Trailing Stops to Protect and Maximize Gains

Though your initial plan should be to exit near likely resistance, remember that you have the option of using a trailing stop.

Instead of fixed stop losses, use trailing stop loss orders whenever possible because they give you the best of both worlds, the protection of a regular stop loss without the limitations of a fixed exit point. Until price retraces and hits the trailing limit, you ride the move as high as it goes. Once your trailing stop is above your entry point, the only question is how much you'll profit. As part of our drive to maintain a high rrr, we try to get even better than 1:3 rrrs when we can. Using trailing stops allows us to get those extra gains. These big winners help compensate for losing trades and for winners in which you were forced to exit with minimal gains to avoid a loss.

It isn't always practical to use a trailing stop when you begin a trade. In these cases, you simply change the switch from a fixed to a trailing stop loss once the trade has moved a certain number of pips in your favor, at minimum so that your loss would be less than your initial fixed stop loss.

ENTRIES AND EXITS: SINGLE VERSUS MULTIPLE

Because s/r levels occur over areas or zones rather than precise points, selecting entry, exit, and stop loss points can be stressful because you're never sure if you're right. To lower the risk and stress level, many find it helpful to enter and exit positions in stages.

For example, if your planned position is two mini account lots, you could take profits on one lot at a more conservative price, and leave the other lot to continue with a trailing stop loss (defined in Chapter 2).

If your trailing stop loss is set to trigger at no worse a position than your first exit point, you at least lock in a smaller profit as a worst-case scenario. This first exit should bring profits on that first lot that are at least equal to the loss risked by your trailing stop, thus allowing a 1:1 rrr on that lot. Set your trailing stop so at worst it triggers at your initial exit and you lock in at least a modest profit and a 1:1 rrr on the trade. If price continues to run higher, the second lot gives you added returns though not as much as if you'd let both lots run with a trailing stop once the first exit. Safety usually comes at a cost of lower returns.

Taking partial profits not only eases stress levels, it also helps build your confidence while you are learning and finding a trading method and style that works for you.

Unlike stock brokers, forex brokers' fees are based on spreads (number of pips between bid and ask). That means they make money on your trading volume (the amount of currency you trade) rather than your trading frequency, so you pay no extra for partial exits and entries. How often you use these will depend greatly on your confidence in a given exit or entry point. When you're very confident about a trade, you're more likely to keep the full position open until you hit your planned exit point.

RISK-REWARD RATIOS (RRRS)

Favorable rrrs are another key part of good RAMM. We seek 1:3 risk-reward ratios (aka 3:1 reward-risk ratios, same thing) or better, though we will certainly consider trades with 1:2 rrrs, as shown next. In other words, we seek trades where the entry point (which is near strong support of course) is ideally at least three times farther away from the profit-taking point (near resistance) than it is from the stop loss. That way your winning trades bring gains triple the size of your losses. That allows you to be profitable with an achievable winning trade percentage of just over 25 percent.

By all means, try strategies that seek lower rrrs and higher winning ratios, and these may be a better fit for those needing frequent wins. At times, market conditions will almost force us to accept lower rrrs. However, be cautious with such approaches until you've made those strategies work in practice accounts and then with small positions. Start out by trading less frequently and only when your loss is smaller than your likely gain if you're right.

Example: How 1:3 RRRs Make Winners
Out of Losers

Here's an illustration of the math:

Assumptions

You have $20,000 in trading capital. You will follow good RAMM practice and not risk more than 1 to 3 percent of that on any given trade, in this case, $200.

You place 10 trades with a stop loss that risks no more than $200 on average, 1 percent of capital risked per trade on average, $1,000 total capital risked. So, you could lose 10 straight trades and still have $19,000 or 95 percent of your capital.

Trade selection criteria

You enter trades only when the distance in pips from your planned entry to stop loss (see setting stop losses) does not risk more than $200 on average.

You will only take trades that offer a minimum of 1:3 rrr. In other words, if our stop loss is hit, we lose $200. If our sell limit is hit, we earn at least about $600.

1:3 rrr: Profitable with over 25 percent winning trades

If 50 percent winning trades: Percent gain from $1,000 risked

$5 \times -\$200 = (\$1,000)$
$5 \times \quad \$600 = \quad \$3,000$
_____

$2,000   200 percent

If 40 percent winning trades:

$6 \times -200 = (\$1,200)$
$4 \times \$600 = \quad \$2,400$
_____

$1,200   120 percent

If 35 percent winning trades:

$6.5 \times -200 = (\$1,300)$
$3.5 \times \$600 = \quad \$2,100$
_____

$800   80 percent

If 30 percent winning trades:

$7 \times -200 = (\$1,400)$
$3 \times \$600 = \quad \$1,800$
_____

$400   40 percent

If 27.5 percent winning trades:

$7.25 \times -200 = (\$1,450)$
$2.75 \times \$600 = \quad \$1,650$
_____

$200   20 percent

As long as you're right more than 27.5 percent of the time, you'll be profitable. The only question is whether your ego can handle that many losses. That's a function of your sensitivity and ego. If you're humble and mature enough to focus on your profits, you'll be fine. Hey, a baseball player with .275 batting average is a good hitter.

If 25 percent winning trades:

$$7.5 \times \quad 200 = (\$1,500)$$
$$2.5 \times \$600 = \quad \$1,500$$

                         $0   0 percent

If 20 percent winning trades:

$$8 \times \quad 200 = (\$1,600)$$
$$2 \times \$600 = \quad \$1,200$$

                      ($400)   −40 percent

This ideal of 1:3 rrr can often be found when markets or at least an individual currency pair are at the start of a trend reversal or at either extremes of a wide trading range.

However, the rest of the time, such opportunities may be much harder to find. Usually they are still available, and you need to spend more time searching for these optimal situations rather than trading. That's fine; better to trade less often to take only the lowest risk and highest yielders that don't require any special skill level or information sources. That's how we trade like a great beginner and make money without the advantages of the big institutions.

Example: How 1:2 Risk-Reward Ratios Make Winners Out of Losers

If you can't find compelling opportunities offering 1:3 rrr (that can happen in certain markets) and you feel confident about the trade, then a 1:2 rrr will be acceptable and may often be a more realistic criterion under the circumstances. If your winning trades bring gains double the size of your losses, you can still be profitable with an achievable winning trade percentage of under 35 percent.

A 1:2 rrr allows you to find more trade opportunities because resistance need only be twice as far from the entry point as the stop loss rather than three times as far. There are legitimate reasons to take trades that offer only a 1:2 rrrr. For example:

- Sometimes that's as much as the market is offering and you spot a setup with high odds of success, so you accept a lower rrr rather than miss a likely profit.
- Sometimes you're too late in spotting what would have been a 1:3 rrr with a very strong trend that still has room to run, so you accept a later, less optimal entry with a lower rrr because you're particularly confident that the trade will be profitable.
- If you're still using a practice demo account and want the experience of the trade.

Alternatively, you can choose to stand aside until you find a 1:3 rrr trade, which is especially wise if you've reason to be especially risk averse. For example:

You've recently graduated to trading real money and want your first few months to show a net profit. Your trading capital is limited and you need the gains from your winners to far exceed your losses from losing trades.

Here's the math:

Assumptions

The same assumptions and trade criteria apply, except the rrr changes to 1:2.

Trade selection criteria

You enter trades only when the distance in pips from your planned entry to stop loss (see setting stop losses) does not risk more than $200.

You will only take trades that offer a minimum of 1:2 rrr. In other words, if our stop loss is hit we lose $200, if our sell limit is hit we earn $400.

1:2 rrr: Profitable with a bit less than 35 percent winning trades

If 50 percent winning trades: % Gain from $1,000 risked

$$5 \times -\$200 = (\$1,000)$$
$$5 \times \$400 = \$2,000$$
_____

                          $1,000   100 percent

If 40 percent winning trades:

$$6 \times -200 = (\$1,200)$$
$$4 \times \$400 = \$1,600$$
_____

                            $400   40 percent

If 35 percent winning trades:

$$6.5 \times -200 = (\$1,300)$$
$$3.5 \times \$400 = \$1,400$$

$$\$100 \qquad\qquad 10 \text{ percent}$$

If 30 percent winning trades:

$$7 \times -200 = (\$1,400)$$
$$3 \times \$400 = \$1,200$$

$$(\$200) \qquad\qquad -20 \text{ percent}$$

What started out as a planned 1:3 rrr often becomes a 1:2 or less if you're using a trailing stop loss order that gets triggered if the trade starts to move against you. That's fine. Though it makes sense to aim for a 1:3 rrr level, markets aren't always that cooperative, and we'll take what's available. More on the value of using trailing stops later.

Applying 1:3 RRR: An Example

Here's an illustrated example (see Figure 5.3).

On August 11, 2011, we see an opportunity to enter near strong support of the 38.2 percent Fib at 1.4110. These Fib lines were drawn for the longer-term uptrend from January 9 to May 1, 2011, not shown here.

We can set a reasonable stop loss order at the recent low of August 4 and 5 around 1.4060 for a maximum loss of 70 pips. Strong resistance is formed by a combination of the upper descending channel line drawn from May 1, 2011, and the 23.6 percent Fib line converging around 1.4410, but we'd prefer a more conservative profit target below the closing price of August 9 around 1.4340. Do we have a 1:3 rrr? Here's the math:

Enter August 11, 2011 at	1.4130
Stop loss order set at August 4 low of	1.4060
Maximum loss 70 pips	0.0070
Profit-taking exit via sell stop order	1.4340
August 11 entry via buy limit order	1.4130
Planned gain 210 pips three times planned loss	0.0210

So, we have our 1:3 rrr. Figure 5.4 shows how it worked out on August 15.

If we had stayed with a fixed sell limit order at 1.4340, we would have made out 210 pips. Sounds great, and it would be. However, most of us would be kicking ourselves for missing so much of the move, which peaked

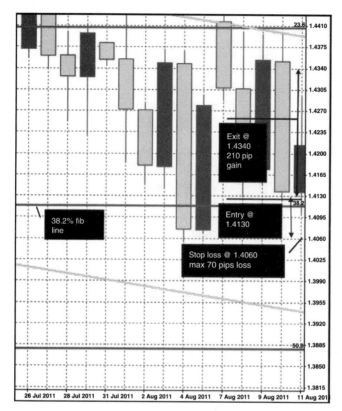

FIGURE 5.3 URUSD Daily Chart, July 28 to August 11, 2011
Source: MetaQuotes Software Corp.

below 1.4480 for another 140 pips gain. An exit around there would have given you a roughly 1:5 rrr.

But there's no way you'd have known and been able to play that, right? Actually, there is. *All you had to do was use a trailing stop* instead and ride the move higher while locking in most of the profits. Others who are more conservative might have taken partial profits and let the rest run with a trailing stop. This brings us to our next point.

Acceptable RRR Can Vary with Market Conditions

Consider market conditions when deciding whether to use a more aggressive 1:2 rrr. In a strongly trending market (up or down), more justification exists for loosening your standards and accepting a lower rrr if the

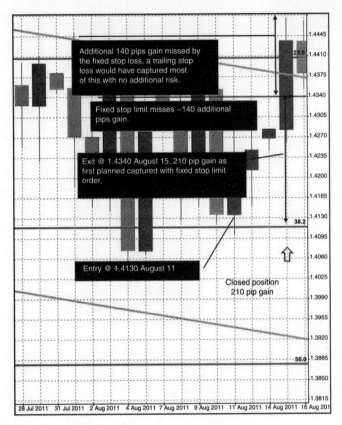

FIGURE 5.4   EURUSD Daily Chart, July 28 to August 16, 2011
Source: MetaQuotes Software Corp.

trade is in the direction of the strong trend and you risk missing the trade altogether.

More on Stop Loss Orders: An Example of Using ATR to Gauge Volatility and Place a Fixed or Trailing Stop Loss Order

We refer to the above example.

In Figure 5.5, we show the same EURUSD daily chart showing the daily candle for the entry date of the trade on August 11, but this time we include an ATR, which shows that over the past 14 days or daily candles, the average price range was about 210 pips. Those interested in how ATR is calculated can look it up online.

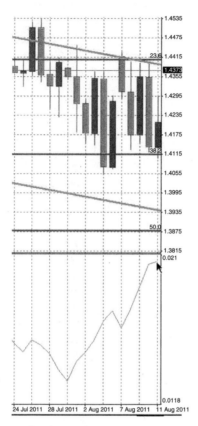

FIGURE 5.5   EURUSD Daily Chart, July 24 to August 11, 2011
Source: MetaQuotes Software Corp.

In this example, we based our stop losses on the other factors mentioned previously. However, if we wanted to lower the chances of getting stopped out of the trade in exchange for the risk of more loss if the trade turned against us, we could have set the stop loss at a distance 50 percent or more of the ATR, 105 pips, beneath the entry point, or some different percentage of ATR.

The point here is that there are different ways to determine how far away you set your stop loss. In the previous example, we used the recent lows as a guide though we could have used ATR instead. Much depends on factors like your risk appetite, market conditions, and confidence in the trade. For example, if you've caught a pullback to strong support in an overall strong uptrend, you might have more confidence that this uptrend will resume and allow a wider stop loss to avoid getting stopped out by random price movements. When you're less confident, you might keep stops tighter.

IF YOU FAIL TO PLAN, YOU PLAN TO FAIL

Planning each and every trade is another aspect of RAMM that separates the professionals from the amateurs. The benefits more than justify the work. Writing out a plan:

- Insures that you go through the full planning process, particularly if you prepare a trading plan form (like that shown in Table 5.1) that reminds you of each step in the planning process.
- Forces you to articulate the pros and cons of the trade, helping you decide if you should take it or not. You go into the trade clear on why it should work, what could go wrong, and what you're risking.
- Leaves you a written record of your thinking and results from which to learn from what you've done right and wrong, and spot repeated mistakes or chronic weaknesses that need to be addressed.
- Makes it easier to keep track of your profits and losses.

Let's look at these benefits in more depth.

To insure that you actually use the ideas taught in this book and learn from both your winning and losing trades, you need to write a plan for every trade that includes such basics as the following.

What's Your Rationale for Taking This Trade?

First, consider the basics that determine whether you've got a favorable risk-reward ratio of at least 1:2, preferably 1:3.

S/R   How strong are the s/r points where you plan your entries and exits?

RRR   Based on the strong s/r points near your planned entry and exit and the needed distance from your entry to your stop loss (to avoid it being triggered by random price movements), does it appear to offer an adequate rrr of at least 1:2 or better, 1:3?

To determine that rrr, in addition to your likely entry and exit, you need to know the distance from your entry point to your stop loss. So, think through where you'll place your initial stop loss and why.

Entry and Exits: Stop Loss   Where are you placing your initial stop loss and why? How do you know it's far enough from your entry point so it won't get hit by random price moves? Recent highs and lows? Or an estimate of average volatility per candle? How large a move would you define that? Based on what? ATR or a visual inspection of recent volatility? Is the planned exit two to three times further from your entry point than your stop loss to allow for a safe stop loss yet still have a 1:3 rrr?

Trend Strength   Assuming your rrr is acceptable, is the trend or trading range likely to continue? How strong is the trend if there is one? What's your evidence for that trend strength? Do the underlying fundamentals look like they'll continue to fuel the continuation in the trend that you need to reach your planned exit near strong resistance?

Other Fundamental and Technical Evidence Pros and Cons

What fundamentals are fueling the move?

What technical or fundamental evidence suggests the trade won't work?

Why do you believe the balance of evidence favors the trade?

What new fundamental or technical evidence might cause you to exit or add to your position?

Scenarios or Decision Trees   If the trade moves in your favor, when would you switch from your original stop loss to a trailing stop to lock in gains or minimize losses?

If trading multiple lots, at what point would you take partial profits? Would you let the whole position ride? Are there possible news events or other fundamental factors, which if announced, would cause you to alter your plan? Are there any planned news announcements (central bank rate statements, U.S. monthly jobs reports, a meeting expected to resolve a major geopolitical crisis, etc.) that could change your opinion of the trade and cause you to exit or to add to your position?

The mere act of writing it forces you to examine whether the analysis and RAMM of each trade is sound. The collected trading plans become your trading journal, one of the most important learning tools you'll have.

You'll need two kinds of plans:

1. A plan for each individual trade. The collection of these forms your trading journal.
2. An overall trade business plan that covers your goals, trading methods, performance monitoring, feedback methods, etc.

No. 1: Plan Every Trade and Record It in a Journal

You know how they say that those who don't learn from the past are destined to repeat it? So, learn from your trading mistakes and correct moves. Keep records of your trade plans, review the trade afterward, and note why it did or didn't work and what that tells you about what you need to do to avoid the same mistake or ensure that you repeat the successful trade.

All the theory you'll learn about TA and fundamental analysis, trader psychology, and RAMM is worthless unless you can implement it. A written trading plan for each trade, stored in a trading diary, is one of the most effective means of doing that because it:

- Serves as a checklist to see that you've taken all of the analytical and RAMM steps needed.
- Forces you to think through the trade rationale (the balance of fundamental and technical pros and cons) and RAMM, so you can develop a step-by-step method for deciding whether a trade provides the right combination of low risk and high potential yield.
- Provides a record of your methods for later review so you learn from what you did right and wrong. Combined with each written trade plan and post-trade analysis you record, it forms a trading diary or journal. You'll want to review these trades periodically. This kind of review is especially valuable when (not if) you hit a losing streak and are figuring out what you're doing wrong. You can examine the common denominators of your winning and losing trades. Include screenshots of the relevant charts at the times of entry and exit. They provide a complete visual picture of the technical evidence, and they take less time to create than a written description. I often print these and scribble notes all over them as I notice things I didn't catch the first time. If you don't have screen capture software, you can get it free online.[8]
- Provides a personal database to identify mistakes, strengths, weaknesses, shows what kinds of trades and trading styles work or don't work for you, and highlights which produce less stress, more fun, and are better suited for your personality.
- Becomes a tool for knowing what kind of trader or investor you are. There many different ways to trade or invest. One of the prime keys to success is to find the methods and styles that fit you rather than adapting to a given way of trading.
- When using a prepared trade plan form as shown in Table 5.1, this can serve as a checklist to insure you consider and record each aspect of the planning process.

TABLE 5.1 Sample Trade Plan Form For Trade Illustrated in Figure 5.3

0 Trade	1 Date and Time	2 Pair	3 Long/ Short	4 Chart Time Frame and Estimated Duration	5 Entry (E) Stop Loss (SL) Take Profit Point (TPP)	6 Amount and % of A/C at Risk from Stop Loss Mini A/C~ $1.00/PIP	7 RRR	8 Lot Size Margin Leverage	9 Comments Rationale for Entry See Page	10 Gain or Loss	11 Comments Post Mortem See Page	12 Screenshot Entry and Exit See Page
124	110811	EURUSD	Long	Multi-Day or Week	E: 1.4130	$70/$20,000						
					SL: 1.4060 TPP: 1.4340	0.003	1:3	$10K $100 100:1	Page XXX	$210	Page YYY	Page ZZZ

Note: At bottom of column 5 E = Entry Point, SL = Stop Loss Point, TPP = Take Profit Point.

- The basic form can include cross-references to more detailed notes than possible on this form. I've always been a big fan of including screenshots of the charts, so I have a picture of the scenario before and after and can scribble notes right on the chart.

Table 5.1 is an example of how the trade example from the previous Risk-Reward Ratios section would be recorded in your trading journal.

Explanation of Columns   Columns 0 and 1 are for reference. Most of the others are self-explanatory, just there to remind you to consider essential elements of RAMM.

Columns 9, 11, and 12 are meant to reference separate pages where there would be enough room to include your thoughts and where most of your thinking will be recorded and reviewed later for what you did wrong or correctly.

Column 9 is Comments Rationale for Entry. There isn't room in this column for your comments, so you'd put in a reference number of some page in a separate journal where you could include the full rationale for the trade like the answers to the sample previous questions.

For example, you could enter these comments:

- Why you believe there is enough room for a 1:3 rrr.
- Whether this trade is going with a longer-term trend, and if not, why you believe the counter move is worth trading.

Sample Trade Rationale as Recorded in Journal

Here's what I recorded, referring to the scenario shown in Figure 5.6.

Column 9: COMMENTS, RATIONALE FOR ENTRY

- I'm going long the EURUSD, trading with the daily trend (my chosen time frame, I usually trade based on daily charts) but I'm going against the longer-term trend on the weekly or monthly charts. I wouldn't normally do this but am making an exception here because I have a chance to enter at 1.4130, above what I believe is a strong support level comprised of the 38.2 percent Fib level at 1.4110, and a price support level of 1.4060 that was tested and held twice (on August 4 and 5) within the prior seven trading sessions. Placing an initial stop loss there, my maximum loss is 70 pips. As shown, this allows a likely rrr of between 1:2 and 1:3.
- There is no significant resistance until at least the 1.4340 level, the closing price on August 8 (175 pips from my entry point, a better than 1:2 rrr).

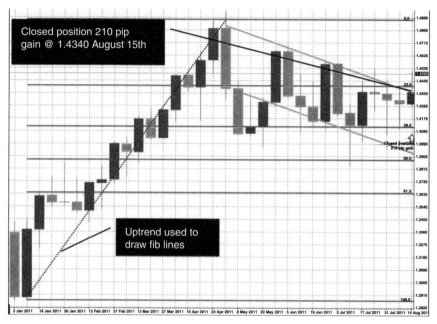

FIGURE 5.6 EURUSD Weekly Chart, January 2, 2011, to August 14, 2011
Source: MetaQuotes Software Corp.

- After that, the next significant resistance is at minimum around 1.4340, based on the opening and closing prices of August 9 and 10. That allows for a 210 pip gain for a 1:3 rrr.
- Neither of these resistance levels are especially strong, so if there are any positive EURUSD developments, they could easily be reached and exceeded.
- There is potential for even greater rrr. No strong resistance at all until the area around 1.4410 where two kinds of strong resistance converge: the 23.6 percent Fib level and the descending upper channel line dating back to the first week of May.
- There are reasons not to take this trade.
- Long-term fundamentals are mostly "risk off," that is, not supportive of this trade. Given that the planned duration is 1 to 2 weeks only, long-term fundamentals are less important than the short-term technical picture noted previously. U.S. credit rating downgrade and ongoing EU crisis. However, short-term fundamentals have had little direct impact on this pair, given that the fundamentals of the underlying economies of the EUR and USD stink, so predicting multiday moves for the pair based on these has been a waste of time. We don't make trade

decisions based on these. Besides, we suspect the Chinese are buying the EUR on dips.

- Overall technical picture for risk assets like stocks and the EURUSD as represented by the Standard & Poor's 500 Index (S&P 500) daily and weekly charts for this period is bearish and not supportive of long EURUSD positions (this pair tends to rise and fall with this index). The index is in a downtrend on daily and weekly charts during this period.

Again, however, the short-term technical picture takes priority. We'll see if this works.

Column 11: COMMENTS, POST MORTEM

- Trade worked, support held, weaker resistance gave way, no clear fundamental driver though a number of possible ones. Just speculation. Switched to trailing stop and achieved better than 1:3 rrr, which I hope will compensate for those trades in which my trailing stop takes me out before achieving at least 1:2 rrr.

Column 12: SCREENSHOT ENTRY and EXIT

- Includes a reference to a page in the trade journal with the screenshot shown in Figure 5.7 of the chart for a visual record which at times,

FIGURE 5.7 EURUSD Weekly Chart, January 2, 2011, to August 14, 2011
Source: MetaQuotes Software Corp.

when reviewed later, yields clues about why things did or didn't work out or hints that I didn't pick up originally.

It can include handwritten or other additional comments, observations, or questions for future investigation. For example, look at this same chart later with some momentum indicators like DBBs, MA crossovers, or others, to see if there were additional clues I didn't see at the time.

No. 2: Your Overall Business Plan

This is the other, bigger picture plan you'll need to make though it comes later than the trading journal shown previously, which you should be keeping from your first practice account trades.

This comes later, after you've had enough study and practice trading on demo accounts to have an idea about how to answer some of the following. If at that point you decide you want to pursue trading as a serious money-making venture, you need to make a business plan.

Much of this business plan will be similar in most ways to any business plan, for example:

- Qualifications/skills your staff (you) possess to justify success, and if others are needed, how to attain them. Some skills you'll still need to learn yourself, others can be bought via paid information services. Some can be attained from your circle of trader contacts either in person or via online forums or email contact. If you want exposure to different kinds of trading, you may allocate time and funds to invest with a proven pro through one of the social networks mentioned in Chapter 11.
- Time allocated, day or week.
- Trading capital.
- Equipment or training costs.
- Training period.
- Profit goals.
- Your market niche: trading style, and so on.
- Assorted goals: profitability, education.
- Feedback methods and periodic review of whether these goals are met and what you'll do if they are or aren't met.

Again, you'll need a number of months' background before you can answer some of these. That's okay; you can always adapt your plan as you learn more.

As with any business, management must review monthly or quarterly performance to measure progress and identify what's going well and what needs fixing. You are management.

WHAT CONDITIONS DO YOU NEED FOR SUCCESS?

We conclude this chapter with a review and another look at the commonly neglected questions that you need to ask yourself to understand what kind of trading style and conditions you need to succeed. If you don't clarify these questions, you may find yourself doing everything else right yet somehow dissatisfied even if you're successful.

Are you an extrovert? Do you prefer to learn by doing rather than by reading? Do you want to hear what others are doing and thinking? You may progress better by hanging out in online trade forums or virtual (or actual) trading rooms. Being shut in a quiet room doing research online or from other sources may leave you drained and bored.

Are you more of an introvert, scholar, or natural systems builder? Do you find most chat rooms or forums filled with more noise than signal, so you've no patience for sorting through mounds of mindless half-baked ideas to find a few pearls of serious, well-thought-out ideas? You'll progress better by researching the best books, online sources, or courses to take.

If you need a lot of action and don't mind risk, you'll gravitate to shorter-term day trading styles. Though we don't urge these for beginners, some succeed with this kind of trading, especially if they've enough RAMM skills and the discipline needed to implement them and survive the learning period. If you're averse to risk and more patient, you'll gravitate to longer-term trading methods.

If you're not the introspective type and don't have a clear idea, then you need to invest some time to find out because you'll get a better idea of what trading or investing suits you. Being aware of the questions we've raised at the beginning of this chapter on trader psychology will help. Knowing the question is halfway to the answer. Experimenting with different trading methods via a demo account will go a long way to helping you.

For those with the time and money, you can find online trader coaches who might provide the answers in less time.

SAFETY IN NUMBERS: BUILD A TEAM

You'll reduce your mistakes and increase your rate of progress if you've both mentors and colleagues with whom you can evaluate trading or investing ideas. This powerful combination is standard operating practice in most kinds of professional education (in law and business schools these roles are filled by professors and study groups).

As we'll discuss in Chapter 11, it's easier than ever to find them without even needing to leave your home via the advent of online trader forums and social trading networks.

As with any fruitful marriage or partnership, you want your teammates to share similar goals. That is, short-term high-risk traders should seek out their own kind, as should longer-term more risk-averse traders, and long-term investors seeking to diversify their assets by currency exposure as well as by asset and sector type.

Ideally, your like-minded mentors and colleagues should offer talents and perspectives that differ from yours, so that your collective wisdom is greater than the sum of your individual members. For example, technicians seek out fundamentalists—those focused on Europe pair up with those more familiar with U.S. or Asian markets, etc. Alternatively, scholars can focus on reading a wide range of analysis and charts, and seek out less academic types with trader and other financial industry contacts. Those who are more verbally inclined and read a lot of fundamental analysis would benefit from contact with more quantitative types who want to build algorithms.

CHAPTER 6

Essentials of Fundamental Analysis

T his chapter will cover:

- Using Fundamental Analysis (FA) and Technical Analysis (TA) Together
- An Overview of FA: Main Fundamental Drivers of Forex Trends
- News Trading: Day Trading on Short-Term Fundamentals
- FA Basics: Easy to Understand, Hard to Apply
- Therefore, Get Thee to an Analyst
- Combining FA and TA: An Example

While technical analysis (TA) focuses solely on patterns in price movements with no attempt to discern what drives them, fundamental analysis (FA) does the opposite. It attempts to identify all the economic, social, and political forces that affect supply and demand for an asset, and ideally, use them to forecast its future price.

Leaving aside the debate over which is more important, the practical fact is that you need both. Here's the short version of how you combine them.

Use FA to attempt to forecast both the longer term trend and the short term market reaction to news events, and plan your overall strategy accordingly. However, its very hard to know when deeper fundamentals will actually start to influence price movements.

Therefore, use TA to time entries and exits. It may not tell you much about what's behind a given trend or chart pattern, but it's great for telling you when price has actually started to move, how markets are actually behaving, how they're feeling, how strongly they're feeling it, and what is a low or high price for a particular period.

TA vastly improves your ability to buy low and sell high over a given period because it tells you about the likely s/r areas and their relative strength. However, in the long run it's the fundamental drivers of currency supply and demand that are behind those price patterns and s/r levels, so your ability to forecast them over many weeks, months, or years depends on your FA skills, or those of the analysts you trust and follow.

In the most general sense, fundamentals influence a currency pair's price through their influence on:

- The macroeconomic conditions of its relevant countries and regions. If China is doing well, the Chinese Yuan Renminbi (CNY) and the currencies of its chief materials suppliers like Australia tend to be strong relative to those with no China connection.
- Overall market sentiment. When markets feel optimistic or anticipate growth, those pairs with base currencies that have much higher risk rankings than their counter currencies, like the AUDJPY or NZDCHF tend to perform best. Under the opposite conditions, those pairs underperform, so you'd sell (or short) them, and buy pairs with the opposite characteristics, like the USDCAD. That general sentiment can determine a currency's performance even if the driver of that sentiment has no direct relation to the currency. For example, a great U.S. economic news or earnings report could easily fuel a rally in risk assets that would benefit risk currencies like the EUR far more than the USD.

Not surprisingly, in periods of global economic expansion, the risk currencies like the Australian Dollar (AUD) form long-term uptrends against most other currencies. In times of contraction, the safe haven currencies can trend higher for long periods against the risk currencies.

This last point is critical for longer-term buy-and-hold investors. In addition to their usual need to consider safety, return, and sector diversification, they'll need to consider what currency exposure they want. For example, *in periods of expansion, those with portfolios of stocks, bonds, real estate, or other assets will favor such assets with exposure to the healthiest risk currencies with the firmest uptrends. During down years, they'll favor assets tied to the better safe haven currencies.*

For day traders, fundamental analysis is almost irrelevant except that daily news announcements to the extent that these events may influence prices during their short holding periods or when they attempt to trade news events (covered below).

USING FUNDAMENTAL ANALYSIS (FA) AND TECHNICAL ANALYSIS (TA) TOGETHER

We gave you the short version earlier. Let's review it and then delve into greater detail.

Most traders and investors use some combination of technical analysis and fundamental analysis. Here's how we combine the two forms of analysis in combination.

In sum, first use FA for determining your big picture view of what kinds of currencies or other assets should do better over a given period, and TA for determining when and at what price to enter and exit positions. Once you have an idea of what kinds of risk or safety assets should be best for buying or selling, you will use TA for determining entries and exits and for determining which specific pairs or other assets offer the best risk-reward ratios (rrrs) in your chosen time frame.

Technical analysis tells you where there's strong support for safe entries, where price shouldn't move much against you if support holds as you expect it should. If it doesn't, you find out quickly and get out with a small loss via a well-placed stop loss order. TA tells you where price is likely to hit resistance and where you should plan on closing some or all of the position or at least plan to switch to a trailing stop to lock in profits.

Understand, however, that over the longer term, your charts are pictures of market reactions to the fundamental factors we'll discuss next. Most of the time, fundamentals are the drivers of the multiweek and longer movements you see on the charts.[1]

So, *use fundamental analysis for forecasting trends for the coming weeks, months, and years, and use TA for timing your entries and exits.*

Some additional warnings about FA and the need to combine it with TA include:

1. Good FA is time consuming and very often inaccurate, even if you have the requisite background. Therefore, until you're experienced, you'll need to read a lot of analysis from professionals who have the time and skills to boil it down for you. Over time, you'll learn which analysts to follow on a regular basis. We recommend a few starting points for finding them in Appendix A.

2. Timing the effects of fundamentals on currency prices is very difficult—often impossible—due to the number of possible fundamental influences on forex prices. For example:
   • Many top analysts were calling for a drop in Japanese stocks years before they began their 20-year (and counting) decline around 1990.

• Similarly, the fundamental picture for Japanese and U.S. government bonds has been troubling for many years as both nations continue to pile on debt, yet neither has begun their anticipated long-term downtrend.

The problems of the Euro-zone (EZ) and of the excessive debt loads of the peripheral economies were known for years before a December 2009 default in tiny Dubai focused markets on sovereign debt trouble in the European Union (EU) and sparked the 2010 outbreak of Europe's sovereign debt and banking crisis. As of this writing, the seemingly "inevitable" wave of sovereign defaults has been repeatedly delayed since it was recognized in early 2010, as the ECB and Fed ignore their own rules and prior ways of operating in order to ward off economic collapse. For a variety of reasons that can't continue forever, no one can tell whether the end is a matter of weeks, years, or decades away. In other words, no matter how compelling our fundamental analysis may be, we don't open or close positions until price actually starts moving accordingly, because it often never does. That's because, in the words of legendary economist John Maynard Keynes: "The market can stay irrational longer than you can stay solvent."[2]

In sum, though fundamentals drive trends in the long term, we use TA to determine entries and exits. No matter how logical or inevitable a coming trend may appear to be, those who don't wait for technical confirmation that their predicted move has begun, risk losses from getting into a trade too early or too late.

However, anyone who trades purely based on TA (except perhaps for day traders), without any reference to the bigger fundamental picture, risks missing critical information that will not show up on a chart until it's too late.

For example, consider the EURUSD weekly chart shown in Figure 6.1.

For the period covered in Figure 6.1, based on simple technical evidence, it appears that we may be approaching another good buying opportunity because price is pulling back to a strong support level comprised of

• The 1.4000 level
• The well-established rising trend line from June 6, 2010

However, an awareness of how seriously the EU sovereign debt and banking crisis was worsening would likely cause a conservative trader to defer opening a long position. Greece's second bailout package was in doubt, a longer-term default looking more likely, and markets were

FIGURE 6.1 EURUSD Weekly Chart, May 30 to September 4, 2011
Source: MetaQuotes Software Corp.

expressing doubts about the creditworthiness of the other weaker EZ economies and of the stability of the EU banking system.

In the weeks that followed, that support didn't hold, and the EURUSD trend continued to follow the EU's deteriorating fundamentals lower, as shown in the chart in Figure 6.2.

Figure 6.3 is another example of why anyone except day traders needs to pay attention to fundamentals.

According to the EURCHF weekly chart in Figure 6.3, the pair is in a strong, well-established downtrend. This trend was halted by rumors of coming Swiss National Bank (SNB) intervention to prop up the Euro versus the Swiss Franc (CHF), which had become so strong it was hurting Swiss exports to the EZ. The rumors proved true when on September 6, the SNB began a massive EURCHF buying campaign aimed at pushing the pair up to 1.2000 and keeping it there.

Regardless of whether you believed this unilateral intervention would work, it was an important consideration for anyone contemplating opening a new long-term position in the EURCHF. It would be important for any U.S. dollar (USD) or Japanese Yen (JPY) trader because the CHF is a fellow safe haven currency. Until this intervention, the CHF had been the market's favorite safe haven currency in the prior months because

FIGURE 6.2   EURUSD Weekly Chart, May 30 to November 4, 2001
Source: MetaQuotes Software Corp.

FIGURE 6.3   EURCHF Weekly Chart, December 21, 2008, to September 11, 2011
Source: MetaQuotes Software Corp.

Switzerland's finances were better than those of the other safe haven currency nations, the United States and Japan. The SNB was taking away the long CHF trade, which would drive safe haven demand to the USD and JPY.

The point is that fundamental analysis matters because fundamental factors like those just cited are what ultimately drive longer term trends.

In sum, everyone but the day traders need a firm grasp of fundamental analysis, so here's an overview. As always, you can find lots more via an online search. For more on an overview of fundamental analysis, use search terms like:

- "Fundamental Analysis" AND forex.
- "Fundamental Analysis" AND forex trading.
- "Fundamental Analysis" AND long-term forex trends.
- Forex AND introduction, and after clicking on some search results, select sections on fundamental analysis.

For more on specific topics, substitute these for the forex-related terms in the above suggestions. See the Binary Options Appendix on the website for specific suggestions.

AN OVERVIEW OF FA: MAIN FUNDAMENTAL DRIVERS OF FOREX TRENDS

The eight classic fundamental drivers of forex trends are, in order of importance:

1. Overall risk appetite
2. Short-term interest rates
3. Macroeconomic data and indicators
4. Geopolitics
5. Capital and trade flows
6. Merger and acquisition (M&A) activity
7. Short-term illiquidity: A lack of buyers and sellers
8. Government and central bank special interventions in times of crisis

Let's look briefly at each one.

Overall Risk Appetite

The most influential fundamental factor that determines the fate of a currency pair in a given period is overall risk appetite, otherwise known as market sentiment or, in plain English, whether markets are feeling optimistic or pessimistic.

If they're feeling optimistic, be it over a period of hours, weeks, or longer, risk assets tend to rise and safe haven or safety assets tend to fall, and vice versa.

Here are the obvious questions:

- What creates this overall market sentiment?
- How do traders and investors gauge it? What do they watch to determine whether markets favor risk or safety assets at a given moment or planned holding period?

The purported causes of market optimism or pessimism are debated and discussed daily in the financial media. Over time, you'll develop your own preferred sources of news and analysis and will form your own opinions or at least a core group of analysts you trust. Sometimes the causes of the market's mood are clear, other times they aren't. However, the actual mood of the market is typically quite clear, even when its underlying cause is not. Look at the charts of the following risk appetite barometers, note the price action and trend, and you'll have a reliable picture of whether markets are optimistic (showing risk appetite) or pessimistic (showing risk aversion).

Risk Appetite Barometers   There are many, of varying degrees of effectiveness and sophistication. Here we'll provide just a few that are very easy to use and find. They usually provide a reliable picture of whether markets are feeling optimistic or pessimistic. That information in turn can tell you a lot about how almost any asset class should be performing in a given period.

- The S&P 500 Index (S&P 500)
- Major sovereign bond prices or Credit Default Swap (CDS) spreads
- Indexes of the major currencies
- Growth-related commodity prices like copper and oil
- Gold and silver for gauging confidence in the most widely held forms of cash, the USD and EUR

The S&P 500 Index (S&P 500)   If I had to choose one measure of market sentiment, this would be it. If it's moving higher, expect risk assets and currencies (led by the AUD, then NZD, CAD, EUR and GBP) to follow it higher. Expect safe haven assets and currencies (led by the JPY, then USD and CHF) to do the opposite and move lower.

For a variety of reasons, major stock indices are considered the single most important indicator of global risk appetite. Though there is some room for debate about which index is best in which circumstances, the S&P 500, the largest cap index of the world's largest economy, tends to be the most popular single barometer of risk, and it also enjoys a degree of self-fulfilling prophecy power. In other words, markets follow it intensively, so it has influence. Its big drawback is that though its futures may trade around the clock, the index itself is open only during EST work hours. If you trade during Asian or European market hours, you'll want to choose a leading index for that market as a supplement, like the Nikkei, Shanghai, or Hang Seng (Hong Kong) for Asia, or the Deutscher Aktien Index (DAX), CAC for Europe, or one of the numerous composite indexes for these regions.

Global indexes tend to move together over time, so no matter which ones you choose, you'll tend to get the same general result over the course of a few days. The trading day starts in Asia, followed by Europe, then the Americas. Each region's major index's "default behavior" is to continue in the direction of the region before it, unless they encounter either

- important news that changes market sentiment
- significant technical s/r levels that block further progress as traders believe the current picture is now fully priced in and doesn't yet justify a break past these levels.

For example, if U.S. stock indexes close strongly, we would expect Asia to open strong and stay that way unless they either hit significantly negative news or significant resistance levels that prompt selling from profit takers and short sellers.

Here's an example of how forex markets are influenced by the major stock indexes. These indexes are risk assets. Some currencies move up and down with these and other risk assets, and so are called risk currencies. Some behave in the opposite way, and so are called safety or safe haven currencies.

Here again is the table (shown earlier) of how they rank on the risk to safety spectrum.

RISK						SAFE HAVEN	
RISK CURRENCIES					SAFE HAVEN CURRENCIES		
AUD	NZD	CAD	EUR	GBP	CHF	USD	JPY

Thus when the S&P 500 is higher, we expect to see currencies that are higher on the risk spectrum (like the AUD and NZD) outperforming lower-risk and safe haven currencies like the JPY and USD. When the index is falling, we'd expect the opposite.

Again, the rankings are a useful guide, not an ironclad rule. Currencies rarely perform exactly as their risk ranking over the short term because daily or weekly events can influence one or more specific currencies more than others.

For example, in Figure 6.4, even though risk appetite as per the S&P 500 (top) was in a mild downtrend in early September, the more risk-sensitive AUDUSD performed better than the EURUSD, a relatively safer haven pair, which dropped more sharply. Why? Most of the bad news

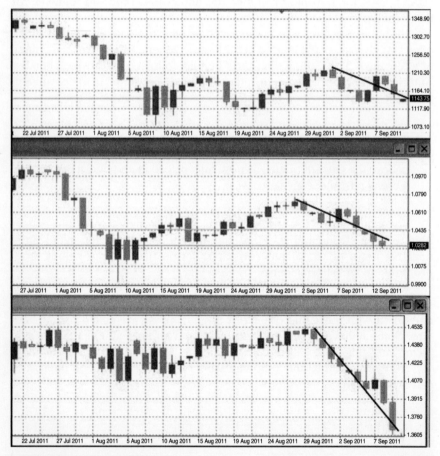

FIGURE 6.4 Daily Charts of S&P 500 (top), AUDUSD (middle), and EURUSD (bottom), July 22 to September 7, 2011
Source: MetaQuotes Software Corp.

was related to the EU debt and banking crisis, which hit the EUR particularly harder than the AUD.

Major Sovereign Bond Prices or CDS Spreads Since the advent of the EU debt crisis in early 2010 and rising risk of numerous sovereign defaults, these have been critical barometers of anxiety about the solvency of specific states, the EU in general, and the very survival of the EUR and Euro-zone as we know it., Unless you hear otherwise, discussions of bond prices, yields, and CDS spreads (measures of default insurance cost) focus on the benchmark 10-year bonds (or more technically speaking, bills). Though they are not the headline numbers like the major stock indexes, you can find their price data and charts easily enough on any major financial media outlet. Top-rated bonds are classic safe haven assets and as such move in the opposite direction of stocks. As with stocks, the U.S.-based barometer, the 10-year Treasury bond (technically, a Treasury bill), is the most widely followed indicator of bond prices and yields though German Bunds and Japanese government bonds are also followed. Sovereign bonds of major economic powers have long been considered to be the ultimate safe haven asset, and U.S. bonds are first among these due to various factors, the first of which is the liquidity (availability) of U.S. bonds and stability of the U.S. economy. Even the loss of the AAA rating from S&P 500 hasn't changed that. Because the EU crisis has been the single greatest threat to the global economy, the bond prices and yields of the EU nations that have been in greatest danger of economic collapse and insolvency (Greece, Italy, Ireland, Portugal, and Spain, aka the GIIPS or PIIGS) have also become important risk barometers.

Here's a brief bit of background information for those not familiar with the basics of bonds. A bond's periodic coupon payment is fixed. Thus when a bond's price falls, its yield rises, and vice versa. One of the main reasons (we'll ignore the others for the sake of simplicity) bond prices fall is when they're deemed riskier so changes in creditworthiness of the bond's issuer can be expressed in terms of bond prices or yields. The terms are used interchangeably. For example, if one media outlet reports that Italian bond yields are rising and another says Italian bond prices are falling, they're reporting on the same thing with the same implication—falling confidence in Italy's creditworthiness and thus its rising borrowing costs.

Related to these are CDS (credit default swap) spreads, which are the difference or spreads between the cost of insuring a bond against default versus the cost of insuring some safer benchmark bond (like German Bunds). The higher the spread or difference between CDS (default insurance) cost of a given bond versus the safer benchmark bond like the German Bund, the riskier the bond. When there are questions about the solvency of individual sovereign states or large companies, CDS spreads serve as a barometer of market confidence in them.

Rising spreads for the bonds of a given sovereign state or private business indicate that confidence is falling in that entity's creditworthiness. For example, throughout the EU crisis, the CDS spreads of the bonds of the weaker EU members and the major EU banks became a prime barometer of the state of the EU and EUR. When a given country's bond yield or CDS spread started spiking, that signaled the country was in trouble.

Taken together, the movements of both the stock indexes and CDS spreads of the GIIPS or other Euro-zone nations have literally defined the level of fear or calm about the EU debt crisis. Because the EU crisis has been the dominant driver of the dominant fundamental market driver-overall market sentiment or risk appetite, these two measures have been among the very most important barometers, even drivers, of market sentiment. As long as the EU crisis remains unresolved, a spike in Spanish bond yields or CDS spreads can send markets plunging; a drop in Italian bond yields or CDS spreads can spark a global rally. While changes in CDS spreads are a superb barometer of debt crisis related fear, they suffer from one significant disadvantage. Unlike the other risk barometers, it's harder to find free sources for tracking their daily changes. The popular financial press mostly ignores them except to mention when specific ones are making dramatic moves related to the EU debt crisis.

There are two subscription services that do provide a degree of free information:

- cmavision.com
- Markit.com

Check these sites for their current free and subscription offerings.

Indexes of the Major Currencies   The relative performance of risk or safe haven currencies provides a quick look at risk appetite.

The USD has its own index. Because the USD is a safe haven currency, a rising USD index is a sign of pessimism and vice versa. Its usefulness is somewhat limited by its structure, which only includes certain currencies, each given a specific weighting. Each major currency has at least one ETF that tracks its performance, though you need to check whether that ETF compares that currency to the USD or to a basket of currencies.

A more demanding but more thorough way to check the performance of a given currency is by comparing charts of its different pairings in one window. Most decent charting platforms, provided free from forex brokers when you have an account with them, allow you to do that.

For example, on the popular Metatrader 4 charting software, I set up a special USD "profile" window, which shows me how the dollar is fairing versus other majors, as shown in Figures 6.5 and 6.6.

Considering that the USD is a safe haven currency, what do the charts tell us about risk appetite? The USD gained against all the currencies that are higher on the risk spectrum, and this tells us this was a "risk off"

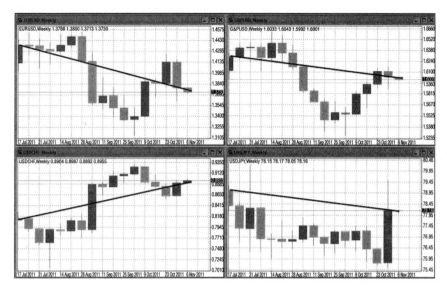

FIGURE 6.5 Clockwise: EURUSD, GBPUSD, USDCHF, and USDJPY Weekly Charts
Source: MetaQuotes Software Corp.

period. As we see from the S&P 500 chart (Figure 6.4 top), that was indeed the case.

As a side note, the USDCHF and USDJPY charts are another illustration of how charts alone don't provide enough of a basis for a trade, and that you need to attempt an understanding of what fundamentals are behind them. The USDCHF showed a spike higher in early September 2011, and the USDJPY did the same thing later that November. Both of these spikes radically altered the trend. What happened? Both price spikes were due to central banks, the Swiss National Bank, and the Bank of Japan (BOJ) selling the CHF and JPY to devalue them after the strength of these currencies had become a hindrance to their nations' exports.

Growth-Related Commodity Prices Like Copper and Oil Copper is often referred to as "Dr. Copper" because copper prices are supposed to accurately diagnose economic activity given copper's widespread applications in manufacturing, infrastructure, and other growth-related activities. Oil consumption is tied tightly to market perceptions of the future pace of economic activity. When investors believe better times are coming, prices of growth-related commodities tend to rise. Their big disadvantage is that at times their prices are subject to temporary manipulation by big players or speculators rather than by genuine supply and demand.

Gold and Silver for Gauging Confidence in the Most Widely Held Forms of Cash, the USD and EUR Contrary to popular belief and what you

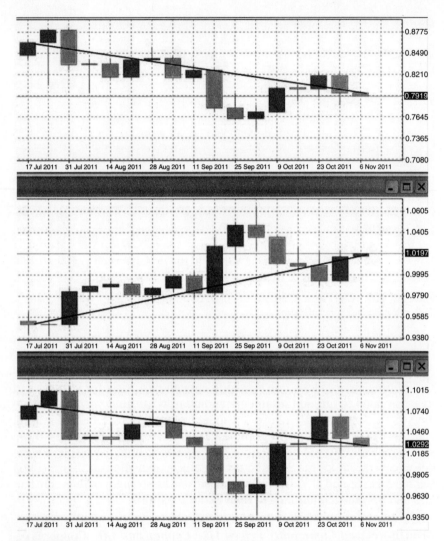

FIGURE 6.6 Top to Bottom: NZDUSD, USDCAD, and AUDUSD Weekly Charts
Source: MetaQuotes Software Corp.

see in most of the financial press, gold is neither a safety nor a risk asset. Instead, it is an inflation hedge that rises and falls with the level of fears about inflation and confidence in the value of fiat money (currency not backed by any hard asset).[3]

When markets are pessimistic about either the USD, EUR, or both (rare but can happen), gold tends to rise and vice versa. See Chapter 9, the section on intermarket analysis, for details on this correlation and how you can use it. I've written extensively on the causes and interpretation of gold price movements. Just use the search term: Cliff Wachtel AND Gold to find further details and applications of the concepts covered here and in Chapter 9 regarding gold.

Again, the previous list of risk barometers is a partial list meant to include some of the most popular and easily accessible measures of risk appetite. There are many others, like rail traffic, Dow theory-related indicators, the Baltic shipping index, and so on, all worth research as time and priorities permit.

The previous sentiment barometers generally apply to all major asset markets. As we'll discuss later, having a basic awareness of intermarket analysis, how and why different asset classes tend to move in similar or opposite directions, is something you'll need to learn.

Though market sentiment may be the most influential fundamental driver of currency and other asset prices, there is no single universally agreed-upon means of measuring it, and in the end, it's really an aggregate result of a combination of other fundamental factors.

Now let's move on to more specific and easier to measure fundamental drivers of asset prices.

Short-Term Interest Rates

After overall market sentiment, the single most influential driver of currency prices is central bank benchmark interest rates and any data that change expectations about the direction, timing, or size of increases or decreases in these benchmark short-term rates. Indeed, one could argue that most of the other fundamental drivers of currency prices that follow below are influential only to the extent that they influence interest rate expectations or the rates themselves. They are influential because rising yields allow traders to profit in two ways:

1. "Carry Trade" profiting on interest rate differences between currencies.
2. Capital appreciation (much of that driven by carry trade).

Carry Trade: Forex for Income Investors One reason that interest rates influence currency pair movements is carry trade. We'll return to carry trading in Chapter 12, but here are the basics so you can understand how interest rates affect demand for a currency via carry trade.

The carry of an asset is the return or cost from holding it due to related interest rates. Whenever you buy or sell a currency pair, your broker credits your account for the interest you earn at the prevailing short-term rate for the currency you bought. The broker also debits your account for the interest you owe on the currency you sold because, as covered in Chapter 2, you borrowed that currency to pay for the one you bought.

The goal of carry trading is to earn income on the interest rate difference between two currencies by either:

1. Buying a currency pair with a higher interest rate base currency (the one on the left) and lower interest rate counter currency (the one on the right).

2. Selling a pair with a higher interest counter currency and lower interest base currency.

In either case, the investor earns interest income on the difference between the two yields. The more leverage used, the more daily income earned because you get paid based on the total amount controlled and not on the margin deposit.

For example, let's say we buy the AUDJPY using 100:1 leverage, committing a $1,000 margin deposit to control 100,000 AUD (see Chapter 2 if these terms are unfamiliar). If the Reserve Bank of Australia's benchmark annual rate for the AUD is 4.75 percent per year, and the BOJ's is 0.10 percent for the JPY, then those holding the AUDJPY earn a net return of 4.65 percent per year.

The rate differential is magnified by the leverage. Using 100:1 leverage with a $1,000 margin deposit to control $100,000 of AUD via having borrowed $100,000 of JPY (as covered in Chapter 2), that annual income is based on the full $100,000 of AUD controlled and not the $1,000 margin deposit. The annual income here is 4.65 percent of $100,000 or $4,650, (paid out on a daily basis) using $1,000 allocated to that position, meaning a 465 percent return before considering changes in the AUDJPY's price.

The net return of 4.65 percent per year is on the interest, before considering changes in the price of the pair.

There lies the high risk. If the JPY starts appreciating against the AUD, at a high leverage of say, 100:1 (a 1 percent move brings a 100 percent profit or loss), an entire year's interest income is quickly wiped out. For leveraged carry trades to work, the higher-yielding currency needs to hold steady or appreciate against the lower-yielding currency.

When risk assets are trending higher, this trade is a real win-win situation as you gain interest income and capital appreciation.

Carry Trade Requires Flat or Rising Risk Asset Trends
Because higher yielding currencies are risk rather than safe haven currencies, carry trade only works when risk assets, and hence higher

yielding currencies, are flat or rising. That's because any drop in the price for the currency you're holding via leverage will usually outweigh your income gains. Carry trades work best when risk assets are in long-term uptrends, and carry trades can be held for long periods if your account has enough capital to handle the normal price swings. If not, you can settle for shorter holding periods and move in and out long positions in carry trade pairs (discussed later in Chapter 11) as you would with any trade, picking up income when the pair is trending higher or flat as long as you use the full RAMM techniques to keep losses low relative to gains from interest and price appreciation.

Higher Yields Support Demand Because They Discourage Short Positions   For example, this interest rate differential not only encourages traders to be long high-yield differential pairs like the AUDJPY whenever possible for the sake of the interest income, it also discourages shorting the pair because that would involve owning the low-yield JPY while needing to pay much higher interest for the borrowed AUD. In other words, a trader shorting the AUDJPY must pay out 4.65 percent annual interest on a daily basis while holding a short AUDJPY position. For the big institutions that do much of the total trading volume and trade in huge blocks of currency pairs, that daily carry charge becomes a material consideration.

Capital Appreciation   The other reason that interest rates are the single biggest fundamental driver of currency prices is that, all things being equal, the higher the yield, the higher the demand for a given currency. (As always, there are exceptions to this rule.)

In addition to the support lent from carry trade, and from the higher cost of shorting high yielding currencies, higher interest rates by their very nature raise demand for a given currency, because:

1. Higher yields tend to suggest higher growth as central banks raise interest rates to keep healthy growth from becoming too rapid and causing inflation.

2. Assets denominated in that currency, like bonds and commercial paper, will yield higher returns than comparable assets denominated in currencies with lower central bank benchmark rates. That's because central bank rates are for relatively low-risk assets, and so as these rise they push up yields on higher-risk assets.

For example, the primary driver behind the EURUSD uptrend in the spring of 2011 (in Figure 6.7) was that the European Central Bank (ECB) was expected to raise its benchmark short-term interest rate in April and

FIGURE 6.7 EURUSD Daily Chart, February 23 to May 3, 2011
Source: MetaQuotes Software Corp.

later in the year. At the same time, the Fed was expected to leave its rates unchanged at much lower levels.[4] Though the EU sovereign debt crisis was worsening, there were no immediate threats of defaults and markets focused on the shorter-term benefit of carry trade income from being long the EURUSD.

All else being equal, currencies with a higher benchmark overnight lending rate will be in demand and in an uptrend versus currencies with lower rates, unless markets turn pessimistic. In risk off environments, higher yielding currencies tend to sell off versus the lower yielders, as carry traders close their positions, selling high-yield currencies and buying lower yielders.

What Drives Short-Term Interest Rates? Why do central banks change short-term interest rates? Generally speaking, they lower them to stimulate growth, and they raise them to keep inflation low. Their benchmark overnight lending rate is typically an attempt to strike a balance between these two needs. Economic conditions determine which need takes priority. In bad times, promoting growth is usually the main concern, hence lower rates. In good times, cooling inflation is the priority, hence higher rates. It's common to see nations with stronger economies have stronger currencies because their central banks will be raising rates, both to minimize inflation threats and to buy themselves more room to lower rates (which encourages growth) when their economies weaken.

From a trading perspective, forex movements are more influenced by changes in market expectations about the direction or pace of rate change than actual rate changes themselves (which are usually anticipated and already priced in when they actually do occur). For example, imagine central banks A and B announce equal interest rate increases. Currency A shoots higher, and currency B sells off. Why? The two most common reasons would be:

1. The rate hike for currency B was expected and priced in, whereas for currency A, it was a surprise and markets view it as more valuable and bid up its price.

2. For whatever the reasons (usually correct), markets believe the rate hike from central bank A is just one in an ongoing series of future rate increases. However, for currency B, markets believe the rate hike will not be followed by further increases, or worse, the next move may be rate cuts, so it's time to take profits and sell currency B.

This situation is analogous to earnings announcements for equities. Whether or not a given stock rises after its quarterly earnings announcement depends on both whether the announcement beats expectations and whether it raises or lowers expectations for the future. Even if a company reports stellar results, if it doesn't beat analysts' expectations, or if the company issues lower guidance for coming quarters, the stock is likely to sell off, because markets reflect expectations about the future. News that affects interest rate expectations affects currencies just like news that affects earnings expectations influences stocks. If expectations remain unchanged, the currency is likely to remain stable versus others currencies. If expectations are lowered, the currency is likely to fall.

Similarly, any change in conditions that suggests a central bank is more or less likely to change its rate policy can also influence interest rate expectations and thus forex prices.

For example:

• Inflation data influences rate expectations because rising inflation makes central banks more likely to raise interest rates in order to keep inflation acceptably low.

- Reports related to growth, like jobs, spending, or GDP influence rate expectations because strong growth makes central banks more likely to raise rates, both to minimize the risks of inflation that can come with faster growth, and to buy themselves room to cut rates when growth slows.

Indeed, it's no exaggeration to say that the importance of a given, new item is typically a function of how strongly it's believed to influence central bank interest rate decisions.

In sum, expectations of rising rates are a reliable and potent fuel for higher currency prices, and expectations of falling rates are the opposite.

What causes market expectations around rates about to change? Funny you should ask.

Watch Monthly Central Bank Announcements on Rates and Economic Outlook   Central banks issue monthly rate statements along with their views about economic conditions. Though many data points influence market expectations about rate changes, none are as important as the monthly central banks' comments on its outlook for the economy.

Though changes in rates don't occur that often and are rarely surprises when they do (markets are good at predicting them), the real newsworthy events are these comments about their economies because they contain hints about the gradual evolution of central bank policy. These alone can move markets. Any subtle change in the wording from prior months that hints of changing rate policy will be widely reported and can be enough to move a given currency or group of currencies as in these examples:

- On March 3, 2011, ECB President Jean-Claude Trichet convinced markets that he'd raise interest rates the following month by adding the phrase "strong vigilance" to his comments on the ECB's attitude toward fighting inflation.
- On September 8, 2011, when commenting on Trichet's post-monetary policy meeting press conference, Kathy Lien of Bkassetmanagement .com wrote:

> *EUR/USD bulls were sorely disappointed when Trichet said uncertainty in the market was unusually high. The number of times that he used the words "downside risks" in his statement reflects his degree of concern about the outlook for the Eurozone economy and drove the EUR/USD below 1.40. He used the words "downside risks" 2 times more than August.... The tone of Trichet's press conference makes crystal clear that not only is he done with raising interest rates but the central bank as a whole has now moved to a more dovish stance.*[5]

Note her careful attention to such subtle details like the number of times Trichet used the words "downside risks." She was clearly studying his prior statement to the press and was comparing it to the current one line by line. This alertness to subtle wording changes in central bank statements is common among forex analysts because both central banks and analysts understand that these subtle changes in wording are how central banks communicate to the markets (although some are moving to more explicit communication in the future).

Anything That Influences Central Bank Rate Policy Influences Forex Markets   That markets can and do move on such subtle hints again underscores how it isn't fundamentals that move markets but rather the markets' collective perceptions of them. It highlights the power central banks have to influence forex and other markets. So, it's no surprise that anything that might influence central bank policy may influence forex and other financial markets regardless of whether it has any immediate impact on the economy.

What influences central bank policy? Again, funny you should ask.

MACROECONOMIC DATA AND INDICATORS

These influence currency prices because they're barometers of the following:

- The health of the underlying economy: That means increased demand for that economy's currency from exports and foreign investment in local hard assets like businesses and real estate.
- The direction of interest rates and central bank policy: As noted earlier, faster growth makes inflation more likely and thus further rate increases more likely because:
  - Central banks use rate increases to reduce inflation risk
  - They like to raise rates in times of growth to allow room to lower rates when their economies start slowing and need a boost.

Example: EURUSD Uptrend Reverses in Late 2009 as Data Show Europe Slows, U.S. Grows

From early March until December 4, 2009, the EUR/USD had a strong uptrend but that trend stalled between November 26 and December 4, reversed hard, and the dollar began to gain against the EUR (see Figure 6.8).

Here's why.

FIGURE 6.8 EURUSD Daily Chart, August 11, 2009, to January 28, 2010
Source: MetaQuotes Software Corp.

On November 26, 2009, Dubai announced that $59 billion in government-related bonds were at risk of default, which in turn caused markets to focus on the creditworthiness of a number of other potential sovereign default risks in the EZ (Euro-zone), lowering expectations for EZ growth and benchmark interest rates.

On December 4, 2009, the United States reported employment data, which were vastly better than forecasted and which raised expectations for U.S. growth, spending, and interest rate increases. The following week on Dec 11, those expectations were confirmed by consumer spending data that were much better than expected. The U.S. economy still had troubles galore, from weak jobs and housing to troubled banks, yet the EU was looking worse.

Over the coming month, credit rating downgrades to Greece and Spain, with more threatened, further weakened EZ growth expectations, sending the pair lower.

This example underscores a key point about currency strength—that it's truly all relative. You don't have to find a currency with a perfect underlying economy, just one with an economy that's improving relative to that of another against which it's traded. Both the U.S. and EU economies (with some exceptions) had deep problems that would not be solved soon.

In short, the underlying fundamentals of a currency don't have to be objectively good, just better than enough of the others and voilà, you have an uptrending currency.

Which fundamental data are most important? Here are some guidelines:

The more directly it affects interest rate expectations, the more influential it is: Because economic conditions change, some indicators become important to central bank policy.

What most affects rate expectations varies over time and place: During recessions, when inflation is less of a concern, growth-related data like GDP, jobs, consumer spending, etc., become most important. In boom times, when inflation is more of a concern, inflation data like the CPI and PPI become more important.

If the central bank of a large economy indicates what macroeconomic data are most important in guiding its rate policy, these data become a market focus. For example, throughout the recession that began in 2007

- The U.S. Federal Reserve said that jobs and spending data were its main guides for when it could begin raising rates, so these reports took on added prominence.
- Whereas fast growing China's central bank was most concerned about inflation, so Chinese inflation data took on special importance. Data that suggested higher inflation meant more steps to slow China's economy, which would be bad for global growth as China was the primary growth engine in the world.

Thus monthly U.S. jobs and spending data as well Chinese inflation were especially strong market moving data. Why were United States and Chinese data so influential? Take a wild guess, then read on.

The larger the economy, the more important the data: Major fundamental data from the largest economies like the United States, the European Union, China, and Japan are more influential on global economic health, and forex markets than data of smaller economies like Switzerland, New Zealand, or Canada (beyond their effects on the related forex pairs).

Influence varies with type of economy: For export-based economies like Japan and Brazil, Russia, India, and China (the BRIC nations), data on exports and industrial production are more important than for nations for which GDP is more based on consumer spending and financial products like the United States and United Kingdom.

Rather than focusing on each of the key fundamentals, we'll provide a brief listing of the macroeconomic indicators and data to watch and research as needed. Details of these may vary from country to country. You'll find abundant free resources about them online. You need not memorize them. Rather, check any good online economic calendar like those of ForexFactory.com and DailyFX.com. These rank events by importance and include explanations of the significance of the data. ForexFactory.com's calendar is better on the general significance, and DailyFX's explanations are at times specifically updated to reflect specifics about the current announcement.

- Quarterly Gross Domestic Product (GDP): Typically, there is an advanced or preliminary reading about four weeks after the quarter ends, and a final one about three months after the quarter ends. The preliminary reading is what carries the most influence because the final reading rarely deviates from it.
- Monthly jobs reports: Again, the more important the economy, the more important the report. Jobs take on even greater significance in economies like the United States or United Kingdom, where consumer spending is a more important component of GDP than manufacturing or exports.
- Monthly retail sales: Same as above.
- Inflation data: Typically monthly CPI and PPI.
- Purchasing Manager's Index (PMI) for both manufacturing and service sectors: The key point is that a reading over 50 suggests expansion, and under 50 suggests contraction. They provide a measure of the health of manufacturing and service sectors, respectively.
- Housing data: This includes a range of monthly reports like housing starts, new home sales, existing home sales, new building permits, etc. Considered an indicator of what stage the economy is in within the current business cycle. It is also a sign of the health of the banking sector and consumer lending, consumer spending, and jobs, given the significant impact housing has for these sectors. Remember that the Great Recession that began in 2007 started with irresponsible and excessive mortgage lending that created a real estate bubble ending in what became known as the subprime crisis. This in turn lead to a banking solvency and liquidity crisis, which spread and essentially crashed much of the developed world's economies.

Again, you could follow more indicators and reports, but these are enough to get you started. As you develop your trading style and preferred news and analysis sources, you'll develop your own list.

Geopolitics

Though all financial markets can be influenced by major geopolitical events like news of political instability in key countries or military actions, few are as sensitive as the forex market because of its extremely international nature. Of course, certain currencies and their related pairs will be especially sensitive to related local developments. As stock prices reflect market sentiment about companies, so do currencies for countries. Thus, they are responsive to geopolitical changes insofar as these affect expectations for interest rates, growth, trade and capital flows, and so on for the underlying economies.

Because the professional traders who manage the big money in forex focus first on risk management (take the hint, so should you), the first rule of trading based on geopolitical unrest is that markets tend to sell first and ask questions later. In other words, markets are prone to volatility in times of serious unrest. Remember, whenever professionals fear any threat to their capital, they quickly retreat into cash, especially safe haven currencies, until the political risk fades.

In sum, a general rule of thumb in all kinds of financial markets including forex is that politics usually trumps economics. In other words, very good or bad geopolitical data tend to outweigh economic data.

Capital and Trade Flows

Another key factor in analyzing the demand for a given currency is whether the underlying economy is more dependent on trade flow or capital flow. In other words, is the economy based more on exports or attracting foreign investment? Trade flow refers to a country's income from trade, i.e., exports. Capital flow refers to how much investment it draws from abroad. Export-oriented economies depend more on trade flows, and countries more focused on financial industries are more dependent on capital flows.

The export-oriented economies, whose currency strength depends on their trade flows include:

- Canada: oil, gas
- Australia: industrial and precious metals
- New Zealand: agricultural products, particularly dairy products
- China, Japan, and Germany: finished high value-added manufactured goods, heavy industry

In contrast, for the United States and United Kingdom, which have large liquid investment markets, capital flows are of far greater significance. In these countries, financial services are a larger part of GDP compared to the export nations. For example, in the United States, financial services contributed about 40 percent of the total profits of the S&P 500. No wonder the economic crisis that began in the summer of 2007 in the United States and spread worldwide originated in the U.S. banking sector with the subprime mortgage lending crisis.

All recent U.S. economic downturns (which usually become global due to the size of the U.S. economy) originated out of the financial sector, particularly bank lending (Latin American debt crisis of the early 1980s, savings and loan crisis of the early 1990s, the dot-com stock market collapse in 2001, and the subprime mortgage lending crisis of 2007).

The United States exemplifies why it is critical to understand which kinds of flows affect which country. Given America's trade and current account deficit, one would think the USD would be worth little. However, throughout the past decades, the USD has performed much better than that. The United States' highly liquid, diverse, relatively well-regulated, and transparent capital markets allowed it to attract more than enough surplus capital from the rest of the world to offset the negative effects of its massive trade deficits. If, however, the United States should suddenly cease attracting adequate capital flows to balance its trade and current account deficits, the USD would likely plunge. Badly.

There are two basic kinds of capital flows:

1. From investment in physical assets like factories, real estate, and businesses.
2. From investment in financial assets like equities and bonds or other debt instruments.

Indeed, it's possible to view financial products as just another kind of product sold that builds demand for the local currency, just like exports of tangible goods. The result is the same: steady demand for the local currency.

Here's another example of how capital flows can affect a currency pair. During part of 2009, as part of its economic stimulus program, the Japanese government allowed Japanese exporters to repatriate profits earned abroad at reduced tax rates. As the deadline for this reduced rate approached, pressure increased on the USDJPY because whenever the pair would rise (i.e., the USD would go up relative to the JPY), dollar-loaded Japanese exporters would sell some of their accumulated piles of U.S. dollars and buy bargain-priced yen.

Merger and Acquisition (M&A) Activity

Remember how we warned earlier that short-term price moves can be unpredictable because they are driven by short-term money flows that are often impossible to foresee? Here's one reason why. Merger and acquisi-tion (M&A) activity can be the most powerful force behind near-term cur-rency moves, even though it's the least significant long-term driver of forex prices. M&A activity refers to when a company from one economic region wants to buy a corporation or large capital asset like a division of a com-pany or a major real estate acquisition in another currency.

For example, if an Asian company wanted to buy an American asset for $30 billion, it would have to go into the currency market and acquire U.S. dollars to pay for it. Typically, these deals are time sensitive because the acquirer has a contract to pay by a certain date. This time pressure can cause a sudden spike in demand for a given currency, so M&A flow can exert a strong albeit temporary force on FX trading, sometimes influencing currency prices for days or weeks as the buyer attempts to buy slowly to prevent a self-inflicted loss from rising conversion costs. It may continue longer because certain market conditions can promote a wave of such pur-chases. For example, when a booming economy in one country leaves its companies flush with their native currency that is suddenly unusually high versus another currency, assets denominated in that cheaper currency are at bargain prices, resulting in a wave of acquisitions and a spike in demand for the cheaper currency. Look at these examples:

- In the late 1980s and early 1990s, Asian buyers became significant ac-quirers of major U.S. assets such as film and music companies, and landmark real estate projects like New York's Rockefeller Center.
- In the fall of 2006, Canada surprised markets, announcing that the pop-ular Canadian income trusts would lose their tax-advantaged status. The Harper government exacerbated the situation by not grandfather-ing any of the long-term investors who held positions in income trusts. The next day, despite the lack of good USD news, the USDCAD rose as traders dumped the CAD in anticipation of tens of billions in in-vestment capital fleeing Canadian stocks. Most of the companies were healthy, and it was years before the law took effect. Again, politics trumped economics.

Short-Term Illiquidity: A Lack of Buyers and Sellers

Periodically, typically in the final days or hours before long weekends or holidays, the number of traders drops off sharply as they head home to start vacations early. That can mean quiet uneventful trading. It can cause wild price movements should a sudden imbalance occur between buyers and sellers as is the case when major surprises hit illiquid markets.

For example, on Wednesday afternoon (EST) November 26, 2009, most traders in the United States and the Middle East had already ceased

FIGURE 6.9   EURUSD Daily Chart, September 7 to November 10, 2009
Source: MetaQuotes Software Corp.

trading for holidays in both regions. Then came a shocking announcement of a major bond default concerning the Dubai government's sovereign investment fund. Whether or not the timing of the announcement was intentional, the resulting price movements were exaggerated by the lack of buyers for suddenly unwanted risk currencies and of sellers of the newly desired safe haven currencies.

As shown in Figure 6.9, risk currency pairs like the EURUSD were in strong uptrends at the time. Indeed the EURUSD was at a multiyear high and had just made another strong move higher. Yet the announcement brought a sharp reversal even though, on the surface, the Dubai debt could be seen as a minor event. For those seeking to take profits on the high EURUSD, few buyers were on hand, and the move down was significant and signaled a longer-term drop in the EURUSD.

Because low liquidity can amplify volatility if surprises occur, many traders will avoid trading on known low liquidity days though they can provide great bargains from panicked sellers.

Government and Central Bank Special Interventions in Times of Crisis

One of the most enduring lessons of the "Great Recession" that began in the summer of 2007 is that in desperate times governments will take desperate measures that by definition are unique and thus unpredictable.

After the subprime crisis in the United States morphed into a global banking crisis with the fall of Lehman Brothers and global markets appeared to be at the brink of the abyss in early 2009, intensive government intervention produced a rally in risk assets that lasted until late 2009, with the start of the EU sovereign debt and banking crisis.

In the fall of 2010, when it appeared that risk asset markets might again be in trouble, the U.S. Federal Reserve Bank (Fed) came riding to the rescue with a new stimulus plan, called QE 2. Risk asset markets perceived this would provide at least a temporary boost for risk assets.

In July 2011, when the EU sovereign debt and banking crisis worsened, a series of policy blunders caused too-big-to-bail Italy's bond yields to spike. For the rest of 2011 and in to 2012, markets started moving mostly with speculation about what EU and U.S. officials would do to prevent the EU crisis from going global.

Indeed, as of this writing in mid-2012, the policies of the central banks of the largest economies, the Fed, ECB, PBOC, BoJ, and so on have arguably become more influential than any time in the past half century.

NEWS TRADING: DAY TRADING BASED ON SHORT-TERM FUNDAMENTALS

The only day traders with any interest in fundamentals are news traders, those who base trades off of major news announcements. Like any other forex day trading:

- It's mostly based on technical analysis and methodologies, with news serving as the catalyst.
- Few succeed at it though some claim to prosper handsomely from it.
- Like most investors, this not my area of preference or expertise, so I can only advise you to treat this like any other form of day trading. Study it well, and don't risk much money on it until you've built a method and track record, first on practice accounts and then with small positions using real money.

I'll mention a few points to get you started. From there, you can find plenty of online material, often free. The same prior warnings about day trading forex apply.

What News Traders Watch

Certain news items change expectations about these and can move markets within moments of their announcement. Here is a list of news items that can move markets within minutes and tend to be most followed by news traders.

This list was prepared based on the behavior of the USD as of the time of this writing, but it applies to the economic news of any currency, and only the names of the reports may vary somewhat from country to country:

- Any major geopolitical event: For example, political unrest or heightened military tensions involving in a major economy or commodity supplier (especially oil) will have an impact.
- Threats to global banking: Every global recession of the past 40 + years began in some form in the banking sector. Big bank failures tend to make markets nervous, especially if they signal that third parties could be destabilized because they, too, have third parties that could suffer, and voila, a spreading banking crisis or contagion.[6]
- Monthly jobs reports: Nonfarm payrolls change month to month, unemployment rate, and so on, can have an impact.
- Central Bank interest rate announcements and comments on economic outlook.
- GDP (preliminary, not final reading).
- Inflation (CPI, PPI).
- Consumer spending: Retail sales, personal spending.
- Housing: New and existing home sales, building permits, and so forth.
- Durable goods orders.
- Business sentiment: PMI for nonmanufacturing and service sectors, etc. Within these, pay attention to the price (indicates degree of inflation) and employment (an advance indicator of nonfarm payroll direction) components, or at least what your preferred commentators say about them.
- Consumer Confidence Report: Like the Conference Board and University of Michigan Consumer Confidence.
- Industrial Production: Most important for export-oriented economies.

Again, the relative importance of economic data changes with time and circumstances. For example, during the ongoing recession that began in 2007, all major central banks cut interest rates and increased money supply to stimulate growth. These may have been necessary steps to help their economies, but they made financial assets like currencies less attractive to hold and more prone to losing purchasing power.

Thus, the more a news item had the power to change expectations about the rate and extent of stimulus withdrawal or interest rate increases, the more it influenced currency markets. In the early 1990s, however, U.S. trade balance was a foremost concern for dollar traders and a major market mover.

As noted earlier, the more influence something is believed to have on short-term interest rates or growth expectations, the greater its market moving potential. For example, because markets understood that the Fed wouldn't raise rates until there was a significant and sustained improvement in the monthly jobs and consumer spending reports, those reports became especially important.

FA BASICS: EASY TO UNDERSTAND AND HARD TO APPLY

As with technical analysis, take rules for fundamental analysis to be guidelines and not absolutes. Because all of the preceding and other factors are endlessly exerting influence in the markets to varying degrees, basing trades on fundamentals is not recommended except for those planning long holding periods who aren't concerned with buying as low as they can or selling at near-term highs.

The price of a given currency pair is the product of numerous forces acting on it at any one time.

For example, though news that raises expectations about rate increases for the EUR should mean the EURUSD rises, enough bad news for the EUR can overwhelm the good news. How much bad news is enough to override rising rate expectations? No one one can easily say; it's a matter of watching how markets respond.

We saw such a thing happen in the spring and summer of 2011 with the EURUSD. As noted previously, from March 3 to September 8, 2011, the ECB was believed to be raising interest rates faster than the Fed, and until early May, this advantage in rate expectations kept the EURUSD rising. Yet as we see from the EURUSD weekly chart (shown in Figure 6.10) from the start of May 2011, the EURUSD entered a multimonth downtrend despite the rate advantage.

Why? One reason is that the EUR was being undermined by a new phase in the EU sovereign debt and banking crisis. Another reason was that this crisis, combined with evidence of slowing growth in nearly every major economy was causing traders and investors to take profits in risk assets like the EUR and flee into safe havens like the USD.

In other words, though differences in interest rates and expectation about them are arguably the primary fundamental driver of currency prices in general, there will be times when this and other principles of analysis won't apply. Also, overall risk sentiment can easily override considerations about interest rate increases.

In sum, fundamental analysis is valuable for getting a big picture long-term strategic view, but when deciding whether to enter a trade, we prefer technical tools for our final screening of the lowest risk, highest reward trades and their entry and exit points (as discussed in depth in Chapter 7).

FIGURE 6.10   EURUSD Weekly Chart, March 6 to September 8, 2011
Source: MetaQuotes Software Corp.

THEREFORE, GET THEE TO AN ANALYST

Though some will enjoy doing their own analysis, most of us will find it more efficient to locate some analysts we trust and follow them, for their views on the technical and fundamental picture. This speeds up the learning process. The better ones will read the most important reports and summarize the key points, saving you the time and trouble. See Appendix A for some suggestions to consider.

COMBINING FA AND TA: AN EXAMPLE

Though we must introduce fundamental analysis and TA separately, everyone except day traders (who ignore fundamentals beyond near-term news events) needs to consider fundamental and technical evidence together. Here's an example and quiz to give you an experience of this.

Any good analysis for multiday or longer positions must include fundamental as well as TA. Indeed, over the long term the technical picture is driven by underlying fundamental forces, so good fundamental analysis is key to predicting longer-term trends.

Analyze This!

To illustrate this point, try the following quiz, which refers to Figure 6.11 originally introduced in the Fibonacci retracement (Fib) section of Chapter 4.

On August 4, 2011, note two kinds of support converge @ ~1.3880, a 61.8% Fib retracement and the lower channel line

FIGURE 6.11 EURUSD Daily Chart, September 2, 2010, to August 5, 2011
Source: MetaQuotes Software Corp.

Question: Imagine you were back at August 4, 2011. Do you think the above price support level at ~1.3880 will hold and make a good entry point for a long EURUSD position? It's comprised of two strong support indicators:

- The 61.8 percent Fib level of the EURUSD uptrend of July 2010 to May 2011.
- The lower line of the descending channel.

Before you answer, consider the fundamental background. The sovereign debt and banking crisis in the EU was steadily worsening. Over the past months, Greece had been granted its second bailout within about a year. The new rescue plan for Greece contained what was appearing to be a fatal flaw in that it imposed losses on private bondholders. Though this may have seemed fair to various EU electorates, it was scaring off the bond buyers the EU was depending on to keep demand up for these bonds from the weak EU economies and keep their yields down so these nations could continue to borrow at affordable rates.

Until this new imposition of haircuts (losses) on bond holders (mostly the big EU banks), it was assumed that the EU would protect private bond buyers from losses, but no more. Not surprisingly, borrowing costs for these nations began soaring to compensate buyers for the greater risk of loss. Italian and Spanish bond yields were soaring and their stock markets were crashing on fears that their governments and banks could be sliding towards bankruptcy. These nations were too big to bail out, yet scared credit markets, fearing losses would be imposed on holders of these bonds, were demanding yields these nations couldn't afford. The risk of an eventual wave of sovereign and bank defaults leading to a banking and economic crisis was much higher.

Growth was slowing in nearly every major economy. The United States had defaulted on a bond payment for the first time ever due to a political stalemate, casting doubt on its ability to deal with its own debt problems.

The broader technical picture for risk assets like major stocks was breaking down. The bellwether S&P 500 had fallen in 9 out of 10 sessions, and on August 4, it fell 5 percent, its worst one-day drop since the October 2008, as deterioration in the EU and United States, and the belief that the United States would no longer attempt major stimulus plans due to political opposition combined to create a dark mood in financial markets.

Answer: Given the fundamental background, I'm not at all that sure the 1.3900/61.8 percent Fib levels or other price supports would hold. We'd need further confirmation from technical indicators of a coming bounce higher, which would almost certainly be preceded by some easing in the fundamental tensions described above.

Therefore, if there is no improvement in the fundamentals, I might be watching for a break below the 1.3880 level, in which case I'd consider opening a short position. Based on the indicators used here (in reality, we'd want to check some others like the major moving averages, etc.), there appears to be no major resistance for this short until the 50 percent Fib level. Whether we open a short would depend on:

- Whether the fundamental situation continues to deteriorate.
- What other resistance may be offered from other types of support and resistance (s/r) mentioned earlier.

- How far we need place our stop loss from our entry point and so can tell if we have a 1:3 rrr. Were the fundamental situation bad, we might feel so good about shorting the EURUSD that we'd consider accepting a 1:2 rrr.

Post Mortem: Was I right?

Yes. As shown in Figure 6.12 below, by the end of August 2011 the bearish fundamentals, particularly the EU crisis, began exerting their influence, and drove the EURUSD sharply lower for the rest of the year and beyond, from nearly 1.4000 to well below 1.3000.

FIGURE 6.12 EURUSD Daily Chart, July 20, 2011, to January 6 2012, *Source:* MetaQuotes Software Corp.

The Lesson: Your trading decisions need to consider both technical and fundamental analysis. TA is great for timing lower-risk entries and exits, but fundamentals give you critical insights about what's behind the price moves and the future reliability of the trends, s/r points, and other indicators.

CHAPTER 7

Pulling It All Together with Trade Examples

C ongratulations; at this stage you've already seen the basics.
Now it's time to pull together some of what we've covered thus far and apply it in real-life trades.
In this chapter we'll:

- Review the steps to identifying and executing low-risk, high potential yield trades.
- Introduce some of the common types or styles of trades.
- Apply these ideas in a few real-life trades from my personal trading journal.

IDENTIFYING AND EXECUTING LOW-RISK, HIGH POTENTIAL YIELD TRADES

You should be trading from daily, weekly, or monthly charts for all the reasons we mentioned earlier in Chapter 3, particularly because indicators and trends are more reliable and stable in these time frames. That means your likely holding period will be days, weeks, or months.

Begin Your Search On Longer Time Frame Charts, Then Zoom In

Here's the basic idea behind how we locate simple, low-risk, high potential trades. Start your search for low-risk trades by scanning charts with time frames that are 4 to 5 times longer than the time frame from which you intend to trade. The first goal is to find low-risk entry points by identifying the long established, and therefore most reliable, s/r areas, because they're where the risk of opening a position is lowest. Here's why.

If price breaches long-term strong support, that's a clear signal that price is moving decisively against you. By entering close to strong support, you can also set your stop loss order relatively close to that support, using the methods discussed in Chapter 5, so that you escape with only a small, affordable loss, ideally one that is ever less than your maximum allowed loss of 1 to 3 percent of your account.

Like a bird of prey, you begin your hunt where you can view of lots of territory. The longer time frame chart allows you to view key s/r points over months or years. Then, if you see something interesting (a pair approaching one of those levels) you swoop in for a closer look on the shorter, time frame chart from which you actually trade, in order to make your final trading decisions. That's where you'll see if you've got a situation that combines a low-risk entry near strong support, with a likely resistance area far enough away from your entry point so that you've a good chance of earning three times as much as what you'll lose if your stop loss is hit, for a 3:1 reward/risk ratio.

This process will be clearer in the following examples.

Consider the Fundamental Context

Note that the longer you think the trade will need to play out, the more important it is that the trade fits with your fundamental analysis for your planned holding period. This is less important if you think the trade will last less than a week or so, unless you're trading based on a specific news item that's due out during that time. However, trades that may take weeks or months are typically based at least in part on some theory you have about how certain fundamentals are likely to play out.

For example, you go long the AUDJPY because you believe markets will be optimistic over the coming weeks or months (favoring risk over safety currencies), or you believe Australia's economic data will be much better than Japan's. You'll see examples of this kind of thinking in the following trade examples. Now let's look at the concepts just covered in greater detail.

Initial Screening on Longer Time Frame Charts

The purpose of your first screening is to find a currency pair that meets the following four criterias:

1. Risk Management Criterion #1: The currency pair is approaching a strong support area that provides a low-risk entry point. For example,

by definition, strong s/r levels on a weekly chart will be even stronger on a daily chart, because they're more established than the s/r levels you see on daily charts. You then set your stop loss just far enough beyond this area so that it doesn't get hit by random price movements, but rather only when price has turned far enough against you that you know you were probably wrong about the trade and it's best to escape with a small loss. Thus the stronger the s/r area where you enter, the lower your risk of a losing trade (barring any unforeseen change in fundamentals and sentiment). Once you know your likely entry and stop loss points, you can check if the trade may meet your second criteria

2. **Risk Management Criterion #2:** Find the nearest major resistance area, because that's where you'd expect to exit and take profits. If the distance from entry (at support) to exit (at resistance) is 2 to 3 times farther than the distance from entry to stop loss, then you may have a 2:1 to 3:1 reward/risk ratio (rrr). We'll know for sure only when we do the second screening.

3. **Risk Management Criteria #3-Stop Loss Placement:** The stop loss should be far enough away from your entry point so that it does not get hit by normal random price movements, but only by larger moves against you that suggest price may be making a sustained move against you.

4. **Money Management Criterion #1:** The stop loss should be close enough to your entry point so that you don't lose more than 1-3 percent of your account on the trade.

These are the first criteria for low-risk, high-reward trades. Remember that definitions of support and resistance are the opposite for short and long positions, as discussed in Chapter 3.

Again, we scan for situations that look like they might fulfill the preceding criteria on charts with a time frame approximately four to five times longer than the time frame on which we trade. *For the examples that follow, we trade off daily charts, so we scan weekly charts in the first screening.*

This first screening doesn't take long because we generally prefer to trade only the most liquid pairs. There are only about eight really liquid pairs, and maybe about 20 liquid enough for most of your trading.[1]

In short, we're scanning the weekly charts of these pairs for an entry near strong support, with any likely resistance far enough away so that there's a chance of getting a 1:3 or 1:2 risk-to-reward ratio (rrr).

As we'll see, *the deciding factor in whether you take the trade is if the second screening on the daily charts shows you can get a combination of stop loss, entry, and exit points that allows the desired rrr yet does not cost you more than 1 to 3 percent of your account if the stop loss is hit.*

For the purpose of illustration, assume just one entry and exit, and mostly avoid consideration of variations like trailing stop losses and partial or staged entries and exits.

When we talk about strong support or resistance, that means we want to see at least one well-tested kind of support, ideally as many kinds as we can get, all converging on a narrow price range. Just to remind you, these include:

- Prices that have clearly been support or resistance in the past; often these are some kind of round number, because traders tend to think in round numbers.
- Trend lines and/or their variations like channels, moving averages, and Bollinger Bands.
- Fibonacci retracements.
- Chart patterns, besides being useful in their own right, also provide additional evidence of s/r points. For example, if a head-and-shoulders pattern is about to complete its second shoulder or if price is about to hit the neckline of that pattern, that price level takes on added significance as a possible s/r point.

Again, there are many more indicators you could use, and we haven't even covered momentum indicators yet. But these give us enough for some trading examples from my trading journal.

Second Screening

Once you've found some situations that meet these criteria on the weekly charts, the next step is to see if the same criteria for low-risk, high potential reward trades are present in your chosen time frame, in this case, daily charts.

Why bother with the first screening? As noted previously, the longer time frame chart shows you stronger s/r levels. We're hoping to find an entry point on the daily charts that is near the stronger s/r areas found on the longer time frame, in this case the weekly charts. If we find that a pair nears its weekly s/r, we'll know it's worth doing a second screening on the daily chart.

Again, the deciding factor in whether you take the trade will be if the daily chart (or whatever timeframe from which you trade) shows the combination of stop loss, entry, and exit points that allow the desired rrr, yet will not cost you more than 1 to 3 percent of your account if the stop loss is hit. To reiterate:

- The stop loss is far enough past strong support so that it would get hit only by strong price moves that signal your trade idea was mistaken, and close enough so you're out with a small but affordable loss that doesn't exceed 1 to 3 percent of your trading capital, so you can afford lots of mistakes, recover your losses, and be profitable

- It's two to three times closer to your entry point than is your profit-taking point, so you have a 1:3 or at worst 1:2 rrr.

Regarding stop loss placement, remember that there are different methods. These include:

- The Intuitive Approach: Study the chart for the relevant period and define the price range for the normal up and down oscillation of price. You want your stop loss to be no closer to your entry point than that distance, ideally a bit more than that, while still not causing a loss greater than your 1–3 percent limit. This is a very simple approach and hence the one we choose to use in the example that follows. This method involves a heavy dose of personal judgment.
- The Somewhat More Objective Approach: Set distance from entry point to stop loss based on fixed percentages (also a judgment call) of the Average True Range (ATR), as mentioned in Chapter 5, or other formula or statistically based methods to ensure you don't get shaken out of your trade due to normal price fluctuations.

Regarding rrr, if the trade is in the direction of a very strong trend, it's safer to be more aggressive, so we're more likely to accept a 1:2 rrr.

In the end, you're always trying to strike a balance between the size of the loss if hit versus the risk of being stopped out. In other words, the farther away your stop loss is from your entry point, the bigger the loss if hit but the lower the chance of being hit by random price fluctuations rather than a real move against you.

If the second screening shows that you can get the desired rrr without risking more than 1 to 3 percent of your capital, you take the trade near strong support. The precise entry level you choose is a judgment call. You're trying to strike a balance between entering at the best price and not being so greedy that price never hits your order and you miss the trade altogether.

Third Screening to Monitor Trade Progress

This screening occurs on a chart time frame four to five times shorter than your trading time frame. For example, if you're trading on daily charts, then use two- to four-hour candles. This one usually doesn't determine whether you take the trade. Instead, it's mostly just to identify short-term s/r points that are likely to be temporary, so you're not surprised if the trend halts or reverses around these zones. Rather than getting worried, you expect a progressing trade to temporarily halt or even reverse. These areas can also serve as points where you augment or reduce your position if you're using staged entries and exits.

At times, this screening may alter your strategy. For example, if price repeatedly struggles to break through the resistance you see on the four hour chart, that might indicate that the longer-term trend may be failing, especially if important new information just came out. Similarly, if there's too much quality short-term resistance too close to your entry, you might elect to enter in stages, saving most of your planned position until price clears that resistance area. Alternatively, if there are better opportunities or if breaking news casts doubts on your conclusions from the second screening, you might change your mind about the trade and just get out.

For the sake of brevity and simplicity, the following trade examples omit the third screening.

TYPES OF TRADES

While any good trader should be using most of the techniques we cover, within these guidelines there are different types or styles of trading for any given time frame. Here's a brief listing of the most popular styles. The idea is just to acquaint you with these terms. There are whole books written about each of these trading styles, so use this listing as both an introduction to the vocabulary of trading styles and as a starting point for further research into the styles that interest you. Just take these as general labels, because trades often combine elements of more than one style. The most popular types of trades include:

- Position trading—taking a longer-term position to ride a trend: Trading a longer-term trend (multiple days, weeks, or months) typically involves entering on some kind of pullback to strong support, waiting to see if that support holds, and then going long soon after longer-term trend bounces back up from support and resumes (and vice versa for short positions). This style is associated with longer-term trends (so pay attention to the relevant long-term fundamentals).
- Trend trading: This type is essentially the same as position trading but is associated with shorter-term trends, and is thus mostly based on technical analysis of trend strength. Again, the goal is usually to enter after some kind of support, and to ride the trend as it resumes. Also, when shorting in order to ride a downtrend, a pullback means a brief move up to a near-term high that serves as support.
- Swing trading: This type involves entering just after a trend reverses briefly, then resumes. You enter just as price is pushing or "swinging"

past its former resistance, which indicates that the trend has found new strength. Your technical analysis will need to focus not only on s/r points but also on:

- Momentum indicators (Chapter 8) that either telegraph a possible coming trend reversal or confirm it.
- Timing or wave indicators like Elliott Wave, Fibonacci, or Gann style analysis (Chapter 9).
- Range trading: This is when you identify a pair that is locked in a sideways (or nearly so) trading range or channel and you attempt to go long at the lows and short at the highs. As mentioned earlier, when doing this with strongly trending channels. This kind of trading works when you have both flat or weak trends, and wide channels.
- Momentum trading: This involves locating pairs showing signs of accelerating trends via momentum indicators covered in the next chapter.

Like swing traders, momentum traders are less focused on entering on a bounce off support. Instead, they want to enter just after price as broken through key resistance, which suggests a new stage in the trend.

In sum, position, trend, range, and swing traders seek to buy low and sell high. Momentum traders seek to buy high on breakouts past resistance because these suggest price is making its next run higher.

Again, with all of these styles, the longer you think you'll be holding the position, the more you need to consider longer-term fundamentals because they'll have more time to influence the pair.

TRADE EXAMPLE 1: A SWING TRADE

Here's a simple example that pulls together much of the previous discussion. I label it a swing trade, though as I'll discuss in the conclusion it's really a hybrid combination of a position or trend trade with an attempt to play a brief reversal that gives the trade its "swing" element. One of the reasons I chose it is to illustrate how the trade types are just general labels, as the distinctions between them are often blurred.

Initial Screening

On Sunday, September 18, 2011, while scanning weekly charts, I find the following intriguing situation for the EURUSD shown in Figure 7.1.

What Initially Attracts Me   The pair has been in a strong downtrend for the past three weeks but bounced in the prior week, putting it back near

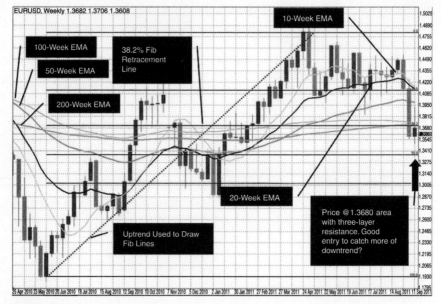

FIGURE 7.1 EURUSD Weekly Chart, May 16 to September 11, 2011
Source: MetaQuotes Software Corp.

strong support for a short trade if the downtrend resumes. Specifically, we note that the pair's most recent weekly close is 1.3680 and it has recently broken a major support at 1.3700, a level that included the:

- 100 week exponential moving average (EMA)
- 200 week EMA
- 38.2 percent Fibonacci retracement level of the uptrend from the week of June 6, 2010, to the week of May 1, 2011

We also note that the shorter duration (and more sensitive to recent price momentum) 10-, 20-, and 50-week EMAs have begun turning lower, a sign of downward momentum that further supports the case for shorting the pair. We'll discuss more on using moving average crossovers to discern momentum changes in Chapter 8.

Fundamental Analysis Context—Weekly Chart During the prior week, the pair had bounced higher, back close to this support level. As I noted in my weekly review at the time, I believed the move was based on false hopes that the EU situation would improve soon and that the EURUSD would rise.[2] The prior week's bounce seemed like a possible new chance to enter a short EURUSD position right back near strong support around the 1.3700 area (remember that support for a short position is the likely high for the period in question).

So I suspect we may have a "short the rally" situation—that is, a rally unlikely to last that may allow promising entry points for new short EURUSD positions near strong support.

Technical Analysis (TA)—Weekly Chart   First, there are the technical factors that initially attracted me to this trade, on the weekly chart, like the strong three-week-old downtrend that is still very much intact after the prior week's small bounce back up to near the 38.2 percent Fib retracement line. So we may have a safe entry point around there.

Then, we also may have a temptingly distant exit point. According to the indicators displayed, there's no significant resistance to a further downside until the 1.3400 to 1.3275 area, where there may be resistance from both:

- The 1.3400 price level itself (note how often it served as an s/r point in the past).
- The 50 percent Fibonacci retracement nearby at 1.3366.

With the current price around 1.3680, that leaves almost 300 pips of room for profit according to this first look, assuming an exit around 1.3400. The question is: can I find a low-risk, high potential yield entry point? That is, an entry point with a reasonable stop loss that allows both:

- Enough room so that I don't get stopped out by random movements but rather only if the pair is really moving higher and my thinking was wrong.
- A loss that is a third or less the size of my gain according to what I see as likely strong resistance.

Second Screening

To find out, let's zoom in to look at this possible entry point on a daily time frame, because we appear to have a good entry point at a near term high for a short EURUSD trade in this time frame.

TA and RAMM Considerations—Daily Chart   We now need to see where resistance might be on the daily chart shown in Figure 7.2. First we look for s/r points over a longer period.

No real resistance until about 1.3455, which was an s/r point from November 2010 to February 2011 (highlighted with the ellipsis). The

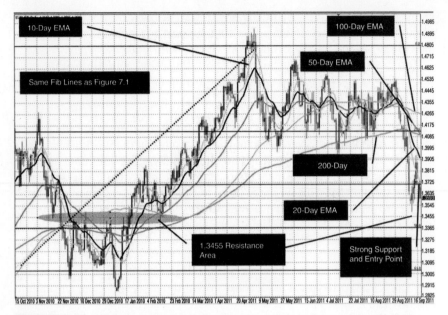

FIGURE 7.2   EURUSD Daily Chart, October 15, 2010, to September 16, 2011
Source: MetaQuotes Software Corp.

Fibonacci retracements are the same as in the weekly chart (Figure 7.1). Note the strong downward momentum indicated by the shorter-term moving averages crossing below the longer-term moving averages.

I zoom in further for a closer look on the daily chart shown in Figure 7.3 to the period of August 10 to September 16, 2011, in order to get a sense of where my stop loss should be.

We see that the nearest meaningful high (support) is in the 1.3915 to 1.3865 area highlighted by the ellipsis.

RRR Evaluation

In sum, the daily chart for the EURUSD indicates the potential gain and potential loss on the trade.

Potential Gain: Likely Profit-Taking Point   There's no likely resistance until around 1.3455 per the chart, though it's possible the 38.2 percent Fib level at about 1.3700 could stop us, so I'd consider switching from a fixed to a trailing stop loss order just before that level.

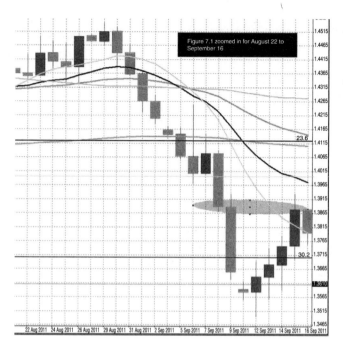

FIGURE 7.3 EURUSD Daily Chart, August 11 to September 16, 2011
Source: MetaQuotes Software Corp.

It's now Friday, September 16, 2011.

Planned entry point:	1.3815
Planned exit point:	1.3455
Potential gain:	0.0360 or 360 pips

Potential Loss: Stop Loss Placement and RRR   I'll keep it simple and just refer to recent highs as a guide for setting a stop loss, and see if that's small enough compared to the likely gain from the pair falling to the 1.3455 area.

The recent highs are around the 1.3915 to 1.3865 area.

If I use those as a guide for placing my stop loss at 1.3915 (the high of the prior week), then if this stop loss is hit my loss is:

Planned entry point:	1.3815
Planned stop loss:	1.3915
Potential loss:	0.0100 or 100 pips
Risk-reward ratio	100/360 = 1:3.6, exceeding our 1:3 criterion

Assume that 100 pip loss represents less than 3 percent of my total trading account equity, so I'm within my money management guidelines.

I'd plan on switching to a 50 pip trailing stop loss order at around 1.3720. I choose 50 pips because it represents a good chunk of the recent daily volatility, while still allowing me to break even (or do slightly better) after expenses.

Fundamental Analysis Context   I know there is a meeting of European finance ministers Friday and Saturday discussing the latest Greek bailout package. Greece has failed miserably to meet its deficit reduction targets, so there's a good chance of the meeting producing either its usual disappointing lack of results (bearish for the pair) or even a chance they'll get tough with Greece and demand further budget cutbacks, which would put the Greek bailout in even greater doubt, which would likely send the EURUSD down.

In sum, it appears that we have a low-risk, high potential reward trade on the daily chart from the perspectives of:

- Money management
- Risk management
- Technical analysis
- Fundamental context

If the price moves in our favor, we might do better than the 360 pips by switching to a trailing stop once we gain ~150 to 200 pips (so that we get at least a 1:1.5 to 1:2 rrr as a worst-case scenario) and the EURUSD moves below our anticipated 360 pip drop. I'd have to consider conditions at the time to determine how wide the trailing stop should be.

Conclusion: We Take the Trade

We take this trade with the stated entry and stop loss points, and probably move up our stop loss and change it from a fixed to a trailing stop once price moves in our favor, as noted. However, we're going to take only a relatively small position, half of what I'd like to do. Why?

Note again that this is *not* really a classic swing trade, which would wait until we clear the recent low around 1.3570, and thus truly swing past this most recent resistance. I'm being more aggressive and getting in earlier for two reasons:

1. The fundamental considerations suggest the odds favor more downside. That was decisive.
2. The entry point is near strong support for entering an existing trend (making this a mix of position and swing trade).

So I want to take a more aggressive position. There are many who would say I'm being too aggressive and should wait. However, my stop loss and position sizes are not large, and the rrr is excellent, so I make a judgment call and enter with half of what I would like to put in, and may add to the short when the EURUSD closes below 1.3565.

Here's one last word about the importance of trying to understand the fundamental context in which the trade occurs. Throughout the EU sovereign debt and banking crisis, trading the EURUSD was hazardous. There was constant risk that the crisis could become another Lehman Brothers event that could crash global markets and spark another recession or worse. Thus the real drivers of this crisis were political decisions that are inherently difficult to predict. Just when a default would seem imminent, a last-minute rescue deal, or a mere rumor of one, could send the pair higher. The opposite kind of news could send the pair crashing lower.

Trade Postmortem: What Happened

As shown in Figure 7.4, the trade worked as planned.

Specifically:

- Anticipated support (or resistance for our short position) held due to hopes that there would be a decisive solution to the EU debt crisis in the coming weeks.

FIGURE 7.4 EURUSD Weekly Chart, June 6 to October 30, 2011
Source: MetaQuotes Software Corp.

- As the long down candle for the week of October 30 shows, these hopes proved incorrect. Our bearish view of the EU situation continued to be correct after a brief rally as the EURUSD pair put in another lower high, setting up another move lower in the continued downtrend of the EURUSD.

So this trade had a happy ending. However, there's a reason we want those nice high risk-to-reward ratios when we can get them. We want to make enough on the winners so that we can be wrong more often than we're right, or to provide extra cash reserves so that we can afford to be patient when we're having trouble finding low-risk, high potential yield trades.

TRADE EXAMPLE 2: A BREAKOUT TRADE

Here's another simple trade example, this time a breakout type of trade.

First Screening

On Sunday, July 11, 2010, while scanning weekly charts, I find the situation for the EURUSD shown in Figure 7.5.

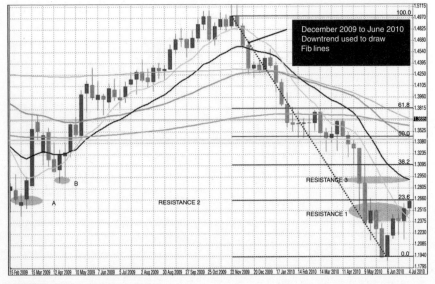

FIGURE 7.5   EURUSD Weekly Chart, February 15, 2009, to July 4, 2010
Source: MetaQuotes Software Corp.

What Initially Attracts Me If the EURUSD can make a decisive break above the 1.2700 area labeled Resistance 2, this would then become a strong support and possible low-risk entry point ~1.2700, which we'll then examine more closely on the daily chart in the second screening.

The EURUSD has already broken through two resistance levels at 1.2375 (bottom of ellipsis labeled Resistance 1) and at 1.2515 (middle of ellipsis labeled Resistance 1). Now it may be ready to break through the next area at around 1.2660 to 1.2700 (labeled Resistance 2), which would be a bullish sign of strength for the current uptrend because:

- This price level was a significant s/r point in the past, from the weekly candles of February 15 to March 15 (ellipsis A), and also for the weekly candles of May 2, 16, and 23.
- It has the 23.6 percent Fibonacci retracement level for the downtrend that ran from the weekly candle of November 29 to that of June 6.
- The prior week's high was around 1.2720.

If the pair can make a decisive break above the prior week's high of about 1.2720 (the upper extreme of the July 4 candlewick), that breakout could signal the next move higher, so I might want to enter a long EURUSD position around that price.

Fundamental Analysis Context—Weekly Chart Though long-term prospects for the EUR may be very cloudy, we have the ingredients for some kind of further rally:

- The EURUSD is in a five-week uptrend after hitting multiyear lows around 1.2000 on fears that Greece would default. Given that the newly passed €750 billion rescue package is currently believed to be able to cover Greece for the coming year and also the next most likely default threats, Portugal and Ireland, these default threats have passed for now, and no other peripheral economy poses an immediate default threat. None of the long-term problems at the root of the EU sovereign debt and banking crisis have been addressed, but they've likely been deferred long enough for a tradable multiweek rally, as suggested by the current five-week rally. I may not personally believe the EUR has a bright future, but that's irrelevant. The uptrend is telling me that the other traders believe it at least has a tradable rally. If the pair breaks above the area labeled Resistance 2, that will be further confirmation of that belief and an indication that the uptrend has room to run.
- The pair is coming off multiyear lows, and so could well retrace a chunk of the December 2009 to June 2010 downtrend shown in Figure 7.5.

- An upcoming stress test of EU banks will likely paint a rosy picture, and while everyone knows in advance that the results will show that all is in order, this little PR exercise may still provide an excuse for a further rally. I suspect the market wants that excuse, given that the primary fundamental driver of the recent downtrend (threat of Greek default) has passed and the EURUSD pair is coming off multiyear lows and so may be ripe for a further rally.

Technical Analysis (TA)—Weekly Chart   As noted above and shown in Figure 7.5 the pair has broken past recent resistance at 1.2500 (Resistance 1) and now faces resistance around 1.2660 (Resistance 2), which has served as a strong weekly s/r point from mid-February to mid-March in 2009 and for much of May in 2010, and from the 23.6 percent Fib retracement of the downtrend.

As noted earlier, if it can break past the prior week's high around 1.2720 (which would be an entry point), there is no significant resistance until about 1.2900 (Resistance 3), which is the next likely strong resistance because:

- 1.2900 was the s/r price level in April 2009 (ellipsis B).
- 1.2900 was a recent s/r price level in early to mid-May 2010 (Resistance 3).
- The 20-week exponential moving average (the descending line that touches the right side of the Resistance 3 area ellipsis) also converges on this area.

From 1.2720 to 1.2900 we have about 280 pips, depending on our exact entry and exit points. Again, we assume only one entry and exit to simplify our presentation. That implies that for this trade to work we'll need to see if a stop loss can be placed no farther than a third to a half of that distance from the entry point so that we get a 1:3 or 1:2 risk-reward ratio.

Second Screening

The two questions we now seek to answer are:

1. Can we find a stop loss that meets our risk and money management criteria given our planned entry around 1.2700?
   - Risk Management: Not likely to be hit by random price movements but rather only if the breakout is truly failing, yet less than 90 pips from the entry point (about a third of the potential gain for a 1:3 rrr) or at least no more than 140 pips from the entry point (for a 1:2 rrr) from our preferred entry at a price that suggests a decisive breakout.

FIGURE 7.6 EURUSD Daily Chart, April 16 to July 9, 2010 (Ends Week Beginning Sunday, July 4, 2010)
Source: MetaQuotes Software Corp.

The 90 pip limit means a stop loss no lower than 1.2630, and the 140 pip limit means a stop loss no lower than 1.2560.

- Money Management: Doesn't risk more that 1 to 3 percent of our capital.

2. Is there any support or resistance we need to consider for planning entries or exits that we didn't see on the weekly chart?

For the answers to these questions we zoom in on the daily chart for the prior weeks (see Figure 7.6).

TA and RAMM Considerations—Daily Chart   For an entry around 1.2700, the TA and RAMM picture is not great. Here's why. While there is some minor resistance around 1.2735 (Resistance 1), there is stronger resistance around 1.2800 (Resistance 2) from both the price level itself and the 100 day EMA.

RRR Evaluation

To see if this trade offers the rrr we want, we first consider stop loss placement.

Stop Loss Placement   There isn't firm support until around 1.2435, where four kinds of support converge (at the bottom of ellipsis B):

- The 1.2435 price area itself (ellipsis A)
- The 10-day EMA
- The 50-day EMA
- The 20-day EMA

So if we enter at 1.2700, we could get stopped by resistance at around 1.2800 for only a 100 pip gain, and a trustworthy stop loss around 1.2435 would, if hit, inflict a 265 pip loss. That's a 2.65:1 rrr, the opposite of what we want. No, thanks.

Before we give up, here's another idea. What about if we entered at a breakout above Resistance 1 and Resistance 2 at around 1.2830, with an eye to ride the EURUSD higher until the next significant resistance area between the 38.2 percent Fibonacci retracement (the same one as on the weekly chart) and the 200-day EMA at ~1.3145?

Potential Gain: Likely Profit-Taking Point

Planned entry point:	1.2830
Planned exit point:	<u>1.3145</u>
Potential gain:	0.0315 or 315 pips

Potential Loss: Stop Loss Placement and RRR   We still don't have any trustworthy support until around 1.2435, given that the 23.6 percent Fib retracement did not provide strong s/r back in May 2010 on the daily chart.

Planned entry point:	1.2830
Planned stop loss:	<u>1.2435</u>
Potential loss:	0.0395 or 395 pips
Risk-reward ratio	395/315 = 1.25:1

Again, more risk than reward, not tempting. Given that the likely loss is higher than the likely gain, we needn't even bother considering whether this trade risks less than three percent of our account.

Fundamental Analysis Context   There is nothing to add from the fundamentals mentioned earlier.

Conclusion: Know When to Walk Away

We pass on this one. Yes, I know you're thinking, Cliff, WTF? This is supposed to be a full real-life trade example. Baby, there is *nothing* more real-life about trading than investing time and effort to study a trade, and then concluding it's not worthwhile.

Is this as exciting a conclusion as opening a new trade? No. So what? If you want action while sitting at your computer, play video games.

Was this analysis wasted time? Hardly. As you'll learn if you start taking questionable trades out of a need for some action, some of your most profitable trading decisions will be to reject trades that don't meet your standards, thus avoiding a loss.

Hey, a penny saved is a penny earned.

Trade Postmortem: Was I Right?

The next question is: did I just blow an opportunity? Have I just become the trading version of Peter Best, the original Beatles drummer, the one whom Ringo Starr replaced just before they made it big? Or much worse, have I become the trading version of Ronald Wayne? He's the little-known third founder of Apple Computer (along with Jobs and Wozniak) who sold his 10 percent stake for $2,300. As of this writing it would be worth about $22 billion, and would have made him among the world's top 20 richest people.[3]

Ah, the road not taken.

Fortunately, we have no regrets this time.

Our maximum affordable stop loss was 140 pips. From our 1.2700 entry that would have been 1.25600.

As we can see in Figure 7.7, my stop loss would have been hit a few days later on July 13, when the low was about 1.2520. So in the short term, I was definitely right.

However, even if I had missed an opportunity, that would have been okay, because the rrr was terrible. With a 1.25:1 rrr, I'd have to be right on over 60 percent of my trades just to break even. That's too much risk; the odds are against me. Those odds would catch up to me eventually, as surely as they get most amateur gamblers in casinos.

The Second-Guessing Game   However, if I wanted to second-guess myself about this trade, I could look at what happened after that July 13 exit.

If I had taken on extra risk with a wider stop loss (and thus a lower rrr), stayed in the trade, and put on a trailing stop of, say, 20 to 50 pips (depending on a variety of variables) once it moved about 50 to 100 pips in my favor to lock in some profit, I could have probably gotten out during the July 21 pullback (candle A) somewhere around 1.2865 (50 pips from the high of 1.2915, assuming a trailing stop of 50 pips) for a gain of 165 pips from our 1.2700 entry at about an rrr of about 1:1, maybe worse. That's

FIGURE 7.7   EURUSD Daily Chart, July 9 to October 1, 2010
Source: MetaQuotes Software Corp.

poor risk management because it means I have to be right on most of my trades to be profitable, which isn't a great assumption for most traders.

If I had somehow stayed in the trade, either with a wider fixed or trailing stop, I might have ridden it higher to somewhere around the early August highs of 1.3200 (candle B on the chart, a gain of 500 pips from our 1.2700 entry). Again, however, this would have required a very wide fixed initial stop loss or a nearly 200 pip trailing stop loss in order to have stayed in during the July 21 pullback (candle A). That's a lot of risk considering our initial goal was only 200 pips, and again gives us about a 1:1 risk-reward ratio, which means we need to be right most of the time to be profitable and that we're exposed to much larger losses. As illustrated in Appendix E, big losses hurt us more than big gains help us.

This case of taking on extra risk for potentially winning trades brings us to another very key lesson in how to have a professional trader's mindset.

MORE KEY TRADER PSYCHOLOGY: DISTINGUISHING BETWEEN GOOD TRADES AND WINNING TRADES

A winning trade is not a good trade if you took on too much risk, because that habit is likely to kill you in the end.

A good trade is not necessarily a winning trade. If you had a good plan, stayed with it, incurred a small but affordable loss, and then learned something from the trade, you just had a successful trade. You're keeping the odds on your side, so, like a casino, you should be profitable in the long run as long as you refine your methods and systems and keep risk low.

Would higher-risk alternatives have been better trades in retrospect?

No! *Any profits from higher-risk trades would have been more a matter of luck than skill.* Like a casino, we take calculated risks, but only trade when the odds are in our favor.

Eventually the odds will catch up with traders with poor (or nonexistent) RAMM and who regularly trade with risk-to-reward ratios around 1:1 or worse, and they'll join the 80 percent or more of forex traders who fail.

I'm not saying anything original here, and pardon me for repeating myself, but it's really worth repeating.

If you followed your plan and it included proper RAMM, *that* is a good trade even if you missed out on profits or even took a small but acceptable loss. You'll live to fight another day, unlike the reckless and undisciplined traders. Once you find a system (and style) that works, you'll be able to execute it and be consistently profitable.

Pat yourself on the back, pour yourself a good glass of something, study the trade and strategy for possible mistakes or faults, and move on. These things happen, a lot. That's why we love trades with risk-to-reward ratios of 1:3 or better. Our conservative assumption is that most of our trades won't work out. As long as we're profitable at the end of the month, that's fine.

Markets are hard to predict, and that is what you're trying to do. So part of having realistic expectations is to accept that you'll have a lot of losing trades, even a majority of losing trades.

As mentioned in Chapter 5, if you need a certain percentage of wins to keep from getting discouraged, consider taking partial profits early on trades that are moving in your favor. Your rrr may fall to below 1:2 overall, but you'll be happier and able to continue trading. You'll also be able to build confidence that may allow you to accept more losing trades in exchange for higher profits as you mature as a trader.

CHAPTER 8

Technical Analysis

Basic Momentum Indicators

I n the prior chapter you saw how to use the basic tools that we've taught thus far. If you'd like to practice applying them, visit thesensibleguidetoforex.com, and search for the trade simulations exercises or trade diaries. That's where we'll post trade scenarios, give you the chance to play them, then provide suggested solutions.

Now it's time to add a new and different set of technical tools to your arsenal—momentum indicators. They are useful in helping to answer the following common trader dilemmas.

- What do you do if a currency pair (or any asset) is making historic highs or lows, so there isn't enough, or any, support or resistance to guide you in making entry and exit decisions?
- How do you know you're not buying at the top, or selling short at the bottom, just before the trend ends? Ideally in either case you'd wait for a pullback of some kind, but meanwhile you risk missing out on the trend!
- If you're in a winning trade and it approaches your planned exit, how do you know if you should take your planned exit, or leave at least some of the position in hopes of letting profits run with a trailing stop?

For example, look what happened to gold from May 2009 to August 2011 (see Figure 8.1).

FIGURE 8.1   Gold Monthly Chart, July 2005 to December 2011
Source: MetaQuotes Software Corp.

From May 2009 to August 2011 it kept hitting new all-time highs, and had only eight down months out of 27, rarely pulling back to anything more than very near-term support levels.

Gold hit four new all-time highs from 2008 to 2011, breaking over $1,000, then $1,220, then $1,265, then over $1,350, $1,400, and $1,500. Those waiting for significant pullbacks often never got in and missed the biggest trend of the year.

The basic problem traders and investors face is that we get paid for being right about what happens in the future, yet most of the popular indicators we've covered thus far are more lagging than leading indicators. They tell us about the past, and from that information all we can do at best is to form some hypotheses about the future.

What's a trader to do? Use momentum indicators. They're leading indicators because:

- They can tell you whether a trend is strengthening or weakening.
- They can tell you if an asset is overbought or oversold relative to past activity over a given period, and so indicate if the trend is more likely to reverse direction.

Knowing these can help you forecast changes and be more profitable.

Momentum indicators can give you additional clues to put the odds of being correct even more in your favor. There are many momentum inticators, but for now we will introduce just a few of the most effective and easiest ones to use:

- Double Bollinger Bands.
- Moving average (MA) crossovers.
- Three kinds of basic oscillators: Moving Average Convergence/ Divergence (MACD), Relative Strength Index (RSI), and Stochastics.

As with any indicator, you can use these without fully understanding how they work, though if you do, you'll be able to use them more effectively and know how to adapt them to specific situations.

DOUBLE BOLLINGER BANDS (DBBs)—USE AS MOMENTUM INDICATORS

We noted in Chapter 4 that while standard single Bollinger Bands can provide a degree of support or resistance (s/r) in flat or gently trending markets, Bollinger Bands don't provide reliable support and resistance in strongly trending markets, because they widen with increasing volatility, so a strong trend can continue to climb the upper or lower band for extended periods.

There's lots of material written about standard single Bollinger Bands (much of it free online), so we'll focus on their newer, less covered but far more useful variant, Double Bollinger Bands.

Kathy Lien, one of the most famous rock-star forex analysts around (books, major website, regular TV appearances), devised a brilliant modification. In addition to the standard bands set at two standard deviations' distance from a 20-period simple moving average (SMA) at the center, she added a second set of bands only one standard deviation away from that SMA.

By using Double Bollinger Bands (DBBs), we get a much better indication of:

- Whether a trend is strong enough to continue riding or to enter new positions even if it has been going on for a long time.
- Whether it's time to take profits or to get ready to trade the reversal.

That sounds helpful. Just how useful are DBBs?

In her latest book, *The Little Book of Currency Trading*, Kathy Lien writes:

> *Of the hundreds of technical indicators out there, the Double Bollinger Bands are hands down my favorite ... they provide a wealth of actionable information. They tell me whether a currency pair is in a trend or range, the direction of the trend, and when the trend has exhausted. More importantly, Bollinger Bands also identify entry points and proper places to put a stop.*[1]

As we'll describe later, they are indeed at least as useful as any indicator I've encountered.

To create them on your chart, just insert a second set of Bollinger bands at one standard deviation on your moving average. Consult your charting platform's help menu. We'll clarify standard deviations later. For now just know that they are units of distance from the 20-period simple moving average (SMA), which is both the center of the DBBs and the baseline for determining the location of the other Bollinger bands.

Figure 8.2 is an example of what DBBs look like, applied to the same chart shown in Figure 8.1.

A1: The upper BB line that is two standard deviations away from line C, the 20-period simple moving average (SMA).

FIGURE 8.2   Gold Monthly Chart, July 2005 to December 2011
Source: MetaQuotes Software Corp.

B1: The upper BB line that is one standard deviation from the 20-period SMA.

C: The 20-period SMA. Figure 8.2 is a weekly chart, so this is a 20-week SMA. Again, this is both the center of the DBBs and baseline for determining the location of the other bands.

B2: The lower BB line that is one standard deviation from the 20-period SMA.

A2: The lower BB line that is two standard deviations from the 20-period SMA.

Notice how these bands form four separate zones. It's these zones that provide the added information about the strength of a trend, whether it still has the momentum to continue, and where we might attempt to enter trades, even if there is no other s/r to serve as a reference point, as was the case with gold in Figure 8.2.

DBB Basics

- The DBB Buy zone: When price is within this upper zone (between the two topmost lines, A1 and B1), that means the uptrend is strong and has a higher probability of continuing. As long as candles continue to close in this uppermost zone, the odds favor entering or maintaining long positions, and closing or avoiding short positions.
- The DBB Sell zone: When price is in the bottom zone (between the two lowest lines, A2 and B2), the downtrend is likely to continue. That suggests that as long as the candles close in this lowest zone, one should enter or maintain short positions and close or avoid long positions.
- The DBB Neutral zone: When price is within the area bounded by the one standard deviation bands (B1 and B2), there is no strong trend. The 20-day simple moving average (C) that serves as the baseline for the Bollinger Bands is in the center of this zone. Typically one to three candles closing in this area are your signal to exit your trade because the trend is showing weakness.

In other words, DBBs tell us whether we should be trading a trend or a trading range.

- When the pair is in the buy or sell zone (above the top one standard deviation line or below the bottom one standard deviation line), we have a trend that is strong enough to continue trading; it's probably not too late to get in, though you may want to wait for the trend to retreat to the first standard deviation line, and ideally wait for it to begin to rebound back in the direction of the trend.

- When the pair is within the neutral zone (between the one standard deviation lines), it's in a trading range. If there's any trend, it lacks the momentum needed to be tradable. You may be able to trade bounces off the upper and lower channels, but the trend itself lacks enough strength to assume that it will continue without excessive risk of a reversal that hits our stop loss.

As with most technical indicators, the longer the time frame of the chart on which they're viewed, the stronger the momentum indicator that DBBs provide.

The Four Rules for Using Double Bollinger Bands

Here's a short summary of how to use Double Bollinger Bands (DBBs). The rules are a combination of what I've gleaned from Kathy Lien, other sources, and my own experience. This short version focuses on just the rules for how to actually use DBBs. Search online for further details.

We'll be referring to Figure 8.3.

Rule 1: Go Short When Price Is Within or Below the Double BB Sell Zone (Bounded by the Lower Two Bollinger Bands)   As long as price remains within or below the lower two BBs, the downward momentum is strong enough so that there is a high probability that the

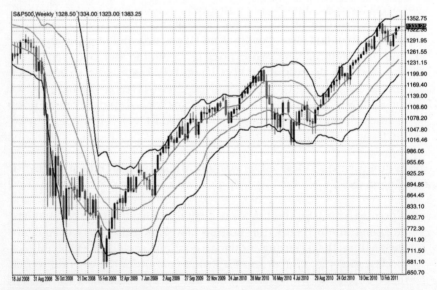

FIGURE 8.3   S&P 500 Weekly Chart, July 18, 2008, to April 3, 2011
Source: MetaQuotes Software Corp.

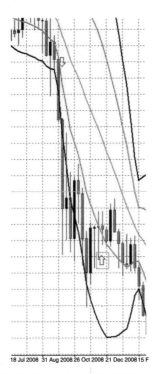

18 Jul 2008   31 Aug 2008 26 Oct 2008 21 Dec 2008 15 F

FIGURE 8.4   S&P 500 Weekly Chart, July 18, 2008, to February 15, 2009
Source: MetaQuotes Software Corp.

trend will continue lower. This is the time to enter new short positions. Exit and take profits when price moves above this zone.

For example, looking at the S&P 500 index weekly chart in Figure 8.4, if we zoom in on Q3 of 2008, from the week of September 7 (down arrow) until the week of December 14 (up arrow), the odds favored maintaining short positions for those trading off weekly charts.

Rule 2: Go Long When Price Is Within or Above the Double BB Buy Zone (Bounded by the Upper Two Bollinger Bands)   As long as price remains within or above the upper two BBs, the upward momentum is strong enough so that there is a high probability that the trend will continue higher. This is the time to enter new long positions. Exit and take profits when price moves below this zone.

For example, looking at the S&P 500 index weekly chart in Figure 8.5, if we zoom in on July 27 to September 27, 2009, bounded by the arrows, the odds favored maintaining long positions for those trading off weekly charts. If we look at the previous chart for the period of July 2008 to

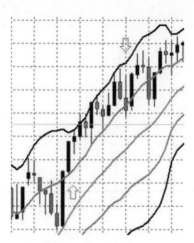

FIGURE 8.5   S&P 500 Weekly Chart, Highlighting the Week of July 27 to September 27, 2009
Source: MetaQuotes Software Corp.

mid-March 2011, it's clear that this indicator would have kept you in for most of the multiyear uptrend and gotten you out before most of the major sell-offs played out.

Rule 3: Trade the Range, Not the Trend, When Price Is between the Buy and Sell Zones

When price is in the middle zone of the one standard deviation Bollinger Bands, the trend isn't strong enough to trust, so don't trade it unless you have enough fundamental evidence or signals from your other technical indicators that suggest the trend will continue. Otherwise, shift your thinking into range-trading mode and start looking for lows and highs that can serve as potential entry and exit points if the channel is wide enough.

See Figure 8.6 for examples of when this did and didn't work during the EU debt crisis (Greek stage) of 2010.

For example, in late April 2010, according to this Rule 3, I should not have been short until the week of May 16, highlighted by the left-hand up arrow.

However, there was a growing chance that the EU might not bail out Greece in time to avoid a market collapse, so I didn't wait to start taking at least some short positions—the fundamentals (and other technical signals I was watching) were enough to justify ignoring Rule 3.

My fundamental thesis: If the collapse of just one major bank (Lehman Brothers) crashed markets in September 2008, imagine what a national

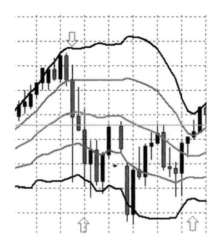

FIGURE 8.6 S&P 500 Weekly Chart—Greek Stage of EU Debt Crisis, 2010
Source: MetaQuotes Software Corp.

default (and wave of defaults that would follow as no one would lend to the other weak EU economies) could do.

So that was a classic case of when to ignore Rule 3, and of the need to find that balance between using too little evidence to see the full picture and using so much that it paralyzes you and prevents you from taking action. In the spring of 2010, DBBs were just not enough.

However, Rule 3 would have worked well in keeping you out of the choppy range-bound action into the spring and early summer of 2010, highlighted by the two up arrows in Figure 8.6. It's harder to trade profitably when there is no clear trend.

Rule 4: Minimize Risk by Waiting Until Price Retraces to the Cheaper End of the Buy or Sell Zone, or Take Partial Positions

This rule attempts to reduce the risk of buying at the top or selling at the bottom that comes when chasing a strong trend.

This rule is not easy to implement. Your success depends on how well you read the other technical and fundamental evidence, and how well you are able to understand whether you're catching a bargain or a falling knife.

Thus the key qualification to Rule 4: There should be no major contradictions from other technical indicators or fundamental data that suggest the trend is in fact exhausted. If there are, stand aside, and don't trade until the situation clarifies.

For example, look at Figure 8.7.

The rule worked well if you bought at the cheap end of the buy zone during the week of September 27, 2009 (first down arrow); there you caught

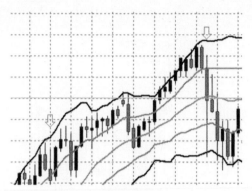

FIGURE 8.7   S&P 500 Weekly Chart, Week of September 27, 2009, to April 25, 2010
Source: MetaQuotes Software Corp.

a bargain. However, if you bought at the close of the week of April 25, 2010, you caught a falling knife, as a threatened Greek default set off a sharp four-week pullback. *The key was to recognize that the fundamentals were so bad at that point that they outweighed the suggested bargain of Rule 4.*

What would have saved you? In addition to reasonable stop losses (which we always use, right?), Rule 4 also suggests taking partial positions when entering strong trends, like one-third of your total planned position if you can't wait for the retracement to the cheaper end of your buy or sell zone, another one-third if or when you get the retracement, and the final one-third when or if you get a bounce back into the buy or sell zone.

See the Appendix on Binary Options at www.thesensibleguidetoforex .com for examples of how we use Double Bollinger Bands to time entries and exits.

Combine DBBs with a Leading Indicator

Because the downtrend needs time to build up the strong momentum to enter the buy or sell zones, Double Bollinger Bands are distinctly lagging indicators and thus not suited for catching less sustained though perfectly tradable trends. For example, if you had solely relied on DBBs during the Greek stage of the EU debt crisis that occurred in the spring of 2010, you would not have gone short the index until the trend was mostly finished. (See Figure 8.8.)

So as good as DBBs are, like any other indicator they need to be used in combination with other technical and fundamental evidence. They're much more effective when used in combination with a leading indicator like moving average crossovers or oscillators like MACD, both covered

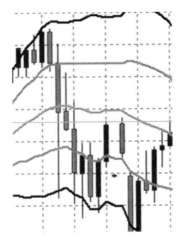

FIGURE 8.8 S&P 500 Weekly Chart, Week of April 25, 2010, to August 1, 2010
Source: MetaQuotes Software Corp.

later in this chapter. These additional indicators can provide earlier signals to open partial positions as a nascent trend forms. Then when the trend is confirmed as it enters the DBB buy or sell zone, you open the rest of the position.

DBBs: Conclusion and Summary

Double Bollinger Bands are incredibly useful, but, like any other technical indicator, they must be used in combination with other evidence, the precise nature of which depends on your style of trading and time frame.

Use DBBs with a Leading Indicator   To avoid missing much of the trend while it works its way into the buy or sell zone, use DBBs in combination with a leading indicator that signals you to begin taking partial positions if you're willing to accept the risk that the trend might fail, in exchange for the greater profits of establishing part of your position at a better price.

MOVING AVERAGE CROSSOVERS

Like Bollinger Bands, moving averages can also be adapted to be leading momentum indicators. By placing multiple moving averages with different durations on our charts, we create a useful momentum indicator, the moving average crossover.

There are two common types of moving average crossovers used to signal possible trend reversals.

1. Price itself crosses over or under a moving average.
2. Shorter-duration moving averages cross over or under longer, slower-moving averages.

Each type signals changing momentum that could be the start of a new trend.

Price Crosses Over or Under a Moving Average

The first type of MA crossover is when the price moves through an important moving average. For example, see Figure 8.9. When price moves below its 50-period simple moving average, or SMA (candle A), it's a sign the trend may be moving lower. When price moves above its 50-period SMA, (candles B and C) it's a sign that the trend may be reversing higher.

Traders who exited long positions on July 1 (A) when price closed below the 50-day SMA avoided a month of losses (and the risk that the

FIGURE 8.9   Gold Daily Chart, June 10 to September 30, 2010

This chart has two sets of BBs, one and two standard deviations from the 20-day SMA baseline in the middle. Here we've added a 50-day SMA, which price crosses at points A and B. Thus we can use a combination of both Bollinger Bands and moving average crossovers of the 20- and 50-day SMAs.

Source: MetaQuotes Software Corp.

pullback could have turned into something far worse). If they entered new long positions when price closed above the 50-day SMA on August 6 (B) or August 11 (C), they caught the beginning of the next move higher.

Note also that there was another sign on August 6 (B) that the trend had resumed. Gold closed the day in its upper Bollinger Band buy zone, providing additional confirmation that the uptrend had resumed.

As noted earlier, moving average crossovers and DBBs make a potent combination for timing entries and exits. The moving average crossovers provide an earlier advanced warning of a trend change, and the DBBs confirm it. More conservative traders or investors might choose not to enter positions until price enters the DBB buy or sell zone. More aggressive ones will enter at least partial positions when they get the moving average crossover. Regardless of your risk tolerance, the fundamental context should be considered before deciding to take a more conservative or aggressive approach.

Two points to remember:

1. Adjust your risk appetite to market conditions. If your analysis makes you confident in the trend, you should be more inclined to open partial positions based on whatever moving average crossover tends to signal the start of a trend. If the evidence is equivocal, you might want to wait until price enters the DBB buy or sell zone, or have some other further confirmation of the move.

2. Which moving average should price cross over to give you a signal for a new trend? While we used the 50-period SMA in the example, that will depend on which one(s) you find provide(s) the best results: that is, those MAs that provide signals early enough to catch most of the move, but not so early that you get more false signals than you're willing to accept. You can learn this from:
   - Trading experience, as recorded in your trade journal.
   - Back testing: This can be as simple as just scrolling the chart backward and observing which moving averages price had to cross before the trends tended to last long enough for a profitable trade, or doing more sophisticated testing via specialized software. We'll do more on back testing in Chapter 9.

The More Indicators in Our Favor, the Better

Note that in Figure 8.9 there was dual confirmation of the new uptrend at points B and C by both:

- Price crossing above the 50-day SMA.
- Price entering the DBB buy zone.

This was a classic case of what we want to see when we enter or exit trades: multiple kinds of indicators confirming each other without any contradicting ones.

How Many Indicators Should You Use?

This is ultimately a judgment call, but the consensus appears to be to use about five (which can mean anything from three to seven) indicators, carefully chosen to complement each other as a mix of trend following, momentum, lagging, leading indicators, and timing or cycle indicators. We've provided enough from which to choose those indicators in order to put the odds in your favor without overloading you with too much information. Combine these technical tools with a solid understanding of:

- The fundamental analysis context, which will help you decide if the underlying fundamentals support or contradict the technical picture.
- Risk and money management (RAMM) techniques, including trade planning and monitoring via your trading journal.

Do all this and you'll be far beyond the typical lay trader. We'll offer some more concrete ideas and examples of combinations of indicators to use as part of your normal toolbox later at the beginning of Chapter 9.

But RAMM Is Key

Beware, however, that indicators are only tools, not crystal balls. That's the reason why we focus so much on risk and money management (RAMM). Assume you'll be wrong a lot. If you've any doubts, please review the quotes at the beginning of Chapter 5 on RAMM from some of the most successful money managers of our generation.

Look at Figure 8.10 to see what happened from late January to March 2010.

During this period we saw the same two indicators pointing to an uptrend, and price crossing the 50-day SMA and entering the DBB buy zone; but they were wrong twice within one month:

- On February 15 we had the same signals as earlier giving dual confirmation of a new uptrend. Price crossed over the 50-day SMA, and also closed within the upper DBB buy zone. Yet the trend reversed lower five sessions later.
- On March 1 price again not only had crossed its 50-day SMA a few days earlier but had also now entered its BB buy zone, only to fall back lower six sessions later.

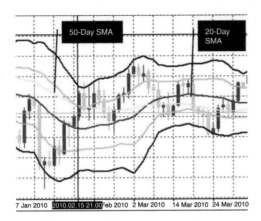

FIGURE 8.10 Gold Daily Chart, January 7 to April 1, 2010
This chart has two sets of BBs, one and two standard deviations from the 20-day SMA baseline in the middle. Again we've added a 50-day SMA. Thus we can use a combination of both Bollinger Bands and moving average crossovers of the 20- and 50-day SMAs.
Source: MetaQuotes Software Corp.

The point is again that indicators are only useful tools that increase the odds of being right; that's all. So we stick to trading only when we have:

- An entry near strong support to serve as a barrier against price moves against our position.
- A risk-to-reward ratio (rrr) at least 1:2, preferably 1:3.

Under these conditions, the odds are heavily in our favor for gains being much larger than losses. That way we can afford to be wrong a lot and still prosper.

While they can never eliminate the risk of loss, the right combination of analysis and RAMM can greatly increase your odds of success.

Moving Averages Cross Each Other

The other type of trend reversal indicator using moving average crossovers is when:

- A shorter-duration moving average crosses *over* a slower, longer-duration moving average, signaling upward, bullish momentum.
- A shorter-duration moving average crosses *under* a slower, longer-duration moving average, signaling downward, bearish momentum.

That is, instead of price crossing over or under a moving average, two separate moving averages cross.

Examples of Simple Trading Systems Using MA Crossovers

As mentioned earlier, your goal is to develop a trading system, which in its simplest form is just some rules for when you enter and exit trades for a given currency pair or other asset. It doesn't have to be complex. Typically even a simple system that you've found works most of the time with a given asset is better than no system at all. To clarify, let's look at a few cases of very simple trading systems using MA crossovers.

For example, if the 20-day MA crosses *above* the less responsive 50-day MA, it's a sign that the trend is more likely to be moving higher. Similarly, if the 20-day MA crosses *under* the 50-day MA, it's a sign that the trend is more likely to be moving lower.

The movements of the shorter-term moving averages are the trigger because, as noted earlier, shorter-duration moving averages like the 20-period MA are more responsive to recent changes than longer-duration ones like the 50-period MA. Thus when a shorter MA crosses above or below a longer one, it's an alert that a longer-term change may be coming, even when this trend is not so clear from the candlesticks themselves.

For example, look again at the daily gold chart we saw in Figure 8.10, reproduced in Figure 8.11. Note that while I use a 20-day SMA here, I also

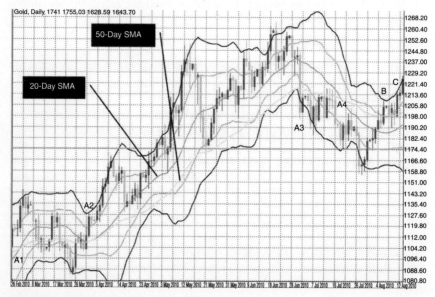

FIGURE 8.11 Gold Daily Chart February 26 to August 12, 2010
Source: MetaQuotes Software Corp.

use a 50-day exponential moving average (EMA) (more responsive than SMAs) in order to make their interaction a bit more sensitive to recent price action. You can do this kind of mix and match of EMAs and SMAs as experience warrants.

Note how the 20-day SMA (used as part of the DBBs) crossed over the 50-day EMA on March 2, 2010 (A1). Even though gold continued to fall for a few more sessions, the MA crossover signaled that the overall trend over the past 20 periods (days on a daily chart) was rising, and in fact this crossover would have alerted you that gold might soon break higher, which it did.

If you did nothing else but stay long in gold until the 20-day SMA crossed below the 50-day EMA on July 19, 2010 (A4), you'd have caught a long uptrend and gotten out before some of the downtrend that followed.

Of course we don't rely on just one indicator. Depending on other indicators you may have used, you might well have had better results. For example, having studied gold's past performance, you may have added some rules that might have improved your performance over the February 26 to August 12 period. For example, you might have only added the application of DBBs along with the MA crossover to form the following overly simple system:

- The 20-day SMA is above the 50-day EMA.
- Once that happens, apply the four rules of Double Bollinger Bands (DBBs). That is, once the 20-day SMA has crossed the 50-day EMA and you are looking to be long gold:
  - Buy when gold has a daily close within or above its DBB buy zone.
  - Sell if gold has a daily close below its DBB buy zone.

Note how well combining just these two rules would have worked. Look again at Figure 8.11, and at the continuation in Figure 8.12.

A few choppy weeks after your initial entry on March 2 (A1), on March 31 (just before the candle labeled A2) gold crossed and closed above both its 50-day and 20-day MAs, then the next day on April 1 (A2) gold crossed into the DBB buy zone. By *just using this simple rule of entering and staying long while gold was in its DBB buy zone, and exiting when it closed below that zone,* you would have caught most of the uptrend in gold over the following eight months, avoided almost all of the drop on July 1 (A3) and the choppy sideways movement from July to early August, and caught virtually all of the uptrend from mid-August onward when the 20-day SMA crossed back over the 50-day EMA on August 22 (D1). You'd have missed the first weeks of gold being back in the DBB buy zone that began in early August (B and C), but that's the price you pay to avoid the choppy market.

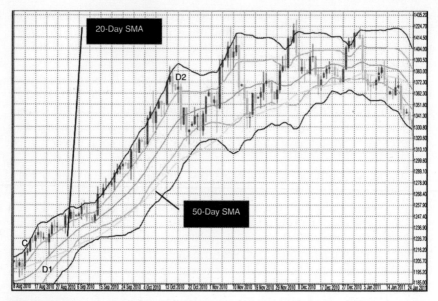

FIGURE 8.12   Gold Daily Chart, August 8, 2010, to January 24, 2011
Source: MetaQuotes Software Corp.

Note what happened from mid-August to mid-October (D1 to D2).

Welcome to Back Testing

By the way, this kind of examining how different indicators have worked together in the past is a simple example of what we call back testing. As we'll discuss later, any truly serious trader or investor will adopt this practice with a passion. We'll revisit this topic in Chapter 9.

In the preceding simple example of back testing the combination of DBBs with MA crossovers, we saw that this overly simple system did very well during this period of a strong trend. Afterward, it clearly didn't work well, highlighting the need for further rules to deal with choppy, range-bound markets. For dealing with such conditions, traders typically turn to oscillators. What are those? Funny you should ask.

OSCILLATORS

Oscillators are a class of technical indicators that measure momentum by comparing the current price to the price range over a given period. These are useful in range-bound markets because that's when price highs and

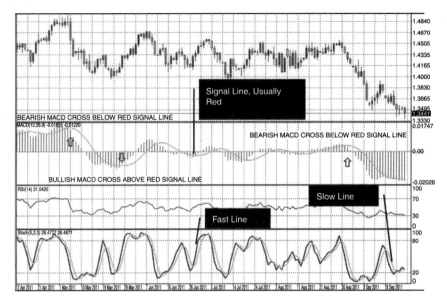

FIGURE 8.13 EURUSD Daily Chart, April 12 to September 26, 2011
Source: MetaQuotes Software Corp.

lows for a given period provide meaningful s/r, and thus are indicators that a reversal is more likely when price approaches these limits.

Figure 8.13 is an example of a daily EURUSD chart with three of the more popular types of oscillators, Moving Average Convergence/ Divergence (MACD) on top, Relative Strength Index (RSI) in the middle, and Stochastic on the bottom.

As their name implies, they oscillate between extreme levels or around a center line. Extremely low readings indicate an exceptionally low price for a given period and theoretically oversold condition. Extreme high readings suggest the opposite. Again, this information is very useful in range-bound markets, but meaningless in strongly trending markets, when the highs and lows that the oscillators depict are obsolete.

There are many oscillators, and there is plenty of good material on their theory and use online if you just enter their names into your search engine of choice. Because our focus is more on providing material on the practice and theory of profiting from forex that you *can't* easily find elsewhere, and because so many of the oscillators are similar, we're going to keep this section brief and recommend that you do some further study of these three so that you understand how they work, and include at least one of them as part of your usual toolbox of four to seven indicators.

Regarding the oscillators shown in Figure 8.13:

- MACD: This one deserves a bit more explanation. Assuming the following standard settings, the histogram shows the difference between a 12-period EMA and a 26-period EMA. Its length and direction show the strength of the bullish or bearish momentum. The signal line is a 9-period SMA that serves as a trend change signal. For particularly good sources on MACD search online, particularly for the books of Dr. Alexander Elder.
- RSI and Stochastic: Both are variations on the basic idea of comparing current price to the price range over a given period. There's plenty of material on both of these online that you can find by just entering the names of these into your search engine of choice, or just search major financial educational websites like investopedia.com or others noted in Appendix A.

How They're Used to Generate Buy/Sell Signals

Oscillators generate buy/sell signals by showing:

- Crossovers: Crossing extreme overbought or oversold levels. With oscillators that use multiple lines such as MACD and stochastics, the crossing of those lines can also generate a buy or sell signal.
- Divergences: When oscillators move in the opposite direction from the trend, that divergence with the trend suggests price may soon change direction.

Crossovers Crossovers occur when price crosses an indicator, or two indicator lines cross, for example:

- Moving average crossovers: As we saw in Figure 8.13 with MACD, one or more moving averages shown cross each other.
- Oscillators cross extreme readings: If they show that price is high relative to prices over the period they cover, that suggests the asset may be overbought and due for a pullback. If they show that price is at the low end of the range for the period in question, that suggests the asset is oversold and is due for a bounce. For example:
  - The RSI can generate buy and sell signals when it goes beyond the 70 and 30 lines shown in Figure 8.13 and then reenters the middle zone between these lines, suggesting a reversal is coming.
  - The stochastic does the same when it exceeds either the 20 line or the 80 line as shown in Figure 8.13 and then reenters the middle zone between these lines. The crossing of the faster line over or under

the slower line also suggests a change in trend momentum that can signal a coming bullish or bearish reversal.

- When the MACD histogram crosses under the (usually red) signal line, that's bearish, suggesting further reversal lower. When it crosses above the (usually red) signal line, that's bullish, signaling possible reversal higher. Again, see Figure 8.13 for examples, with bullish and bearish crosses highlighted and labeled.

When Price and Oscillator Trends Diverge   Momentum oscillators generally move in the same direction as price. However, because the momentum oscillators are measuring not just the direction of price change but also the *rate of change in price*, their direction will diverge from the direction of the price of the asset when the rate of change slows. In other words, when price is moving higher or lower, so should the oscillator. However, when the speed of that trend slows, the direction of the momentum oscillators will start to diverge from that of price. *Those divergences can be valuable leading indicators of a possible trend reversal. For example, slowing momentum, as reflected by these divergences, suggests a trend reversal may be coming.* (See Figure 8.14.)

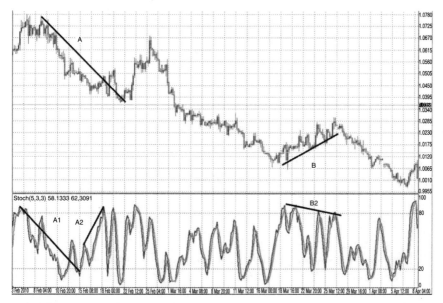

FIGURE 8.14   USDCAD Four-Hour Chart, February 3 to April 8, 2010
Source: MetaQuotes Software Corp.

Here's some explanation.

- Lines A and A1: These are examples of how an oscillator typically moves in the same direction as price, in this case reflecting the same downward momentum.
- Lines A and A2: Even though the USDCAD is moving lower, A2 shows how the stochastic oscillator is suggesting a reversal is coming, as it reflects increasing bullish momentum (or fading bearish momentum). In other words, recent prices have been higher over the period it measures, hence the uptrend in the stochastic that foretells the coming uptrend.
- Lines B and B2: Again, while the USDCAD itself is moving higher, the momentum of the move is weakening over the dates covered; hence, while the pair itself keeps moving higher, the stochastic starts trending lower, forecasting the coming reversal.

When to Use Oscillators

We repeat: Oscillators are not that useful in strongly trending markets because prior highs or lows are not especially relevant. The perception of value is changing, hence the irrelevance of old highs and/or lows.

That said, in range-bound or gently trending markets they're very useful in providing evidence of coming turns. The wider the trading range or channel, the lower the risk and the higher the potential yield. As we noted earlier when discussing channels, be wary of trading against the direction of the channel unless the channel is wide enough to allow you to profit even as time erodes your room to profit and pulls resistance closer each day.

Other Oscillators to Consider

There are many. First do some more research on the ones we've mentioned. Not only are they as useful as any, they are also among the most popular and thus help you to understand what other traders are thinking and to anticipate their moves.

Here's a partial list of other very popular oscillators you should certainly consider:

- Commodity Channel Index (CCI): Despite its name, the CCI works equally well with forex and stocks, too, and provides both oversold/overbought as well as divergence indicators.
- Rate of Change (ROC): This indicator measures the percent change from the price a given number of periods ago. It is useful as both a

divergence and an oversold/overbought indicator as it oscillates around a zero line.

- Williams %R: Generates buy/sell signals via overbought/oversold, crossover, and divergences. It's very similar to Stochastic %K, except that Williams %R is plotted a bit differently, using negative values ranging from 0 to –100. It's the creation of Larry Williams, who, in addition to being a star commodities trader and investor, has published nine books on investing and won the Robbins World Cup Championship of Futures Trading in 1987.

Designer Genes

Williams's daughter grew up watching him, was homeschooled by the man himself, and 10 years later in 1997 won the cup herself—at age 17! Not only did she win it, but she also crushed the competition and all that followed ever since then. No one has yet topped her returns of 1,000 percent. Talk about talent; trading isn't even her focus. She's the actress Michelle Williams, whose credits include the TV series *Dawson's Creek* and three Oscar nominations, if you don't mind, for her roles in *Brokeback Mountain, Blue Valentine,* and *My Week with Marilyn.* Still, as Momma Wachtel would say, good that she has something to fall back on in case acting doesn't work out.[2]

MOVING AVERAGE LAYERING INDICATES TREND STRENGTH

If you insert 10-, 20-, 50-, 100-, and 200-period MAs on your chart, the way they are layered or ordered can tell you a lot about the strength of the current trend.

Here are the basic rules.

The Stronger the Trend, the Clearer the MA Layering

By "clearer" we mean that the distance between the MAs will be greater and the slope will be steeper.

Specifically:

The Stronger the Uptrend, the More the MAs Will Be Layered with Shorter Durations on the Top   The most bullish MA layering is when the shortest (most responsive to price changes) duration MA is on the top and the longest (least responsive to price changes) duration MA is

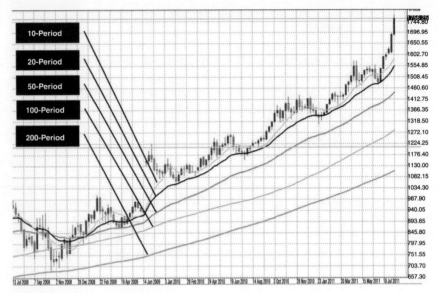

FIGURE 8.15   Gold Weekly Chart, January 13, 2009, to August 9, 2011
Source: MetaQuotes Software Corp.

on the bottom, and the trend itself is sitting above them all. For example, see Figure 8.15.

In case you're wondering why I'm using a gold chart in a forex book, it's because gold is primarily a currency hedge when markets are feeling concerned about the long-term buying power of the major currencies, particularly of the USD and EUR. Thus forex traders often trade gold, and most retail forex firms offer it along with other commodities. Demand for either of these currencies falls when there's anxiety about their purchasing power, making gold a useful alternative way to play weakness in either or both of these currencies.

Currency traders and investors may wind up trading gold (as well as oil, silver, copper, etc.) and other currency-related commodities as another way of playing currency trends or hedging currency bets, particularly those involving the EUR and USD. We'll look further at the relationship between gold and the EUR and USD in Chapter 9.

Figure 8.16 is another example, which we include because it connects so well with the following examples illustrating the other MA layering rules.

Note how until the week of June 17, 2007, the EMAs were layered exactly as we'd want to see to confirm a strong uptrend, with the 10-week

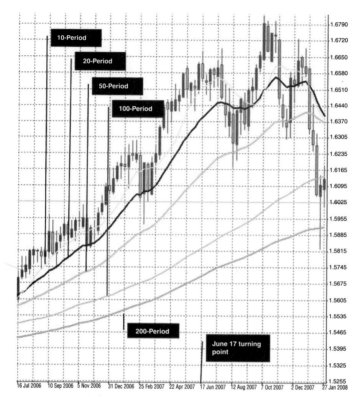

FIGURE 8.16 EURCHF Weekly Chart, July 16, 2006, to January 27, 2008
Source: MetaQuotes Software Corp.

EMA on top, followed by the 20-, 50-, 100-, and 200-week EMAs, all sloping higher.

But wait! Note how from that point onward, the 10-week, then 20-week, then 50-week EMAs' slopes flattened, then turned down. From early July to late October 2007 the 10- and 20-week EMAs were flattening out, hinting at a trend reversal. By early December the EURCHF had begun a downtrend (a series of lower highs and lower lows). By late December 2007 the 10-week EMA had turned down and was about to cross beneath the now falling 20-week EMA, and both would then cross the now descending 50-week EMA (see Figure 8.17). This brings us to our next rule.

The Weaker the Trend, the More Mixed the MA Layering By "mixed" we mean that the orderly EMA layering starts to break down, with the shorter-duration EMAs flattening out and then crossing below or

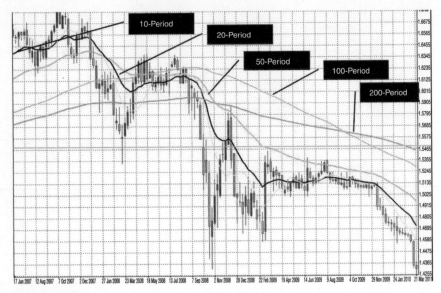

FIGURE 8.17   EURCHF Weekly Chart, June 17, 2007, to March 21, 2010
Source: MetaQuotes Software Corp.

above the longer-term EMAs, signaling that the trend is losing momentum (in either direction) in the trend and a possible reversal up or down. Such moving average crossovers are classic momentum indicators.

For example, when previously rising shorter-term moving averages start falling and crossing beneath longer-term EMAs, that's a classic sign that an uptrend is losing momentum and could be reversing. Look what happened to the EURCHF from late December 2007 to mid-December 2009 in Figure 8.17.

Note how the layering that began flattening and then reversing from July to December 2007 suggested that a much longer-term reversal was coming. This brings us to our third rule.

The Stronger the Downtrend, the More the MAs Will Be Layered with Shorter Durations on the Bottom   The most bearish MA layering is when the longest-duration MA is on the top and the shortest-duration MA is on the bottom, and the trend itself is sitting beneath them all. As we saw in Figure 8.17, the downtrend was already well established by September 2008 as the world fell into recession and the more safe haven CHF began a long-term uptrend versus the EUR; the process was already

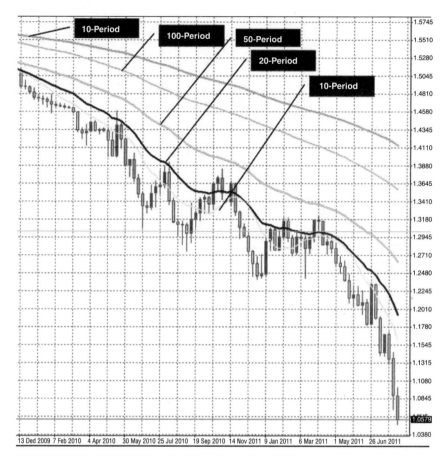

FIGURE 8.18 EURCHF Weekly Chart, December 13, 2009, to August 9, 2011
Source: MetaQuotes Software Corp.

completed by December 2009. Figure 8.18 better illustrates the completed layering confirming a classic strong downtrend.

Due to length limits for this book, I couldn't provide trade examples using momentum indicators. Look for them at www.thesensiblegui detoforex.com under the Practice Trade Simulations tab and other parts of the website where we'll feature trading ideas.

CHAPTER 9

Technical Analysis

Future Study

A central principle of good teaching is that it gives the student a clear path on which to continue once the teacher exits. A common fault in trading books is that either they provide insufficient guidance about what to learn next or they presume that they've taught you everything you need to succeed. Unfortunately that's impossible to do.

Trading books tend to focus on what is most relevant to the author's own trading style, and there are just too many ways to trade for any one book to possibly cover them all well.

After having studied this book, you're ready to start applying the specific methods and tools we've taught on practice accounts, and then with real accounts. These are good starting points, but it's quite possible that you'll grow in other directions.

Regarding what to learn next, this chapter is meant to introduce you to the next technical analysis (TA) topics you'll want to learn as part of your continuing education, to expand your analytical skills and find the trading style that best fits you.

CATCH A WAVE: TIMING OR CYCLE INDICATORS

Be it in surfing, comedy, investing, or anything else, the right timing is critical. In addition to Fibonacci retracements, covered in Chapter 4, there are a number of other indicators that help you understand the inner rhythm

255

of price movements. Like electricity, we can use them effectively without really understanding why they work. As with Fibonacci retracements, deploying these others successfully depends on correctly identifying the relevant trend on which to draw your retracement levels. It's not hard, but you do get better with practice. Fibonacci retracements are an excellent starting point, but you eventually want to be comfortable with a few of the following, particularly Elliott Wave analysis and Fibonacci extensions.

Meet the Fibonaccis

In addition to Fib retracements, there are also:

- Extensions or expansions.

After retracements, they get my vote for next most useful fibonacci indicators. They are attempts to indicate how far the next move in the direction of the trend will be, as opposed to Fibonacci retracements, which indicate how far the pullback will retrace from the current trend.

There are also Fibonacci:

- Time zones.
- Arcs.
- Fans.

... And the Ganns

From the work of William D. Gann we get:

- Gann Lines.

and also:

- Fans.
- Grids.

Catch the Most Popular Wave: Elliott Wave Theory and More

Everyone should have some familiarity with Elliott Wave analysis, one of the oldest and most popular forms of timing or cycle analysis. Again, popular indicators have the added bonus of telling you what the crowd is thinking. Other approaches to surfing the waves of price movements include

DiNapoli levels, Goodman Wave Theory, and more, but let this much suffice. You've got enough to investigate as time permits.

COMBINING TECHNICAL INDICATORS: WHICH ONES AND HOW MANY?

One of the hardest, most time-consuming aspects of trading is figuring out what trading style(s) and time frame(s) suit you best. From the technical analysis perspective, that means finding the right toolbox of indicators you habitually use and learn very well.

As noted earlier, the consensus is that about five indicators is the right balance between enough information to make informed decisions and not too much so that you suffer from information overload, aka paralysis by analysis. Practically, that can mean anywhere from three to seven; it's ultimately your choice. You don't have to stick with the same tools all the time; just limit the number you're watching at any given time. Those trading longer time frames have more time and can afford to look at more indicators. They also need to be better informed about the long-term fundamentals of both:

- The underlying economies of the currencies they trade.
- The big macroeconomic drivers of the global economy that drive risk appetite and influence *all* markets *all* the time.

This is critical. At minimum it involves following a few good fundamental analysts to read and at least one big picture indicator like the S&P 500 Index (and what's driving it for your chosen time frame). I write weekly reviews of the past week's top market drivers and the likely ones for the coming week, simply because I couldn't find anyone who was already providing the big picture of the prior and coming weeks' top market drivers (which I generally post both on my own sites, as well as on SeekingAlpha.com, ForexFactory.com, and others. John Kicklighter at DailyFX.com, and Kathleen Brooks of Forex.com provide some of my favorite weekly reviews for forex, and there are often excellent weekly reviews from top banks on FXstreet.com. Joel Kruger of DailyFX .com and Boris Schlossberg and Kathy Lien of Bkassetmanagement .com are always part of my daily forex reading. For commodities (closely related to forex, as we'll see later), Oil N' Gold (oilngold.com) usually has a very good weekly review of what was driving commodity markets. I read these and many others and try to sort out the big drivers influencing all markets in my weekly articles. For more on my favorite daily and weekly reads, see Appendix A.

Your Tool Kit Needs a Gang of Four

While your exact choice of indicators can vary with preference, needs, and trading style, the overriding principle in selecting your tool kit of indicators is to have a balance that gives you a "gang of four" of different kinds of information you need, specifically:

1. Trend or trading range.
2. Momentum.
3. Support/resistance.
4. Timing or cycles.

Trend or Range   Examples are trend lines, channels, moving averages, and Double Bollinger Bands. DBBs are really a hybrid trend and momentum indicator. In range-bound markets, DBBs provide support and resistance (s/r) points. When there's a trend, they show the trend's momentum and likely staying power.

Momentum Indicators   You should strongly consider using Double Bollinger Bands and one or two oscillators of choice, especially moving average convergence/divergence (MACD). A set of moving average lines like we saw earlier (10, 20, 50, 100, and 200 period) not only serves as a momentum indicator, it also provides s/r points, too.

Support/Resistance Points   In addition to obvious price levels that stand out on your chart (and on time frames four to five times shorter and longer), you should always watch:

- The s/r points generated from trend or range indicators.
- The s/r points formed by Western-style chart patterns, both their trend lines and implied breakout targets, as shown in Chapter 4. See Figures 4.14, 4.16, 4.18, 4.19, 4.20, 4.21, 4.23, and 4.24 for examples.

Timing or Cycle Indicators   Fibonacci, Elliott Wave, Gann, DiNapoli, and similar studies are timing or cycle indicators.

For example, your typical technical tool kit might include, in addition to an awareness of any obvious s/r points:

- A set of moving averages of 10, 20, 50, 100, and 200 periods: Again, these serve as both s/r points as well as momentum indicators if they show crossing or layering as discussed in Chapter 8.
- Trend/channel lines show the trend and provide s/r points.

- Double Bollinger Bands and MACD show changes in momentum.
- Fibonacci retracements of the most recent trends in each given time frame suggest possible s/r points. You'd need to redraw these for each time frame that you examine, as the primary trends may differ dramatically in different time frames.
- If you spot any Western-style chart pattern forming, note the implied s/r levels (highs, lows, necklines, shoulders, etc.). Japanese candlestick patterns provide shorter-term signals of trend continuation or reversal.

Apply Indicators to Each Time Frame When Screening Trades

You'd then apply this group of indicators to the time frame in which you trade, as well as those four to five times longer and shorter. For example, if you trade off daily charts, you'd also look at weekly and two- to four-hour charts (depending on whether you define your trading day as 24 hours or 8 to 10 hours).

A good charting program like that included with MetaTrader 4 will allow you to store any group of indicators you like as a chart template that can be applied to any chart of any asset or time frame your broker offers.

As shown in our trading examples in Chapter 7:

- The purpose of your first screening on the longer time frame (weekly, in our examples) is to find longer-term s/r points than you would see on the charts on which you trade, and hopefully, find a currency pair that looks like it might reach that s/r area and provide a low-risk entry point. That's the first step in locating low-risk, high-yield trades.
- Your second screening would then examine the likely entries and exits on the shorter time frame chart from which you trade, to see if you can find situations where your entry point is two to three times farther from your exit than it is from your stop loss. The profit-taking point is usually easy to spot. It's whether you can get the right stop loss point that usually determines whether you take the trade. See the description of the second screening in Chapter 7 for a review of the criteria for a low-risk stop loss that isn't too close to your entry point so that you don't risk getting stopped out by random price movements.
- Your third screening would check your shorter time frame (two- to four-hour charts in our examples) to look for any short-term s/r points, just so you're aware of temporary s/r points. If those hold too long or too often, your trade may be showing signs of failing and you might want to reduce your position size. If, however, these are quickly breached, that's a sign of progress and a signal to consider adding to your position.

BACK TESTING: LEARNING FROM THE PAST

> Those who do not learn from history are doomed to repeat it.
> —*Philosopher George Santayana*

At some point, any serious trader will develop his or her own sets of rules or conditions for entering and exiting trades. These sets of rules are called trading systems, and they are of vastly varying degrees of complexity.

The only way to avoid losing money on bad systems is to test them using prior market data. That's called back testing, and it is as essential as risk and money management (RAMM) practices and trading journals for developing good trading rules and habits.

The goal of back testing is to discover a set of rules for a given time frame and currency pair (or other instrument) for entering and exiting positions so that over time you're consistently profitable. That profitability can come from a high percentage of winning trades, high profits on fewer winning trades that outweigh the losses, or anything in between. Typically these rules work only in certain market conditions. In other words, for a given asset or currency pair, you'll develop different systems for trending markets, range-bound flat markets, and so on. You may also find that you need different systems for different kinds of assets.

Back Testing Software: Play It Again, Sam

Today any serious back testing is done via computer software designed for that purpose. It works by simulating trades when the programmed signals or conditions appear on the historical price data. The goal is to test the system's potential profitability and maximum drawdown or risk over the given historical data.

Computerized back testing works for technical trading strategies as long as their rules are clear and unambiguous enough to be translated into programming code. It can also be applied to fundamental strategies as long as the strategy can be reduced to a set of clear, quantifiable criteria like interest rates, growth statistics, or other quantifiable macroeconomic data and/or the logical or mathematical relationships between them.

A quick online search will yield a wealth of information about various software packages. Online forex forums will provide a venue to benefit from the experience of others. There are many such venues. A few off the top of my head include (look under their "forum" tabs or links):

- ForexFactory.com: Has a trading systems forum on the homepage.
- Currensee.com: Under the Social Network tab of the homepage.
- DailyFX.com: Under the Forum tab.

These sites have active forums that should provide a good place to start along with a diligent online search for information on how to back test and which software to use.

The preceding also applies for researching automated trading systems. More on these in Chapter 10.

A Manual Back Testing Example

Before you're ready to work with back testing software, you should first go through the experience of manually back testing. You will learn a lot, improve your technical analysis skills, and be a better testing software user. Manual tests also give you a quick-and-dirty way to play with indicators and get a sense of what combinations deserve further investigation.

We'll take a deeper look at manual back testing so that you better understand how back testing works.

Technical Tools   To keep the illustration simple, we'll use:

- Double Bollinger Bands (DBBs).
- A set of exponential moving averages (EMAs): 10, 20, 50, and 200 period.
- Awareness of established s/r price levels.
- MACD standard settings (12, 26, 9).

Together these will provide our gang of four indicators: s/r, momentum, trend, and timing/cycle indicators as discussed earlier.

The Purpose   To see if these provide leading (predictive) and/or lagging (confirming) indications of the start and/or end of a tradable price move. In other words, you'll want to scroll back in time on the charts and observe how these interacted with price when trends both began and ended. If you see that they behaved the same way each time (or most of the time) a trend began and/or ended, you then have a set of rules to follow for when to enter and exit a trade.

In its simplest form, our overall goal is to develop rules for entering and exiting trades. Specifically, we want to distinguish the real signals from the false ones; that is:

- Entry rules that provide early entry signals only at the start of real trends, yet don't issue entry signals at the start of false trends.
- Exit rules that don't issue exit signals until the trend has fully run its course, do issue exit signals before you lose profits to a trend stopping or reversing.

The reality is that you'll need to strike a balance between rules that offer higher profits with higher risk of loss versus those that offer lower profits and lower risk. In other words, you'll probably need to choose between sets of rules that offer higher reward and risk versus those that offer the lower reward and risk.

That means you must choose between rules that offer more risk and reward or less risk and reward:

- Higher risk/reward versus lower risk/reward entry rules: The former get you in sooner but catch more false trends; the latter miss more of the trend as they wait for more trend confirmation and safer entries.
- Higher risk/reward versus lower risk/reward exit rules: The former keep you in the trade longer to both ride the trend longer (for greater profits) and its reversal (for greater losses); the latter get you out faster, and miss more of the trend (for lower profits) and its reversal (for lower risk).

If all of this sounds abstract, the examples that follow should clarify what you're trying to do with back testing.

Time Frame   Let's assume we're long-term forex investors looking to develop some rules for trading long-term trends with the above indicators for the AUDUSD on its *monthly* chart. Figure 9.1 presents the AUDUSD monthly chart from September 1, 1996, through September 2008. The same process applies to any time frame.

The Thought Process   Here's a simple example of how we create a simple set of rules. The following example refers to Figure 9.1.

First, start looking for the strong, clear trends—defining a strong trend as one that entered and stayed in the DBB buy zone (between the upper two Bollinger Bands) for at least three to four months. Alternatively, you could look for well defined trading ranges too, but for this example we'll seek clear trends.

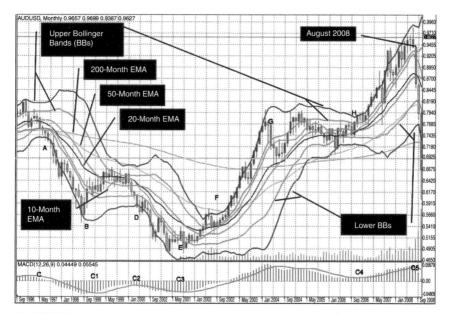

FIGURE 9.1 AUDUSD Monthly Chart, September 1, 1996, to September 30, 2008
Source: MetaQuotes Software Corp.

Then we'll look at how the DBBs and EMAs reacted (and interacted with the candles) both before and after these started to identify leading and confirming indicators.

To identify leading indicators, look at what tended to happen before the trend started. If we can identify a pattern of behavior for how these indicators interact with price, we'll know how these may signal the start of a trend (aka be a leading indicator).

To identify confirming indicators (to help us trade only real trends not false moves), we look at how these indicators acted (and interacted with the candles) at the start of real trends that lasted versus those false-start trends that didn't follow through. More specifically:

- To find leading indicators, we're looking for what lines were crossed before or at the start of the trend.
- To find confirming indicators, we're looking for what lines were crossed after the successful trends got started, and want to see that these same crossings didn't occur for trends that failed (the ones that didn't stay in the DBB buy or sell zones for an extended, tradable period).

So, what do we find with this simple back testing exercise?

In April 2000 (D), the AUDUSD began a nice long dip into the DBB sell zone (lower two Bollinger Bands), our definition of a tradable downtrend. To find possible leading indicators, let's see if our indicators would have given us any clues in advance that this downtrend would start.

Starting at the earliest part of the chart to the left, we note that in July 1997 (A) the AUDUSD entered the DBB sell zone and stayed there for a strong, very tradable long-term downtrend until it rose out of the sell zone in October 1998 (B). The fact that the AUDUSD was already below its 200-, 50-, 20-, and 10-month EMAs already gave us a clearly bearish sign, but what signaled that the pair would enter and remain in its DBB sell zone, our definition of a strong downtrend?

From July 1997 to October 1998, note that as long as the 10-month EMA was below the 20-month EMA *and* the MACD histogram remained below the signal line (from C to C1), the AUDUSD stayed within a strong downtrend, defined as the pair being in its DBB sell zone. So the tentative rules for shorting the AUDUSD from studying this period would be that all three of the following conditions must be present for us to short the pair:

1. The AUDUSD is in its DBB sell zone.
2. The 10-month EMA is below the 20-month EMA (A to B, D to E).
3. The MACD histogram is below its signal line (C to C1, C2 to C3).

From April 2000 (D and C2) to August 2001 (E and C3), following these same rules would have worked again, keeping you in a profitable AUDUSD short position at any time you entered until the final months for most of the downtrend.

Applying these same three criteria for being in long AUDUSD positions also worked. That is, to be long the AUDUSD we would need the following three conditions in place:

1. The AUDUSD is in its DBB *buy* zone (F to G): Note this was the first indicator to issue a sell signal (price falls below buy zone) and to get us out in April 2004 (G) so we would miss the choppy price action that occurred until October 2006 (H).
2. The 10-month EMA is above the 20-month EMA (F to G).
3. The MACD histogram is above its signal line (C4), which occurred in December 2006. Waiting for this indicator to give us a bullish signal would have kept us from taking any long position until then, even though the AUDUSD had entered the DBB buy zone. That's fine; the price action from October to December of 2006 was choppy even though the pair was in the buy zone, so it was no big loss.

Again, this example was simplified for illustration purposes. It was also shortened. Normally, we'd scroll back and look at multiple past examples of what happened with our indicators before and during major trend changes.

My point was not to give you a complete system for trading the AUDUSD during the time period covered. Rather it was to show you the kind of thought process you go through when doing simple back testing. If we had wanted to do a full back testing we'd have looked at a longer period, asked a lot more questions, and at some point inserted some Fibonacci retracements to see how the pair would respond at different retracement levels.

Here's a final word about manual back testing. In the example we looked at this 9.5-year period all at once just to get an initial quick idea of a set of rules that might work and show you the basic thought process. Part of your further testing would involve scrolling back in time on the chart, then scrolling forward one candle at a time so that you can't see subsequent price movements, and simulating the strategy as if you were implementing it in real time. That process helps avoid the temptation to trade using hindsight that wouldn't be available in real trading. Remember, you can trade only from the far right side of the chart. You can't trade from its middle.

Back Testing Is a Tool, Not a Solution

History doesn't repeat itself—at best it sometimes rhymes.
—Mark Twain

Back testing is a valuable tool for any serious trader. However, just because a system seems to have worked in the past doesn't mean it will remain effective in the future. Even if you do design a system that works, market conditions and the correlations they produce change over time, and because others will eventually discover a similar system on their own and eliminate your advantage.

So by all means learn more about back testing and how to do it better via software. Just know that it's only a fallible tool, not a foolproof route to fast riches. Apply full RAMM practices when using back tested systems.

INTERMARKET ANALYSIS: READING INTERMARKET CORRELATIONS AND DIVERGENCES

Another area for further study will be learning how to do intermarket analysis. A full treatment of this topic alone could cover multiple books, big books. However, we just want to introduce this area of analysis so you understand what it is, why it's important, and thus why you need to pay attention when you read analysts talking about what another market may be telling about what could happen in forex.

Specifically, we'll introduce how to use price movements in other markets to predict what could happen to a given currency pair.

Background

In essence, intermarket analysis is all about

- Knowing how different assets, asset classes, and markets correlate— that is, whether they tend to move in the same direction (positive correlation) or the opposite direction (negative correlation).
- Watching for divergences from those correlations: Those divergences are often leading or coincident indicators of changing market conditions. Over time you'll see how some markets tend to react before others, and so provide advanced notice of changes from which you can profit.

We noted in Chapter 2 that currencies can be classified as either risk or safe haven, depending on whether they behave like risk or safe haven assets. That is, currencies have either a positive or a negative correlation with other risk assets. In fact, virtually every tradable financial instrument can be classified as a risk or safe haven asset. For a variety of reasons, most global asset markets share some kind of general correlation. *That is, they generally move in either the same direction or opposite directions*, either because:

- Causation and thus correlation: One market acts on another. For example, because most commodities are priced in U.S. dollars, if the dollar gets stronger, that puts pressure on commodity prices and vice versa. This rule doesn't always hold, because there are a variety of other forces that influence both commodities and the dollar. Another example, crude oil, is usually a risk asset that moves in response to the popular risk asset barometers like the S&P 500. However, when oil prices spike suddenly as they did during the Arab Spring of 2011, those suddenly much higher prices hurt growth and thus risk assets. Oil was now not only moving in the opposite direction of other risk assets, but actually directly driving them higher or lower, not merely reacting to macroeconomic data along with them.
- Correlation without causation: Both markets are influenced by the same underlying drivers, either in similar or in opposite ways, but

aren't influencing each other. For example, when markets are feeling optimistic, the classic risk assets like equities, commodities, and higher-yielding and commodity-driven currencies *all tend to rise together because they're reacting to the same things in the same way.* Meanwhile, classic safe haven assets like the lower-yielding currencies and bonds fall together. When markets are fearful, the opposite happens. Both groups of assets are responding to the same good or bad news, just in opposite ways. They are usually not causing each other to rise or fall.

For example, in recent years the USD and equities tend to move in opposite directions, leading many ill-informed journalists to blame a rising USD for falling stocks. Typically the flimsy rationale was that a rising USD made U.S. exports less competitive. The point is true, but not relevant. By the same reasoning, a rising USD should be accompanied by rising stocks in nations dependent on exporting to the United States. Yet, in fact, global stock indexes all move together with those of the United States, invalidating the above rationale. In fact, the real reason that U.S. stocks and the USD move in opposite directions is that stocks are risk assets and the USD is a safety asset. By definition they tend to move in opposite directions.

In fact, there are times when news favors both risk assets and the USD, like when the United States reports strong jobs or consumer spending data. This news not only raises optimism about U.S. growth (good for stocks), it also raises expectations for U.S. rate increases and reduces the chances of additional U.S. stimulus (both bullish for the USD).

Just be aware that these relationships can and do change over time, as noted earlier with crude oil and risk assets.

When the normal relationships don't apply, it could well be a sign of important trend changes coming. Let's look at a few simple examples.

Currencies versus Equities: The S&P 500 as Forex Indicator

The S&P 500 may be the most widely watched single barometer of risk appetite. That's not so surprising, given that it has the largest market capitalization of any stock index and is the prime index of the world's largest economy. However, if you trade at times of the day when the U.S. markets are closed, you'd need to watch the major indexes for the markets that are open. For example, those trading during the Asian session would want to keep an eye on the Nikkei, Shanghai, and Hang Seng indexes at a minimum. The only warning with watching these is that they often simply play catch-up to whatever happened the night before in New York, unless some significant news breaks while these regions are trading.

Risk Currencies versus Safe Haven Currencies

Again, (it's worth repeating) as noted in Chapter 2, certain major currencies are referred to as the risk currencies, because they tend to move in the same direction as other risk assets like these major global stock indexes (*not* because they are any less safe a store of value). The risk currencies are, ranked in order of riskiness (i.e., starting with the most correlated to other risk assets):

RISK	⟶				SAFE HAVEN		
RISK CURRENCIES					SAFE HAVEN CURRENCIES		
AUD	NZD	CAD	EUR	GBP	CHF	USD	JPY

For example, when stocks are moving sharply higher, we would expect the AUD to be doing best, followed by the NZD, CAD, and so on. In reality they rarely perform in that precise order, but that's the general idea.

The other major currencies, referred to as safe haven currencies, tend to move in the opposite direction of risk assets like global stock indexes (not because they are necessarily any safer as stores of value). In times of fear, stocks and risk currencies tend to sell off, and these safe haven currencies, along with other safe haven assets like AAA-rated bonds, tend to rise in value. The safe havens are, ranked in order of how well they generally perform in times of fear (and how poorly they do when risk assets are rising): the JPY, USD, and CHF.

Because currencies trade in pairs, in times of optimism (aka risk appetite) the classic pairs to buy are those with a highly ranked risk base currency and safe haven counter currency, like the AUDJPY, AUDUSD, NZDJPY, NZDUSD, EURUSD, and so on. Remember, pairs move up or down depending on whether the base currency (the one on the left) is moving up or down relative to the counter currency (the one on the right).

Similarly, in times of fear, traders do the opposite. Risk pairs like those just mentioned are shorted, and traders go long on pairs with a relatively safe base currency versus its counter currency, like the USDCAD.

WHY THESE RELATIONSHIPS MATTER

Here are reasons why these relationships are important.

They Give You a Fast, Big Picture

Just knowing how certain currencies and pairs are supposed to move relative to stocks, as represented by the major global indexes like the S&P 500, is incredibly valuable for giving you a quick big picture of how forex markets should be behaving.

For example, if during the Asian session you see that the major Asian indexes are up, you'd expect to see the AUD, NZD, CAD, EUR, and GBP up versus the safe haven currencies, more or less in that order. If not, that's something you may want to investigate if one of the currencies or pairs you're watching is not behaving as it should. Sometimes the answer is obvious, sometimes not.

For example, if China comes out with great monthly data, that's usually very bullish for risk assets given China's importance as a major growth engine. Risk currencies on the daily charts should be strong, especially the AUD, because China is Australia's biggest export customer. If, however, the AUD is weak that day, or weak against a specific currency, an AUD trader would want to know why.

Let's say on this day of great China data the AUDUSD is flat or down. Possible explanations include that there was some bad Australian economic news, or there was some U.S. economic news that raised expectations about U.S. interest rates that is helping the USD more than the Chinese data helps the AUD. Those watching or trading a pair involving the AUD would want to check further in order to know if the explanation influenced their current trading plan.

Divergences from Normal Correlations Can Be Significant

In the previous chapter we saw how divergences from normal correlations between trends of momentum oscillators and an asset may warn of a coming trend reversal.

When trends of assets that normally correlate suddenly diverge, that kind of divergence can signal a coming trend reversal for one of them, because divergences often mean that one of the markets hasn't yet recognized a change in conditions. When it does, its trend will reverse and fall back into its normal correlation with the other trend. Those who identify these divergences first and interpret them correctly get advance notice of a trend change and a chance at big, easy profits.

For example, note how in the charts in Figure 9.2, during the period of July 4 to 8, 2011, the S&P 500 (top) was moving higher, suggesting rising risk appetite. Yet the EURUSD (bottom) trend, which tends to move in the same direction as other risk assets like this index, was falling. Which market was right, and which market was due for a reversal?

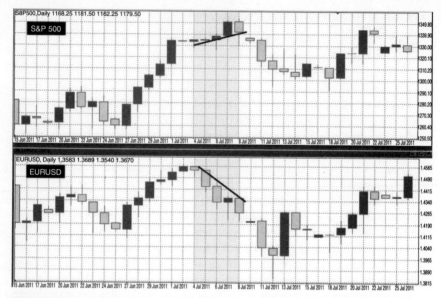

FIGURE 9.2   S&P 500 versus EURUSD Daily Charts, July 15 to 26, 2011
Source: MetaQuotes Software Corp.

Figure 9.2 is a great example illustrating why any investor or trader needs to be familiar with forex markets, especially those involved with equities. Forex markets often lead equities markets. Those watching the EURUSD had advance warning that the S&P 500 could be pulling back, which it soon did. Those who understood the fundamental drivers of the EURUSD knew why.

They knew that the reason for this divergence in trends was a rising risk of a Greek sovereign bond default, which could set off a wave of other sovereign defaults. Borrowing costs for other EU nations with high debt/GDP ratios would rise beyond their means with perceived higher risk, pushing them toward default as their normal bond payments became due. That in turn risked a wave of defaults among the banks that held the bonds, and so risked another systemic banking crisis similar to that of 2008 when Lehman Brothers bank collapsed. Indeed that risk was rising for a variety of reasons.

This information was valuable in a number of ways. For example:

- Currency traders who noted this divergence knew that market anxiety about Greece and the EU was rising, and that could easily drag down all other risk assets and boost safe haven assets, as it had in the spring of 2010.

- These investors would thus be better prepared to short major indexes like the S&P 500 (and other risk assets) once these indexes showed signs of reversing lower.
- Traders viewing the EURUSD would rightly suspect the USD should be stronger versus other currencies, given the extra push it would be getting from the EUR's decline.

As we mentioned in Chapter 1, one of the reasons that everyone needs some forex background is that forex markets (perhaps due to their more international focus) often reflect changing conditions before other markets do, certainly before the equities herd, who are typically the last to know (perhaps because equities traders tend to focus on the national or regional stock exchange). That advance knowledge can make you a better trader or investor, no matter what market you're in.

By the way, on July 13 the EURUSD also provided advance warning that the S&P 500 would be heading higher. Note the strong upward candle, suggesting optimism about the EU crisis. Fears about the EU had been pressuring the S&P 500, so it's not surprising that calming about the EU, as reflected by the rising EURUSD, would soon bring a move up in the S&P 500. Stock traders smart enough to follow forex trends had a profitable advantage in this case.

These examples highlight another key point about intermarket analysis: the cause/effect relationship between asset classes can change.

Sometimes the EURUSD moves the S&P 500: In these examples markets in general were moving with the EU crisis, so not surprisingly the EURUSD was leading the S&P 500. Most of the time, however, the EURUSD will move with general risk appetite reflected by (but not necessarily caused by) the moves in the S&P 500.

As we saw above, we can also see temporary changes in correlations between the S&P 500 and oil. Usually oil follows the S&P 500 because signs of growth suggest rising demand for oil. However, when oil prices really spike, both the correlation and driver of that correlation change completely. Not only do oil and stocks start moving in opposite directions, but also oil prices drive stock prices. That's because when oil prices spike too quickly, that acts like an added tax that drains cash away from consumer and business spending and so limits growth.

The USD versus Equities

The USD is the most widely traded currency by far; as we saw in Figure 2.5 in Chapter 2, it's part of over 80 percent of all forex pair volume. It is also usually the most popular counterpart for all other currencies, so its strength influences everything in forex. That's why we're giving it some extra attention.

As previously noted, USD tends to move in the opposite direction of major stock indexes like the S&P 500. So if you see the major indexes rising, the USD is generally moving lower versus higher-risk currencies and other risk assets.

Why is this? In recent years the USD has behaved as a safe haven currency. The U.S. economy has been struggling and the Federal Reserve has kept rates very low. Thus there has been little reason for investors to hold low-yielding dollars when stocks and other risk assets have provided higher returns, except in times of fear. So risk assets like stocks or higher-yielding currencies do better in times of optimism, aka "risk on" environments. Similarly, when markets are scared, risk assets sell off as demand rises for safe haven assets like the USD (as well as other safe haven assets like the JPY, CHF, and AAA-rated bonds).

The USD and Stocks: Correlation, but Not Causation

Again, as previously noted (but well worth repeating) a common misconception, often repeated in the popular financial media by writers who should know better (but don't because they don't watch how currencies and stock indexes interact), is that the USD directly influences stocks, and that a weak USD sends stocks higher and vice versa. This is incorrect, a confusion between correlation and causation. While the two move in opposite directions, that's only because the USD is a safe haven and stocks are risk assets.

The mistaken reasoning behind the supposed direct USD-U.S. stocks connection is that a higher USD hurts U.S. exports and thus drives stocks lower. However, based on that reasoning, non-U.S. stock indexes, like the DAX, Nikkei, or Shanghai, particularly of nations that export heavily to the United States, should rise when the USD rises, because a strong dollar makes *their* exports cheaper. Yet, in fact, global stock indexes tend to move in the same direction as US indexes (on a weekly if not daily basis) *opposite* the USD.

Why? Because these, too, like U.S. stock indexes, are risk assets. Why the confusion about the nature of the relationship between stocks and the USD? Probably from the sheer ignorance that comes from having a single region market focus, like following only the U.S. financial markets or not having a basic understanding of intermarket analysis. That can be a costly mistake.

Like we said at the start, everyone who manages one's own investments needs some forex (and commodity, bond, and macroeconomic) background.

Currencies versus Currencies: How They Correlate

Like all the intermarket analysis topics we're introducing, currency correlations are a large and worthy topic. So as time permits, learn how the pairs and currencies you trade behave relative to others. To get started, use search terms like:

- Common currency correlations.
- USD correlations.
- USDJPY correlations *and* currency pairs.

We already know that risk currencies should all move in the same direction, and so should the safe haven group.

There are other important correlations between currencies, and you need to be aware of them because when they break down, that can be a signal of changing conditions from which you can profit if you understand what's happening before the rest of the crowd does. Here are just two examples.

Trade-Driven Correlations   If one nation does a large part of its foreign trade with another, that trade relationship will influence the related currencies. As with many typical correlations, these don't always hold, especially in the short term, but they are worth knowing. For example, a number of currencies have a degree of positive correlation due to their close trade relationships of their respective economies. We've already mentioned the AUD's strong connection to China because China is Australia's primary export customer. Here are a few other trade driven forex correlations.

- AUD versus NZD: Their correlation goes beyond their both being risk currencies. They tend to be very highly correlated, even though their economies are quite different, because they are major trading partners with each other.
- USD versus CAD: While the CAD and USD are on different sides of the risk spectrum, the US accounts for about 75% of Canadian exports. Thus a rising CAD versus the USD hurts Canadian export revenues, and that fact limits the pair's volatility.
- EUR versus CHF: About 60 percent of Swiss exports go to the surrounding Euro-zone and the rest of Europe. So even though the CHF is a safe haven currency and the EUR is a risk currency, when times in the EU are very bad, the CHF tends to drop, as we saw during both bouts of EU debt crises in the spring of 2010 and latter part of 2011. The direct reasons were somewhat different (in 2011 the CHF dropped on direct Swiss intervention to keep the CHF from rising too much versus

the EUR), but the underlying driver was the same. Switzerland needs to export to the EU, and so a falling EURCHF hurts Swiss exports and growth.

Risk versus Safe Haven Currency Correlations   Of course, safe haven and risk currencies will tend to move in opposite directions. That means that pairs comprised of currencies on extreme opposite ends of the risk spectrum tend to move most with changes in risk appetite, because each half should be moving strongly in the opposite direction. For example, take the AUDJPY. The AUD has tended to be the highest-yielding currency and hence the highest-ranking risk currency. It's the first currency traders think about when considering a carry trade. The JPY has tended to be the lowest-yielding currency and hence the most safe haven currency. It's a classic funding currency, one that's sold in order to buy a higher-yielding currency (though the USD has been competing for this role, too, with its ultralow yields). Thus the AUDJPY is a match of the highest-ranking and lowest-ranking risk currencies, so we expect it to be especially sensitive to changes in risk appetite. One way to play strong risk appetite is to be long the AUDJPY. However, in times of fear, this pair can be heavily sold. The same can be said for the AUD or NZD versus other safe havens like the USD and CHF.

USD and EUR: A Negative Correlation Driven by Both Risk and Liquidity   The EURUSD is one pair everyone in any market needs to follow. Here are the key things to know about it.

With its low yield and high liquidity (availability), the USD has been a safety currency in recent years, especially in times of great fear when liquidity is the top priority, and the USD is the world's most liquid currency by far. When big market-moving players need to be in cash, they can always get dollars. In contrast, with its higher rate, the EUR is a risk currency. That alone would cause the two to move in opposite directions.

However, their negative correlation is driven not only by risk appetite, but also by their being the two most widely held currencies. After the USD, the EUR is the next most widely traded currency.

The EURUSD pair comprises almost a third of all forex trade. So every time three Euros are bought, almost a dollar is sold, and vice versa. Thus these two currencies tend to push each other in opposite directions like children on a seesaw; strength in one of these tends to bring weakness in the other. They have a very strong, consistent negative correlation.

For example, during the July 4 to 8, 2011, period (shown in Figure 9.2), the EUR's weakness meant the USD should be rising versus most currencies. In fact, the USD was flat to lower versus most other major currencies,

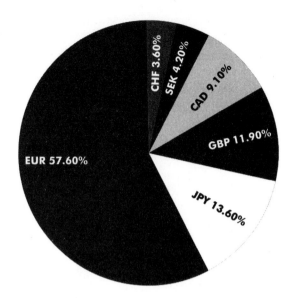

FIGURE 9.3 U.S. Dollar Index Composition

a distinct sign of short-term USD weakness that might well have kept you away from going long the USD versus most other currencies.

Warning: The U.S. Dollar Index Isn't a Substitute for Studying Charts

You can't rely on the dollar index chart (Figure 9.3) as a shortcut for assessing the USD's strength versus other currencies, because the EUR is such a large component of the basket of currencies that comprise this index.

Even though the USD was flat to lower against other currencies, the USD index was higher (see Figure 9.4) because of the EUR weakness we saw in Figure 9.2.

You need to look at the individual charts of the USD versus the other majors. That's not a big deal; there are only seven other major pairs besides the EURUSD.

That strong negative correlation between the EUR and the USD means that you can't get a full picture of either of these currencies by just looking at the EURUSD.

To get a better picture of the true health of each of these currencies individually—that is, to see them in a way that is not as influenced by movements in the EURUSD—we can do two things. We can compare each of these currencies either to other currencies or to gold.

Cross Currency Analysis   As noted back in Chapter 2 when we discussed the importance of cross currencies, we can check how these two

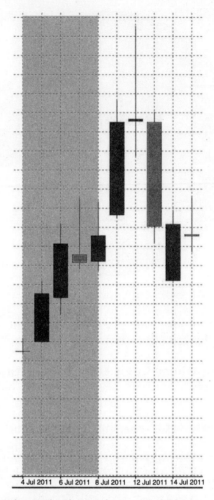

FIGURE 9.4   USD Index Daily Chart, July 1 to 15, 2011
Source: MetaQuotes Software Corp.

are faring against other currencies. For example (see Figure 9.5), in recent years one of the favorite major currency hedges for the Euro in
times of anxiety about the Euro-zone was the CHF, due to Switzerland's
healthier economy and smaller debt load compared to the United States or
Japan, homes of the other chief safe haven currencies. If the EURCHF was
falling, that was a sign of EUR weakness, regardless of what happened with
the EURUSD. This correlation doesn't always work because at times the
Swiss central bank intervenes in currency markets to keep the CHF artifi-
cially low versus the EUR. Fortunately we can get a read on currencies by
looking beyond forex market.

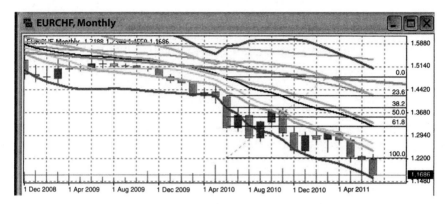

FIGURE 9.5   EURCHF Monthly Chart, December 2008 to July 2011
Source: MetaQuotes Software Corp.

Another way to get perspective on each of these currencies is to watch gold.

CURRENCIES VERSUS COMMODITIES

Now let's look at how we can use gold prices to help analyze the strength of the two most widely held currencies, the U.S. dollar and the Euro.

Gold as a Barometer of the USD or EUR

When the normal market and intermarket correlations stop working or even reverse, that's usually a sign that something important may be happening. For example, earlier in the chapter we saw how the divergence between the EURUSD and S&P 500 told of trouble brewing. Back in Chapter 2 we discussed how cross currency pairs could tell us much about the true health of a currency. Another excellent indicator is gold, particularly for the USD and EUR. Normally we expect it to move in the opposite direction of the USD (in which it's priced) or, during times of anxiety about the EUR, gold can move opposite the EUR along with the USD as both move up as investors move out of the EUR into these. More specifically, we watch for divergences from gold's normal correlation with the USD or EUR.

The relationship of gold with currencies and other assets is a broad topic by itself, but here's some must-know background on gold and its importance to forex traders and investors.

Unlike almost any other asset, gold is typically neither a safety nor a risk asset, though the popular financial media have often called it both over the years (depending on how gold has been performing in recent months). Instead it's a currency hedge for which demand rises when there are concerns about inflation diluting the purchasing power of fiat currencies (particularly those most widely held, like the USD and EUR). In other words:

- In times of optimism (aka risk appetite), gold can either appreciate if markets believe growth will lead to inflation, or it can fall if the desire for higher yields overrides inflation concerns and investors move into more classic risk assets which they believe will provide better returns.
- In times of pessimism (aka risk aversion) gold can either rise if markets believe that stalling growth will lead to rising deficits and/or money printing that could ultimately cause inflation, or it can also fall on fears of deflation or of a market crash that feeds demand for cash. In times of panics, traders seek cash either in order to cover margin calls or other obligations or to be ready to go bargain hunting. If pessimism turns to panic, then gold could either:
  - rise if markets are more concerned about the USD or EUR losing their purchasing power than about near-term liquidity needs, as was the case at times from 2009 through 2011.
  - fall if markets are more concerned about liquidity than loss of purchasing power, as was the case in late 2011.

Gold is very useful for assessing the health of the USD and EUR, because they're the most widely held currencies and so any selloff in these tends to cause a rally in gold, the most popular fiat currency hedge.

For example:

- In the wake of the Great Financial Crisis that began in late 2007, the U.S. dollar's prior multi-year decline versus gold accelerated because markets feared that the U.S. would engage in massive stimulus programs that risked devaluing the USD. The same thing happened to the EUR versus gold during the same period, for essentially the same reason, a fear of loss of purchasing power for the EUR.
- The EU sovereign debt and banking crisis raised doubts about the very existence of the EUR. When anxiety about the EU crisis was high, gold tended to do well. Throughout much of 2010 and 2011, plotting long-term strategy for the EURUSD was tough because the fundamentals of the underlying economies for both currencies were terrible; it was a contest of which currency was uglier, and there was no clear winner in the short term. However, gold benefited because both the USD's and the EUR's underlying economies looked bad. I soon stopped trading the EURUSD and found going long gold a far simpler way to make money.

Again, however, as noted above, there are exceptions to the rule that anxiety about the USD or EUR is bullish for gold.

In particular, when markets aren't concerned about fading purchasing power, the major currencies tend to gain against gold. That can happen due to:

- Low inflation expectations, as we saw starting in late 2011. Concerns about the global economy kept inflation fears low, and so gold began a multimonth downtrend.
- Panic periods when markets fear a financial crisis, and liquidity becomes the top priority. We saw gold sell off during times of peak anxiety about the US or EU. During these periods, investors tend to sell gold in order to raise cash.

Investors seek cash for a variety of reasons. Some need to cover margin calls as they suffer losses on losing positions they hold with leverage (borrowed funds). Others want cash ready either to take advantage of the drop in asset prices for bargain hunting or out of fear of losing jobs, businesses, or other income sources. Under these conditions, cash, especially the USD (in which gold is priced), appreciates and gold drops.

Note the monthly gold chart in Figure 9.6 covering August 2008 through September 2011.

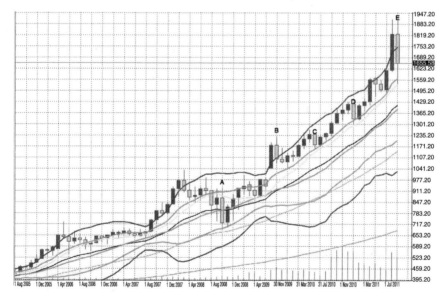

FIGURE 9.6   Gold Monthly Chart, August 1, 2008, to September 28, 2011
Source: MetaQuotes Software Corp.

Gold had few significant monthly drawdowns during this period. Every one occurred due to a major bout of fear that drove up the demand for cash at the expense of gold, other currency hedges, as well as risk assets.

Monthly candlestick A: The October 2008 panic from the Lehman Brothers bank collapse that threatened to bring down the global banking system and introduced the term *systemic risk* into the mainstream media.

Monthly candlesticks B through E: Assorted bouts of panic that a Greek sovereign default threatened, which in turn could start a wave of sovereign and/or bank defaults.

Look at the monthly charts in Figure 9.7 comparing the EURUSD and gold from December 2008 to July 2011.

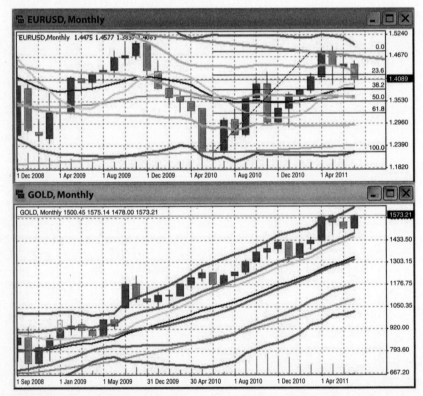

FIGURE 9.7 EURUSD (top) versus Gold (bottom), December 2008 through July 2011
Source: MetaQuotes Software Corp.

Note that the EURUSD was in a flat trading range while gold kept steadily rising. This was one of many signs, both technical and fundamental, that markets were dumping both currencies during this period and seeking refuge in other kinds of assets, be they commodities or other currencies. A look at commodities like gold, silver, oil, and copper would have confirmed this move out of cash into hard assets.

In short, if you see gold rising, chances are good that demand for the USD, EUR, or both is falling.

The EURUSD will tell you which one is stronger.

If one of them is stronger than most of its crosses, then you know that its strength is genuine, which in turn tells you something deeper about the state of the markets. If not, the opposite would hold.

Here are some very simple examples of how you'd compare gold, the EURUSD, and the EUR and USD crosses to gain a deeper understanding of what's happening and how you might profit. My goal here is to just introduce you to the thought process involved rather than cover every possible scenario.

- If gold is up and the EURUSD is down (the USD is the stronger of the two), then (assuming the USD is still a low-yielding safe haven currency):
  - If the USD is up versus most of its counterparts, that USD strength is real, not just relative to the EUR. That could mean it's a risk off environment (because the USD is a safe haven currency) and you should start thinking about moving into safe haven assets. It could also signal a fear-driven flight to liquidity instead of U.S. economic strength, as we saw in the summer and fall of 2008 and 2011.
  - If the USD is down versus most of its counterparts, that USD strength is only *relative to* the EUR. That could mean it's a risk off environment because both the U.S. and Euro-zone economies are struggling, and that markets are worried about a loss of purchasing power in both currencies from policies of both the Fed and ECB that risk cutting the purchasing power of both the USD and EUR.
- If gold is up and the EURUSD also is up (the EUR is the stronger of the two), then:
  - If the EUR is up versus most of its counterparts, that strength is real, not just relative to the USD. That could mean it's a risk on environment (because the EUR is a risk currency) and you look to go into risk assets, or it indicates that something good is happening with the Euro-zone economy relative to the rest of the world.
  - If the EUR is down versus most of its counterparts, then sentiment about the EUR, and particularly the USD, is negative. Given that the EUR is a risk currency and the USD is a safe haven currency, that

dual weakness shouldn't be due to overall market sentiment in favor
of either risk appetite or risk aversion. Instead it is likely due to policy decisions from both the United States and the EU that are slam-
ming both currencies. For example, both the European Central Bank
and the U.S. Federal Reserve could be in strong easing modes or en-
gaging in potentially inflationary stimulus programs that threaten the
purchasing power of both currencies.

Again, other scenarios are conceivable. The goal here is to demonstrate
how to do some basic intermarket analysis using gold, the EURUSD, and
the relevant EUR and USD crosses.

Other Currency versus Commodity Correlations

There are many currency versus commodity correlations, and like other
kinds of correlations they can change over time.

USD versus Commodities   As with the EURUSD, the USD and commodities tend to push each other in opposite directions (though not as
strongly). Here's why.

- First, the U.S. imports many commodities, like oil, so higher prices for
  oil and other imported commodities pressure the U.S. economy and
  the USD.
- Second, commodities are usually priced in U.S. dollars, so higher commodity prices also imply a less valuable USD.

Also, remember that the USD is a safe haven asset and commodities are
risk assets, so by their very nature they respond in opposite ways in times
of optimism or fear. Note that this correlation may change over the coming
years. We are seeing signs of exporter nations making deals to conduct
trade among themselves without using dollars.

Gold Supports the AUD and NZD   Australia is one of the world's
top gold producers, so rising gold prices help the AUD. Because of the
strong trade relationship between Australia and New Zealand, what's good
for the AUD often also benefits the NZD. The United States is one of the
world's largest gold buyers, and also gold is priced in dollars, so higher
gold prices usually pressure the USD. So the AUDUSD and NZDUSD can
also be bought to ride rising gold prices, or sold when gold is falling.

**Oil versus Risk Currencies: An Example of How Correlations
Can Change**   Oil is a risk asset like the AUD, NZD, and CAD, so these all

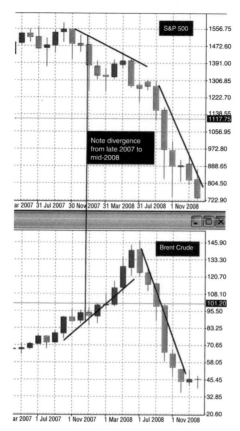

FIGURE 9.8 S&P 500 versus Brent Crude Oil Monthly Charts, March 2007 to January 2009
Divergence between the S&P 500 (a risk appetite barometer) and oil eventually ends as higher oil prices hurt growth, which in turn reduces oil prices.
Source: MetaQuotes Software Corp.

tend to move together. When there is growth, economies consume more oil. Because oil is so essential, its price is built into almost all economic activity. As noted before, so if oil prices spike too far too fast, they hurt growth, and that positive correlation with risk assets, which rise or fall with growth prospects, becomes negative. This negative correlation tends to be short lived, however. Rapidly rising oil prices have eventually led to their own correction, as they bring fears of slowing growth, and so lower prices.

Note in Figure 9.8 how this divergence (oil rising and the S&P 500 falling) from September 2007 to June 2008 ultimately corrected and the positive correlation resumed (both the S&P 500 and oil fell together) from July 2008 to December 2008.

Oil versus the CADJPY   Canada is a major oil exporter, so higher oil prices generally support a higher CAD. Japan is a major oil importer, so higher oil hurts Japan and the JPY. The same holds true to a lesser degree for the USDCAD. Why a lesser degree, even though the United States is an oil importer? Remember the trade relationship between the United States and Canada noted earlier. What hurts Canada's biggest export market ultimately hurts Canada and thus the CAD. This tight trade relationship tends to limit the CAD's short-term gains against the USD. However it hasn't been strong enough to halt the USDCAD's ongoing decade-plus decline, which reflects Canada's better economic performance.

We see a similar relationship with the EUR and CHF. If Europe is getting hurt, that weakness eventually hurts the CHF because Europe buys most of Switzerland's exports. Here too, however, the tight trade relationship may limit the EURCHF'S short-term volatility, but it hadn't prevented the decade-plus downtrend as Switzerland's better economic fundamentals ultimately drive the pair lower. Over the long term, fundamentals are the true drivers of price trends. That's why long-term investors must consider longer-term fundamentals so carefully.

Again, there are exceptions to these rules.

THINKING LIKE A PRO, ONE STEP BEYOND TECHNICAL ANALYSIS

While you've learned a lot so far, beware that a little knowledge can be a dangerous thing.

As we have said from the beginning, we don't claim to teach you any secrets to fast riches. While learning what we've taught will put you far ahead of the masses of the typically ignorant, reckless forex beginners and casual gamblers who fill the ranks of the 70 percent of traders that fail, there is *nothing* in this book that isn't known to the elite professional forex traders, including those who run the forex trading departments of large financial institutions and thus control most of the daily volume traded. If you feel you've got an insight into what's happening, assume the big boys and their supercomputers have already seen the same thing. They have probably correctly anticipated what most traders are likely to do, and probably have plans ready to exploit their advantage.

Mind Games

Some of these traders have enough capital to move markets in the short term and will do so when they think they can fool the masses. They, too, understand support and resistance, know that buy and sell orders cluster in swarms around the most popularly recognized s/r levels, and will attempt to profit from them by a variety of means, like starting the false breakouts we saw in Chapter 4 when discussing chart patterns.

Learn to Think Like These Pros

This includes the following. Remember the quotes from the start of Chapter 5 on trader psychology and RAMM.

First, as always, remember that smart, low-risk trading and investing starts with the right attitudes and expectations. Always assume that if you see a strong s/r point at which to place an entry or exit, Big Brother and his machines have long ago seen it, positioned for it, hedged it, and planned to use it against you. Sorry if I'm bursting your bubble. Fear not—there is hope, even for those of us who aren't going to create sophisticated computerized trading systems or hire someone to do so.

Second, (once again) avoid day trading forex until you've tested (first on a practice account, then with small positions on real accounts) and found methods that keep you profitable most months over at least a six-month period. Until then, focus on multiday, multiweek, and multimonth positions. Short-term money flows from the big boys, whether from attempted price manipulation as seen in our false breakout examples or from simple random money flows from daily multinational business activity, and can move markets over a matter of hours, perhaps days. Beyond that time frame, nobody except for a few central banks has the cash to fuel a sustained price move in a given currency pair. The fundamental and technical analysis that you can do, based on publicly available information and basic technical indicators that are easily available to you, matters much more in these time frames.

Third, consider entering a bit later and exiting a bit earlier. That is, if you need to use entry and exits entered in advance because you can't be sure you'll be monitoring the markets when your chosen s/r levels are hit (usually the case), then enter at least some of your planned position after price has moved well past support, and exit a bit earlier, just before where selling near resistance would begin. You will sacrifice some profit, but you will be less prone to getting sucked into the false breakouts or other manipulations that the big players love to orchestrate. Alternatively, use trailing stops to ride the move until it reverses. The tighter the stop, the less of the move you give back, but the more likely you are to be shaken out by short-term price movements. The looser the stop, the opposite applies. Many traders will tighten their trailing stops as price approaches resistance. This reduces risk of loss from reversals, but at a cost of being shaken out by normal price gyrations before the move has finished.

Fourth, if you believe you can be at your computer actively monitoring markets when your entry or exit levels are hit, then:

- Instead of using a preset entry point, wait to enter near support until after price has clearly bounced higher per whatever trend-confirming indicators you use.
- For exits, in addition to using trailing stops as discussed earlier, consider leaving at least some of your position in the trade until you get confirmation from your indicators that the trend is probably finished.

CHAPTER 10

Alternatives to Traditional Methods

This chapter is specifically for those who are smart enough to know that they need currency diversification, would like some exposure to forex trading (versus more passive long-term buy-and-hold investing) but are:

- Unable or unwilling to do their own forex trading.
- Seeking simpler, less time-consuming, lower-risk trading methods than those we've covered thus far.

In this chapter we present the more traditional alternatives for those seeking currency exposure and diversification with less risk, time, and effort.

- Auto-trading systems.
- Currency funds.
- Managed currency accounts.

Then in Chapter 11, for the first time in any forex book, we'll look at two newer, smarter, easier, and less demanding ways to get forex exposure.

AUTO-TRADING SYSTEMS: WELCOME TO THE MACHINE

As the name implies, automated trading or algorithmic systems go beyond mere testing of systems to actually applying them in real time to make real trades with live market data. When the programmed system generates a buy or sell signal, the software automatically places the trade. These systems have been widely used by institutional traders for many years in all financial markets. In recent years more affordable versions have become much more popular with private traders, particularly those with programming and testing expertise, or the means to hire it.

Assuming the system is well designed, it is back tested, and its performance is monitored, programmed trading has some obvious advantages:

- Never miss an opportunity: they can work 24/7.
- No emotion, full discipline: they take the emotion out of trading as long as you're disciplined enough to let the system work even when you believe the rules don't apply under current conditions.

So if:

- You develop a clear, unambiguous set of trading rules that can be expressed in programming code.
- You have the time and expertise to translate the rules into a program and back test it, or can hire someone to do that.

Then auto-trading is the best way to execute that system.

However, those conditions don't apply to most of us, so the way most of us would exercise this option is via the retail forex trading system market. Many forex brokers offer a wide variety of trading systems as part of their offerings. There's nothing wrong with trying these, especially if they allow you to paper trade them for a while to see for yourself how they work. There are legitimate providers and there are scams, so four caveats are in order.

1. Trading systems are generally designed to work in specific kinds of environments, typically either trending or range-bound markets, but not both. Before choosing a system, be clear on what kind of markets and conditions it's designed for. A legitimate vendor will provide clear information on what kind of conditions the system is designed for, its performance and length of track record, likely profit and maximum drawdown, and so on. If your broker offers a variety of systems and allows you to place and remove funds from a given system as quickly as you would any other kind of trade, then you can just move in and out of these systems as market conditions warrant.

2. As with any business proposal, if it sounds too good to be true, chances are that it is. If the returns seem outsized and the price very low, well, I hope they let you paper trade it first or start with very small amounts at risk. Otherwise, move on.

3. You want to see as long a track record as possible, and understand what the market conditions were during the sample period. For example, in a time of growth and rising rates, systems that buy carry trades will work well as risk currencies are favored. However, during global downturns these systems will suffer.

4. Typically, the higher the returns claimed, the higher the risk of loss. If a system vendor claims both high returns and high maximum drawdown, that's a sign of honesty. If vendors claim high returns without a correspondingly high risk level, then be suspicious.

There are many online trader forums dedicated to the auto-trading topic; for example, ForexFactory.com has links to one right on its homepage. Do an online search for these, and use them to tap the experience of others. There's no reason that you shouldn't be able to access reputable, cost-effective systems if you just do your homework.

CURRENCY FUNDS: FOREX ETFs, ETNs, AND MORE

As part of my research on forex currency funds, I asked one of the experts on exchange-traded funds (ETFs) for his input. John Nyaradi is publisher of WallStreetSectorSelector.com. He's also a prolific writer on ETFs whose credits include the book *Super Sectors: How to Outsmart the Market Using Sector Rotation and ETFs*, which was included among the Year's Top Investment Books in the 2011 *Stock Trader's Almanac*. What he sent back was so good, I thought why not just pass it on as a quick introduction? Here's what he wrote:

> *Exchange-traded funds (ETFs) offer investors the ultimate in flexibility and portfolio construction by making previously unavailable asset classes easily accessible to retail investors. One of these major asset classes is forex, which, until recently, has been the domain of specialists, and traders/investors have been required to open separate accounts and trade forex as a separate segment of their investment portfolio.*
>
> *However, with the advent of ETFs, investors can now get exposure to the benefits (and risks) of forex trading in traditional brokerage accounts, including IRAs and qualified defined contribution and 401(k) accounts.*
>
> *Many investment avenues are available when using currency ETFs. One can go "long" a particular currency with standard*

currency ETFs or one can "short" a currency, either by shorting the particular ETF or by buying an "inverse" ETF that changes value in the opposite direction of the underlying index. One can also leverage positions with ETFs that offer 2X leverage to the underlying currency's index. Finally, ETFs that simulate the action of currency pairs are available which can replicate the trading action of the underlying forex pairs themselves.

Currency ETFs trade just like a stock, move with the underlying foreign exchange rate, and offer a convenient, easy-to-understand way to participate in this market. While there are differences between currency ETFs and spot forex trading, ETFs offer investors several unique advantages.

Foremost, you can use currency ETFs within the confines of a standard brokerage account and so all of the things you're used to with a standard stock account apply to currency ETFs. ETFs allow margin, short selling, stop loss entry and exit opportunities, and reasonable commission structures. Currency ETFs also offer standard stock market margin leverage, and for more aggressive investors, options strategies on currency ETFs are available, including covered calls and buying either puts or calls to amplify potential returns.

Beyond single-currency ETFs, investors can also use currency pair exchange-traded funds that are available in major markets, including the British Pound/U.S. Dollar (GBP/USD) Euro/U.S. Dollar (EUR/USD), and U.S. Dollar/Japanese Yen (USD/JPY).

Like all currency pairs, these ETFs reflect the relative value of the two currencies and fluctuate in value as the underlying relationship of the currencies changes. In the case of the EUR/USD, for instance, when the Euro appreciates relative to the U.S. Dollar, the value of the ETF increases, and when the Euro loses value to the U.S. Dollar, the ETF declines in price.

Investors also can get exposure to the so-called "carry trade" via Barclays Capital Intelligent Carry Index (ICI) that is designed to capture returns from investing in high-yielding currencies with money financed by borrowing low-yielding currencies. The Barclays Carry ETN (ICI) uses a pool of currencies for this strategy that includes major currencies like the U.S. Dollar, Japanese Yen, Euro, Swiss Franc, British Pound, and Australian and New Zealand Dollars.

So it's easy to see that currency exchange-traded funds offer a simple, convenient way for investors to develop and deploy a potent and flexible arsenal in the world of foreign exchange trading.[1]

For a more complete, practical guide to currency funds visit thesensibleguidetoforex.com, under the Bonus Materials tab click through to

Chapter 10—Guide To Forex ETFs, ETNs, and More. It covers:

- Key Differences between ETFs and ETNs
- Pros & Cons of Currency Funds vs. Trading Forex Pairs
- Advantages of ETFs versus ETNs
- For Further Investigation: Free Online ETF Resources

MANAGED ACCOUNTS: SHOULD YOU SEEK PROFESSIONAL HELP?

You don't always have to be a successful trader to succeed at trading, if you can identify a professional willing to trade for you.

The appeal of this approach is obvious for those who want forex exposure and lack the time, will, or ability to do it themselves. As with anything else that requires skill and experience, most people will get much better results by hiring a professional.

The whole trick is in knowing how to locate a trustworthy, competent, and cost-effective professional. As with packaged auto-trading systems, the quality of product offered varies dramatically. The big problems with picking professional managers are:

- There is a lack of reliable information about a given professional's performance.
- Most people don't have the expertise or time to evaluate a professional using whatever information is available.

The one huge lesson I've learned from sitting through so many unconvincing, amateurish presentations from reputable institutions seeking to manage funds under my control is this: if these clowns are getting people's money despite their weak presentations, flimsy qualifications and/or short track records, then there must be vast herds of investors who seek professional assistance yet don't know how to pick the winners.

If you're one of them, that's fine. We all have to start somewhere. Just use common sense and do your homework. If that's beyond your resources, seek the advice of someone both trustworthy and qualified who can refer you to trustworthy forex professionals, or at least guide your decision-making process and feed you the right questions to be asking.

Here are some pointers.

Unless you've got some very sharp and trustworthy advisors who can steer you to someone proven, and are among the high-net-worth types they seek, skip down to the next section on social trading for what may be the best way to find competent pros to follow. For those who do go the managed account route, keep the following in mind.

- Realistic risk/reward: As with any business or investment proposal, apply the smell test. Anyone offering above-market returns without higher risk is most likely misleading you. If the reward-risk ratio seems unrealistically high, then move on to someone else.
- Registered and regulated: As the past years have demonstrated, oversight and enforcement even in well-regulated markets are not always reliable, though it's still a mark of some legitimacy if the advisor is registered with some official licensing body that in theory imposes some standards, oversight, and accountability. If nothing else, it's a sign of greater seriousness on the part of the management, and gives you an address for complaints and possible redress of damages or improprieties.
- Incorporated in countries with reliable rule of law: Not that the United States hasn't had its share of lapses. Still, this feature would theoretically allow for easier redress and oversight.
- Seek references: Even if you don't have a trusted referral source, search online for references and credentials of the advisor. The greater the number of years and money invested in the business and its reputation, the more the advisor has to lose. For example, if you want forex exposure via ETFs and have the funds needed to get started with the likes of a Tom Lydon or Roger Nusbaum, or anyone else who has clearly invested a lot in building a business and reputation, you should be fine with them.

If you find this search process intimidating or lack a trusted advisor, there's a new alternative to traditional managed accounts with significant advantages that make it much better suited for most investors—forex social trading. As we'll discuss in the next chapter, the list of advantages inclues:

- Much better transparency: They provide rankings and extensive performance, risk, and trade style information on which to base your selection, and you can then monitor your chosen trader's performance in real time.
- Lower entry costs: With some vendors you can start with a few hundred dollars and have a proven expert trading for you.

- Ability to easily switch to different expert traders: You've a variety to choose from and can easily move funds between them.
- Active Trading for Passive Investors: Using the social trading site's software, you link your account to your chosen expert traders, and the software automatically matches that trader's every trade.

See Chapter 11 for further details on social trading and another innovation in forex for a smarter, simpler way to trading success—binary options.

CHAPTER 11

Newer, Smarter Methods

F or those seeking simpler ways to tap the potentially faster profits from short- to medium-term (ranging from minutes to weeks) trading of forex, with more controlled risk, we introduce two new and very useful instruments:

- Forex social trading.
- Forex binary options.

Both have come out only over the past few years, and are the fastest-growing sectors of the forex industry for good reason. They meet an important need of traders to tap forex trading in ways that are easier and less time-consuming, and for many traders they offer a better chance of profiting.

FOLLOW THE LEADERS: FOREX SOCIAL NETWORKS AND TRADING

Between 2007 and 2009, the first social networks and social trading sites showed promise for stock investors,[1] so it was natural that the idea of tapping crowd sentiment via social networks, and copying the moves of top traders via social trading, would quickly be applied to the rapidly growing forex trading scene.

The first social trading networks appeared in late 2010 and are on their way to becoming ideal solutions for many investors seeking forex exposure and diversification but who lack the time or expertise to trade successfully on their own.

The trading networks evolved from an only slightly older and equally valuable new tool, forex social networks.

What Are Forex Social Networks?

As retail forex trading gained popularity over the past decade, forex social networks arose to fill a massive information vacuum. Compared to other financial markets like stocks, retail forex is still in its infancy and is still largely unknown to mainstream investors. It's neglected by the mainstream media, and whatever coverage it gets tends to be superficial and often misinformed, as noted earlier in Chapters 1 and 2. Retail forex trading was born online; it was only natural that this information vacuum would be filled by online sources. These were filled by a combination of:

- Dedicated forex content sites: DailyFX.com, ForexFactory.com, Forexpros.com, DailyForex.com, and others.
- Content sections of forex broker sites: Some provided good analysis, some little more than news summaries. Unlike the content sites, however, they avoided specific trading advice given brokers' legal and liability concerns.

A huge part of any professional's on-the-job training is the input from mentors and co-workers. Because most forex traders typically work alone at home, online forex social networks have filled much of that workplace role as a source of practical advice and news. Whether they're seeking new opportunities or trading the same pairs and time frames, traders can easily share information and critique or validate each other's trade ideas or methods.

The first to attempt to fill these voids were Forex forums found on some of the content sites like BabyPips.com, ForexFactory.com, ForexP eaceArmy.com, Forexpros.com, and DailyFX.com. They offered a venue for exchange of information and advice among traders but lacked the more personal, user-profile-oriented interface of a true social network like Facebook. There are also sites such as ZuluTrade and Tradency that solely offer automated strategies, which could be seen as a kind of social trading, but these still lack the complete social interaction of the forums. Then, over the past three years, came the first true forex social networks that better filled these needs. The most prominent are such websites as Currensee, eToro's OpenBook, FxStat, and Myfxbook.

While the definition of a social network is not clear-cut, for the purposes of this discussion we'll loosely define it as a website that puts greater emphasis on user profiles and trading credentials than a typical trader forum does.

In their original forms as of 2009, these nascent forex social networks offered lots of advice and interaction, but they still lacked a way to distinguish the real experts from the mere posers who were better at getting attention than at trading. The sites lacked a means of accountability, an easy way for users to identify who was worth following and who was just good at getting attention.

What Is Social Trading?

Then in late 2010, Currensee and eToro took social networks to the next level. They went from being marketplaces of actionable ideas to those of actual traders. They began offering social trading, a service that allows your account to automatically mimic the trades of one or more chosen expert traders. To help you identify the top traders most suitable for your needs, these services include trader rankings complete with detailed data on their styles, performance, maximum drawdown, and other risk data, experience, and so on.

Most major brokers are either linking up with existing social trading services or building their own. Why? Because social trading fills an important unmet need, a shortcut to trading success without needing to trade yourself, but with better transparency and lower entry costs than with traditional managed accounts.

As we'll see later, you're more likely to actually make money by letting an expert do it for you. For those interested in becoming star traders themselves, they can raise their chances of making money sooner by using a portion of their accounts to trade via experts until they reach a similar level of performance. For those who just want some exposure to forex trading without as much work, here's the solution.

How It Works: The Highest Form of Flattery

Basically, you select one or more of your favorite experts based on the data available on them, and set up an account that mimics their every trade, either automatically or only after your approval (depending on the broker).

Experts are compensated based on performance measures that vary from site to site, such as profitability and number of followers.

We'll focus on the two big players, Currensee and eToro.

EToro is a forex broker, and requires having an eToro account in order to follow its experts.

Currensee is not a broker; it's a pure social network and social trading site. You set up an account, or part of an account, with a third-party broker and link that account to Currensee. You then select the trader(s) that your account will mimic.

When that star trader makes a trade, your linked account simultaneously makes the same trade automatically, or notifies you and awaits your approval. This use of hired expertise makes social trading similar to managed accounts, with the advantages of lower entry costs, greater accountability, more transparency, and far greater ease of switching between experts. You always know how your chosen traders are performing in real time by a variety of measures and how they compare to others. If you see that a chosen trader is underperforming, you can switch over to another.

Risks of Social Trading

In theory, having a proven pro trade for you should vastly improve your odds of making money. There are still risks, though. Because pros focus on risks before profits, let's consider risks first.

Trade Replication Risk   Will your results accurately reflect those of your chosen experts? That is, do these accounts accurately mimic the trades of the expert trader you're following? Because currency prices can change so quickly, followers' trades might be executed at slightly different prices than those of the trader they're following. For trading styles that seek to eke out very small gains from minute-to-minute moves, that difference could turn a profitable trade into a loser for the followers.

Different sites deal with this trade replication risk differently. For example, Currensee.com doesn't accept this style of trading when selecting its trade leaders.[2] Even by eliminating this style of trading from the mix, CEO Dave Lemont admits there can still be minor differences in the price received by the Trade Leader and that subsequently received by the followers at both the open and close of the position. He notes:

> *All of this is transparent for you in the portfolio performance page in the platform. A negative number in parentheses [see the Open Price and Close Price columns in Figure 11.1] indicates a better price for the Trade Leader and a positive number in parentheses indicates a better price for the investor. In addition, all of these prices and their correlation to the Trade Leader can be exported to Excel for further analysis.[3]*

EToro.com does allow you to follow Guru traders using this approach and attempts to minimize any differences in execution time and thus price. With eToro's social trading, the accounts of both the experts and followers are all in-house under one integrated trading platform. That tighter

Portfolio Performance CUTBTA								Account Balance: 8,327.63 USD		

Open Time	Close Time	Type	Ticker	Lots	Currency	Open Price	Close Price	Gain/Loss	Comments
03/08/2011 01:12:53 PM	03/08/2011 03:43:10 PM	Close Long	ANBZN.A	0.02	USD/JPY	82.637 (-1.1)	82.646 (-0.3)	0.22 USD	Followed
03/07/2011 02:01:03 PM	03/08/2011 09:53:09 PM	Close Long	WIHFG.A	0.01	EUR/USD	1.39613 (+0.7)	1.38652 (+3.2)	-9.60 USD	Followed
03/07/2011 02:00:56 PM	03/08/2011 09:53:07 PM	Close Long	WIHFG.A	0.01	EUR/USD	1.39613 (+1.7)	1.38660 (+3.0)	-9.52 USD	Followed
03/08/2011 01:01:22 AM	03/08/2011 09:11:24 AM	Close Long	WIHFG.A	0.01	EUR/USD	1.39613 (+1.3)	1.38825 (-1.5)	-10.02 USD	Followed
03/04/2011 09:13:35 AM	03/08/2011 09:08:44 AM	Close Short	ROICU.A	0.01	AUD/USD	1.01009 (-0.7)	1.00672 (-0.3)	-3.10 USD	Followed
03/04/2011 09:03:25 AM	03/08/2011 09:07:27 AM	Close Short	ROICU.A	0.01	AUD/USD	1.00945 (-1.2)	1.00735 (-0.7)	1.83 USD	Followed
03/08/2011 03:30:07 AM	03/08/2011 08:45:03 AM	Close Short	LIWWK.B	0.02	EUR/USD	1.39332 (-1.2)	1.38936	7.92 USD	Followed
03/08/2011 03:45:06 AM	03/08/2011 07:30:09 AM	Close Short	LIWWK.B	0.02	EUR/USD	1.39256 (+0.1)	1.39035 (+0.2)	4.42 USD	Followed
03/02/2011 05:45:34 AM	03/08/2011 02:45:51 AM	Close Long	DOCGM.A	0.07	EUR/USD	1.38350 (-1.5)	1.39461 (-0.2)	77.95 USD	Followed
03/02/2011 09:01:16 AM	03/08/2011 01:01:20 AM	Close Short	WIHFG.A	0.01	EUR/USD	1.40028 (-1.2)	1.39828 (+1.2)	1.97 USD	Followed
03/07/2011 06:16:04 PM	03/07/2011 07:03:30 PM	Close Long	ANBZN.A	0.02	EUR/GBP	0.86214 (-0.8)	0.86238 (-0.8)	0.78 USD	Followed

FIGURE 11.1 Portfolio Performance

integration may better minimize any time lag between the actions of the experts and the accounts that are linked to them.

Selection Process and Quality of Experts Vary As with managed accounts, your success depends on your ability to pick winning traders and know when to switch to others. That gets easier if you have all the information you need to make that choice, a range of choices from a qualified pool of applicants, and an ability to move to different experts quickly and easily without needing to close and open different accounts. Both Currensee and eToro fill these requirements, though in distinctly different ways.

To get an initial feel for the quality of the selection of experts, it pays to be familiar with:

The rigorousness of the selection process EToro allows traders to become Guru traders, who can then recruit followers, if they:

- Have a documented "positive trading history" in the three months prior to admission.
- Continue to meet certain performance, trade frequency, and recruiting targets.

At last count, eToro has about 400 Guru traders with around 200 having at least 10 followers, between 50 and 100 of whom are full-time professional traders.[4]

Currensee takes a much more selective approach. It accepts only about 2 percent out of thousands who apply. There are typically between 10 to 20 selected Trade Leaders available at any one time that have both survived that screening process and met ongoing performance goals needed to remain in this very exclusive club. At the time of this writing, 11 of the 14 Trade Leaders were full-time professionals or trading firms rather than solo traders.[5] Currensee is clearly the more selective of the two. As we discuss later, that's no guarantee that you will succeed, though it should improve your odds.

If Currensee's more limited selection of traders doesn't suit your needs, you'll have a wider selection at eToro, though you'll have many more to sort through and most won't sport the same level of credentials.

Note that because both Currensee's and eToro's programs began in late 2010, the track records of most experts in the programs are measured in months rather than years. While Currensee may have checked farther back, keep in mind that you're dealing with shorter, hence less reliable, performance records than you'd normally see with other asset classes. That should improve over time as these services mature.

How well the expert compensation system aligns trader interests with yours   Logically, we want to see compensation systems that:

- Connect the experts' earnings directly to those of their followers.
- Pay very well for good performance in order to attract better expert traders. You get what you pay for, so if the network can provide a handsome income for top traders, it should in theory attract them.

Both eToro and Currensee attempt to do this, but in different ways.

EToro pays its Guru traders $10 per follower per month up to a maximum of $10,000 per month while they have live accounts that can be copied, its theory apparently being that top performers will attract more followers. Assuming the system quickly makes that performance well known throughout the network, then that would connect performance and reward. If not, then this method is rewarding a mix of the trader's marketing skills as well as performance. The advantage of this approach is that it encourages top traders to respond to questions or comments and serve a mentor role. That could be a real plus for educating traders, as long as top traders aren't put off by this extra demand on their time.

Currensee pays 15 percent of the amount by which the expert trader actually increases a follower's account measured from its highest value (high-water mark). So if the account loses money in a given month, the experts don't start getting paid again from that follower until they recoup those losses. They then get 15 percent of any additional gains beyond the prior high water mark. There are no limits on how much a Trade Leader can earn.

This method appears to more directly connect reward with performance, and in theory allows for a higher income than from eToro. Currensee does not reward or encourage Trade Leaders to be mentors. Indeed the Currensee website explicitly states that users should not expect to have contact with Trade Leaders. This makes sense given that Currensee seeks only a very small, elite group of mostly professional traders who may well be unwilling or unable to commit the time needed to assume the correspondence and mentoring roles of eToro Gurus.

Your costs to participate EToro is a forex broker and earns its money from your trading volume, without charging anything to follow another trader.

Currensee is not a brokerage but rather a pure forex social network and trading business. It charges an annual service fee of 2 percent charged monthly, based on the average capital in your account, plus a 20 percent performance fee paid to your Trade Leaders on whatever profits they generated for you.[6] For example, if you had an average monthly balance of $10,000 and earned $1,500 for 15 percent annual profits:

EOY balance:	$11,500 (assuming the 2% fee is collected only at EOY for sake of illustration)
Annual service fee:	200
Performance fee:	300
Total EOY:	$11,000
Net annual yield:	11%

To participate in Currensee's social trading program, you need a minimum $3,000, though a Currensee spokesperson told me the average account is around $25,000, increasingly from satisfied customers starting with small accounts and subsequently adding funds in the hope of averaging up, like one would do with any other winning investment in a firm uptrend.

EToro's initial deposit for the social trading is a much easier to digest $100, and you're not permitted to have more than 20 percent of your account balance at risk from one trade or one guru trader.

Note that with either site, you're ultimately using the same leverage as the trader you follow for a given trade. Given that most traders use significant leverage (anywhere from 20:1 to 400:1), you'd need the appropriate cash reserves in your account, and very good risk and money management (RAMM) skills, to have any realistic chance of surviving normal price fluctuations and account drawdowns expected if following the more leveraged traders, as we covered in Chapter 5 on RAMM.

Regulation The sites are essentially unregulated, so there are some gaps in oversight. As this industry matures, we expect that situation to get better as firms seek to improve their standing as legitimate alternative investment vehicles and so work with relevant regulatory agencies like the National Futures Association (NFA), in the case of U.S.-based firms, on their risk disclosures and marketing materials.

Success at Social Trading Still Ultimately Depends on Your Own Skill and Judgment Though social trading is a huge shortcut to success, it's far from an idiot-proof solution. There's skill involved in knowing how to select expert traders, how long to stick with them, and how to deal with one's own psychological, risk, and money management issues. You are still responsible for these. These issues are critical, yet they are difficult to master and often neglected in the mistaken focus on finding the magical mix of trade setups or analytical tools.

In other words, you still need enough of a background in analysis, trader psychology, risk, and money management to be able to:

- Select the experts that best fit your own risk tolerance, account size, style preferences, and current market conditions, and know how long to stay with them even when normal drawdowns tempt you to switch prematurely to another expert.
- Be responsible for your own RAMM.

In sum, there are plenty of decisions left in your hands once you've selected your expert(s). For example:

- As a senior manager of one social trading venue told me, most profitable traders tend to use the riskiest strategies. When selecting which expert(s) to follow, you can't just rely on the sites' rankings or one profitability metric. You need to consider whether you can psychologically and financially accept large drawdowns that might not ever be recovered. The experts are human, and thus liable to have cold streaks and at some point lose their touch altogether, as with managed accounts.
- You need to assess which traders might be best for current market conditions. Like top hedge fund managers, star expert traders tend to have their winning and losing streaks, and tend to do better in certain kinds of markets. At minimum, you need to be able to have some idea about whether the coming weeks or months are likely to favor risk or safety assets, and to trend strongly or stay within a range. Then you need to assess whether a given expert's track record was formed under similar

market conditions to those you anticipate, or you have some reason to believe that the trader will succeed under the likely coming market conditions. As every site warns, past performance is no guarantee of future returns. You should be able to clearly articulate why your chosen expert(s) should continue to perform in current and near-term market conditions.

- You are still fully responsible for your own money management. The available performance metrics can tell you about the likely risk and maximum drawdown of given experts; however, these traders are making decisions based on their own account balances and risk tolerance, not yours. That is, you must still be sure you have enough funds in your account to cover those possible drawdowns. This is especially true for those following multiple experts, because their accounts must be able to absorb their combined losses at any one time or risk facing margin calls. As we noted earlier, you *must* be clear that you have enough cash in your account to be able to survive the possible drawdowns of your chosen experts given what you know about their leverage and maximum drawdown data. *If you have any doubt, back off until you are clear that you have the cash.* Otherwise it's very possible you will hit a margin call and lose your money just as your expert starts to turn around and get profitable.

Huge red flag and flashing lights warning: Before linking with any expert, you should first be very clear on how much leverage they use, what is their expected and maximum drawdown, and therefore how much cash you need to keep in your account to avoid a margin call and survive a likely worst-case scenario losing streak that most traders hit at one time or another. If in doubt, ask:

- The customer service reps: My experiences with them at both eToro and Currensee have been good.
- Fellow traders in the social network: This is exactly what they are there to do—provide advice.

As easy as social trading appears, don't even think about trying it until you know you have the needed cash to ride out possible drawdowns and losing streaks of your chosen expert. Otherwise you are *so* not ready for this.

To eToro's great credit, it has recognized that too many new traders make far too many mistakes with RAMM (not having read this book yet), *and has actually done something to help these poor innocents.* It has taken a number of steps to promote more responsible, less reckless trading. These include:

- Adjustable leverage and default leverage settings to reduce the risk of excessive leverage. *Note:* Unless regulations of the user's country of residence are lower, eToro's default leverage is 100:1. That's still quite high.
- Real-time "Guardian Angel" guidance system: an automated trading guide to help traders avoid some of the worst mistakes that can kill accounts and self-esteem. While the system is mentioned on the home-page, there's no easy-to-find link to more information on this. Instead, just do an online search (eToro and Guardian Angel) for full details.
- Maximum 20 percent of available balance with any given trader. That is a good diversification for most, who may not be both very well capitalized and very capable of identifying the right trader at the right time.
- Maximum 20 percent of available balance on any one trade. That may still be high (depending on account size and available balance), but does allow for an exceptional situation when a trader is willing to take on more risk than usual. In the end, users must be responsible for their own RAMM, and eToro wants to keep its rules simple.
- Users can not only copy others' trades but also automatically allocate the same proportion of their account to that trade as the expert trader's allocation, allowing users to not only copy trades of Gurus but also at least some of their risk management.
- The ability to practice social trading even on demo accounts. Currensee allows social trading only with real accounts.
- Exceptionally detailed screening tools to allow users to set criteria for selecting whom to copy or follow. That makes it far easier to find safer, lower-risk traders that suit your needs among the thousands of possibilities in the social network. Ease of use raises the chances that users will make the effort to do careful screening and selection. Users can even choose only one instrument of a given trader to copy. For example, if that trader is really an expert only in the AUDJPY or gold, you can choose to copy only trades in these instruments.

We hope more forex brokers will invest in providing these kinds of safety features, as well as in quality analysis, training, and other tools to help you survive and prosper, and so prove that they want to make money with you rather than from you.

So while using expert traders should improve your results (see the following page for details), until you attain a similar level of expertise, you still need a background in forex, analysis, and RAMM in order to best exploit social trading, even with the aforementioned safety features.

Rewards of Social Trading

Now that the risks are clear, let's look at the advantages of the social trading approach.

Higher Chances of Success   Not surprisingly, leaving the trading to those better qualified should produce better results than if you did your own trading, at least until you become an expert trader yourself.

According to a report by the Aite Group, a Boston consulting firm that specializes in the financial services industry, up to 50 percent of social traders are profitable in a given quarter versus only about a third (at best) of do-it-yourself retail traders, according to data from the major retail forex brokers.[7]

EToro reports even better results, claiming that between 80 and 90 percent of all copied trades are profitable, and that investors who copy are showing "significantly higher gains than manual (self) traders."[8] As noted earlier, only about 20 percent to 30 percent of forex traders are profitable according to broker reports gathered by the U.S. government.

While it's not so surprising that copying experts should produce better results for most people, early results suggest that a decent picker of top traders could beat markets in general, regardless of whether conditions are bullish or bearish. As shown in Figure 11.1, Currensee's Trade Leaders have been doing just that.

As the social trading sites become more adept at making it easier to identify and track top performers, this performance advantage is likely to grow, regardless of how many followers are attracted. As noted in Chapter 1, the forex market dwarfs that of the major stock indexes, so it is very hard for anyone except for a few central banks to generate enough volume to move markets for more than a matter of days.

Time Saved   While it still takes skill to succeed with social trading, you save an enormous amount of time and effort compared to the time and effort invested to become and remain a top trader.

Even if you do expect to become a star trader, you still need to consider whether your results are likely to justify the extra time and effort invested.

We suspect that the advantages of better results and time saved will cause many to decide to study forex with a goal of becoming adept selectors of trading talent rather than traders themselves. Just like there are funds comprised of shares in other funds, and investors who focus on mutual funds and exchange-traded funds (ETFs), there will be forex investors who prefer to build portfolios of traders as part or all of their forex activities.

Better Way to Play the Lower Correlation with Other Markets
As we covered in Chapters 1 and 2, the very nature of currency trading allows traders and investors to profit in down as well as up markets. There's always a trend to be played in some pair or time frame, and the almost interchangeable nature of retail forex and commodity trading means that skilled forex traders can as easily exploit developments via certain commodities, making it easier still to find worthwhile opportunities when other retail markets are more challenging.

In other words, forex's low correlation to other markets means you're not forced into the same crowded and often overpriced assets like investors in other markets are.

In good times, cash pours into the most popular risk assets, bidding them up so that they quickly become expensive, and you risk paying too much and missing the gains. In bad times, the same thing happens with the popular safe haven assets. It's every asset manager's dream to find an asset class that can do well in any market conditions.

Given the nature and size of forex markets, *skillful* (yes, there's the catch) forex trading is a uniquely effective solution for those seeking assets with little correlation to other markets. The problem for most people, even otherwise sophisticated investors or fund managers, is that they aren't skilled forex traders. Social trading provides the shortcut to the benefits of professional forex trading without the requisite investment to build that skill.

With social trading, it's much easier for average traders to exploit that low correlation by automatically mirroring the trading of those who do it best. Again, there's a skill to identifying these experts, but that's still easier and less time-consuming than doing it all yourself. Study this book well and you've got most of the background you need to pick the right experts to follow.

For a more complete discussion of how uncorrelated expert trader returns can be to other markets, see Appendix G.

Transparency: You Know Your Experts' Track Records and Current Performance   You have the records of the other experts against which to compare the results of your own. This is critical, because even the most exclusive private account and hedge fund managers at some point go cold. You need a way to monitor them. Social trading provides past and current performance information that is at least as good as and usually better than traditional managed accounts, and come with the added bonus of community for consultations about your chosen experts and their competitors.

The Growth of Social Trading

Given these advantages, the appeal of better returns for less effort at a reasonable (or no additional) cost, and the added benefit of having an entire community to consult about how and whom to choose, social trading has been growing dramatically since it began in late 2010. For example, as of the end of 2011, Currensee reports the following for its Trade Leader program:[9]

- There has been $6 billion trading volume since the program began, and a 50 percent increase since April 14, 2011.
- There is $12 million in assets under management since launch.
- More than 400 individual investors are actively participating.
- Average investor account size is over $25,000.
- An average of 3,500 trades are executed daily.
- Investors from more than 50 countries are using the service in English, Chinese, French, Italian, and Spanish.
- Nearly 50 percent of the growth in assets during the prior 60 days has come from investors achieving success in the program and depositing additional capital.

As a purely social trading site, Currensee's growth figures are all attributable to the growth of social trading.

EToro reports that now 50 percent of all trades in its network are copied trades, up from 0 percent when the program began in late 2010.[10] Because eToro offers both self-directed and social trading, its figures suggest the potential future growth of copied trades versus traditional self-directed trades that we could see throughout the retail forex industry.

How eToro and Currensee Compare

EToro allows you to try their social trading platform with demo accounts. Currensee accepts only real money accounts. There is a reason for this difference.

EToro runs its own forex brokerage, which provides both a revenue stream independent of social trading and a preexisting infrastructure for demo accounts. If you see social trading as a key part of your forex activities, then strongly consider starting your social trading career with an eToro demo account. The chance to social trade on a demo account alone is enough to justify opening a demo account with eToro. Of course if your research shows other brokers to be more suitable, there's nothing stopping you from having demo accounts at different brokers as well, but you'll be able to practice social trading only on the eToro account.

Currensee, in contrast, is not a forex broker. As a pure social network and trading business, Currensee depends on its broker referral and social trading service fees, which come only with real accounts. Its lack of a social trading demo account is a distinct disadvantage for newer traders because, as we noted earlier, although social trading is easier than doing it yourself, it still demands skill, and demo accounts help build skill.

However, precisely because it's not a broker, Currensee allows you the flexibility to choose the broker that best fits you and still engage in social trading. Once you're past the entry-level stage, that flexibility becomes a huge advantage because different brokers do different things better, be it uniquely valuable members-only content, better prices, a wider range of assets to trade, a particular trading platform or language support, or something else. Also, eToro is available only to residents of certain countries (see: www.etoro.com/trade/etoro-and-brokers.aspx for details), so depending on where you live, Currensee may be your best social trading option because you're more likely to find a broker registered where you're a resident.[11]

As noted earlier, Currensee invests much more in selecting its expert traders, so your chances of picking a winner with less time and effort are better. While eToro claims between 50 and 100 full-time professionals among its roughly 400 trade Gurus, Currensee's team of experts is intended to be a small, elite all-star team, so any trader(s) you pick should be highly qualified.

Not surprisingly, these trader studs pump out some impressive documented returns compared to other asset classes. See Figure 11.2, which compares their average cumulative monthly performance versus some

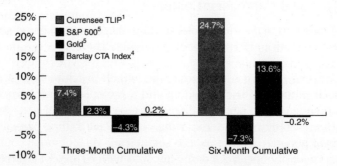

FIGURE 11.2 Currensee.com versus Other Asset Classes
Note: TLIP stands for Trade Leaders Investment Program.

other popular asset classes over three- and six-month periods ending October 31, 2011.

Admittedly this isn't a long time period, though it's an auspicious start. Not only has Currensee's dream team beaten the other asset classes, but it has shown very low correlation to other markets. That's another huge advantage, because it means you have a better chance of profiting regardless of market conditions. This is such a big deal that I've dedicated all of Appendix G to explaining it.

So in sum, how do the two social trading leaders compare? If you're new to forex or have very limited capital, and if you reside where eToro is available, it may well be a better one-stop solution. It is a brokerage that's as equipped as any to deal with beginners, so you need only deal with it. While other brokers like FXCM offer more extensive education for their members (via its superlative content site, DailyFX.com), eToro has some potent advantages for those who are newer or have yet to find themselves as traders, including:

- Numerous features noted earlier to help reduce (though not eliminate) RAMM mistakes. Until you're solid in these skills, this feature matters—a lot.
- Ability to practice social trading via demo accounts—also very, very significant for less experienced forex traders or investors.
- A stronger emphasis on trader education. In particular, it claims to have the largest social network, which may, in theory, make it easier to find more of the advice and mentoring a beginner would need. Moreover, you have a chance to be in contact with those you follow.
- Guru trader compensation more heavily tied to number of followers than is Currensee's trader compensation. While that may not be the most precise alignment of compensation and performance as measured by profits, it should better reward those Gurus who do more marketing via mentoring. Currensee's traders operate more like traditional fund managers, and are generally not available for consultation.
- Much larger selection of traders to copy. Not only are there hundreds of certified Gurus, with 50 to 100 full-time professionals among them, but also you can choose to copy any one of the many thousands in the social network. That could be a distinct advantage for those seeking an unusual trader profile to copy. Yes, that could require a much greater time investment than if operating with Currensee. However, eToro has extensive screening tools to speed that process of sifting through thousands of potential experts to copy.
- Much lower minimum deposit, only $100, versus about $3,000 for Currensee. Again, however, I'd warn that $100 seems far too little to have a realistic chance of surviving any kind of temporary setback, though it's

certainly possible for those with good RAMM skills to begin with less than $3,000. However, even $3,000 is dangerously small when dealing with any kind of moderate to high leverage or high-risk trader who experiences significant drawdowns in the normal course of business.

- For those who are already successful traders and seek to build at least a part-time career in trading, but lack the trading style or track record for Currensee's elite club, eToro is the place to build a track record and reputation among the many successful part-time traders and full-time professionals there.
- If you've the skill, time, and energy to sort through the hundreds of Guru traders to find the top performers for your particular trading style and risk preferences, you could build a portfolio of star traders producing stellar results at a significant discount to what you'd pay with Currensee, possibly with greater diversification due to the greater choice available. With eToro's screening tools, that shouldn't be any harder than using stock-screening software to screen stocks.

In sum, eToro may be the better bet for traders with less capital, less RAMM skill, and/or those who are willing to dedicate the time to exploit the educational benefits of the larger social network and access to input from trade experts. It's also definitely the place for those seeking to build a following of traders. While only registered Guru traders get paid for having active copiers, anyone can be copied and build a following and reputation as a good trader. Also, eToro will offer a much wider range, albeit less selective, group of traders to follow. So if Currensee doesn't have a trader that fits your needs, eToro's wider selection might.

On the other hand, Currensee is likely to be a better choice for:

- Those who can afford the higher minimum required investment (typically between $2,000 and $4,000) or, better still, $20,000 or more to allow for diversifying into a number of traders.
- Finding a top trader, or for building a portfolio of traders faster and with less effort, due to the smaller size and more selective composition of its Trade Leader team. Heck, for somewhere between $30,000 and $60,000 you can have a small diversified portfolio comprised of each Trade Leader.
- Flexibility of broker choices, an important point if you're particularly attached to a given broker and want all your trading done through that account. As good as eToro may be, it can't be all things to all people. That said, even if eToro allows social trading via other brokerage accounts, the mere fact that Currensee is not a potentially competing broker may simplify its ability to connect with additional brokers.

- Those who already have enough RAMM skills so that the assistance eToro provides in this critical area for beginners is not decisive. Currensee's selection process considers risk management, that's built into its system, although some of the Trade Leaders still experience significant drawdowns and volatility, so RAMM is more in your own hands.
- Those with less time or interest in actively monitoring their trading experts or alternative experts, given the higher bar set for its Trade Leaders and much more limited selection of them.
- Those with less interest in using the site for trader education via exploiting a larger social network or being able to contact those whom you follow. We suspect wealthier, busier private investors, as well as institutional investors and money managers, will be more comfortable at Currensee.

GREAT TOOL, BUT REQUIRES SKILL TO USE

For most aspiring traders, using proven traders should work better, at least until you're on their level. The available data shown earlier suggests you have a much better chance of profiting, and with less effort, too.

If optimal returns are your top priority, it's hard to argue against having at least some of your forex-dedicated funds allocated to copying experts, even if you're an aspiring star trader yourself. If you're not set on becoming a successful trader, then your time is probably better spent learning enough about forex to evaluate market conditions and traders, focusing on becoming adept at choosing the best traders, building a portfolio of them, and leaving the actual trading to them.

Yes, you'd probably be a better selector of talent if you're active in the social network, doing some trading and constantly growing your own skills. However, as with everything else, there's a time (and probably money) price to pay. It's your call if the price is worth it.

That said, even if you're totally sold on the efficiency of social trading, keep in mind that, as with any other professional services business, while you needn't be a great practitioner to succeed, you do need to be a good judge of the talent you hire. Also, as we noted earlier, you need to be competent at:

- Knowing yourself and what styles and risks you can comfortably handle: That is, are you okay with seeing your account fall dramatically if you're using a trader with a volatile high-risk strategy?
- Risk and money management: You need to thoroughly understand, given the leverage and risk data provided for a given expert, how much

you could lose at a given time, and you must be sure to have enough cash on hand to survive that drawdown until the longer-term profitability statistics kick in.

- Assessing whether a trader's style fits current market conditions: Different traders succeed under different circumstances, so you want to have some idea of why your chosen trader should succeed in the future. Consulting your colleagues in the social network may help, and so would diversifying your holdings among multiple traders.

In other words, with social trading, as with managed accounts or automated systems, while you don't need to be a great trader yourself, you still need enough of the core four skills mentioned in Chapter 2 to select which delegated or outsourced trading solution to follow, and how long to stay with a given trader or system.

No matter how good the experts may be, you still have plenty of chances to screw up. So continue to educate yourself so that you can better exploit social trading through better selection of the right traders and solid RAMM practices.

In sum, social trading is a potentially extraordinary tool and shortcut, but still requires skill, or trustworthy, competent advice, to use it properly. By all means consider it, but don't view it as a substitute for building your own knowledge and skills, at least to the point where you can manage your talent choices and RAMM.

An Auspicious Start

Given that social trading only began in late 2010, it has shown great promise for reasons mentioned earlier. However, given that it is still so new, be aware that its track record is very limited.

When you start trading, strongly consider allocating at least a portion of your capital to following one or more experts, compare your results to theirs over a period of months, and draw your own conclusions.

Do Your Homework Before You Decide Which to Use

In addition to the obvious wisdom of not relying solely on my information, both sites are constantly upgrading their services, so it's possible that each may offer new features or copy features from the other over time. Given how useful social trading services could be, it could be well worth your while trying both, and even continuing to use both, depending on your needs. Also, by the time you read this, new players may have emerged that may also be worth a look.

Social Studies: Further Reading on Social Networks and Trading Forex isn't the only market where you can tap experts via social trading. For more on social trading, read the seminal work on the topic, *TradeStream Your Way to Profits* by Zack Miller (John Wiley & Sons, 2010). For the latest in social trading across different markets, and other new ways to apply technology to investing, see his superb website, www.tradestreaming.com.

Consider Market Conditions in Choosing Strategy and Risk Tolerance

Just as you'll find that your preferred trading or investing style works best in certain conditions, the same holds true for anyone, or anything, to which you delegate your trading decisions, be it a computerized or human trader. They will work better in some markets than in others. *That's why we strive to get a sense of the longer-term trend, the one that's four to five times longer than the time frame in which you trade, and then make sure our chosen strategy, system, or trader is in harmony with that trend.* That's easier said than done, and why you'll seek out reliable sources of good analysis to use for guidance.

How much risk you accept for a given trading strategy, be it manual, automated, or professionally managed, depends on two factors.

1. Your own personal risk tolerance in general: That's a personal decision, no matter what the time frame, be it five minutes or five years.
2. How well that chosen strategy fits the anticipated conditions: In other words, if the trend is strong, you may accept more risk with strategies that work well with very clear trends. The longer you hold positions, the more trustworthy the trends and indicators are and hence the more important it is to move in harmony with them.

If you believe you're at the early or middle stages of a long-term bull market in risk assets, you should be biased to more aggressively bullish strategies, whether you implement them manually, via auto-trading systems, or via professional managers. If you believed the opposite, you'd be looking for solutions that are likely to do best in bearish conditions.

For the sake of illustration, let's say your time horizon is very long term, say five to 10 years or more.

How would you know if you're in a long-term bull or bear market? Study one or more of the risk appetite barometers we introduced in Chapter 6; this is what they're for. For example, look at some long-term charts

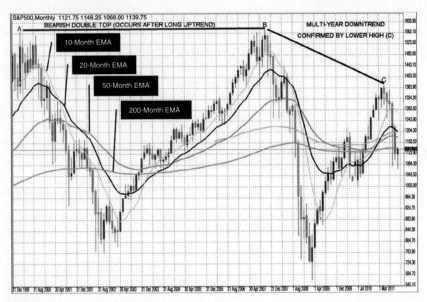

FIGURE 11.3　S&P 500 Monthly Chart, December 1999 to September 2011
Source: MetaQuotes Software Corp.

of 10 years or more of some major market stock indexes like the S&P 500.
(See Figures 11.3 and 11.4.)

Some key points to note:

- We have a bearish double top as discussed in Chapter 4 in the section
  on Western chart patterns. A valid double top pattern needs to be preceded by a long uptrend.

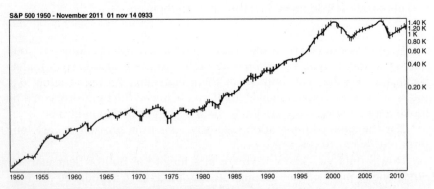

FIGURE 11.4　S&P 500, 1950 to November 2011
Source: MetaQuotes Software Corp.

Figure 11.4 of the S&P 500 dating back to 1950 shows that we do indeed have a prior uptrend and also shows the 60-plus-year perspective to demonstrate how significant this double top is, the first decade-long topping pattern since the 1970s.

- In Figure 11.3 note the double top formed in 2000 and 2007 (A and B) with the lower high (C) in May 2011 that confirmed the double top.
- Additional confirmation of the longer-term bear market in risk assets that began in the summer of 2007 includes a close below the 200-month exponential moving average (EMA) as well as all shorter-term EMAs in September 2011.

Our conclusion is that as of September 2011, for our long-term portfolio, we should seek strategies that will benefit from a bear market. In other words, it should involve shorting risk assets and being long safe haven assets.

So when selecting an auto-trading system, professional manager, or social network trade expert to manage a long-term portfolio (or a trade strategy), you'd want one with a track record that suggests success when risk assets are in a long-term downtrend.

In theory, the same thinking could be applied to even short-term time frames, though as we've noted repeatedly, shorter-term trends are less stable, and those that occur over a matter of hours or days are even less so. Short-term trading works only for those good at RAMM and technical analysis. Until you're proven with short-term trading, stick to proven systems or traders for that.

How low could the S&P 500 (and by implication other risk assets) fall given the Head and Shoulders reversal pattern? As we learned in Chapter 4, the general rule of thumb is that the potential pullback is double the distance from the tops to the neckline. The tops were at about 1,500 and the neckline was at about 800—a 700-point or 46 percent drop! Another 700-point drop would bring the S&P 500 to 100, a 93 percent drop!

Obviously you wouldn't base your long-term portfolio strategy on this one indicator, though. Also, you'd refer to fundamental analysis for confirmation or refutation of that bearish analysis. There is significant fundamental evidence that as of this writing, markets are in a multiyear downtrend. See some of the most important financial books in recent years on the topic:

This Time Is Different: Eight Centuries of Financial Folly, by Carmen M. Reinhart and Kenneth S. Rogoff (Princeton University Press, 2009).

Endgame: The End of the Debt Supercycle and How It Changes Everything, by John Mauldin and Jonathan Tepper (John Wiley & Sons, 2011).

> *Planet Ponzi: How Politicians and Bankers Stole Your Future,* by Mitch Feierstein (Bantam Press, 2012).

Both suggest the fundamental outlook for the coming years could be very bleak. Both are also considered to be among the most important books in recent years on financial markets, and very worthwhile for framing your longer-term perspective.

BINARY OPTIONS: TRADING MADE EASIER

The other big innovation in forex trading that has shown dramatic growth in recent years is the binary option (BO; aka digital or fixed-return options). Like forex social trading and social networks, it's so new that there's little objective information out about it. So for the second time in one chapter, and for the first time in any forex book, I'll introduce a new approach to forex that, when done intelligently, can provide exceptional gains without exceptional risk.

The following is a summary of my full study, *Binary Options: Pros and Cons*, which is available on the website, thesensibleguidetoforex.com. It is one of the more valuable parts of this book, because the information is both very worthwhile and currently unavailable elsewhere. Binary options are an incredibly useful tool. While their popularity has grown enormously since they became available to retail traders just a few years ago (they were formerly reserved for the big boys), they remain an underutilized tool, particularly for traders seeking a simplified way to ride a multiday or multiweek trend with very controlled (though not insignificant) risk.

Make 70 percent in under an hour! Limited risk! Just forecast the trend and rake in the dough! No experience necessary!

Try to research binary options, and that's the typical way they're presented. The material is more focused on attracting reckless speculators than on reaching and teaching prudent, serious traders and investors how and when to use binary options.

Like most rational adults, I gave up believing in get-rich-quick schemes shortly after I abandoned belief in Santa Claus and that Mom was still a virgin. Too bad (not for Mom) but reality beckons.

The popularity of binary options for forex and other assets has literally exploded since 2010[12] because their combination of simplicity, high profit potential, and controlled risk makes them an ideal introductory trading vehicle.

Unfortunately, that same simplicity has attracted gamblers and thus gambler-oriented websites, hence the unfortunate casino feel of many brokers as they aim their marketing at the ignorant and reckless, undermining the credibility of binary options among the more serious traders and investors.

However, it would be a big mistake to ignore binary options. Like a junkyard, it isn't the most posh venue, but there's very serious money to be made without exceptional talent or effort if you're willing to put in the requisite work.

As compelling an option as social trading is, most of us should aspire to do at least some part-time trading in order to improve our skills and market awareness; and if you're going to trade, you will want to use binary options at least some of the time, perhaps regularly. There are just too many situations in which they can't be beat for quickly exploiting a trend, exceptional potential returns, low entry cost, and clearly predefined maximum loss.

Ignore the suspicious-sounding claims of many binary options brokers and the gambling mentality that pervades some of their websites. When used intelligently, mostly *via binary options with weekly or monthly expirations*, binary options in fact can be an extremely useful complement or substitute to traditional spot market instruments. Their simplicity, availability at very small and low-cost position sizes, and more controlled risk make them at times an ideal vehicle for:

- Beginning traders or anyone else seeking a simpler way to trade that allows for faster decision making.
- Those with limited capital.
- More advanced and well-funded serious traders seeking a way to jump on a short-term trend quickly (because binary options require less trade planning) with strictly controlled downside risk.

When first learning about binary options, I couldn't find any decent objective review of their advantages and disadvantages that made clear when and for whom they are appropriate. The following is the product of my own research and analysis to answer that need. I believe you'll find it very helpful and objective despite my affiliation with the industry.

Full disclosure: As of this writing I provide analysis for one broker, Anyoption.com, the only broker I'd consider using (were I not a related party and thus prohibited) because as of the time of this writing:

- It is the only broker I know that provides weekly and monthly expirations. That is a critical advantage for the trader. These are time frames in which individual traders with some analytical skills have a very

realistic chance of being profitable, if they're selective about which
trades they enter and follow the principles we've discussed.

- The support, resistance, and other indicators are old enough to be
  meaningful. There's enough time for the publicly available fundamental data (interest rate trends, growth rates, jobs and spending
  trends, etc.) to have some predictable impact on the trend, and binary options are all about being right about the direction of that
  trend.
- Whereas options that expire within an hour or a day are usually suitable only for the reckless gamblers or skilled day traders. As we've
  noted earlier, intraday (never mind intrahour) price movements are
  mostly based on unpredictable short-term money flows from big
  players. Admittedly, these short-term options can be useful for news
  traders.
- It offers one of the widest selections of instruments found among binary options brokers.
- It offers a wider range of ways to trade binary options than most other
  brokers.
- Anyoption.com has its faults, but they aren't disadvantages relative to
  other brokers because these same faults are shared by the entire binary
  brokerage industry (like limited charting tools, inability to place limit
  orders for entries and exits, etc).
- It typically ranks at or near the top of every binary options broker survey I've seen, so I'm not the only one it has impressed.

Most binary option brokers offer only very short-term daily or hourly
expirations—too short a period for most traders to make any reliable forecast about the trend.

The industry is growing very rapidly, and new brokers and offerings
appear regularly, so by all means do your own online research to find the
most updated information on which brokers are offering what features.

To cover binary options properly requires almost 50 pages, because
binary options are so new to most people and I can't be sure you'll find
other trustworthy materials elsewhere on whether binary options are right
for you. Thus more coverage is needed.

In order to avoid interfering with the continuity of the book, this full
review is in the appendix on binary options found on the website. The following is a brief summary of the key points you should know to give you
an overview of what's covered.

Background

The five most common types of binary options are the asset-or-
nothing, cash-or-nothing, no-touch, one-touch, and double-no-touch/

double-one-touch. The most popular of these is the cash-or-nothing binary option, which is typically what's referenced when describing binary options and what is most commonly offered by most brokers. The other varieties are not always available, with most brokers at best offering a few but not all of them and not for all instruments. *Unless stated otherwise, we'll be covering the cash-or-nothing type.*

How They Work

With regular plain-vanilla options:

- When you buy an option, you're buying a right, but not an obligation, to buy or sell the underlying asset (a stock, commodity, currency pair, etc.) at a certain price called the *strike price*, at any time until the *expiration date*, after which time the option contract expires and is worthless.
- If you think the price will go higher than the strike price, you buy a *call option*, which is the right to buy at the lower strike price. You buy calls when you think the trend will rise over the given expiration period.
- If you think the price will go lower than the strike price, you buy a *put option*, which is the right to sell at the higher strike price. You buy puts when you believe the trend will fall during the expiration period.
- You can place orders in advance to buy or sell an option as you would in forex or other kinds of spot market trading.
- If you were right, your profit is roughly proportional to how far the price of the underlying asset moved in your favor (*in the money*) at the time you sell the option. For example, if you bought a call on the GBPUSD and the pair was up 3 percent when you sold, you made about 3 percent. If you bought a put, you lose the full amount, but no more, of what you paid for the option. The opposite would apply if the pair fell by 3 percent at the time you sold the option: the put would be worth about 3 percent more and the call would be worthless if price remained below the strike price when the option expired. Your profit varies with how far price moves in your favor. If there's enough time left before the expiration date, you may still be able to sell a losing option position (*out of the money*) to cut your loss, because your buyer thinks that price could still turn around.

Yes, this is an oversimplification for the sake of illustration. In many cases option prices do not move in the same proportion as the price of the underlying asset.

The main differences with binary options include these four points:

1. Fixed holding period: Generally, binary options can't be sold before expiration, so there is no chance of taking profits or cutting losses before the expiration date.

2. Fixed payout: If the option expires in the money, it generally yields about 70 percent profit regardless of how little the underlying asset moved in your favor. Some brokers credit you 5 percent to 15 percent of the option's cost if it expires out of the money.

3. Shorter expiration periods: Binary option expiration periods range from about one hour (sometimes less) to one month at most. Plain-vanilla options can be held for much longer periods.

4. No advance order placement: Generally you can't place entry limit orders. If you want to be long via a call or to be short via a put at a certain price, you have to wait to place your order until that price is hit.

Pros and Cons

There is much more on these and others in the Appendix (Binary Options: Pros and Cons) on the book's companion website (thesensibleguidet oforex.com), but here are the key points in brief.

Pros

- High potential profit: The fixed payouts are high, especially considering:
  - The short expiration times: You can earn about 70 percent[1] in as little as an hour or at most up to a month. While it's not realistic to expect most traders to be consistently profitable on very short time frames like one hour or one day, the odds are much better when trading binary options with weekly and monthly expiration dates.
  - Strictly defined maximum loss: You can't lose more than the cost of the option. With standard trading, even stop loss orders are no guarantee against unplanned higher losses if the market suddenly gaps past your stop loss price.
  - This makes binary options a particularly lucrative way to play small percentage moves without the added RAMM planning needed with leveraged instruments.
- Greater simplicity can boost earnings: This fixed holding period and payout vastly simplify trading. That can boost profits because:
  - There are just fewer mistakes to make: Once you've bought a call (to be long the currency pair) or put (to open a short position) at a price and position size you deem acceptable, no further planning or monitoring is needed. You need only be correct about the overall price direction over the life of the binary option. That's it. For example, as long as the pair has appreciated, even just slightly, by the time the option expires, the call binary option earns about 70 percent. If it fell, even just incrementally, by the expiration time, the put option

also earns about 70 percent. Usually,[2] risk management is limited to choosing your entry points, and money management is limited to choosing position sizes that don't risk over one to three percent of your account. Beyond these, there's no chance to make fatal RAMM mistakes regarding planned profit taking and stop loss points, etc. Reward-risk ratios, exit points, etc. are generally fixed or irrelevant. See the full "Binary Options Pros and Cons" material on the companion website for illustrations of how binary options' greater simplicity can boost your profitability.

- You can make decisions faster: This simplicity also raises the odds of being profitable because it cuts down the decision-making time when you need to move fast, as is often the case for those trading shorter-term positions or breaking news.
- Low entry cost: Depending on the broker, options can cost as little as $10, maybe less.

Cons

- Negative risk-reward ratio: Winning trades typically yield 70 percent over your investment, while losing trades typically cost you 85 percent, sometimes more, depending on the broker. That means you have to be right over 55 percent of the time just to break even.

    On the other hand, it's much easier to be right most of the time with binary options because the only thing that must be right about is the overall trend during the life of the option, as noted above.

    Throughout this book we've encouraged you to use strategies that allow you to be wrong most of the time and still make money, and for standard forex trading that makes sense given the greater complexity and thus more chances for mistakes. The far greater simplicity of the binary option trading decision, fully detailed in the appendix on the website, balances this disadvantage and for many traders will outweigh it as they hit a higher percentage of winning trades. Still, those who are skilled at RAMM will usually be able to attain better practical risk-reward ratios with standard (spot market) forex trading, though they still risk greater than anticipated losses when price gaps beyond their stop losses.
- No advanced order placement: This means you have to be ready and waiting to go if you want a specific entry point. At minimum that's inconvenient, and for those who are not always watching the markets (who is?), it can mean missed opportunities.
- Less selection: Most binary option brokers don't offer as wide a range of assets to trade as most of the better forex brokers, though all offer the most popular ones, so this is a problem only for some.

- Binary options brokers provide fewer services. For example, charting packages, as well as content offerings (both training and trade guidance) tend to be minimal or non-existent. Any serious binary option trader will need to find their own charting software and data feed in order to do any real technical analysis.

Again, see the Appendix on the website for the full story.

CHAPTER 12

Forex for Income

The Smartest Oxymoron

I know, the title sounds like an oxymoron. The stereotypical private currency trader is a risk-taking short-term speculator. Income investors lean toward steady, reliable long-term returns.

However, the need for currency diversification is one of the most important lessons of the Great Financial Crisis. Ignoring it involves some toxic combination of ignorance, foolishness, laziness, and/or recklessness.

I can help you with only the first one, though if you have read this far the other three probably don't apply to you.

The lesson isn't new. It has been ongoing for decades. Remember *Europe on $5.00 a Day*, or when one U.S. dollar (USD) was worth hundreds of Japanese Yen (JPY), or even just when oil was under $50 a barrel? For those too heavily in the wrong currencies, currency risk has been a slow, quiet but steady drain on net worth.

However there's substantial risk of that draining sound getting louder as the process accelerates. With most developed world central banks keeping rates low and stimulus flowing as they hope to inflate away their debt burdens, it's likely that the purchasing power of most major currencies will continue to erode. That means you've got to get your portfolios diversified into assets tied to the best currencies. Your portfolio needs currency diversification just as much as it needs asset and sector diversificaton.

The past chapters have been mostly for traders, albeit the longer-term, more conservative variety, but still for those who are willing to regularly move in and out of positions over days, preferably weeks or months.

This chapter is mostly for the more passive investors willing to hold quality assets for the long term regardless of short-term fluctuations, as long as these produce either long-term appreciation, a relatively steady, high yield for passive income, or some combination of the two.

This chapter covers just two ways that these investors can use forex markets as another source of steady income:

1. Identify currencies in strong long-term uptrends and allocate portions of your income portfolio portfolio to assets that provide direct or indirect exposure to those currencies for a steady currency diversified income stream.

2. Engage in long-term carry trades either via direct spot market currency pair investments or through income assets denominated in high-yield currencies purchased with lower-yield currencies. Either way, the goal is to profit from interest rate differentials (explained in the following section).

Let this chapter serve as a wake-up call for income investors to diversify by currency as well as by sector and asset type.

RIDE LONG-TERM FOREX TRENDS FOR LOWER RISK, HIGHER INCOME

Until we were well into the Great Financial Crisis, currency diversification was one of the most neglected topics for income investors. With the long-term value of most developed world currencies being undermined by growing national debt levels, investors are starting to get the message.

Even today, much of the advice that purports to cover overseas investing focuses on individual foreign stock or bond picking without regard for the quality of the underlying currency. That brings some diversification, but still fails to consider whether or not you're diversifying into a currency that's any better than what you've already got. The purpose of diversifying into other currencies is to get into those with the best chances for long-term appreciation. A good investment in a bad currency can become a bad investment, and vice versa.

In other words, first you identify the currencies you want represented in your portfolio, then you allocate a percentage of your portfolio to each one, and finally, you choose the individual assets that provide that given percentage exposure. That's the basic idea.

Obviously you'll need to weigh the quality of the stocks, bonds, or other assets versus that of the currency. For example, if there's an abundance of quality high-yield income stocks in Canada and relatively few in Switzerland or Australia, you might allocate more heavily to Canadian income investments.

Here's the short version of the steps involved.

1. First identify the right currencies:
   - Study weekly or monthly charts of currencies or representative currency indexes for your projected holding period. If you're planning on holding for five to 10 years, you want to see trends over the prior five to 10 years. See Figure 12.1 for an example of how I compared the CAD's performance to that of the USD, GBP, EUR, and JPY from mid-2006 to mid-2012.
   - Identify the currencies with the healthiest uptrends over that period.
   - Check that the underlying national economic fundamentals support that trend with relatively good growth, or at least consistently low ratios of debt to gross domestic product (GDP) and a culture of fiscal discipline, not growing budget and trade deficits. For example, the JPY has performed well over the past decades, but its underlying fundamentals have been worsening. Japan's formerly high rate of individual savings that supported demand for JPY is plummeting as its population ages into retirement.
   - Allocate percentages of your portfolio for income-generating instruments denominated in or tied to those currencies.
2. Then shop around for specific assets you want that are denominated in or exposed to those currencies so that you have a set portion of your portfolio in both the right currencies and assets in those currencies. The research method is the same as for any stock, bond, fund, and so on. The only difference is that in addition to your normal screening criteria, you screen by country or currency.

Why Income Investors Neglect Currency Diversification

There are reasons why forex considerations get ignored by income investors.

For individual investors, forex is mostly a short-term speculator's market; it is unfamiliar territory with a discomforting reputation for high-risk, complex, and stressful short-term trading with high attrition rates. Most of the free forex advice found online is either directly or indirectly paid for by the online retail forex brokers. The better ones hire some of the best writers. There are also forex content sites that are supported by broker advertising. Forex brokers make their money on trading volume, and thus have an interest in promoting short-term trading that generates much higher trading volumes. The low start-up costs and high profit potential also help attract the less sophisticated seekers of get-rich-quick schemes and the simple gamblers.

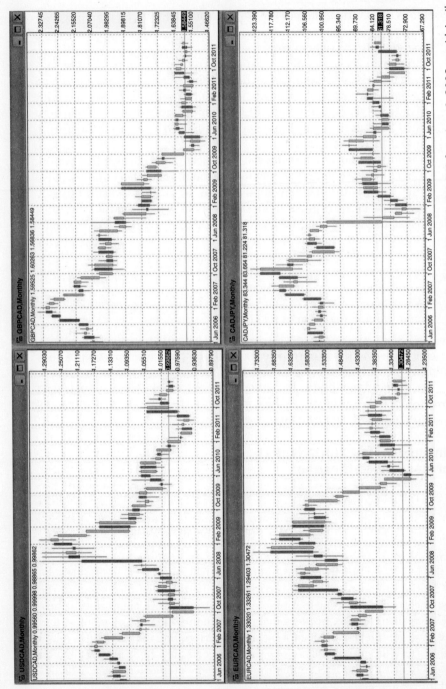

FIGURE 12.1 CAD Monthly Charts Showing CAD performance versus (clockwise): USD, GBP, JPY, EUR from June 1, 2006 to mid-April 2012, almost 6 years

Source: MetaQuotes Software Corp.

Long-Term Trends for Long-Term Investors

As noted earlier when we discussed the advantages of trading in longer time frames, the common focus on short-term trading is sadly ironic. Forex markets produce some of the most reliable long-term trends compared to more traditional stock and corporate bond markets, because the fundamentals of nations change more slowly than those of corporations. These long-term trends are well suited for helping long-term buy-and-hold investors attain greater capital gains and income, with the reduced risk that comes from diversification into other markets outside of their native country.

The trick is to find nations that have both rising currencies and rising asset markets. You'd use monthly charts covering five to 10 years, looking at both forex pairs (as illustrated in Figure 12.2) and major global stock and bond markets.

Being in the right investments but in the wrong currency is like swimming against a strong current. No matter how much you think you're moving ahead, the current keeps pulling you back, impeding your progress or setting you back despite otherwise successful investment choices.

Conversely, being in both the right investments and the right currency is like swimming with the current; you progress much faster if your investments swim well, and even if they don't, they can still get carried forward in value by the current of a rising currency. In other words, even if your investments aren't the best, if they're linked to or denominated in the right currency, your net worth keeps moving in the right direction.

For anyone else hurt by the long-term decline in the USD, GBP, EUR, etc., the need to be aware of long-term forex trends and to diversify into currencies that are in long-term uptrends versus most others is one of the most important and painful lessons of the past years. Large forex-savvy multinational corporations have been aware of the trouble and routinely hedge forex exposure, but many smaller businesses and individual investors are only just beginning to awaken to the need for currency diversification.[1] Even though the USD has been in overall decline versus many major currencies (like the AUD, CAD, and JPY) for a decade or more, or for many decades (down 75 percent versus the CHF since 1970[2]), reputations die hard, and most U.S. investors grew up believing the USD was the safest currency to own, backed by the best economy, and a soundly managed financial and public sector.

Following is a case study illustrating the benefits of picking the right currency for dividend stock investors. The focus is on combining the right currency and stock market, though an appreciating currency is obviously an equally potent bonus for bond investors.

CASE STUDY: CANADA 2000–2011: APPLYING FOREX TRENDS TO EQUITIES INVESTING

Imagine that back at the beginning of 2000 an American investor (No. 1) decided to seek currency diversification for his portfolio beyond the United States, converted $100,000 USD to CAD, and invested the sum in a basket of Canadian stocks that comprise the S&P/TSX index, an index that tracks the Toronto Stock Exchange. His friend, fellow American investor No. 2, took the same sum and invested it in the S&P 500 index.

Note: The following assumes that dividend stock prices of the United States and Canada move in the same direction as the primary national stock indexes just for the sake of comparison, and does not take into account gains from dividends.

The USD versus the CAD: Guess Which Has No Debt/GDP Problem

What happened to the USD versus the CAD is shown in the chart in Figure 12.2 of the USDCAD.

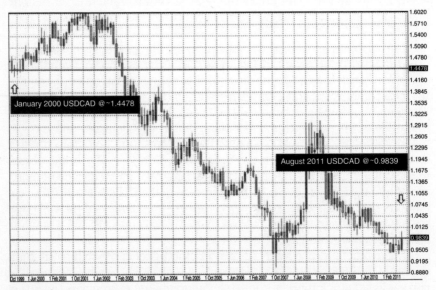

FIGURE 12.2   USDCAD Monthly Chart, January 2000 to August 18, 2011
Source: MetaQuotes Software Corp.

Obviously, we have a strong and overall very steady 10-year downtrend for the USDCAD. Here are the numbers:

USDCAD, January 2000:	1.4478
USDCAD, August 18, 2011:	0.9839
Change:	−0.4639
Percent change:	+32.04%

So, since January 2000, investor No. 1 gained 32.04 percent over investor No. 2 just on currency appreciation.

Equities: Canada Is Not Japan

Of course currency appreciation by itself isn't necessarily enough. If you don't have the right investments in a given currency, you still could lose. For example, just looking at relative currency performance, the JPY looks like an even better investment. If you sold U.S. dollars and bought the JPY in 1990, you did even better than with the CAD in the preceding example.

Figure 12.3 shows the USDJPY chart from May 1990 to August 2011.

FIGURE 12.3 USDJPY Monthly Chart, May 1990 to August 17, 2011
Source: MetaQuotes Software Corp.

Again, it is another obvious long-term downtrend for the USD, this time versus the JPY. Here are the numbers:

USDJPY, May 1990:	159.47
USDJPY, August 2011:	76.45
Nominal change:	83.02
Percent change:	52%

However, if you invested your JPY in the Nikkei 225, look what happened (see Figure 12.4).

Your 52 percent gain in currency appreciation was more than counteracted by a nearly 75 percent drop in the Nikkei over the same period.

Meanwhile, look how your U.S. dollars performed if invested in the S&P 500 over the same period (see Figure 12.5).

The 52 percent currency loss was more than made up for by the vast outperformance of U.S. stocks during this period, particularly during 1990 to 2000.

However, things went better for Canada. Note in Figure 12.6 how the representative index of Canadian shares fared versus the S&P 500, a good barometer for U.S. stocks (and risk assets in general).

The S&P/TSX composite basket of stocks rose almost 50 percent from January 2000 to mid-August 2011. Meanwhile, the S&P 500 lost 20 percent in this same period.

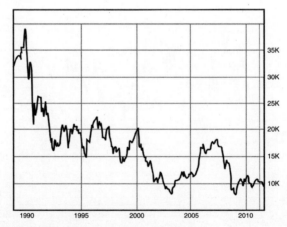

FIGURE 12.4   Nikkei 225, 1990 to August 2011
Source: MetaQuotes Software Corp.

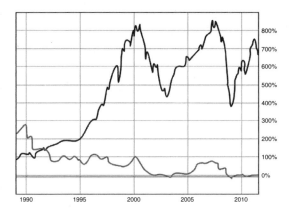

FIGURE 12.5 Nikkei 225 versus S&P 500, 1990 to August 2011
Source: MetaQuotes Software Corp.

For example: If in January 2000 you converted $100,000 USD to CAD, then invested that in the S&P/TSX composite index or a similar basket of stocks:

$100,000 USD put into CAD in 2000 became:	$132,040
That $132,040 invested in stocks grew to be about	
($132,040 * 150% S&P/TSX appreciation):	198,060
That $100,000 USD invested in the S&P in 2000 became about:	80,000
Difference	$118,060

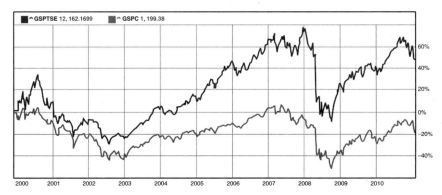

FIGURE 12.6 S&P/TSX Composite Index versus S&P 500, January 4, 2000, to August 15, 2011: Canadian Stocks versus U.S. Stocks
Source: MetaQuotes Software Corp.

In sum, our sample passive investor No. 1 who went with Canadian currency and stocks benefited from both currency and stock trends for a gain of $98,060 versus a $20,000 loss for No. 2, who stuck with U.S. currency and stocks.

Be Aware of Tax Withholdings and Credits

Some countries withhold a percentage of nonresidents' dividends, though it's possible to obtain a tax credit from the United States for foreign tax withholdings on your dividends. For example, Canada withholds 15 percent of dividends of nonresidents. The United States grants a tax credit for that withholding. Obviously, check this with your tax advisor regarding your particular situation, or just do an online search.

A lot has been written about the Canadian tax withholding issue in particular, given that Canada offers some great income stocks and one of the lowest debt/GDP ratios in the developed world. It also has a healthy banking system that largely avoided the reckless real estate lending and resulting losses found in the United States, Ireland, Spain, and so on. That means, barring a deep global financial crisis, the CAD is unlikely to suffer risk of devaluation via money printing and inflation.

For Further Investigation: Online Resources

For learning more about building a currency-diversified portfolio of income-producing investments, here are a few of my favorites to consider.

SeekingAlpha.com   As with ETFs, SeekingAlpha.com (SA) is the best starting point. Its sophisticated readership is very interested in steady income investments that allow you to ride out market volatility, so SA has a rich "Investing for Income" section. There are some good basic educational tools, but its big strength is the enormous daily flow of articles on all kinds of income investments, including those that provide some forex diversification. SeekingAlpha.com has built up a huge archive of articles, which you can search when seeking information on a specific idea or topic, like Chinese dividend stocks. SA has a huge following, so almost anyone seeking to build or maintain a reputation in this area is going to be posting here at some point, including yours truly, so you'll quickly get an idea about writers you want to follow on this topic.

I really hope to get back to writing on quality income stocks that provide diversification out of the USD and EUR at some point. These articles were rewarding for both myself and my readers, one of whom described them as "a top quality subscription quality newsletter free of charge." Stay tuned.

Other Writers to Follow   Here are a few writers to follow in this space. Unfortunately most of their material is via paid-for subscription, but they do offer some free content either in free e-mail newsletters (admittedly with a heavy focus on promoting the paid subscriptions) or on their assorted websites.

Peter Schiff is one of the senior blogger/authors on having a globally diversified portfolio of relatively conservative, high-quality non-U.S. income stocks. Just search his name and you'll find plenty of material worth considering. For those seeking managed accounts in this area, he's principal of a firm specializing in this niche, Euro Pacific Capital, Inc. I can't vouch for the quality of their managed accounts, but they've got the right idea. Peter Schiff's articles are usually good, as are those of his senior market strategist, John Browne (check out the guy's profile on SeekingAlpha.com—just remember to cue the James Bond music).

Roger Conrad is another one of the very best on investing in non-USD-denominated income vehicles. If you search his name online, you'll find he offers some free e-mail newsletters, though he saves his best stuff for his paid subscription newsletters, including ones that focus on Canadian and Australian stocks. He also has newsletters on master limited partnerships and utility stocks, both U.S. and non-U.S. based. They aren't cheap but they are excellent. If you're going to manage your own stock and bond portfolio, these newsletters are well worth a look, and last I checked they allowed readers to cancel at any time with a full refund, so there's little risk in trying them out.

THE CARRY TRADE: USING DIRECT FOREX TRADES AS AN INCOME VEHICLE

While the previous section combined careful selection of forex trends and income instruments for better income investing, carry trading is the classic pure forex play for income. Note right from the start that it uses leveraged instruments, and depends greatly on your forecasting a given currency trend correctly, so carry trading is for more active investors who understand leverage and have the RAMM skills to deal with it. Income investors without the time or expertise should approach carry trading by using a proven trader via a managed account or social trading network. If you want to do it yourself, first get four to six profitable months using practice accounts, then you can more safely consider doing your own carry trading.

In essence, carry trading is just:

- Buying the currency that pays you a higher annual yield and getting that interest paid daily into your account.

- Selling the lower-yielding one and paying out the daily portion of that annual interest.
- Earning an income on the difference.

That means you're either taking long positions in pairs that have base currencies with much higher yields than their quote currencies (like the AUDJPY) or taking short positions in pairs with higher-yielding quote currencies (like the GBPAUD).

Given retail forex's justified reputation as a tool for short-term speculators, you may find it surprising that you can earn steady income via carry trading (which we first introduced in Chapter 6).

Differences between Forex Carry Trade and Traditional Long-Term Buy-and-Hold Instruments

Here's how carry trading differs from typical long-term buy-and-hold income instruments. The carry trade is a classic kind of forex trade and so carries higher risk and demands more time than buy-and-hold investing.

Greater Risk and Reward via Leverage   The use of leverage magnifies both gains and losses.

The Reward: Magnified Interest and Price Appreciation   Concerning carry trading, if you're long a pair that has higher-yield base currency (the one on the left), leverage magnifies the actual interest earned. Recall that back in Chapter 6 we wrote that the net interest of 4.65 percent you collected on the AUDJPY trade we presented was on the full amount of currency you controlled, not the margin deposit.

For example, if you are using 100:1 leverage with a $1,000 margin deposit to control $100,000 of AUD via having borrowed $100,000 of JPY, that annual income is based on the full $100,000 of AUD controlled, not the $1,000 margin deposit. Thus the annual income here is 4.65 percent of $100,000 or $4,650 (paid out on a pro rata daily basis). Using just $1,000 allocated to that position, this is a 465 percent return before considering changes in the AUDJPY's price.

As always, if the pair rises in value, leverage magnifies those gains, too. For example, at 100:1 leverage every 1 percent move is a 100 percent profit on your margin deposit, which would be another $1,000 in the previous example.

The Risk: Magnified Loss   As previously noted, as long as you're going long on pairs that have higher-yielding base currencies compared to their counter currencies, the magnified interest income can only help.

If, however, you were short a pair like the AUDJPY, you'd be paying out that interest for each day you held the short position.

The real risk of loss from leverage with carry trading is no different than with any other kind of forex trade—the risk that price moves against you. Using the previous example, every 1 percent move against you is another 100 percent of your margin deposit. This is why in our chapter on RAMM we recommended having cash in your account equal to at the very least 10 times your typical margin deposit as a general guideline. So while in the previous example you may be earning 465 percent on the $1,000 deposit, you need to keep enough cash on hand (either in your forex account or somewhere else where it's quickly accessible) to absorb whatever percentage move against you you're willing to tolerate. That would cut your overall income yield from your account, but at 465 percent returns on the margin committed, the net yield can still be handsome. You could keep less cash in your account and more in a higher-yielding account elsewhere as long as you're able to transfer funds into your forex account on short notice. In addition to wire transfers, most forex brokers accept deposits via credit cards, allowing for quick deposits over the phone.

Here's another way to deal with the amplified loss risk from leverage: punctuated buy-and-hold.

Using the proper RAMM covered earlier, you can enter and exit positions as needed. So rather than simply buying and holding through possibly crippling losses, just keep entering and exiting your selected high-interest-differential currency pairs over time, riding a multiyear trend for various periods, exiting and then reentering as per our technical analysis and RAMM criteria summarized here.

- Carry trading works only in times of optimism or risk appetite.
- Higher-yielding currencies generally hold their value or appreciate only in times of optimism, so carry trades are generally not successful during bear markets in risk assets. You risk losing more from falling markets than you earn from the interest.
- Carry trading requires more careful use of technical analysis and RAMM.

Because leverage adds to risk compared to traditional nonleveraged income investments like bonds or dividend stocks, we employ the full range of risk and money management (RAMM) techniques discussed in Chapter 5, such as:

- Not risking more than a small percentage of your trading capital.
- Proper setting of stop losses.
- Adequate capitalization.
- Position sizing.

- Entries near strong support.
- Risk-reward ratios of at least 1:2, preferably 1:3 or better.
- Every trade based on a written plan.

The Key to Carry Trading

Ideally, you want to be long a currency with a rising interest rate and short a currency with a stable or falling rate. If there is any significant chance of the opposite occurring in your planned holding period, don't take the trade; your capital losses could easily outweigh your income—remember that leverage magnifies losses as well as income. Using the previous AUDJPY example, assuming you held the position for one year and earned 4.65 percent, a mere 4.65 percent drop in the pair would wipe out your gains for the year. It's not uncommon to see pairs move that much in a matter of days. You can ride out those moves if you're confident in the longer-term trend and have the cash to avoid a margin call. Otherwise, skip the trade.

In sum:

- Your technical analysis should indicate a healthy uptrend for your intended holding period. Those seeking a long-term (multimonth or multiyear) hold should look for pairs with healthy multiyear rising trends on monthly charts.
- Your fundamental analysis, or the analysts you follow, should indicate that the currency you're considering being long has interest rates steady or rising relative to those of whatever currency you'll be shorting.

At minimum, you want to be long one of the higher-yielding currencies and short one of the lower yielders, the difference in their interest rates expected to widen, or at least not shrink.

For example, you want one of the following:

- A long-established long-term uptrend on weekly or monthly charts (again, we want a long-established uptrend) in a currency pair with a high-yielding base currency and low-yielding counter currency like the AUDJPY, NZDJPY, AUDUSD, NZDUSD, AUDCHF, or NZDCHF. The minimum age for the trend is a judgment call, but the longer the better. As we noted in Chapter 3, because economic fundamentals of countries change slowly, forex markets produce some very stable long-term trends or trading ranges, making them well suited to long-term positions as long as a trader or investor can either eliminate or cope with the leverage typically used in most forex trading and the risks it entails. These trends or trading ranges are out there waiting for you to find them.

- If there isn't a long-term uptrend, you should at minimum have good reason to believe one is starting. Because high-yield currencies tend to be risk currencies (i.e., they rise or fall along with other risk assets), these pairs are best played when you believe risk markets have begun at least a multiweek (or longer) uptrend, or your chosen technical indicators suggest there's an established uptrend on the weekly or monthly charts.
- Instead of a trend, a long-established trading range combined with a chance to open either a long position at the low extreme or a short position.

Here is one important note about playing bounces off support, be it for long or short positions. These dips to support should only be technical pullbacks, *not* those pullbacks fueled by a major news item or other sign of breakdown in the longer-term underlying fundamentals of the pair; that might suggest support is likely to break down. You're trying to buy low or sell high, not catch the proverbial falling knife. So pay attention to fundamentals, to what's going on in both the global economy and the economies of the specific currencies involved.

The Key to Trading Range-Bound Markets   By their very nature, trading ranges imply that conditions haven't changed. If, however, you have reason to believe that the big fundamental factors behind a long-established trading range may be changing, be cautious when attempting to trade bounces off of the lows and highs of that range.

For example, remember the EURUSD weekly chart from Chapter 6 on fundamental analysis shown here in Figure 12.7.

Based purely on a simple technical picture, the convergence of two kinds of support for the EURUSD, the 1.4000 level and the rising trend line from June 6, 2010, it looked like we had a dip to strong support that could be an entry point for going long the EURUSD.

However, the European Union sovereign debt and banking crisis was entering a new crisis stage for a variety of reasons, including:

- A rising risk that Greece would not receive its second round of bailout loans in little more than a year, due to both Greek failure to meet conditions for the loans and rising opposition to further loans in funding nations.
- Dangerously high Spanish and Italian bond yields that indicated rising risks that these countries, considered too big to rescue with bailout funds available at the time, would need assistance to avoid default.
- EU banks having increasing trouble getting funding in global credit markets because their large exposure to Greek, Portuguese, Spanish,

FIGURE 12.7   EURUSD Weekly Chart, May 30 to September 6, 2011
Source: MetaQuotes Software Corp.

Italian, and Irish bonds made these banks themselves questionable
credit risks.
- Reports that Germany was preparing plans to stabilize its banks in the
  event of a Greek default, which was at the time becoming increasingly more likely on growing doubts that it would receive additional
  aid needed to keep it from defaulting on its bonds in the coming weeks.

Thus a conservative trader or investor trading off daily or weekly
charts would likely avoid being long EU-based assets, particularly the EUR,
until there were further fundamental and technical signs of stability.

Carry Trade Steps

Here are the basic steps. As with much in this book, we are merely introducing a topic worthy of a book in itself.

Part 1: Use Fundamentals to Screen Pairs   Like any currency
trade, you've still got to be right about the overall direction of the pair.
The only difference is that the pair doesn't have to rise for you to win; all
it has to do is hold steady. However, the relatively narrow interest rate

differentials on which you earn your income won't outweigh any material move against you. So the first step is to evaluate fundamentals and be looking for pairs with the best chances of longer-term appreciation, because the longer you hold the pair, the more carry income you earn. You can move in and out of the pair, but doing that often will eat into your income earnings.

Wide Rate Differentials Find currency pairs with a wide enough interest rate differential, at least 2.5 percent (250 basis points), to justify holding it as a long-term carry trade. As a quick guide, Bkassetmanagement.com and other top content sites typically keep a table of current benchmark central bank rates on their homepages.

Best Prospects for Rising Rate Differentials Identify pairs with the best odds for significant changes in the interest rate differentials between the two currencies. In other words, you'd look for currencies that are most likely to see improving expectations about the extent and pace of changes in rates relative to the other currency in the pair. You'd do that by studying the fundamental data most directly related to interest rate expectations, like recent central bank statements, economic conditions, and inflation outlook, and quality commentaries on these. For example, from 2009 to 2011, the AUD was in a period of rising rates, whereas the rates for the USD and JPY were clearly not going anywhere. The rate differences between the AUD and these others were significant, so the AUDJPY or AUDUSD was a good carry trade as long as risk assets were rising.

If you're not sure which pairs to investigate, don't worry; plenty of traders already have. Do your online searches, and ask around in trader forums. It's a hot topic.

Part 2: Apply Normal Technical Analysis Criteria After applying fundamental analysis to screen for the currency pairs with the best potential for a change in interest rate differentials between the two currencies, then apply technical analysis and RAMM to find the pair(s) with the lowest-risk, highest-yield entry and exit, as we would for any other trade. For example,

- Stop losses should risk no more than 1 to 3 percent of your capital, yet be far enough away to avoid being stopped out of your position by normal price moves for a selected period.
- Entry at strong support, and consider staged entries with partial positions.
- Choose only trades in which the loss implied by your stop loss is no more than a half to a third of the distance from likely resistance.
- For additional criteria, refer to relevant chapters for details.

Because it takes time to accumulate income from the interest differentials, these trades are ideally done off of weekly or monthly charts, but there's nothing wrong with using daily charts and aiming for shorter holding periods in which you move in and out of your selected pairs as conditions warrant.

Note that there are numerous variations on this basic form of carry trade, you don't have to actually buy or sell currency pairs. For example, you can convert currencies and buy stocks, bonds, or other assets denominated in the currency of your choice as multimonth or multiyear investments.

CHAPTER 13

Now What?
Next Steps

H ere's what we've covered and what you should do next.

WHERE YOU'VE BEEN

Chapters 1 through 9 give you the very basics, which you'd find in some form in most forex books, but with the advantage of greater:

- Clarity and detail.
- Detail and emphasis on keeping your losses and stress lower, via obsessive RAMM, and focus on longer-term holding periods needed to exploit the more reliable longer-term trends and ranges.
- Detail and emphasis on discovering which kinds of trading styles fit you best.

While these were of more direct use to traders, long-term passive investors should be very familiar with this material as well because it will help them make better decisions and lower their risk by getting better entry points, and by knowing when a planned long-term investment is best abandoned as a mistake, at least for the time being.

Chapters 10 through 12 are for the more passive long-term investors, showing how you can still benefit from forex markets even if regular online leveraged spot market trading isn't for you. For many of you, it won't be appropriate, and that's fine. You can still profit handsomely from forex markets using the alternatives presented. No one talks about these (maybe because they're relatively new), but they should, because everyone needs some forex exposure for reasons cited in the introduction, Chapters 1, 2, and 12. It can lower your currency risk, which can be substantial when you're overexposed to currencies of mismanaged economies, and can increase your returns.

WHERE YOU'RE GOING

Following are some suggestions for how to proceed now that you've finished the book.

For Traders or Those Seeking Exposure to Forex Trading

- Select one or more brokers to start using their practice accounts. You may find after just a few weeks that you start getting friendly calls from their representative checking on your progress and encouraging you to start trading with real money. Politely but firmly tell them you want to first use the practice account for a "number of months" until you become consistently profitable on a weekly or monthly basis. Usually they'll give you all the time you want. If they don't, then they're not even making a pretense of looking out for your interests, so move on. See Appendix F, tips on selecting a broker.
- Once you have your practice account, start creating a basic trading system, which again is just some rules for how you select trades, when you enter and exit, what RAMM rules you'll use, etc. You'll draw primarily on what we covered in Chapters 2 though 8 (especially 5 through 7). Your simple systems should include the technical and fundamental indicators you're going to try, your likely time frame, what percentage of your account you'll risk with any given trade, the risk-reward ratio you seek, and so on, as illustrated in Chapters 5–7. Don't drive yourself crazy making elaborate plans at this stage. The first ones will be glorified guesses. You will change your systems repeatedly as you experiment with them by simple manual back testing, and gain experience and insight into what sets of rules work best with which currency pairs. The first goal is to just get used to always trading with some kind of system (set of rules) in mind, and then building trading plans based on the RAMM, time frames, indicators, and so forth of your system. You'll know you're on the right path if you have a written set of rules and can justify every entry and exit based on those rules, and have each trade fully recorded in a trade journal that you periodically review. I assign bonus points to those who include screen shots of the charts on which they based their decisions in their journals, and so on.

Successful trading will come eventually because you, unlike most others, have a way to identify and learn from your mistakes. Conversely, you'll know you're on the path to failure if you start trading based on hunches that "just feel right," or tips, or anything other than a set of rules that you followed. If they don't work, analyze what the problem is and change your system. Using a trade journal is invaluable because it forces you to articulate your rules and reasons for what you're doing, including why you may chose to depart from them in a given situation.

- When choosing your technical indicators, remember what we taught in Chapter 9, apply the "gang of four" principle to select three to seven indicators that give you the different kinds of information you need. You want to know about the s/r points, trend direction and momentum (or strength), and have some indication of where the move is likely to halt or make a normal retracement. Then start manually back testing these indicators for a given currency pair (or other asset) and time frame (daily, weekly, monthly, etc.) as discussed in Chapter 9. The goal is to find a set of rules, using these indicators, that tells you when to enter and exit a position. With time and experimentation you'll find some. The goal isn't to come up with a foolproof system. You just want to get used to the thought process and find some rules that increase your odds. Again, your plans and systems may not be great at first; that's normal. They should become successful in time as you learn from your mistakes and find what kinds of trading styles suit you. If time permits, do an online search for the various trader forums or social networks and visit them (as well as the ones we've mentioned) and ask for guidance.
- In general, when attempting to refine your system, change only one aspect of it at a time, be it an indicator, time frame, whatever, rather than making multiple changes. That way you'll know how each change affects your performance.
- After trying assorted combinations of rules for a number of months, you should find a set of rules that appears promising. The system needn't be amazing. If it keeps your losses low, appears to produce net profits over a few months, and fits your personal needs (skill level, time to monitor, risk level, etc.) then you've got a starting point. Start applying this system consistently over a period of months on your practice account. Get comfortable with using it: how to apply the indicators, change time frames, draw trend lines, enter stop and limit orders, keep track of funds in your account, use tools like pip value calculators (so you know how much cash is at risk from your entry and stop loss points), and so on.
- Start looking for the kind of low-risk, high-potential yield trades we discussed. That is, those that allow you to enter near strong support,

with likely resistance much farther away from your entry than your stop loss, so that you have planned 1:2 risk-to-reward ratios or better.

- At the same time that you're getting comfortable with the mechanics of applying your plan, you should be getting used to using a trading journal as covered in Chapter 5, both to plan trades and to review them afterward, noting what went right, what didn't, and any ideas you have about why and how to improve. You'll find that you'll improve format and organization of your journal to include the information you need and make the review and learning process easier.

- From the preceding steps you should have some idea of how much time you can dedicate per day or week to both practice trading and continuing education. You'll also be getting a better idea of the trading styles and time frames that work best for you.

- Seek out sources of analysis and further education for your daily and/or weekly reading. Consider those mentioned earlier and those suggested in Appendix A on free trader resources. While you're there, explore the available trader forums, and don't be shy about asking for guidance on the various aspects of how to proceed, like recommended reading, trading methods, and so on.

- Strongly consider joining at least one social network as another source of advice and guidance.

- Those simply looking for some forex exposure to hedge currency risk and who aren't interested in trading should stick to the ideas covered in Chapters 10 through 12.

- Finally, visit www.thesensibleguidetoforex.com periodically. In addition to bonus material, we're planning to have a growing archive of training material, as well as conservative trading ideas.

For Those Seeking Currency Diversification for Longer-Term Investment Portfolio

- Study long-term forex trends as mentioned in Chapter 12 and make a list of the currencies and currency pairs with the strongest long-term trends. As of this writing, I'd be seeking exposure to the CAD, AUD, CHF, NOK, SEK, and SGD. The CNY is likely to make the list when China produces trustworthy data, but currently I view the AUD as a safer way to play China, for a variety of reasons. Those without USD exposure should have at least some, possibly a lot if your long term outlook for the EU, Japan, and UK is very bearish, or you believe China is due for a major slowdown. As reckless and inept as the US deficit management has been, leaders of the aforementioned nations appear determined to be as bad or worse. Moreover, most of the USD's fundamental troubles can be corrected by a change in political will to do so. It does not suffer from an ungovernable currency union like the EU, or a terminally aging population like Japan. As bad as the USD may look, it may yet prove to be one of the relatively stronger currencies by default. Moreover, if things get really ugly, the US is still arguably the least vulnerable of any nation to economic or military coercion. Should the Euro-zone ultimately contract to include only the nations with a hard money tradition, the EUR could then be attractive.

- Decide what percentage of your portfolio of stocks, bonds, or other assets you want denominated or exposed to these currencies. Then research them as you would for any domestic asset. You may need to locate new research sources and identify salient differences in tax and transactional details, but otherwise the research and criteria you seek are similar.

- Research which currency pairs or other assets to be long or short:
  - Using sources recommended previously and others you find, research which specific stocks, bonds, or other assets in those specific currencies you want to own, and acquire them, using your technical and fundamental analysis (or that of those analysts you follow) to time your entries. As of this writing, as noted earlier, stocks and many other risk assets remain in a long-term downtrend. If that remains the case, whatever you buy should be with money you can afford to let sit, and should have a relatively high and sustainable dividend so that you're relatively well paid while you wait until the next multiyear bull market looks like it's coming.
  - Similarly, one could consider a mirror image of this strategy, picking the weakest currencies and shorting weaker assets denominated in or exposed to these currencies. This is a bit more complicated, especially if global exchanges continue to ban short selling whenever it becomes most likely to be profitable. There are ways around these rules, but they're beyond the scope of this book. There are also short exchange-traded funds (ETFs) for all kinds of currencies and stock sectors, though beware of the rebalancing issues that tend to make these poor vehicles for long-term holds. See the bonus material for Chapter 10 on the website for details on the hazards of ETFs that short specific asset classes or currencies.

I could go on and on, but I won't. Beyond these or other general comments, what would be the right advice for you would depend on what kind of trading or investing you want to do. If you don't know, experiment. If you do, seek out online gathering spots of like-minded individuals (found in trading/investing forums and social networks). The whole topic of conservative forex trading and currency diversified investing is vast and changing, and so all additional thoughts, insights, and teachings will be on www.thesensibleguidetoforex.com.

May the time you've spent reading this book prove to be among your most fruitful investments. For further updates and ideas, you're likely to find my current thoughts on one or more of the following websites.

TheSensibleGuidetoForex.com, the book's companion website, I hope will become a gathering point for the community of traders and investors to which this book is dedicated: those interested in smarter, safer ways to use forex for both lower currency risk and higher portfolio returns.

In addition, you can always just search my name online to see the websites where I often post, like SeekingAlpha.com or ForexFactory.com. I've received a variety of kind invitations from some excellent forex and financial sites, so there could well be others. If you need to reach me, try either the Contact Us tab at thesensibleguidetoforex.com, or, you can leave a message for me via the Send Message button on my profile page at seekingalpha.com (http://seekingalpha.com/author/cliff-wachtel). Like everyone else, I'm also on LinkedIn and other major online hangouts, though I don't always check them regularly.

Good luck!

Recommended Free Online Resources

M any of the following websites were mentioned earlier, but here's a one-stop guide to my favorites for forex traders and investors at all levels. Not only will these websites prove useful from the start, you're also unlikely to ever outgrow them. They'll lead you to further resources as well. I'll just hit the highlights: The "About" pages on these sites will provide a more complete picture.

FOREX SITES

Here are my favorite pure forex resources.

Thesensibleguidetoforex.com

If you like the book, you'll love the website. Your online home for continuing education, as well as trade and investment ideas for those seeking a range of ways to diversify currency exposure either via active trading or currency diversified income investing. Includes a variety of bonus materials to supplement the book.

BabyPips.com

BabyPips.com focuses on beginning traders, providing a wide array of lessons and tools needed to develop the fundamental skills of forex trading and analysis. Don't be put off by the site's more light-hearted, informal take on forex. This is a great site for those seeking an unintimidating, clear, well-organized, and illustrated introduction to forex.

Its most outstanding feature is its School of Pipsology, an organized multitopic intro to the forex course. A stand-out feature of the school is that readers can mark the lessons "completed" to track their progress. New traders looking to build a solid foundation should read through the lessons in order. More seasoned traders can jump ahead to later lessons as needed for reference or to refresh their skills in more advanced topics.

On top of educational content, readers can find news, analyses, and trade ideas in the site's blog. BabyPips.com also provides features like a forex forum, a "Forexpedia," forex-specific calculators, and an economic calendar.

DailyForex.com

While there are many sites that offer forex broker reviews, they are for the most part submitted by volunteer contributors of unknown reliability and objectivity. In contrast, DailyForex.com provides reviews that incorporate the results of its own in-house testing and research of each broker's trading platforms, customer service feedback, trading conditions, and so on. In other words, DailyForex puts its reputation at stake with each review, which should provide much better quality control and reliability.

The site is funded by broker advertising, but this presents no more of a conflict of interest issue than there would be, for example, with accounting firms that get paid by the clients they audit, and for the same reason. DailyForex.com's need to preserve its reputation for reliable reviews is worth more to it than any one broker's patronage. Practically speaking, the site's visitors appear to get consistently reliable reporting (I'm familiar with some of the organizations covered and those reviews were objective and fair) although they will view ads in the process.

Still, don't be shy about seeking second opinions on trader forums regarding a given broker's pros and cons. Each review also includes screenshots and explanations of each broker's site to give viewers a quick feel for what's offered.

There are also reviews of forex binary options brokers, as well as of some forex training courses, and automated trading programs. Credible reviews of these are hard to find, so these really add to the site. Also, there are a variety of news, analysis, and educational offerings, trader tools, and forums.

DailyFX.com

This is one of the most widely-viewed forex content websites, and justifiably so. It's a one-stop shop for news, analysis, analyst picks, extensive educational materials, trader tools, and forums. It's as good a dedicated forex content site as any, beautifully designed, and easy to navigate. My personal favorite features include:

- One of, if not the most extensive offerings of consistently quality analysis from full-time in-house staff. John Kicklighter and Joel Kruger are among my regular reads for daily and weekly analysis.
- Real-time news feeds of tweets from its staff of obviously sharp analysts. It's the best of its kind that I've seen, and the analysts are not above wry comedic observations about the markets and responses to each other's tweets, an added bonus.
- A growing archive of quality training materials. What sets apart DailyFX.com from most other brokers is its serious investment in useful quality content, both analysis and training. It reflects an all too rare business plan based on profiting from long-term relationships with successful traders, rather than just marketing to new suckers and getting them to trade and lose money before they're ready. Which kind of management team do you think is likely to look out for your interests?

Forex.com

Kathleen Brooks' weekly analysis is excellent and one of my weekly reads. As one who does these myself, I know how hard it is to deliver consistent quality, but she does it.

The site's research team does a solid job covering the market 24×5, and provides intraday, daily and weekly research and analysis, including:

- Daily session updates at the end of each major trading session.
- Weekly research including a newsletter that analyzes events that just occurred, with predictions for the upcoming week and a weekly strategy, providing actionable trade ideas.
- Research notes released just before major economic reports, plus an economic calendar.
- Periodic commentary on topics ranging from emerging markets to commodities.
- 24×5 twitter coverage (http://twitter.com/FOREXcom)

Trader education is provided under the "Learn" tab on the website. FOREX.com offers a variety of resources including a limited library of video tutorials, training modules, articles and other text-based content, as well as a schedule of regularly held webinars.

ForexCrunch.com

Forex Crunch has news, analysis, and educational materials along with some good links to other forex sites and articles. Check out the popular posts section.

ForexFactory.com

Along with DailyFX.com, this is one of, if not the most widely viewed forex sites, so you're likely to wind up here at some point—possibly as a regular viewer, if you become a serious trader. ForexFactory.com offers news and opinion via an editor-vetted selection of daily articles, forums, and a variety of trader tools, including one of the best forex economic calendars. Full disclosure: I'm a contributor as well as daily reader.

ForexMagnates.com

Forex Magnates is the leading site for forex brokerage industry news, such as what's happening with individual brokers, hot new products, and so on, and consequently is particularly useful as you narrow your broker selection. To aid in that process, the site has an active forum on broker selection and other topics of interest, as well as a searchable archive. For the larger brokers, it sometimes publishes useful data on the percentage of their clients who are profitable.

Forexpros.com

Another one of the more popular forex content portals, it offers a range of news, analysis, trader tools, and educational materials.

FXstreet.com

This content portal is another of the best content sites in both quantity and quality, from both regular and guest contributors, many of whom are first rate. This is another one of my regular research sources. My favorite features of FXstreet.com include:

- One of the few content sites to publish high-quality macroeconomic and forex-related research from leading international banks, a brilliant idea that I wish more content providers would copy. I try to read this every weekend.
- Exceptional educational materials that go beyond the basics.

Bkassetmanagement.com

Another of the very best content sites, lead by Kathy Lien and Boris Schlossberg, arguably the best one-two combination of analysts anywhere—certainly among the most widely read. The site has excellent daily and longer-term analysis and is another of my daily reads.

OTHER FAVORITE FINANCIAL SITES

BusinessInsider.com

This is a popular hybrid financial site that combines:

- A focus on financial market and business topics with a wide range of other popular verticals (topic categories organized on the homepage's horizontal navigation bar).
- Both in-house reporting and an aggregation of externally produced blogs.
- The result is a combination of financial analysis and news mixed with a variety of tech and tabloid topics ranging from cars, sports, and celebrities to other topic verticals.
- Especially useful, the site features a daily preview before the U.S. markets open ("10 Things You Need To Know Before The Opening Bell") and an even more useful review of the day's top stories and events after the U.S. close (no set title). These are useful time-saving tools for staying up to date with minimal effort, and the bullet-pointed items are often hyperlinked to their sources for further details.

Full disclosure: I'm an occasional contributor.

Investopedia.com

As the name implies, this site is a virtual encyclopedia of financial markets and investing. It's one of, if not the best general financial education websites. Whenever you're researching an unfamiliar topic on markets, this is a great place to start. For those seeking a structured free intro to a forex course that's got a more academic feel than that of BabyPips.com, this is the place to go. The archive of forex training articles is as good, or better than any I've seen in both quantity and quality.

SeekingAlpha.com

Seeking Alpha aggregates about 250 financial and investing articles per day, mostly from 400-plus amateur and professional investors worldwide who serve as regular contributors, augmented by thousands of irregulars. In other words, the articles and comments are by and for fellow investors and traders. To help you find the articles you want, you can subscribe to e-mailed lists of daily offerings on a variety of specific topics. The articles are archived by topic and author, so you can find "that thing I read about three months ago" fairly easily. In its Investing for Income section, it has extensive daily articles on US and international dividend paying stocks, to help those seeking to build a currency diversified income stream, with quality ranging from mediocre to excellent.

While its emphasis is on U.S. equities and related topics, SeekingAlpha.com (SA) also includes some quality forex and commodity articles, but those aren't necessarily what will keep you coming back. Here's my take on the five most useful features for forex trading or investing:

1. Extensive daily selection of archived, searchable articles on:
   - The macroeconomic forces affecting all markets, including daily pre–U.S. market-opening review of top stories.
   - The SA *Market Currents* blog (see number two following).
   - Income investing (including articles on global dividend stocks). The articles on global stocks tend to focus on the prospects of the company and its dividends without considering the long-term strength of the currency to which it's tied. So that's still up to you. However, once you know what percent of your income you want tied to CAD, AUD, CNY, or other currencies, then SA is a good place to go looking for ideas.
   - ETFs, including currency and commodity ETFs.
2. *Market Currents* blog: Imagine you hired someone to keep a diary of the top news and commentary for global and forex markets, making entries every five minutes, which become hyperlinks to the sources for those seeking further details. Now imagine you hired a whole team to do this for general market news and the more popular market sectors or asset types. That's the *Market Currents* blog. It's your personal market diary, hyperlinked to sources and searchable by date. For anyone trying to keep track of the most important news and comments of the day, or what happened concerning any major asset class on any given day, there is nothing else like it. In 10 minutes you can read the entries for a given day and get caught up fast. It's as good as any

10-minute market overview available for any given day. It's among my daily reads.

3. An especially active and useful stream of comments. This is one of the few sites where I actually read the comments because they're often as useful as the article itself—a tribute to the quality of the often savvy readership. Full disclosure: I'm a contributor.

4. Investors can set up portfolios and get alerts sent by e-mail whenever something comes up on that stock or ETF, making this feature very useful for keeping up on currencies represented by an ETF.

5. "Wall Street Breakfast: Must Know News," a daily premarket review. There's also a small paragraph summarizing the U.S. stock market activity that serves as a useful shorter complement to BusinessInsider.com's more comprehensive wrap of the major events.

Wall Street Sector Selector (wallstreetsectorselector.com)

A leading ETF portal, this a good place for those seeking information on forex ETFs and related news and analysis.

INDIVIDUAL ANALYSTS

In addition to the sites already mentioned, the following are names I tend to read regularly. All offer free content; some offer paid subscriptions as well. You can just search their names online for more information. In no particular order, these are the writers or blogs that get my attention. For the most part, they cover the overall macro picture and, at times, include specific investment advice. The list is far from comprehensive. Unless otherwise noted, they cover general markets, though many have particular specialties.

Fundamental Analysis

John Mauldin, Cullen Roche, Mike "Mish" Shedlock, Ed Harrison, Reggie Middleton, ZeroHedge.com (all writers use pseudonyms), Patrick Chovanec (China specialist), Michael Pettis (China specialist), Ambrose Evans Pritchard, Martin Wolf, Marc Chandler (forex), Bruce Krasting, Cullen Roche and Ralph Shell (forex).

Technical Analysis

While there are many worthwhile technical analysts and signal providers, one of the best that you've probably never heard of is Charles Nenner. Unlike anyone else I've seen, this former Goldman Sachs analyst provides a unique application of sophisticated cycle analysis to forex and related markets that can be particularly useful for the longer-term and intermarket-focused trading styles we've covered. While most of his material is subscription only, he regularly appears in interviews, many of which are archived on his website, CharlesNenner.com, or searchable online. He offers free trials, so you can sample his work for yourself at no risk.

How to Calculate Pip Values and Examples

DEFINITION

A *pip* is the smallest unit of price movement for any currency pair. For pairs with the JPY as the counter currency, it's 0.01 Yen. For all other pairs, it's 0.0001 of the counter or quote currency.

For example:

- For the EURUSD and most other pairs, movement from 1.4000 to 1.4001 is one pip.
- For the USDJPY, a movement from 80.00 to 80.01 is one pip.

Its cash value is always in terms of the quote currency (the one on the right), which you then convert to whatever currency your account is denominated in, using the currency pair price, which is the actual exchange rate.

CALCULATION

Happily, you needn't go through the following, because there are plenty of free pip calculators you can find online, and the better brokers will provide pip calculators, or their dealing platforms will show pip values in whatever currency your account is denominated.

Still, just so you know, here's the calculation.

The basic formula for calculating a pip value (in the quote or counter currency—the one on the right):

- Pip value per lot equals 1 pip (0.0001 for most currency pairs, or 0.01 if the JPY is the counter currency)
- Divided by the exchange rate or current price of the pair
- Times lot size (in base currency)

Or,

(1 pip/exchange rate or price of the pair)

$\times$ lot size [in base currency—the one on the left]

= pip value in the quote currency [the one on the right]

You'll then need to convert the result into the currency in which your account is denominated if that is different from the base currency. (This will all become clear in the following examples.)

Note that a standard lot size is 100,000 units of the *base* currency (the one on the left). Most online retail brokers offer mini accounts in lot sizes of 10,000 units, and micro accounts in lot sizes of 1,000 units.

EXAMPLE: EURUSD

Assuming a standard 100,000 lot size, and EURUSD price of 1.4000, account denominated in USD:

$(0.0001/1.4000) \times 100,000 = \$7.14$/pip for a standard lot

(\$0.74/pip for a mini lot, \$0.074/pip for a micro lot)

If you are trading 3 lots, each pip would be worth 3 times that amount. If your account is denominated in USD, you'd be finished.

If it is in EUR or JPY, then you'd need to convert the \$7.14 into that currency.

For example, if the account is denominated in EUR, then:

$\$7.14 \times 1.4000$ dollars per Euro = €10.00/pip/standard lot,

€1.00/pip/mini lot, €0.1000 per micro lot

HANDY RULE OF TENS

When the account is denominated in the base currency, pip values are in units of 10 (except when the JPY is the counter or quote currency).

This illustrates how, when the account is denominated in the base currency, the pip value is:

Standard (100,000 lots base currency): 10 units of the currency in which your account is denominated.

Mini (10,000 lots base currency): 1 unit of the currency in which your account is denominated.

Micro (1,000 lots base currency): 0.10 units of the currency in which your account is denominated.

For instance:

In the earlier EURUSD example, if the account is denominated in Euros, then each pip would be worth €10 for a standard lot size, €1 for a mini lot, and €0.1 for a micro lot.

With any currency pair in which the USD is the base currency (with the majors, that only happens with the USDJPY and USDCAD), the pip value of the USDCAD in a USD-denominated account would be $10 per standard lot, $1.00 for a mini lot, and $0.1000 for a micro lot.

This rule is handy for those who trade the major pairs with EUR or GBP denominated accounts, because these are usually the base currencies. The EUR takes precedence over all others as the base currency, followed by the GBP. Thus the EURGBP is the only major pair with the GBP as the quote or counter currency.

EXAMPLE USDCAD

Assuming a standard 100,000 lot size, and USDCAD price of 1.01935, denominated in USD:

$$(0.0001/1.01935) * 100,000 = 10.1935 \text{ CAD/pip}$$

Divide that value by the 1.01935, and you get $10/pip for a standard lot size, $1 for a mini, and $0.10 for a micro account.

EXAMPLE USDJPY: RULE OF TENS DOESN'T APPLY WITH THE JPY

The exception to this rule occurs when the JPY is the quote currency (all the time with the majors) because pips are in increments of 0.01 not 0.0001.

Assuming a standard 100,000 lot size, and USDJPY price of 80, account denominated in USD:

$0.01/80 \times 100,000 =$

¥12.50/standard lot, ¥1.25/pip/mini lot, ¥0.125/pip per micro lot

Converting that to USD: ¥12.5/80 = $0.15625/pip for a standard lot, $0.01562/pip for a micro lot, and so on.

Pip calculation is a bit more complex for cross currencies. For the sake of brevity I'll leave that for your own online search.[1]

Forex Trading Time Zones, Liquidity, and Why These Matter

The trading week runs 5.5 days per week, 24 hours a day. It begins in Asia Sunday afternoon Eastern Standard Time (EST), or Sunday evening Greenwich Mean Time (GMT), and progresses each day until the close of trading in the United States as follows.

- New Zealand trading is open from 2:00 P.M. to 11 P.M. EST starting Sunday.
- Sydney is open from 5:00 P.M. to 2:00 A.M. EST.
- Tokyo is open from 7:00 P.M. to 4:00 A.M. EST.
- Hong Kong and Singapore are open from 9 P.M. EST to 6 A.M. EST.
- Frankfurt, Germany, the primary European market, is open from 2:00 A.M. to 11:00 A.M. EST.
- London is open from 3:00 A.M. to 12:00 noon EST. London is the world's largest forex trading center.
- New York opens at 8:00 A.M. to 5:00 P.M. EST. NYC is the second-largest forex center. Not surprisingly, then, the greatest liquidity occurs when both London and New York are operating.

Table C.1 shows this graphically.

THREE MAJOR TRADING SESSIONS AND WHY THEY MATTER

There are three major sessions each day: Asian, London/European, and U.S. The timing of these is important because the best times to trade are

TABLE C.1 The Trading Day per EST

1	2	3	4	5	6	7	8	9	10	11	12	13	14	15	16	17	18	19	20	21	22	23	24
													New Zealand										
															Sydney								
																		Tokyo		Hong Kong &			
Tokyo		Singapore																					
		Frankfurt	London			New York																	

TABLE C.2 Trading Day per GMT
(To adjust to GMT, add 5 hours to EST. That is, Tokyo would begin at 12:00 midnight, London at 8:00 A.M., New York at 12:00 noon, etc.)

6	7	8	9	10	11	12	13	14	15	16	17	18	19	20	21	22	23	24	1	2	3	4	5

Markets: Tokyo, Singapore, Frankfurt, London, New York, New Zealand, Sydney, Tokyo, Hong Kong &

when two of the sessions overlap. When they do, the increased liquidity means you get the fairest prices due to the abundance of those willing to take the other side of your trade. These are:

The second most liquid time: 1 to 3 A.M. EST combines the top Asian and European sessions. The most liquid time is 8 to 11 A.M. EST, which combines the most liquid European markets with those of the United States.

> Asian: Relatively quiet, lower liquidity, though the JPY may trade heavily if a major financial event has just happened and Asian markets are reacting to it. It is centered near Tokyo.
>
> European/London: Has the highest trading volume; most active currencies are the USD, EUR, and GBP. Heavily centered around London, *the* traditional center of forex markets.
>
> U.S.: The second-heaviest volume; most active currencies are the USD, EUR, JPY, GBP, and AUD. Centered around New York, although includes other U.S. trading centers like Boston, Philadelphia, and (mostly) Chicago.

The most liquid, and thus best hours for trading are when London and the U.S. sessions overlap. You usually get the most participants, and hence strongest price moves and fairest trade execution.

However, don't make the mistake of thinking that each currency trades heaviest in its local time zones. Instead, they trade most heavily in the most liquid markets, during the London and New York sessions.

MARKETS TEND TO FOLLOW EACH OTHER

In all financial markets, not just forex, one session tends to take its cues from the one before it. For example:

If the U.S. markets are bullish or showing risk appetite, Asia will open the same way and continue to do so until whatever news or sentiment that drive the U.S. markets is priced in.

If Asia closes strongly bullish or bearish, expect Europe, centered on London, to open the same way.

If Europe is still rocking higher when the U.S. session opens, expect the United States to open higher, favoring risk assets and risk currencies.

Similarly, if one session reverses the prior session's moves, chances are good that the next session will open in that same direction.

WHAT STOPS THE FOLLOW-THROUGH?

Obviously markets don't continue in one direction for long stretches on a daily basis. What breaks the cycle of follow-through from one session to the next? The two most common forces that change market direction are:

1. News or How It's Interpreted

Major news events or reports are what tend to drive these changes. For example, the United States could close very bullishly, but if during the Asian session some significant bearish news comes, like evidence of China, the biggest Asian economy, slowing down, that could cause Asia to reverse lower.

New interpretations of news events can have the same effect. For example, there are occasions when a major event occurs late Friday in the U.S. session (like U.S. monthly jobs reports) and markets don't have enough time to digest them before the weekend. In such cases, final judgment isn't rendered until the Asian session begins the following week.

2. Technical Resistance: The News Is Already Priced In

Trend exhaustion from technical resistance can also break the cycle of follow-through from one session to the next. In other words, at some point a rally or pullback hits enough technical resistance to halt the current trend unless there is new news to fuel a continuation of the move. Otherwise, all news is already "priced in," and price either remains locked in a range or reverses as participants take profits or open short positions.

The Prior Session Is Most Influential

Asia tends to lag the New York trading session because Asia is closed when U.S. news comes out, so major U.S. news provides hints about how Asia will open. The European session reacts to early U.S. news but misses later news, and its open is influenced by what happened in Asia. For example, if great news comes from the United States, but then there's bad news in Asia, Europe's opening will reflect how traders are responding to the combination of news from both sessions.

Likewise, the U.S. opening tends to take into account the news of both Asia and Europe.

In sum, short-term moves are heavily influenced by the region that most recently finished its trading day, news, and whether that news justifies moves up to or past the next technical levels. As mentioned earlier, short-term money flows from big players (either from big speculators or simply commercial traders funding normal multinational business operations) can also start short-term price moves.

Beware Holiday Catch-Up Sessions

If Tokyo, London, or New York are closed for a holiday and the other two were open, then you'd expect a catch-up session when markets reopen for that region. For example, if the United States shows strongly improving monthly employment reports on a Friday (during the last session of the last trading day of the week), and closes sharply higher, expect Asia to open strongly to price in that news at the start of the following week.

More on Leverage and Margin

A s the retail forex industry has developed and expanded since its beginnings in the mid-1990s, so too have regulatory controls, as governments seek to protect the unwary from unscrupulous or what they deem excessively risky leverage limits. Leverage limits vary with time and place.

For example, as of October 18, 2010, U.S. retail forex brokers are limited to 50:1 (2 percent margin) leverage for the most liquid currencies, the majors, and the more liquid crosses, and 20:1 for the exotics. While this may seem positively sedate compared to the 200:1 to 400:1 offered in many places outside the United States, compared to the 2:1 (~50 percent) margin offered by most equities brokers, the greater risk and reward offered U.S. forex traders is still substantial, and still demands careful RAMM practices.

Note, however, there is a loophole that allows SEC/FINRA-regulated brokers (like Citi, Deutschebank, etc.) to keep offering higher leverage to retail forex trading regardless of these regulations, therefore becoming potentially more attractive to forex traders than CFTC forex brokers (like FXCM, IBFX, etc.).[1]

There is some confusion surrounding the classification of "majors." In common Forex jargon, the majors are only the seven pairs mentioned in Chapter 2. However, as far as the new rules go, the majors are all pairs which include any two of the following currencies:

- U.S. Dollar (USD)
- British Pound (GBP)
- Swiss Franc (CHF)

- Canadian Dollar (CAD)
- Japanese Yen (JPY)
- Euro (EUR)
- Australian Dollar (AUD)
- New Zealand Dollar (NZD)
- Swedish Krona (SEK)
- Norwegian Krone (NOK)
- Danish Krone (DKK)

This means that a wide range of pairs which are normally considered crosses fall under the majors designation for the purposes of this rule and can be traded at 50:1 leverage (2 percent margin deposit). Trading any other currency pair will demand a margin of 5 percent or 20:1 leverage. The rest can be traded at 20:1 leverage (5 percent margin).

These rules are subject to change, because the new regulations charge the National Futures Association (NFA) with defining which currencies are "major currencies," and require at least an annual review of these designations to potentially adjust them as necessary in light of changes in the volatility of currencies and other economic and market factors.

In Japan, maximum leverage was reduced to 1:25 in August 2011, after it had been reduced to 1:50 a year earlier, as per rules set by Japan's Financial Services Agency in 2009.[2] Other nations, like Israel, had already cut leverage to 1:25 a year earlier.

How the Mathematics of Loss Demands Keeping Losses Per Trade Low

A s noted at the start of Chapter 5, losses hurt you more than gains help you. This is true from both a financial and psychological perspective.

First let's look at the financial side. Losses do disproportionately greater financial damage because in order to recover your losses you need to earn higher returns with a smaller capital base.

For example, let's say you started the year with $100,000 and lost 20 percent, or $20,000, over the course of the year. You now have $80,000 left. To recoup that $20,000 or 20 percent that you lost from your remaining $80,000, you have to make 25 percent on that $80,000. However, if you'd gained just 10 percent over the course of the first year, you would only need a 9 percent return over the coming year on that $110,000 to add another $10,000 to your account.

Which of the two possibilities is more likely? A 10 percent gainer earning 9 percent or a 20 percent loser gaining 25 percent?

Do you see how losses hurt you more than gains help you?

I recommend not risking more than 1 percent to 3 percent per trade. In other words, if you start with a $20,000 account, your stop loss should be close enough to your entry point so that if hit, your loss won't exceed $200 to $600. Assume you follow my advice and risk 2 percent on average.

Here is a more detailed illustration of the difference between risking that 2 percent of your capital and risking 10 percent.

Imagine two traders each starting with a $20,000 account. One risks 2 percent/trade, the other risks 10 percent. Both slide into a losing streak. Look what happens in Table E.1.

TABLE E.1 Difference in Drawdown When Trader Risks 2 Percent versus 10 Percent on Each Trade

Trade #	Trader A: Loss with 2 percent Risk per Trade	Total Account	Trader B: Loss with 10 percent Risk per Trade	Total Account
1	$400	$20,000	$2,000	$20,000
2	$392	$19,600	$1,800	$18,000
3	$384	$19,208	$1,620	$16,200
4	$376	$18,824	$1,458	$14,580
5	$369	$18,447	$1,312	$13,122
6	$362	$18,078	$1,181	$11,810
7	$354	$17,717	$1,063	$10,629
8	$347	$17,363	$ 957	$ 9,566
9	$340	$17,015	$ 861	$ 8,609
10	$333	$16,675	$ 775	$ 7,748
11	$327	$16,341	$ 697	$ 6,974
12	$320	$16,015	$ 628	$ 6,276
13	$314	$15,694	$ 565	$ 5,649
14	$308	$15,380	$ 508	$ 5,084
15	$301	$15,073	$ 458	$ 4,575
16	$295	$14,771	$ 412	$ 4,118
17	$290	$14,476	$ 371	$ 3,706
18	$284	$14,186	$ 334	$ 3,335
19	$278	$13,903	$ 300	$ 3,002

After just seven trades, trader B has lost nearly half his capital, and needs to nearly double his money just to break even on the year. Trader A has almost 80 percent of his capital left. Trader A has a realistic chance of recovering if he's smart and takes a break, goes back to a demo account until he believes he's fixed the problem, and then returns to trading smaller positions, ideally with even smaller amounts risked.

Trader B is unlikely to recover without adding additional capital to his account. Remember from Chapter 5 that the more capital you have, the more trade opportunities you're able to take while still only risking 1 to 3 percent of your capital. Trader B can now only afford stop losses that are half the distance from the entry point as those of Trader A. Trader A has more opportunities to make money, because he can afford wider, more realistic stop losses that allow a greater margin of error. Trader B must be very right, very often. Given his past, that's not likely to happen.

In sum, allowing only small losses allows you to survive and recover from the inevitable drawdowns.

To make the point more vividly, Table E.2 shows the damage done from each 10 percent loss.

TABLE E.2	Losses Hurt More Than Gains Help: Percent Gain Needed to Recover after Each 10 percent Loss		
Trader B Loss of Capital	**% Return on Capital Required to Reach Breakeven of $20,000**
10%	11%
20%	25%
30%	43%
40%	67%
50%	100%
60%	150%
70%	233%
80%	400%
90%	900%

Get the point? Losses hurt you more than gains help you. Until you have a very strong track record, trade defensively. Focus more on surviving losses than scoring fast gains.

Losses also do disproportionate damage on a psychological level. Researchers have found that the pain of losing money is twice as strong as the joy of gaining the same amount of money.[1]

This pain leads to a psychological bias called Loss Aversion. It manifests itself in the variety of mistakes traders make to avoid admitting they were wrong. These include:

- Adding money to losing positions to lower their cost basis
- Staying in a trade after their stop loss has been hit
- Prematurely exiting trades before price hits likely resistance in order to "lock in" profits

We began Chapter 5 with quotes from two of the most accomplished market players of their era, one a trader, one a longer-term investor. After all their successes, they continued to focus on keeping losses low.

How can we be any less cautious?

Choosing a Forex Broker

A s with evaluating any vendor, do your homework.
To maintain maximum objectivity, I will neither recommend brokers nor specific reviews or websites that provide them.
To speed your search, however, I offer the following guidance.

SUGGESTED SEARCH TERMS TO FIND BROKER REVIEWS

Search for reviews using the obvious combinations of keywords like:

- "Forex brokers" AND (reviews OR comparisons)
- "Forex trading" AND "recommended brokers"
- "Online forex trading" AND "broker reviews"

If you're curious about a specific broker, try searching for specific reviews about them. For example,

- FXCM AND reviews
- GFT AND "compared to other brokers"

Criteria to Consider

Once you've seen some reviews and have a list of possible brokers, consider how they compare on the following criteria.

A few must-mentions include:

1. Overall good reviews. While there are many forums you can find on-line, anyone can post anything to many of these, making them great spots for any loser seeking to vent frustration at a broker. Unhappy customers are more likely to post than satisfied ones. You may well do better sticking to websites like DailyForex.com that do their own inde-pendent reviews. When visiting these sites, look for evidence credibil-ity. Does the site reveal weaknesses as well as strengths, or do the re-views sound like they were written by the broker's marketing writers? Also, take note if the same brokers that get top reviews are running ad-vertisements or have links on the site to open an account, which create potential conflicts of interest. Check other sites and forums and try to pick up the overall level of satisfaction. ForexMagnates.com is a site dedicated to industry news and can also be a source of who's doing well and who's in trouble.

   Look for what traders and reviewers say in regard to informa-tion about:
   - Transaction costs: commissions (if any), spreads, rollover rates, quality of execution.
   - Trading platforms: Many offer a choice, from simple platforms to more advanced and complex ones.
   - Where are they located and who regulates them?
   - Customer service and trading support.

2. Overall feel of the site: If the site lacks a professional look and feel, if it feels cheap, is hard to navigate, or behaves poorly, there's no reason to expect that your impression will improve with time. Does it look more like a gambling site (gaudy animation, loaded with promises of returns that seem too good to be true, etc.) than a serious investing site?

3. Check out the "About" page. The longer the company has been in busi-ness, and the more impressive the management team (their profiles are often available at LinkedIn.com), the more likely they have a repu-tation and investment to protect.

4. Clear Links to Quality Analysis and Training: *As detailed in Chap-ter 5, content quality is key, and an excellent way to tell who the quality brokers are.* Brokers that don't offer a variety of qual-ity analysis and training that actually helps you find and execute trades (versus just having generic news items) either don't have the financial resources and stability to help you, or don't care enough to do so. *These sites are probably run by gambling-site types. Their business model is to offer minimal content, just for show, while*

investing heavily in marketing campaigns to provide a needed steady supply of new suckers, gambler sheep, to be fleeced and slaughtered within a matter of months. Remember, unless they're providing useful guidance that helps you survive and succeed, they're probably assuming you'll fail quickly. Move on. Note: Often a broker will have a content site separate from the main site. As long as the content site is easy to access from the main site's homepage and offers quality content, that's fine. That content should ideally include:

- Analysis that guides you to successful long- and short-term trades.
- Big picture fundamental and technical analysis over long and short terms (daily, weekly, and, ideally, quarterly outlooks).
- Trader training: on the full gamut of topics covered in this book, aimed at a variety of levels. If the material is superficial, then it's more likely serving as a way to fool the gullible into thinking they're ready to succeed, when instead they're just ready to be exploited.

5. Range of assets offered to trade: The wider the variety, the greater your chances of finding a reliable trend in one or more of them.

Low Correlations to Other Markets via Social Trading Means There's Always a Bull Market Somewhere*

Global asset markets tend to move in the same direction. More precisely, in times of optimism most risk assets rise and safe haven assets fall. In times of pessimism, the opposite occurs. This phenomenon creates a problem for investors. In good times, the price of risk assets gets bid up as cash floods into risk assets, lowering returns and raising risks that you'll be paying too much and may be buying at the top. In bad times, the same thing occurs, only it's safe haven assets that quickly become expensive.

Through skilled forex trading, it's very possible to achieve market-beating returns that don't correlate closely with other markets. That means it's possible to make exceptional returns even when other risk or safe haven assets are too expensive.

However, the problem for most people is that they aren't skilled forex traders, nor do they have the large sums needed to invest with a top forex account manager, even if they are able to find one.

It is not a problem. Locating top traders is relatively easy via social trading networks. Skilled forex traders are able to achieve returns that are not correlated to other markets. That means, in essence, that they're able to create bull-market returns regardless of what's actually happening in most other markets.

For proof, Currensee.com has kindly consented to let me reprint the following article detailing how its Trade Leaders' results are not correlated to other markets.

---

*Copyright Currensee Inc., www.currensee.com. Used with permission.

TRADE LEADER NONCORRELATIONS TO THE MARKETS

A little while ago I did a basic correlation study. It looked at the markets as well as at the Trade Leaders over the June 2010 to September 2011 time frame. In this post I'll share with you the results.

MARKET CORRELATIONS

Let me first start with the correlations between some of the major market asset classes. They include stocks, fixed income, and gold, which together represent the biggest fraction of the asset allocation for most investors these days. Here's what those cross-market correlations were over that full period.

	USD Index	TLT	HQD	GLD
S&P 500	−0.367	−0.707	−0.338	0.121
USD Index		0.195	0.033	−0.406
TLT			0.658	−0.023
HQD				0.147

TLT is the leading long-term Treasury securities ETF and HQD is an ETF that focuses on high-grade corporate bonds. GLD is the gold-tracking ETF. I opted to use these ETFs to avoid any kind of issues that using cash bonds or futures might have caused in determining period-over-period returns. These correlations are based on weekly figures.

There probably won't be much surprise in the numbers. Stocks and the bond ETFs are negatively correlated, indicating that stocks and interest rates were generally moving in the same direction. Stocks and the dollar were also negatively correlated, but not hugely so (+1 means totally positively correlated, −1 means totally negatively correlated). The negative correlation between the dollar and GLD is also no surprise.

These aggregate figures mask the reality of the markets, though. Correlations are not static things as the chart in Figure G.1 shows.

Here we have the rolling three-month correlation of the fixed-income ETFs, gold, and the USD Index against the S&P 500. Notice how they have moved up and down and all around. For example, the USD Index was mostly negatively correlated to stocks, but for a while there it went to

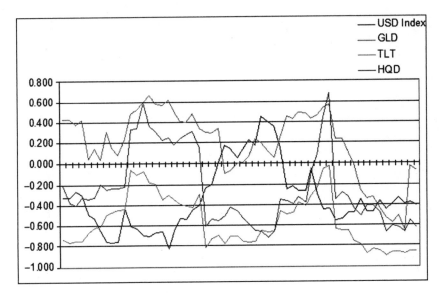

FIGURE G.1   S&P 500 Correlations
Source: Currensee, Inc.

positive. Likewise, gold was mostly positively correlated to stocks, but in the latter part of the covered time it went negative.

LOOKING AT THE TRADE LEADERS

Now let me turn the attention to the Trade Leaders. Here are the figures for how they correlated against the five markets shown in the studies previously mentioned.

USD Index	S&P 500	GLD	TLT	HQD
−0.239	0.059	−0.065	−0.105	0.145

Notice how small these figures are. The Trade Leaders were modestly negatively correlated to the dollar, but otherwise their returns were essentially not correlated against the other markets. Again, we're talking about a comparison of weekly returns here. I used an equal weight average return for the Trade Leader which incorporated all those that were active during a given week.

To see what this looks like, Figure G.2 is a chart which shows a week-by-week comparison of the Trade Leaders and the S&P 500.

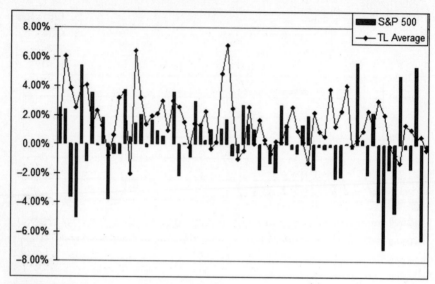

FIGURE G.2   Trade Leaders vs. S&P 500
Source: Currensee Inc.

The S&P 500 weekly returns are indicated by the bars while the line represents the Trade Leaders. It's pretty easy to see how unrelated the returns of the two are in this graph. The directions of the plots are frequently different and the amplitudes are almost never the same. That's basically the definition of uncorrelated.

DIVERSIFICATION OF APPROACH

What we're seeing with the Trade Leaders' correlations is the impact of diversification of trading approach. The index and ETF returns work on the basis of buy-and-hold while the Trade Leaders are employing much more active strategies. Those strategies are somewhat correlated to the direction of the dollar, which will be no real surprise given how much of a focus EUR/USD gets in forex trading, but even that isn't a close relationship. This tends to indicate that Trade Leader performance is mainly a function of skill, not market performance overall.

Notes

READ THIS FIRST: WHAT YOU ABSOLUTELY MUST KNOW

1. Peter Schiff, "Currency Is the Hidden Porfolio Risk," *Business Insider* (October 2011), www.businessinsider.com/currency-the-hidden-portfolio-risk-2011-10.
2. Andrew J. Johnson, "Small Businesses Try Hand at Forex," *Wall Street Journal* (August 2011), http://online.wsj.com/article/SB100014240531119036394045765 14560310571904.html.
3. Joshua M. Brown, "Inside the Currency Boiler Rooms" (August 2011), www .thereformedbroker.com/2011/04/09/inside-the-currency-boiler-rooms/; also, Michael Greenberg, "U.S. Forex Brokers Account Profitability Comparison" (October 2010), http://forexmagnates.com/us-forex-brokers-account-profitabi lity-comparison/.

CHAPTER 1: THE THREE MUST-KNOW FOREX FACTS

1. Neil Woodburn, "50 Year Anniversary of Europe on $5 a Day (Man, How Things Have Changed!)" (May 2007), www.gadling.com/2007/05/02/50-year-anniver sary-of-europe-on-5-a-day-man-how-things-have/.
2. A personification of the Japanese housewife speculators, who are strong enough to affect international markets, especially foreign exchange markets.
3. Vikas Baja and Graham Bowley, "S.E.C. Temporarily Blocks Short Sales of Financial Stocks," *New York Times* (September, 2008), www.nytimes.com/2008/ 09/20/business/20sec.html.
4. In an attempt to halt a run on their banking stocks, Spain, France Italy and Belgium banned short selling them. Their plunge began because as holders of large quantities of Greek bonds they were now being asked to take "voluntary" losses on these as part of the latest failed Greek rescue plan. Markets understood that this set a precedent for similar partial defaults and losses on other sovereign bonds of weak EU nations, which these banks also held in quantity. While wealthy and sophisticated traders and institutions could find other ways to profit from the strong downtrend in these shares, most private traders were now unable to exploit this move.

5. As was the case with holders of insurance against Greek default in July 2011, regulators ruled that "voluntary" acceptance of 21 percent losses by banks holding sovereign Greek bonds did not constitute default, even when it was obvious that these banks did so under official EU threats that the banks would otherwise receive nothing and spark a global crisis.

6. Just do an online search using terms like "online forex brokers reviews." You'll find plenty of sources. The more reliable ones tend to be from established, professional looking websites that obviously have a stake in protecting their reputation and offer their own in-house reviews. Dailyforex.com runs its own in-house professional broker reviews, which are usually more credible than those posted by unknown volunteers in trader forums, because Dailyforex.com's reputation is on the line. Obviously, apply the "smell test." If you see nothing but positive reports on a site with broker reviews, and the site carries ads from those same brokers, seek second and third opinions. There are also online forums, though you've no assurance on the reliability of the contributor. They may be accurate, or just disgruntled losers blaming brokers for their own mistakes.

7. Javier E. David, "Global Forex Turnover Continues to Increase," *Wall Street Journal* (July 2011), http://online.wsj.com/article/SB10001424053111903999 904576468211853284114.html.

8. David Woo is head of Global Rates and Currencies Research for Bank of America, Stephen Jen is a former star forex trader at Morgan Stanley, BlueGold hedge fund, and at last report runs his own hedge fund, SLJ Macro Partners.

9. http://www.forexfactory.com/showthread.php?t=120506.

10. Joshua M. Brown, "Inside the Currency Boiler Rooms" (April 2011), www .thereformedbroker.com/2011/04/09/inside-the-currency-boiler-rooms/ and Michael Greenberg, "U.S. Forex Brokers Account Profitability Comparison" (October 2010), http://forexmagnates.com/us-forex-brokers-account-profitabi lity-comparison/.

11. Brown, "Inside the Currency Boiler Rooms."

12. For example, "... in the year 2000 state regulators in Massachusetts subpoenaed records which showed that after 6 months only 16 percent of day traders (in equities) made money.... Brilliant day traders do exist.... Sadly, it's a very small handful." Quoted from one of the better trading books I've read: *Come Into My Trading Room: A Complete Guide to Trading*, by Dr. Alexander Elder (Hoboken, NJ: John Wiley & Sons, 2002), 100–101.

CHAPTER 2: FOREX BASICS

1. Michael Buek, "Why Index Funds Beat Active Strategies" (October 2009), www .bankrate.com/finance/financial-literacy/why-index-funds-beat-active-strategies-1.aspx.

2. James E. McWhinney, Investopedia, "Massive Hedge Fund Failures" (July 2011), http://finance.yahoo.com/news/Massive-Hedge-Fund-investopedia-71298 9148.html?x=0&.v=1.

CHAPTER 3: TECHNICAL ANALYSIS (TA) BASICS

1. Steve Nison, *Japanese Candlestick Charting Techniques* (New York: New York Institute of Finance, 2001).

CHAPTER 5: TRADER PSYCHOLOGY AND RISK AND MONEY MANAGEMENT (RAMM)

1. Mary Buffett and David Clark, "The Tao of Warren Buffett" (New York: Simon & Schuster, 2006).
2. *Forbes*, "Forbes' 400 Richest Americans" (September 2011), www.forbes.com.
3. Alex Howe, "The 15 Best Things Paul Tudor Jones Has Ever Said About Trading," *Business Insider* (September 2011), www.businessinsider.com/the -tk-best-things-paul-tudor-jones-has-ever-said-2011-8#at-the-end-of-the-day-the-most-important-thing-is-how-good-are-you-at-risk-control-15#ixzz1l9omVe7j.
4. John Tierney, "Do You Suffer From Decision Fatigue?" *New York Times* (August 2011), http://mobile.nytimes.com/article?a=829776&f=37.
5. Boris Schlossberg, "Three Men Doing Time in Israel Prison Are Up for Parole" (August 2011), www.fxstreet.com/education/trading-strategies/forex -trading-strategy/2011/08/19/
6. Joe Weisenthal, "If You Had Bought Swiss Franc in 1970 . . . " *Business Insider* (August 2011), www.businessinsider.com/if-you-had-bought-swiss-franc -in-1970-2011-8.
7. Jeremy Wagner and Timothy Shea, "How Much Capital Should I Trade Forex With?" (December 2011), www.dailyfx.com/forex/education/trading_tips/daily _trading_lesson/2011/12/22/how_much_capital_should_i_trade_forex_with.html.
8. Just enter the search term "screen capture" into your preferred search engine for the latest free versions of such popular software packages as ScreenHunter, Snagit, and so forth.

CHAPTER 6: ESSENTIALS OF FUNDAMENTAL ANALYSIS

1. In times of crisis, however, the usual fundamental considerations become secondary to speculation about government policy or geopolitical events. For example, from late 2010 to mid-2011, risk assets rose largely because the U.S. Federal Reserve was engaged in its second round of easing (aka QE 2), which markets believed would boost risk asset prices. The darkening prospects for virtually every major economy were ignored.

2. John Maynard Keynes, "Keynes the Speculator," www.maynardkeynes.org/keynes-the-speculator.html.

3. Cliff Wachtel, "The Must Know Truth About Gold" (May 2010), http://seek ingalpha.com/article/206487-the-must-know-truth-about-gold.

4. Christian Vits and Jana Randow, "Trichet Says Interest-Rate Increase by the ECB Next Month Is a Possibility" (March 2011), www.bloomberg.com/news/2011-03 -03/trichet-says-european-central-bank-needs-strong-vigilance-on-inflation.html.

5. Kathy Lien, "EUR/USD Sinks on U.S. Trade and Trichet" (September 2011), www.fx360.com/commentary/kathy/6099/eurusd-sinks-on-us-trade-and -trichet.aspx?num=1315487768562.

6. Just going by memory: The Latin America debt crisis of the early 1980s, the Savings and Loan crisis of the early 90s, the dot-com bubble of early 2000s, the subprime lending bubble of 2007 and subsequent Great Recession, and the EU Sovereign Debt and Banking crisis that began in 2010, exacerbated but not caused by the subprime mess in the United States.

CHAPTER 7: PULLING IT ALL TOGETHER WITH TRADE EXAMPLES

1. Because we generally prefer to trade only the most liquid pairs, there are only 8 to 9 really liquid pairs, the EURUSD, USDJPY, GBPUSD, AUDUSD, USDCAD, USDCHF, EURJPY, and EURGBP, NZDUSD. Throw in some of the more popular EUR, JPY, and GBP crosses (like the EURCAD, EURCHF, AUDJPY), and you're up to ~12. Then maybe add the SEK, NOK, HDK, and SGD combined with some of the others for some added exposure to hard money (low debt/GDP economy) currencies, and you have around 12 to 20 pairs at most for almost all of your trading.

2. Cliff Wachtel, "Lessons From Last Week's Market Movers: Faith, Hope and Charity to the Rescue" (September 2011), http://seekingalpha.com/article/294253 -lessons-from-last-week-s-market-movers-faith-hope-and-charity-to-the-rescue.

3. John C. Abell, "Apple Co-Founder Ron Wayne's Long, Strange—and Sad— Trip," *Wired* (June 2010), www.wired.com/epicenter/2010/06/apple-co-founder -ron-waynes-long-strange-and-sad-trip/.

CHAPTER 8: TECHNICAL ANALYSIS

1. Kathy Lien, *The Little Book of Currency Trading: How to Make Big Profits in the World of Forex* (Hoboken, NJ: John Wiley & Sons, 2011).

2. Christine Jenkins, "Here's How Actress Michelle Williams Won the World Cup of Futures Trading Award at Age 17," *Business Insider* (January 2011), www.businessinsider.com/michelle-williams-trader-father-2011-1#ixzz1 l9sYG3z3.

CHAPTER 10: ALTERNATIVES TO TRADITIONAL METHODS

1. Content by John Nyaradi, publisher of Wall Street Sector Selector, wallstreet sectorselector.com, an online newsletter specializing in sector rotation trading using Exchange-Traded Funds. Used with permission.

CHAPTER 11: NEWER, SMARTER METHODS

1. Zach Miller, *Tradestream Your Way To Profits* (Hoboken, NJ: John Wiley & Sons, 2010).
2. Sarah Morgan, "New Tool for Currency Traders: Mimicry," *SmartMoney* (August 2011), www.smartmoney.com/invest/currencies/new-tool-for-curren cy-traders-mimicry-1312324538631/ .
3. Dave Lemont, "Will I Have the Same Profitability as the Trade Leaders I Follow?" © Currensee Inc., www.currensee.com/newsletter/issue4-article1.
4. Interview with Jonathan Assia, Insight Corporate Governance Germany, November 2011, pp. 10–11, and Tom Groenfeldt, "Better Foreign Exchange Investing Through Social Networking," *Forbes* (July 2011), www.forbes.com/sites/tomgroenfeldt/2011/07/26/better-foreign-exchange-investing-through-soci al-networking/.
5. "Currensee Provides Emerging Money Managers with New Route to Alternative Investments," *Wealth Adviser* (April 2011), www.wealthadviser.co/2011/04/04/111575/currensee-provides-emerging-money-managers-new-route-altern ative-investments.
6. "Compensation," © Currensee Inc., www.currensee.com/tradeleaders/compen sation.
7. Sarah Morgan, "New Tool for Currency Traders: Mimicry," *SmartMoney* (August 2011), www.smartmoney.com/invest/currencies/new-tool-for-curren cy-traders-mimicry-1312324538631/ ; Michael Greenberg, "U.S. Forex Brokers Account Profitability Comparison" (October 2010), http://forexmagnates.com/us-forex-brokers-account-profitability-comparison.
8. Alon Levitan, Etoro Head of Strategic Marketing, email message to author, December 26, 2011.
9. "Currensee Alternative Investment Program Surpasses $6 Billion in Trading Volume" © Currensee Inc. (June 2011), www.currensee.com/about-us/news-events/currensee-alternative-investment-program-surpasses-6B-trading-volume.
10. Alon Levitan, Etoro Head of Strategic Marketing, email message to author, December 26, 2011.
11. eToro, Regulation and license (accessed, August 2011), www.etoro.com/trade/etoro-and-brokers.aspx.

12. Forex Magnates Retail Forex Market Quarterly Report for Q1 2011, http://forexmagnates.com/wp-content/uploads/2011/04/Forex_Magnates_Q1_2011_preview.pdf.

CHAPTER 12: FOREX FOR INCOME

1. Andrew J. Johnson, "Small Businesses Try Hand at Forex," *Wall Street Journal* (August 2011), http://online.wsj.com/article/SB100014240531119036394045765145603105719 04.html?mod=rss_whats_news_us.
2. Joe Weisenthal, "If You Had Bought Swiss Franc in 1970..." *Business Insider* (August 2011), www.businessinsider.com/if-you-had-bought-swiss-franc-in-1970-2011-8#ixzz1l9z0UdPr.

APPENDIX B: HOW TO CALCULATE PIP VALUES AND EXAMPLES

1. Here's one source to get you started: www.forexfactory.com/showthread.php?t=8568.

APPENDIX D: MORE ON LEVERAGE AND MARGIN

1. "New Forex Margin Rules Start Today" (October 2010), Fxmadness.com, http://fxmadness.com/2010/10/17/general/new-forex-margin-rules-start-today/.
2. Adil Siddiqui, "Japan Further Reduces Leverage" (August 2011), http://forexmagnates.com/japan-further-reduces-leverage/.

APPENDIX E: HOW THE MATHEMATICS OF LOSS DEMANDS KEEPING LOSSES PER TRADE LOW

1. Tversky, A. & Kahneman, D., "Loss Aversion in Riskless Choice: A Reference Dependent Model" *The Quarterly Journal of Economics*, (1991), http://www.econ.brown.edu/fac/Kfir_Eliaz/LossAversionRisklessChoice.pdf.

About the Author

C liff Wachtel, CPA, is the Chief Analyst of Anyoption.com, a leading binary options broker, and Director of Market Research, New Media, and Training for Caesartrade.com, a fast-growing forex and CFD broker.

He is also publisher of TheSensibleGuidetoForex.com, a website uniquely dedicated to providing safer, simpler ways for active traders and passive long-term income investors to exploit forex markets for lower currency risk and better returns. When the Great Financial Crisis began in 2007, Cliff was among the first financial writers to focus on stocks that provide steady, currency diversified high-yield income for insurance against losses from currency devaluation. He focuses on top income stocks for exposure to multiple quality currencies on safer, simpler, less demanding types of longer-term forex trades than commonly covered on other forex sites, on the macro view of global markets for formulating longer-term strategies, and on trader training. He also posts these via Globalmarkets .anyoption.com, Globalmarkets.com, TheSensibleGuidetoForex.com, and others. Most can also be found at leading financial websites like SeekingAlpha.com, businessinsider.com, on forex sites like ForexFactory.com, and occasionally in print media like *The Forex Journal*. Many of these are translated into numerous languages, including Spanish, French, Italian, Turkish, Arabic, Swedish, German, Japanese, Chinese, and Russian.

Prior to his current positions, he was Chief Analyst at avafx.com, and a 30-year financial market veteran as investor, trader, writer, and adviser to private clients and institutions.

He is married with five children and lives in Jerusalem, Israel, where he can follow Asian markets in the early morning, Europe through the workday, and the United States at night.

Index